LITTLE PRINCE

The Accidental Life of a Lucky Orphan

Kal Wagenheim

WingSpan Press

116 Myrtle Ave. Millburn NJ 07041
Tel: 973 885 6897
Email: kalwagenheim@cs.com
Website: www.kalwagenheim.com

Cover photo taken in the 1940s shows the author with his maternal great-grandma Ida Hoffman Shamberg, in the back yard of their home in Newark NJ.

Published in the United States and the United Kingdom
by WingSpan Press, Livermore, CA

ISBN 978-1-59594-549-5 (pbk.)
ISBN 978-1-59594-884-7 (ebk.)

First edition 2014

Printed in the United States of America

www.wingspanpress.com

Library of Congress Control Number: 2014957519

1 2 3 4 5 6 7 8 9 10

CONTENTS

Preface....................iii
The Early Years....................1
Happiness at 510 Belmont Avenue....................44
South Side High & New Pals....................67
College Days....................78
You're In The Army Now....................86
Civilian Life & Marriage....................95
Single Again....................102
Off to Puerto Rico....................127
Married Again....................139
The San Juan Review....................160
Hired by The New York Times!....................183
Buffalo Days....................203
Back in New Joisey....................218
Another phone call: Clemente!....................223
Finding Family....................228
Phone Calls Out of the Blue....................257
Caribbean Update: A New Career....................292
The Wall Street Journal....................295
Writing Plays and Film Scripts....................307
Teaching at the State Prison....................317
Moving to a New Home....................323
Goodbye to Columbia....................330
My First Novel....................340
50 Years Married....................342

PREFACE

In 1937, during the Great Depression, when I was two years old, my mother, age twenty-two, died in childbirth. Shortly before her death, my father—who had long suffered from severe depression-- left her and went to live with his parents. He never returned.

One might think that I, the little orphan boy, was destined for an unhappy life. Quite the contrary. I was too young to understand what had happened. I was surrounded by so much love (great-grandparents, a grandmother, and a bunch of eccentric great-uncles) that in many ways I was raised like a Little Prince, and enjoyed a happy, carefree childhood in Newark, NJ. It was only later, as an adult—and a parent and grand-parent myself—that I was able to look back and truly understand the nature of the tragedy.

In the past half century, I've had about twenty different jobs. I applied for only two of them. The rest magically appeared, phone calls out of the blue, chance meetings—happy accidents.

Perhaps I'm engaging in fanciful thinking, but so many good people (family, friends, strangers) have intervened in my life that I wonder: does God have a guilty conscience? Has He sought to help me, with divine interventions, in order to compensate for the early tragedy in my life? (On that theme, I have written a one-act play, *"Coffee With God"*, which has been produced dozens of times in the USA,Canada and Ireland.).

I have put together this memoir---a combination of memories, news clippings, letters, and tape recorded conversations-- first of all, for my children and other younger members of our family -- including those yet to be born -- to give them a sense of part of their heritage, and for dear friends and others who might find it of interest. On a deeper level, I have written it for myself, for catharsis, and to savor moments in the past, some sad, and some hilarious. I think the British novelist Graham Greene put it best when asked, in an interview, why he wrote: "We write to heal a wound in ourselves, to make ourselves whole.".

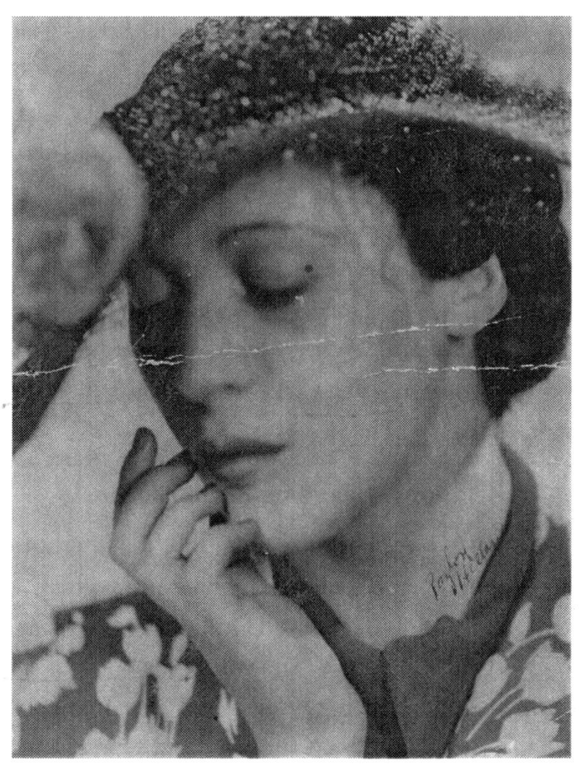

THE EARLY YEARS

The defining moment in my life -- it changed the course of everything -- was the death of my mother, Rozlon Heller Wagenheim, on May 31, 1937, when I was two years old. She was just 22. A photo of my mother rests atop a bookcase near the desk where I work each day. Her illuminated face, surrounded by shadows, is seen in profile, her dark hair combed back in the style of a Spanish flamenco dancer. She is eternally young, and beautiful.

During my childhood I was told that my mother had passed away of an illness. It was not until I was 25, in 1960, that I was told the entire, shocking truth: the day before she died of hemorrhaging, my mother had given birth to a baby girl. The infant girl was adopted. It was not until September 13, 1973, when I was 38, that I met my sister June for the first time. But more about that magical reunion later.

I also learned years later that, when my mother died, she had been separated from my father, Harold Wagenheim, who was a public school teacher in Newark NJ and an amateur dramatist/screenwriter. My father was a man of fragile temperament, who suffered from severe depression, and my mother's death pushed him off the deep end. He lost his teaching job, and drifted to California, where he continued to be plagued by depression and lived on the edge of poverty. We exchanged many good letters over the years, but father and son would not meet face to face until July 1969, when he was 66 years old, and I was 34. He died on January 11, 1981, at the age of 77.

Nanny, Grandma & Cousin Rosie

I was raised by two wonderful women: my maternal great-grandmother, Ida Shamberg (I called her "Grandma"); and her daughter, my grandmother, Lillian (I called her "Nanny"). I adored Grandma, who from age 70 cared for me while Nanny went off to work. She was a gentle, kind soul who probably shaped my character more than anyone else. Grandma spoke to me mostly in Yiddish, and occasional broken English, and I would reply in English. I understood most of the Yiddish, and I regret today that I never learned to speak the language. I also regret that I never took the trouble to write down the full story of her past, her coming to America. But I do recall some details.

She was born Ida Hoffman, around 1868, on the outskirts of Kishinev, the capital of Bessarabia (now called Moldova), a region that is ethnically Romanian, but had long been a part of the Russian Empire. Grandma told me how the people lived in mortal terror of the "Cossacks," sabre wielding horsemen who raided the villages. I first heard the word "pogrom" from her lips. In Bessarabia, Grandma married Israel Shamberg (I called him Grandpa), a butcher, and in 1891 they came, as millions did, to America, settling in the Lower East Side. Since I knew them only as elderly immigrants, it is astounding to me that they arrived in America when they were quite young. According to a 1905 NY State Census, Grandma was then 37. Her birth year was 1868, and she had been in the U.S. for 14 years, meaning that she arrived at age 23. The Census said that Grandpa was 26 when they arrived, but my Aunt Lucille told me that Grandpa was several years older than Grandma.

Grandpa died around 1945, about age 87, when I was 10. Grandma died at age 92 (Nov. 13, 1960) when I was 25.

The 1905 Census shows that the "Schaumberg" family (Grandma and Grandpa) resided on Second Ave in Lower Manhattan. They had seven children, most of whom were somewhat eccentric (*more about them later*). In order of age they were: Anna (the only one born in the old country, in 1887); Murrey (born 1891-2); Lillian (my grandmother, born 1893); Davie (born 1896); Addie, a girl (born 1899, died a few years later); and Eddie and Carl (born some years later) . Since Grandma and Grandpa spoke little or no English when their children were born, although they did their best to pronounce the names of the newborn to the government census takers, the spelling on the papers was different each time. Grandma and Grandpa's surname was "Shamberg." So was Carl's. But Davie's was "Schanberg." Eddie's was "Shanberg." And Murrey's was "Shamburgh"

They didn't come alone. The first member of the family to reach America, I'm told, was Grandma's brother, Kalman Hoffman, who set up a small dry goods store at 120 Ridge Street on Manhattan's Lower East Side. *Years later, after Kalman's death, I was given his name.* I never got the details, but I believe it was Kalman who sent for Grandma and Grandpa. Kalman, the entrepreneur, also eventually sent for his elderly parents, Isaac and Rebecca Hoffman, who were my great-great grandparents and had apparently worked in agriculture in Bessarabia. *They died around 1911 (one of their deaths is listed as Oct. 11, 1911), and are buried in Washington Cemetery, Brooklyn. I have some vague notes that mention "Cem 3, Row 3 left, 13 sec, Bnai Jac An Checkanoffzer" and "Albert Meyer Family Circle, Path 14 left" (Cem 3, Row 3 left, 13 soc).*

The 1940 Census shows Kalman Hoffman, age 66, born in 1874, and his wife Minnie, age 58. Kalman and his wife Minnie had three children: Moe (born 1899, died 1969); Rose (born May 21, 1897, died age 86 on July 21, 1983); and Lillian (born 1905, died in late 1970s). Rose's birth certificate says the family resided at 120 Ridge St. in New York City when she was born, the same address as Kalman's little store. Moe married but neither he nor Lillian or Rose had children of their own. Moe started working for Herring Brothers in New York City, later opened his own business in the NYC garment industry and was very successful. So much so that he provided financial support for his two sisters, and gave substantial donations to Jewish charities. I regret that I never met him.Rose Hoffman, my grandmother Lillian's first cousin (we called her "Cousin Rosie") was an amazing woman, a generous, creative, sensitive soul who wrote plays and poems and—believe it or not—had psychic powers. She really did! Since I was named after her late father, we became quite close and she played an important role in my life. *More about her later.*

My grandma's psychic cousin Rose Hoffman (1897-1983)
as a young lady.

Feb. 5, 1927. Found in a handwritten notebook of Rose Hoffman, my maternal grandmother's psychic cousin. She was 29 years old at the time

Outside snowflakes are softly falling, and everything is so white, and restful. How refreshing each flake is to me—and as my eyes pick out here and there patches of virgin white, my heart within me throbs, lest they be spoiled. And in comparison, my mind wanders back a bit—to a pretty scene in June, when in similar mood, I happened to wander away in the fields—and came to a spot where a little summer cottage stood alone, like a hermit amidst a field of green, and rambler roses of pale pink and deep red set off the dull grey of the little house. I remember I looked inside, and found the place deserted, and rested there a while—I was all alone there and the very same thoughts possessed my mind. Rambler roses, fresh untouched and pretty like the virgin snow, whose hand would in one second rob them of their beauty, and short life, Like the virgin snow, whose feet would soil it—How helpless the roses are, how helpless the snow flakes, and to me something like this dawned upon me. *Humanity*---!!! like the snow flakes and like the flower—Whose hand would rob and soil us—For each one of us are like patches of white flakes, or like the flowers. Millions of hands are there ready to snatch at us, or like heavy feet ready to trample upon us. Hands, feet , in the disguise of thoughts, ideas that enter our brains, brought on by surrounding conditions---But yet unlike the flowers, God had endowed us with understanding, if we would only stop for a moment by the wayside to see the light. And when surging within me, like the roar of the waves the billion impulses within me—tear at my mind, and heart, blinding me in their rage to give them birth—and I choke them back unwillingly, because I stand all alone, but some day those impulses will be given life and it is then I fear for these hands, and feet, who find pleasure in destroying to satisfy their lust. In contrast to this some unknown force is guiding me on to be patient and calm and to love all humanity. Good God, I see a chaos on earth—a downpour of rain, hail, lightning, thunder, fire, water, physical humanity trampled in bloodshed—the world one great ball of darkness, plague and horror, the scene is horrible, my blood seems to freeze—I pray for the light, and behold I see an ark—and all which seemed necessary to life before is wiped out, and spirit takes it proper place and love rules supreme. What beauty, we have it now on earth—but it seems humanity will not take heed. Nature takes its place, all those who did not hesitate before they touched the rose, or trampled on the virgin snow, take heed, because it seems they have learnt their lessons well. The blue skies, the milky ways, the beautiful sunshine, the flowers, the dew, the brooks, the vines, the ocean, all are calm and serene. It's summer all the time, the birds are not afraid to sing. Music—fragrance, beauty, Good Will on earth. It's so beautiful, and then the rainbow. Such colors never have I seen one like it before—the clouds have rolled by, and silver linings enhance the night. Wild beasts, no such things, all the evils that were here before exist no more—even the roses have no thorns because none do take unless it's rightfully theirs. The tower of "Babel" it's there again, but all speak one language because dear God had built a cathedral for all his children. Truth, understanding and Divine Love rules Supreme.

April 19, 1929. Kalman Hoffman died, at age 64. His daughter Rose said her father's funeral cost from $5,000 to $6,000, a fortune in those days (probably paid for by his wealthy son Moe). He had been living at 1240 Bay Ridge Parkway in Brooklyn, and later moved his business to the corner of 20th St. and 4th Ave.

April 21, 1935. When I was born, my great-grandma urged my parents to name me in honor of her beloved brother, Kalman, and they did so.

The day I was born, an Easter Sunday, the front page of The New York Times (cost ten cents) featured several headlines, including: "7-Alarm Fire In Brooklyn Floods I.R.T. with Smoke, Fells Many in Manhattan"; "Earth Is Pictured As Blue To Mars"and "Schultz Jolted As Account Book Appears At Trial", a story about notorious gangster Dutch Schultz.

Rose Hoffman letter to Kal, dated around 1973. Did you know that, shortly after you were born, I wrote a poem about you? When Lillian, your grandmother called me, and said that Rozlon had given birth to a little boy, and that they were going to name the baby Kalman, after my dear Dad, I sat down and wrote this poem. It was 1935, thirty-eight years ago. I still have it. *ROSE*

Darling little one,
So sweet under the stars and the sun,
You are a lucky one,
To be born to such a dear mother.
Remember, there is no other,
And for you, out of the blue,
a heritage of intelligence,
good health and wealth.
In all humility
you will love humanity.
Forward you will march
Leaving behind all stiffness and starch.
You will travel in paths never tread,
And always will be well fed.

In years to come,
You will collect a great sum,
Relating to your children, grandchildren,
and great grand children
The wonders of the coming new age.
In history you will write a new page.
So dear little one,
Always be happy under the stars and the sun.
And even, when the rain, snow or fog does come,
You will still collect your sum.
You will learn and teach new ways,
And the Grace of God will always
send you a bright ray.
Namesake of my Dad
--*From Rose Florence Hoffman.*

April 30, 1935 (nine days after I was born). Typewritten letter on White House Stationery to Rose Hoffman, my maternal grandmother's cousin, concerning Rose's play "Sylvia's Present." My dear Miss Hoffman: I read your manuscript and think it is light and charming and would be suitable for schools. Unfortunately, I cannot give you this letter for publication or for use in any way as so many people send me their manuscripts it is not possible for me to express any opinion about them. Very sincerely yours, *Eleanor Roosevelt*

1935, the year I was born: The depression continued, with unemployment still running at 20.1% , and the war clouds were gathering as Germany began to rearm and passed the Nuremburg laws to strip Jews of their civil rights, and Mussolini's Italy attacked Ethiopia. The Gallup Poll was introduced and a reformed drinker named Bill Wilson formed Alcoholics Anonymous on June 10th.

Events: Persia is renamed as Iran; Amelia Earhart flies solo across the Pacific; President Roosevelt signs the US Social Security Act Providing Unemployment compensation and pensions for the elderly; The China Clipper makes the first Pacific Airmail delivery; The Emergency Relief Appropriation Act on April 8 creates The Works Progress Administration (WPA) to create millions of jobs; 1,200,000 people face starvation in Illinois due to lack of funding; First Public Housing Project launched in New York;

Average Cost of new house $3,450; Average wages per year $1,600; Cost of a gallon of Gas 10 cents; Average Cost for house rent $22 per month; A loaf of Bread 8 cents; A pound of Hamburger Meat 11 cents; Average New Car Price $625; Canada Dry Ginger Ale 20 Cents;

Popular Culture: Babe Ruth hits the 714th and final home run of his career. Parker Brothers releases the board game Monopoly; "Porgy and Bess" opens in New York; Penguin produces the first paperback books; First Orange Bowl. This was also the year of the birth of "Swing" by Benny Goodman and the world was ready to boogie.

Technology: The Peoples car (Volkswagen Beetle) is launched in Germany; First Experimental Radar is developed in UK; GE Starts selling the first Fluorescent Tube for light; First Parking Meters in Oklahoma City designed by Carl C Magee; Toyota Cars are launched in Japan. For the first time, a completely synthetic fiber, was produced by a Dupont chemist. It was called "nylon."

Born in 1935 among the millions of others were: Julie Andrews , Oct. 1; Luciano Pavarotti, Oct. 12: Woody Allen, Dec 1; Sonny Bono, Feb. 16; Dalai Lama, July 6: Elvis Presley, Jan. 8; Donald Sutherland, July 17; Dudley Moore, April 19;

A few folks born on my birthday, April 21: Anthony Quinn (1915); Warren Spahn (1921); Queen Elizabeth II (1926); Elaine May (1932); Charles Grodin and former NJ Governor Thomas Kean (1935); Patti Lupone (1949); Tony Danza (1951).

Lillian: Nanny

My grandmother, Lillian, was 42 in 1937 when my mother died. She worked as a bookkeeper, and to the best of my knowledge was the only person in my immediate family who earned a weekly paycheck at the time. Despite her modest economic circumstances, she dressed with simple elegance. Nanny was a shy woman, not given to open displays of affection, but her quiet devotion to her parents, and to me, was evident each day, in the way she worked hard to support us. In her moments of relaxation, Nanny loved to read. She belonged, I believe, to the Book-of-the-Month Club, and I recall that she particularly liked romantic novels. Daphne Du Maurier was a favorite. Nanny had married Abe

Heller, my maternal grandfather, who was a film editor for Warner Brothers, in the early days of the industry. At the time Warner had offices in either Queens NY or Fort Lee NJ. They had two daughters: my mother Rozlon (born Feb. 8, 1915), and my aunt Lucille (born April 30, 1919). When the girls were young, Abe ran off to Hollywood and married another woman. He remained there, and never provided support for his young daughters. Abe Heller worked in Hollywood for decades as a film editor (I'm told he specialized in editing coming attractions). *The movie database* www.imdb.com *only lists a single credit in his name, showing that he edited a 1928 film Sonia, starring and directed by Hector V. Sarno, with Evelyn Pierce and Rosa Rosanova. (Sarno, born in 1880 in Naples, Italy, died in California in 1953 and acted in 196 films, mostly in small uncredited roles).*

Aunt Anna

My great-aunt Anna, was born in Bessarabia in 1887, and was brought to New York around 1891. I don't know how or where, but at some point she met and married a successful businessman, Mr. Kronenberger, and they lived on prestigious Lake Shore Drive in Chicago, where he operated a clothing business. Anna regularly sent a $25 check to her mother (my great-grandmother), which in those days was quite helpful in covering costs. She had two sons, Dick and Bruce. There was a great tragedy when Dick died, as a young man. Am not sure of the circumstances. Someone in the family said he committed suicide. I do recall that Anna later sent a package to us; it contained a few quality wool sweaters of Dick's, which I (the poor little boy) wore for several years. Anna came east to visit just a couple of times, and we then lost track of her. But I did find a few letters she wrote to Nanny, her sister, who then was living in an apartment on South 13th St. in Newark NJ (*see these letters later*).

Aunt Molly et al.

Molly Hoffman, a sister of Grandma's (we called her Aunt Molly), also came to America, as did a brother, Uncle Herman (many years ago, I heard that Uncle Herman had moved to California, where he operated a tie shop, but I have no further details). Grandma, Molly, and their respective families settled in New Jersey, while Kalman and his family remained in New York. Aunt Molly married Sam Farber, owner of a grocery store at 560 South 12th

St in Newark NJ. Molly and Sam had four children. *It is said that Sam Farber was the one who brought the family from New York to Newark.* Dora, Molly's daughter, married Morris Greenberg, owner of a small supermarket on the main street in Maplewood NJ. They had three children: Buddy, Selma and Arnold. Buddy (who had a reputation as a playboy) married Margie (an attractive woman who was once a Rockette at Radio City Music Hall, I think) and they had two children. Selma married Ed Platter, and they had two children (Billy & Ed). Arnold married, but I have no data about children (I think they adopted a child).

My mother, Rozlon Heller

I was so young when my mother died that I have no memory of her. All that I possess to remind me of her are a few photos, and three letters she wrote to her uncle, Edward Shanberg, who lived with his wife, Elizabeth, in Greensboro, North Carolina. Uncle Eddie and Aunt Elizabeth saved those letters, and mailed them to me many years later. They are among my greatest treasures.

1936: The first, undated, was written in the midst of the Depression, when times were very hard. In that letter, to Uncle Eddie and Aunt Elizabeth, my mother, who was separated from my father, and living with her grandparents at 355 Peshine Avenue in Newark, congratulates them on the birth of their first child, Barbara:

"Hello Pappy!!!!! How glorious - perfectly wonderful that Elizabeth has come thru fine and with a precious bit of heaven - We up north are very happy for you -- and wish you both a world chuck full of good things for your daughter. I wish I could hop-skip and jump down to Aunt Elizabeth and the baby. Give them a big kiss for all of us--and a wet one for Kalman.... Grandma is really alright now -- She wishes she were able to make a trip down South -- But it seems there is a nasty villain called money that always eludes us....Kalman walks all by himself at last -- He is so proud of himself -- He walks about saying *alone - alone - alone* , telling us he doesn't need our help anymore. Very soon you will be writing us and boasting of your daughter's accomplishments - Isn't it a wonderful feeling to have a baby - Something all your own -- A beautiful, soft little body to love and cherish -- It is something to live for -- To cry for -- fight and laugh for...."

October 11, 1936, my mother wrote again to North Carolina: "To

Mommie & Daddie and Barbara...Please - Please forgive me for being so late answering but I have been very busy - I am at last working as a sales girl in a very nice dress shop -- When I get home at night I am so tired I just can't do anything but kiss Kalman goodnite -- and go to bed. How is my darling very new cousin? I almost wrote niece -- I feel like an aunt to her -- Tell us what does she look like -- Does she eat like a little piggy --So that she will get fat and adorable -- Aren't they gorgeous precious things to have --they are expensive and they are troublesome, but one tiny smile and all is forgiven. When I get home at nite I feel so utterly alone and morbid -- so nasty after waiting on picky women all day -- but Kalman runs up to me, throws his chubby arms about me and says *mommie - kiss.* Well -- It's my seventh heaven..."

May 19, 1937: The third letter is postmarked a month after my second birthday, when my mother was very pregnant with my sister (although she does not mention it in her letter). She writes again to North Carolina, probably for the last time: "My dear Aunt, Uncle and Barbara...Your lovely box of candy was received amid exclamations of ohs & ahs! Grandma thanks you from the very bottom of her heart. It was the most delightful surprise. Kalman refused all candy but that which came from Grandma's box. He says it is *Be-e-e-e-u-t-i-f-u-l.* That is the way he talks. He draws his words out and uses much expression... One of these days I will get around to taking pictures of my son. When I do I will forward one. He is the roughest, toughest, kid on the street. Plays ball with all the big boys. And shouts. 'Make a double.' He plays marbles like a veteran, and sings all the latest songs. All that at the age of two. But I have a lot of trouble feeding him. He eats very little. Spinach, eggs, string beans and Kalman are at war. We keep telling him about Barbara, but the poor kid does not understand why she doesn't come and play with him. The weather has been very nice here. All here are well. There is nothing new. So close with love to you all from all. Rozlon."

Twelve days later, my mother lay bleeding to death in the City Hospital. The lights were turned on in at least one movie theatre in downtown Newark, and pleas were made for blood donors, a family member told me years later. Whatever the response to those pleas, she died a few hours later. Each time I re-read those precious letters written by my mother, I feel deeply moved by her love for me, and infinite sadness over her loss.

Sister June

June, my beloved "shvester" (sister), was born May 30,1937 with the given name Dolores Wagenheim. It was later changed to "June" by the couple who apparently adopted her in June 1937. I first connected (on the phone) with my sister on Sept. 10, 1973, when we were both in our 30s. *Later for details.*

May 31, 1937: The death certificate shows that Rozlon Wagenheim, a "housewife" residing at 441 Jelliff Ave, Newark, age 22 years, 3 months, 23 days, died on May 31, 1937, of post-partum hemorrhage, after giving birth. We were so poor we could not afford to pay for the funeral or burial. But Morris Greenberg, husband of Dora, my grandma's cousin, who owned a small business in New Jersey, generously covered the cost. The funeral was held at the Philip Apter Funeral Home, and burial was at the Jewish cemetery off South Orange Ave., Newark. Her parents are listed as Abe Heller, born in New York and Lillian Shamberg (maiden name). Although Rozlon is listed as "married", the space for the name of her husband is left blank. *Since returning to New Jersey in the early 1970s, I have frequently visited her grave, especially on Mother's Day.*

Note: *I shared some of my memories with family, and in 2007, I received an Email from my Cousin Lynn, who told me "One of the few things my Mother told me about your Mother was that after her passing, every day you would look for her to come down the street. What do you say to a 2 year old?"*

June 1,1937: The press carried no notice of my mother's death the previous day. But the *New York Times* (which then sold for two cents) front-page headline screamed: "GERMAN WARSHIPS SHELL ALMERIA, KILLING 20." Inside the paper were reports that Dr. John Wyckoff, dean of the New York University and Bellevue Hospital Medical College, died at age 55. Also, an estimated crowd of 40,000 persons witnessed a Memorial Day parade in Newark NJ, honoring dead soldiers. Two boys, age 15 and 14, drowned when caught in a whirlpool while swimming near Tiffany Falls in the Second River inside the Essex County NJ Park Reservation. And Boris Schwartzburg, 45, was shot and fatally wounded in his drug store in Brooklyn.

About The Wagenheims

My paternal grandfather, Morris Wagenheim (1867-1950), a tailor, came to America from Riga, Latvia around 1892 and at some point settled in Newark NJ. He was married to Ada Barr. They had four children: Nathan ("Nat", 1896-1985); Dora; Frieda, and my father, Harold (1903-81). Uncle Nat had two sons: William ("Bill") and Allan. Bill and his wife Shirley had two daughters, Diane (deceased) and Susan, a psychiatrist, who is married and has two sons. Allan has a son, Steven, from his first marriage, and Steven, married to Donna, has a daughter, Chrissy. Years ago, my Dad's brother, Uncle Nat Wagenheim, gave me the following information, from memory. He said his father told him that in Latvia, they lived at "Kovna Guberna Savolsku Yesk Noverzegora #17, Habeschegassen, Riga." He said they had come to the US by way of England. He mentioned brothers Abraham, Sam, and Hyman, some of whom came to America, and others went to the United Kingdom (perhaps en route to the U.S.). Morris also had sisters, Celia and "M", who also came to the U.S. One or more settled in London and later came to America, while others came directly, settling in Baltimore and Michigan. Uncle Nat told me about a wealthy Wagenheim family in Atlantic City (in the meatpacking business, I believe) but he had no contact with them.

When my wife Olga and I came to live in New Jersey in 1971, we connected with Uncle Nat's son, Cousin Bill Wagenheim and his wife Shirley, who then lived in Union NJ, and we have been very close ever since. Bill, in many ways, is like an older brother to me. Bill, for many years, with a partner (Stanley, a Polish-American) operated a Parts Unlimited retail electronics store on Washington St., near the corner of Market St. in downtown Newark. In the mid 1980s, at age 55, Bill retired, and sold the building to an Israeli. Bill & Shirley moved to an adult community in north-central NJ, where they remained for years. Their eldest daughter, Susan, a psychiatrist based in Albany, has 2 boys (Matthew and Gregory) from her first marriage. She is happily married now to Michael Rosenberg. A few years ago, Bill & Shirley moved up to Delmar, a suburb of Albany, to be closer to Susan and the grandsons, and they are quite happy up there.

My Father, Harold Wagenheim

A copy of a birth certificate made on Feb. 3, 1970 shows that a "Harry Wagenheim" was born on Nov. 27, 1903 in Newark NJ to Morris Wagenheim and Ida Barr Wagenheim. A U.S. Census document taken April 15, 1910, shows a "Harry Wagenheim" (my father), age 6, living with his parents at 212 Broome Street in Newark. When he first entered school, he began to state his name as "Harold E. Wagenheim" with the "E" standing for "Emanuel." The record shows that after graduating from Newark's South Side High School (where I also studied) he had pursued studies at Newark State Normal, Rutgers University, and NYU's Extramural Division.

In 1923, a document shows that "Harry Emanuel Wagenheim" took courses at Rutgers University's School of Education in New Brunswick. On Feb. 23, 1931, he was granted a B.S. in Education from New York University's School of Education. On March 16, 1960, a letter from the Newark Board of Education was mailed to my father who then resided at 127 So. Serrano Ave., Los Angeles 4, California. The letter, said: "To Whom It May Concern. Re: Experience Statement. Mr. Harold Wagenheim was employed as a teacher in the Newark School System. From Sept. 1, 1929 to June 30, 1932 he taught at Montgomery Street Pre-Vocational School, and from Sept. 1, 1932 to June 30, 1935 he taught at Hawthorne Avenue School. On Sept. 1, 1935 (when I was five months old) he was transferred and assigned to Monmouth Street School, at which time he was granted a leave of absence for personal illness until Oct. 7, 1942, when he resigned. Mr. Wagenheim taught in the seventh and eight grade at the above listed schools, and his services were satisfactory. Leon Mones, Assistant Superintendent."

He loved theater. When he was 31, he even played a small role in a Broadway show, *"The Day Will Come,"* a play by Leon Birinski, which had a short run (Sept. 7 to Sept. 23, 1944) at the National Theatre (now the Nederlander Theater), 208 W. 41st St., New York. The program lists "Harold Wagenheim" as one of 25 "Peasants and Villagers". Other Broadway shows that season included *"Ten Little Indians"* by Agatha Christie, *"Catherine Was Great,"* by Mae West, *"While The Sun Shines"* by Terence Rattigan, "*Seven Lively Arts"* with music and lyrics by Cole Porter, *"The Glass Menagerie"* by Tennessee Williams, and *"The Man Who Had All The Luck"* by Arthur Miller.

After my father's death, I found, among his papers, a small printed brochure which on the cover read: "Studio Of the Theatre And Its Allied Arts. Harold Wagenheim, Director. 105 Chadwick Ave., Newark NJ. Bigelow 3-8063." Inside are descriptions of various courses, and a brief bio sketch: "Harold Wagenheim is a teacher of vast experience which includes all the creative arts. He possesses the ability for recognizing the possibilities and limitations of his students. Under his guidance students are treated as individuals and trained to use their native gifts toward some worthwhile creative goal."

He had little or no commercial success as a writer, but he was quite prolific. After his death, among his things I found several receipts for scripts he had written and registered with the the Screen Writers' Guild. These included: "How Did It Start?" (2/27/51, paid $1.50); "The Hodgson Girl And Mr. Dnoyeb" (12/14/51 and 1/21/52, paid $1.50 twice). Later he registered scripts with Writers Guild of America West, in Los Angeles, Calif. These included: "10-20-30, Or: Ye Old Tyme Theater" (11/24/59, paid $4); "Sailors Snug Harbor; TV Filmed Series" (11/24/59, paid $4); "The Moments of Greatness" (3/21/61, paid $4); "Babel Busters" (6/7/61, paid $4); "Two Change Word Game" or "Two Way Word Game" (12/11/61, paid $4); "The Wastrel And Mr. Dnoyeb"(11/6/62, paid $3.50); "The Question Cinquain" (4/7/65, paid $4); "Juan's People" or "The Many Lives of Juan Rodriguez", first draft (12/4/67, paid $3.50); "The Case Of the Changing Habit" or "Box of Sweet Memories" (7/2/68, paid $5). Unfortunately these organizations are required to hold a script for only 10 years, after which they are authorized to destroy them. In 2007, I Emailed them, asking—if by some miracle—the scripts are still on file, but I am not optimistic. The only script that I found among his papers is "The Wastrel And Mr. Dnoyeb" a 79-page typed carbon copy.

Among my late father's papers I found a Prudential Insurance Co. policy, dated May 25, 1948, stating that Harold E. Wagenheim, an employee of The May Company, a department store in Los Angeles, had a group life policy for $1,000, and that the beneficiary was "Kalman H. Wagenheim, Son of the Insured."

My Mother, Rozlon Heller Wagenheim

Taped phone interview, 9/7/97 with Lucille Steltzer (My Aunt, Mom's younger sister, born 1919, age 78 at time of interview. She was living with her youngest daughter Robin and son-in-law Stan Glogocheski in Woodbridge NJ (Robin & Stan have two children, Jamie and Jeff).

Lucille: You know what amazes me? Your mother used to write. Your father used to write. Your mother used to write uneven type of poetry, it didn't rhyme, but it was like very deep.

KW: I didn't know that. No one ever kept it, did they?

Lucille: We didn't think of it at the time. Who knew she was going to die?

KW: How've you been?

Lucille: I'm OK. I'm a diabetic. I take insulin. I give myself my injections. Sometimes Robin or Stan take me shopping. Jamie is a real character. Jeff is taking Spanish in high school. That's the most spoken language in this country. I can read if the letters are three inches high. I can see TV. I'm not blind. There are so many sugar-free foods now, it's easy to be careful. Ice cream. Cookies.

KW: I've been wanting to make a family record, maybe for the kids. You told me where my mother died, in which hospital.

Lucille: We were four years apart. She was very mature in comparison to me.

KW: When she died in 1937, she was 22, and you were 18. How did my parents meet? Do you know?

Lucille: Your father must have had a nervous breakdown before she met him. You know who he was going with? Frances *(my sister June's stepmother)*. And his mother went to Frances' mother and said "don't go with my boy, he's a sick boy, he had a nervous breakdown." She broke up with him, but she never stopped loving him. Then he met my sister. Too bad she didn't come to Nanny. Frances was sitting next to me, that time they came to your house, and her eyes were eating you up. Because of your father. She says, "oh how I loved him". She kept on telling me how his mother came to her. Then I realized it was her we heard about. I remember vaguely me taking walks with him. He was very strange. "You wanna take a walk?" He was very strange.

KW: In what way?

Lucille: Not crazy, but weird. I'm walking with him one day. I was a kid. He stopped real fast, stamped his foot on the sidewalk. There was a dollar bill, or a five dollar bill, I don't remember, on the sidewalk. He didn't want anyone to see him get it. "Don't move," he said. He looked around. Finally he bent over and picked it up.

KW: (laughs) That was a lot of money in those days. Did they go out for a long time before they got married? I never saw a wedding picture of the two of them.

Lucille: I don't remember. I know they got married. .

KW: Would it have been with a rabbi?

Lucille: Yeah. They had a Jewish ceremony.

KW: Cause I know his parents were religious. And Grandma was religious.

Lucille: When she died, of hemorraging, the doctor came in, and he said she gave up, she didn't even try. Whether he could have saved her or not, I don't know. They took her to the hospital. She was heartbroken because your father left her.

KW: I know they were separated when she gave birth.

Lucille: She gave birth to you and he left her. Then he came back. Then he left her again. He was strange.

KW: He left her when I was born? I didn't know that. You mean he left before I was born, or after?

Lucille: She was in the hospital, and came home and he wasn't there. And he stayed away for a while, and then came back. She was madly in love with him and took him back. Then she got pregnant with June, and you know what happened after that.

KW: Do you have any idea what the problem between the two of them was?

Lucille: He had had a nervous breakdown at one time.

KW: It wasn't like he was involved with another woman.

Lucille: No, no. He was just mentally...

KW: Mentally unstable.

Lucille: Yeah. He was a teacher at Hawthorne Avenue school if I'm not mistaken. I think he taught 8th grade school.

KW: He never taught again after she died. In fact, I don't think he ever had a decent job after that. When she died, he was living with his parents. After, did they try to see me?

Lucille: I don't know if they didn't care, or if they didn't think they were welcome. Maybe because of what they felt he did to her. He actually broke her heart. Did you ever see a movie with an old time actor called Richard Dix? He looked a lot like your father. She was madly in love with him. I'll never forget when they took her to the hospital. My Uncle Carlie. I was lying on the couch. Waiting for them to come back. And they said Rozlon just died. I had dozed for a while. Carlie was standing there, and his arms were crossed, and tears were dropping on his arms.

KW: June was born May 30. My mother died the next day.

Lucille: They couldn't stop the hemorraging. Carlie and Nanny were in the hospital. Grandma was in the house, with me. She was waiting for them to come back. And I remember Nanny saying to her, Rozlon died. Carlie standing there, tears dropping on his arms.

KW: When you were a young girl, did your mom tell you how old you were when your father abandoned you?

Lucille: I was a year and a half. Never knew my father.

KW: So my mother was only five and a half when he walked out.

Lucille: I don't remember my life with her as a kid. Isn't that something? She was much more mature and had her own friends. She had a friend Lily, who lived around the corner from us on Belmont Avenue, and later moved to Florida.

KW: Did your father, my grandfather, fall in love with some other woman?

Lucille: She worked for him. I think she enticed him to leave. I never knew him until we went to California, and I was a married woman. Originally he was in Fort Lee, New Jersey, where the movie business started. I was thinking about Rosie, who predicted that years later my mother would meet my father again in my apartment in Newark, and they did!

KW: That was back around 1960.

Lucille: Yeah. We were living in the Seth Boyden Apartments at the time. Frances, his wife called, and said, "Hello Lucille, Daddy and I are in New York and we're going to come visit you." I said fine. Nanny worked. So I figured I'd call her and tell her, but then I said nah. Rosie predicted this three years before. That's why I didn't call her I guess. I figured I'll wait til she gets home from work and call her. They came over . There was a knock on the door. My mother. She said "I'm on vacation this week." It was pathetic. She sat there, all she did was shake. She couldn't drink the coffee.

KW: Yeah, after so many years of not seeing each other.

Lucille: It was very upsetting. She said, "I better go", and she walked out. I wonder how Rosie predicted that.

KW: I don't know. She told me I was going to find my sister June.

Lucille: Rosie told me were were going to ride through red dirt. And that's what we did when we went to California. We went there for about a year, but (*my husband*) Sam couldn't find work. I guess Frances didn't want him there. My father wouldn't find him work, and we came back. Nanny supported us, she went to work, and Grandma raised us. I think I was married when she married Harry Krantz. I think she got the house on Belmont Avenue out of it. One went to the daughter and one went to Nanny. He had been married before. His wife died. He was a nice man.

KW: He was a funny man. Always good humored.

Lucille: His son, Shorty Krantz, was a wealthy man, who owned a bar downtown. Another son was a pharmacist. I know he had a daughter.

KW: I moved over to Belmont Avenue (with Grandma and Grandpa) when Harry Krantz died. She was left all alone, so she asked us to move over there.

Lucille: Your mother was so brilliant,. I know she worked in a toy factory. She wanted to make a few bucks. She went a couple of years to high school. She was such a brain. She kept skipping. She used to write uneven poetry, it didn't rhyme, it was very deep. I do know that she was in a magazine. You know those love story magazines? There was a picture of her, with her elbow on a bar, and her foot on the railing in front of the bar.

KW: Really?

Lucille: I don't remember if it was before she met your father, or when they separated.

KW: I do have some photos of her that look as though they were posed by a professional photographer. A fashion photographer. They were not amateur photos. Did you tell me that my mother had once won a dance contest?

Lucille: She did the tango, a Spanish dance. There used to be a place called the Avon Mansion. It was a place where they had weddings. She wore this white gown. She looked gorgeous.

KW: She gave the name Dolores to her little daughter..

Lucille: I knew she liked the name Dolores.

KW: Why do you think she gave her that name?

Lucille: Dolores del Rio, the movie star, maybe. Everybody said she looked a little bit like Dolores del Rio.

KW: That's what I was guessing. When I found the record of June's birth, it said her name was Dolores Wagenheim. Then, her new parents, they adopted her in the month of June. So maybe that's why they named her June. Did you ever visit the Wagenheims?

Lucille: Once or twice. They lived in a little one-family house, I think on Chadwick Avenue. I remember very little about it. Nice quiet people. I think it was a house wedding. They lived in a little apartment, for a short while, somewhere around the Weequahic section, I think. But he left all of a sudden. She was stuck with the apartment. He was very strange. He taught in Hawthorne Avenue school, so it was up there somewhere. It was a nice little apartment. I can picture him because we used to take walks together. He had a mental problem. He wasn't crazy. It was depression.

KW: Your father offered me a job in California, as an apprentice editor at Warner Brothers. But I was pretty well set on going to Puerto Rico. I thanked him, but I didn't go.

Lucille: When he died, the son was left. She left me in the will, $1000. I wound up with about $500.

KW: When my mother died, what did her father do?

Lucille: That bum, he was a real bum. Nanny didnt have enough money to bury Rozlon. The insurance wasn't enough. She called him. He refused. He sent her a sympathy card.

KW: No money, for his own daughter.

Lucille: Morris Greenberg gave her the money. He said you can pay me back. . When it came to pay it back, he said look, I don't need it, you can't afford it. He was a cousin through marriage. He was a great guy.

KW: Morris used to have a little supermarket in Maplewood. All the rich people in Maplewood used to buy there.

Lucille: My father made a fortune. He did all the coming attractions for Warner Brothers.

KW: He never sent child support for you and my mother?

Lucille: Never. I think it was her. His second wife. Daddy this, and Daddy that. I think she dominated him. Once in a while, maybe once in five years, I got a dollar for my birthday. Very very seldom. You know your father went out to California, and your Uncle Sam and I went out there. We're sitting with them, Frances and my father, and were talking. My father says, "did you go see Kalman's father? I heard he's out here." Sam said, "we don't want to see these bums who desert their wife and kids and run off to California." Frances' face! I was gloating with joy. You should have seen her face! (laughs) Your Uncle Sam was very outspoken.

KW: My father didn't leave to California until 9 years later. He was basically a sick guy. My grandfather had a good job. There was less of an excuse for him to be negligent. My father never had a penny.

Lucille: I think she ran him. Daddy this, and Daddy that.

KW: It was Nanny who told me I had a sister.

Lucille: Grandma said to me: "I'm going to tell Kalman he has a sister. Because if they ever meet, and it's the same blood, they could fall in love"...I knew all along, because I didn't know if you knew or not...

KW: I didn't learn I had a sister until I was 25. The amazing thing to me is how Grandma and Nanny died so close together, a month apart.

Lucille: Nanny had skin cancer, which was curable. She went to the skin doctor, and he said it was an allergy. By the time they found out what it was, it traveled to the lungs. I shoulda sued the bum. He was in the Medical Tower in Newark. A big shot skin specialist. She had thin skin, very thin skin. She wasn't supposed to stay in the sun. She could wear the best jewelry, and her finger would turn black and blue. That's the kind of skin she had. She went to Florida, and instead of staying outa the sun, she didn't. When she got back, it was cancerous. But he told her it was an allergy. So it traveled, and in a month she was gone. She didn't know she had cancer until she was practically dying.

KW: It was so fast. A month after Grandma died.

Lucille: I remember when Grandma died, you and I were sitting in that car. My God, where were we going, Long Island?

KW: That was a long ride. It was some organization she belonged to.

Lucille: The Chekanivtzer.

KW: Right. I think it was Elmont, Long Island.

Lucille: Nanny is buried in Woodbridge, here in New Jersey.

KW: That's where my father is buried, too. There's a Wagenheim family plot. My mother's grave, I went there not long ago.

Lucille: South Orange Avenue, in Newark, right?

KW: Yeah, it's close by. After I met June I took her out there. Yeah, we went out there once. That was at least...for the two of us to go there together...

More about Rozlon Heller Wagenheim (my mother). *Interview with Lucille Steltzer(Aunt). Recorded 9/23/97*

Lucille: She (Rozlon) was very exotic looking. Long dark brown hair. Big brown eyes. She had a beautiful figure. She liked to dance, tango, things like that...Spanish dancing was very popular then. I went to school and came home, and she was working...When she died, we were living on Jelliff Avenue in Newark. She used to sit on the porch with you a lot...The big porch. Living in the house was my mother, Carlie, Grandma, Grandpa. Murrey lived downtown…I was thinking about Grandma today. What a wonderful person she was.

KW: Did anyone from my father's family come visit at Jelliff Ave?

Lucille: No. That's why we resented them so much. We felt that after all, she died, he left this boy, and you don't come to see him?

More about my childhood. 10-14-97. *Recorded interview With Lucille Stelzer, Kal's aunt. Lucille tells Kal that when he was tiny boy, his mother would feed him in the high chair and sing to him...*

Lucille: "Down in the meadow in the itty-bitty poo...fan fings itty bittys and the momma's sitty too...sings said the mamas and and they fammed and they fammed all over the dam...bump-bump-dittum-waddam-waddam watchoo! bump-bump-dittum-waddam-waddam-watchoo! And they fammed and they fammed all over the dam!" There's a black guy, I don't know his name, he sang it on TV not long ago, believe or not. It was a sad thing with Rozlon. The doctor said she didn't want to live. She didn't try. Your father left, when she had you, and he left when she had June. I guess he couldn't take the pressure. When you were born, I think she was living with Grandma already, because he had left. She had to give up the apartment. I think it was the corner of Keer and Hawthorne, but I'm not positive. What I remember most, that June, I graduated high school and I didn't want to go, but Nanny said you're going to get that diploma if it kills me. I'll be there. And she was. That's how I got a civil service job later. I owe that to Nanny. I was a teenager. I don't remember. But I think it was a house wedding. I got married in 1938 to Sam. April. I was living on Bergen Street on the 3rd floor, and I heard the radio, with Orson Welles, War of the Worlds. I would love to get a copy of the newspaper. .

KW: I went down to City Hall the other day, to see if I could find a marriage certificate for Rozlon and Harold. And, also to see about a death certificate for her. Do you know, in City Hall they don't have it? They said try Trenton. So I wrote to Trenton. Then I went to the library. They had microfilms of the newspapers from that time.

Lucille: Did you find an obituary?

KW: No. I looked in the newspaper of the day after she died. June 1. I looked June 2, 3, 4, 5, 6, Ten days. Nothing. It's almost as though she never existed.

Lucille: Maybe nobody reported it. The shame of it all is that your sister

June never met Grandma and Nanny. Grandma would have loved to take care of June. She was strong.

KW: You told me they talked her out of it.

Lucille: Family. You know, Dora...the money people. Morris Greenberg. Sally Pulver. They came over and they talked her out of it. The Weequahic section was a ritzy section that time. They said you're old, you got Kalman, you gotta raise him. The whole bit. And she said to me I'm gonna tell Kalman he's got a sister, because it's the same blood, they could fall in love. Thats why she told you....

KW: When I was in high school, Nan got me part-time jobs after school and on Saturdays in two places where she worked. Mr. Berkowitz, and later Mr. Spritzer (N.J Candy & Tobacco Co. at 39 Ferry St., Newark). That's where Nanny retired from. They liked her a lot. She was very responsible.

Lucille: She went on vacation to Florida. She had such sensitive skin. They didn't know too much in those days. They said it was an allergy of some kind. They gave her medication. By that time it spread. The skin cancer was curable. But it was too late. She died just 30 days after Grandma. The saddest thing I ever saw is when my sister, Rozlon, died. And I remember Nanny staring, staring at the coffin. She never took her eyes off of her. I think a neighbor next door watched you during the funeral. That June I graduated, and Nanny insisted that I go through with the ceremony. That diploma helped me get a job. At the time your mother died, in the house were living Carlie and Davey. Eddie (joined Army in Carolinas, met Aunt Elizabeth, and stayed in N.C.) was living down south. Murrey lived downtown Newark. Didn't want to live at home.

KW: Before he died, I saw Uncle Davey, in North Carolina. He lasted until he was 92. He'd had a stroke. Couldn't talk.

Lucille: Something was wrong with him. He used to punch himself. Have fits. I don't know if he had malaria, or something. It used to frighten me. He would leave home and not come back for a long time. Poor Grandma.

KW: He walked out, said he was gonna get a newspaper, and he disappeared.

Lucille: Murrey once came over our house. Went to the bathroom. After he left, we found a little sign he wrote: "I didn't come in here to sit and think. I came to to sit and stink." When we lived on 13th St. there was a bootlegger that the police were always after. And Murrey had come back from the World

War I with a wound, and he limped. So did the bootlegger. His name was Louie. Grandma was always worried that the police would come by and shoot Murrey, thinking he was the bootlegger, because they both limped. Grandpa in New York may have been a butcher, but in Newark he worked in a place that had to do with burlap bags. He worked near a place that sold figs and dates on a rope, he would bring them home all the time. He was 10 years older than her.

Ana (daughter in Chicago, wealthy) would send Grandma 25 or 50 dollars a month. And , even though Grandma's hand trembled, if she didn't sign her name, Ana wouldn't send her another check. That Ana was a snob. She was born in Europe and ashamed of it. She was very young when she came here. I don't know how she met Mr. Kronenberger. He was very wealthy. In Chicago, had a big business. I think he made hats for the Chicago baseball team. They had two sons, Bruce and Dickie. One committed suicide. The brothers were very very close. Bruce was married, and Dickie went up to see him. The doorman testified that when he came out, Dickie's face was all red, as though he'd been in a fight, and he later killed himself. Ana called Nanny up later, saying she didnt know how terrible it was to lose a child. Was she crazy? What about Rozlon?

KW: All I remember, I was a kid, and a box came in the mail, with a couple of nice wool sweaters. They belonged to her son, the one who died; they sent them to me. I wore those sweaters for several years. I guess she was cleaning out his clothes.

Lucille: She used to send 25 or 50 dollars, and I remember Grandma's hand used to shake, when she would sign the checks. He (Kronenberger) was a nice guy.

KW: I remember, when Rosie used to take the bus from New York to our apartment on South 13th St. and knock on the door. Grandma would put the water to boil for tea, and then go get a deck of cards from a drawer in the kitchen. Rosie would start with the cards.

Lucille: Your Uncle Carlie years before used to pitch in that nearby West Side Park. He was signed up for the Newark Bears (New York Yankee farm team), and he got hit in the nose, a broken nose, and that ended his career. He got scared. His nose was some mess. Left-handed pitcher.

KW: When I was a little kid, he would play catch with me.

Lucille: When I was little he would play, Laurel & Hardy also did it. You took a broomstick and hit a piece of wood...Carlie was very close to your mother. He was close to both of us. He cried like a baby when she died. I can still see the tears dropping onto his bare arms. Sleeves were rolled up. He came in with Nanny and told us that Rozlon had passed away. The doctor said--she might have died anyway--but she had no chance ....she was so heartbroken when your father left...he left when she had you, too.

KW: I guess he couldn't take....

Lucille: She was madly in love with your father ...Then he came back, and she got pregnant with June...and he left again...Grandma wanted to take June home.

Phone conversation with Susan Wagenheim, cousin Bill Wagenheim's daughter, who lives in Albany NY. She is a psychiatrist. Recorded Oct. 8, 1997.

KW: .I was gonna ask you as a doctor, the more I look at the circumstances of my mother's death, and my father's problems over the years, in her case she died of hemorrhaging, giving birth to my sister....and in his case, he apparently had a severe case of depression. If you think back to the 1930s, today there would be a lot more help for both of them. You worked as a nurse before becoming a doctor, and helped to deliver many babies. What caused hemorrhaging? Was this a common thing? What's done today, to prevent it?

Susan: There's a couple of possible causes of intra-partum hemorrhage. You can have an abrupted placenta, in which case a part of the placenta pulls away from the wall; it just bleeds massively. What you gotta do is an immediate delivery. Sometimes the hemorrhage is occult. Because the part of the placenta that pulls away from the wall is up at the top of the uterus, so a lot of the bleeding is contained in that pocket, and you don't see it until pressure builds up and it spills over the sides of the placenta. Another cause, this is less likely, is a low-lying placenta, its low down on the uterus, over the opening of the cervix. When somebody goes into labor, it pulls ...but usually there's bleeding all along during the pregnancy, diagnosed well before labor. A third cause is a rare occurrence. But I've seen a case. Its called DIC, or Disseminated Intervascular Coagulopsy. Nobody really knows what causes it. There's a theory that the force of the uterus puts the amniotic fluid into circulation...and that starts this clotting problem. Basically it's not clotting. Usually the baby's delivered intact. It's right after the delivery that all of a sudden, *pow!* The only treatment is either transfusion of fresh whole blood or all the clotting factors. In the case we had, it was close. This lady almost bit the bullet. But there were three of us right there on the unit who had her blood type, and we ran down to the lab, and gave blood...I gave blood, here I'm a medical student, they hand me my own bag of blood, and I had to run up the stairs. So that's how much of an emergency it was...Hemorrhaging wasn't all that common even then. You had to have this mechanical problem. There's almost no, unless she was a known hemophiliac, which I doubt...It had to be one of the mechanical type problems...

KW So what do they do today?

Susan: First of all diagnosis. With the placentas, they do an ultrasound, and they can see the placenta. They do a C-section. If you have low-lying placenta, they don't let you go into labor. They do a section. You pull the baby up, away from the placenta, and you don't start the bleeding. The Caesarean rate back then was maybe 4%. Now, today, it's something like 40%. They were not quick to do C-sections. The DIC still takes you by surprise, but people know about it. They know what you've got to do, get tons of units of fresh whole blood into the patient. Give you back the clotting factors. Today, it's very rare to die of hemorrhaging. The ultrasound is the key for the placenta conditions.

KW: In the case of my father, according to Neil, who knew my father, he said he was very depressed, and would often break into tears...in those days, the idea of psych. or psychologist...my father was a teacher...

Susan: He could have been treated today... sounds like he suffered from unipolar depression...they run in families. ..Years of untreated depression do something to a person. You become a shell of a person, really. It's so much different today. First of all, there's anti-depressants in any number of classes. If you don't respond to one, you're bound to respond to another. The first class are the tryciclic anti-depressants. They have a chemical structure of three rings. There are the MAOI inhibitors. They work a different way. Then there's the whole new generation of what they call the SSRIs, prozac, and zoloff...you can augment those with a little bit of lithium. I see people...they have a little bit of a response. Sprinkle a little lithium on them, only 300 milligrams, a sub-therapeutic dose for mania, and that just does the trick. ECT, shock treatments, can break a severe depression, and then you put them on maintenance meds, and they do well...

There's no question in my mind that this is something that runs in the family. I've had a couple of major depressions. When I was treated with prozac alone I got high. I've never had a full-blown manic episode. But I got hypo-manic on the anti-depressant. So , it doesn't surprise me to hear there's a confirmed bipolar in the family. It had to come from somewhere. His would be unipolar, if he never had periods of distinctly higher energy...he needed less sleep, was very productive, you don't necessarily ...a full blown manic episode people get psychotic. They really lose...hypomania...if you could be hypomanic forever, you'd be the most productive person in the world! The colors are sharper. the air smells cleaner. You need less sleep. You have a lot of energy. It does seem to run along with higher intelligence. We don't know yet. They're very productive people. Dostoyevsky was supposed to be a bipolar of that type. Hundreds of figures in history.

He could've had the unipolar kind, where you just go down, or if he ever had these periods of productivity, they call it bipolar type II. There's so many forms of treatment today. It would have been more difficult to treat him later in life. The brain is primed to be this way. It gets intractable. We treat depression very aggressively today. We keep people on maintenance meds after a first major depression, we keep them on minimum six months, usually up to a year. If they have another one, we think about keeping it on them, period. Pills plus talk are better than either alone.

Letter from Cousin Neil Simon, Deming, New Mexico. Aug. 31, 1997. Dear Kal: Much of what I am writing here is subject to my memory over a sixty year period, and conversations with Harry's mother (my grandmother) in Yiddish before I was 20 years old! Ada Barr was born in Zahga, a small town near Riga, the present capital of Latvia. The area was under German rule and Yiddish and German were her languages. Wagenheim is somewhat Germanic and it may explain Morris' heritage. I do know that Morris was one of three brothers, who stopped in England, where one of them left for South Africa. All of the children were born in America (Newark). I remember Charlie's parents from visits when I was young. "Uncle" would always give me a quarter, "but don't tell my wife."

Nathan and Frieda were the older children and Harry and Dora were always the babies. Nat drove a truck for Rose Dairy and always had milk and butter for us. I was born May 16, 1932 in an old house at the corner of Waverly Ave. and Hunterdon St. Five months later, during the height of the Depression, we all moved into the house on Chadwick Ave. During the next 7 years we lived together. Harry occupied a small front room where he frequently typed on a noisy typewriter. On Chadwick Ave. labor was divided as follows: Grandpa Morris—coal for kitchen oven and basement steam heat. Churning ice cream with the help of Neil and Greta. Freida and Ada: all cooking and dishwashing. Dora: care for all of the children, sending Jerry and Bernie to school. Harry: when not typing, making beds, setting table, healing everyone. Sam: away all day at work.

It was on Avon Ave. that I got to know Harry. My uncle impressed me with his clothes and manner. Harry almost always wore a suit, tie and white shirt, and shiny black shoes. There was a problem with the shoes; they always hurt him. I was 8 years old and I began to read any and every book which my mother bought for me (5c each) from McRory's used book counter. She brought home everything from Medical Books to Russian Literature. Harry helped me understand them, and showed me how to use his 2-volume dictionary set, tooled in leather. Harry had breakfast late (always an egg cup), fully dressed and his mother sitting with him.

I gradually learned that Harry was in constant turmoil and depression. He bore lifelong responsibility for the death of his wife, and not knowing his daughter. By this time I believe he was not allowed to visit Kal. I myself had seen Kal once, as a little baby in a crib. (I believe this took place when I still lived on Chadwick Ave.). Harry had fairly regular habits. He spent much time looking for work. He also frequented the Hebrew Club on Clinton Ave. My mother told me that he had written many plays that were produced at the YMHA on High Street in Newark. When the time came for applause, Harry was never present to receive honors. I was also told that Harry got an appointment to show his work to Dore Schary in Hollywood. For this single great opportunity Harry brought with him a woman writer who he believed was very talented. Schary became indignant since his time was for Harry alone. He threw them both out of the office and would never see Harry again. (*Note: Isidore Dore Schary, born in Newark NJ in 1905, died in New York in 1980, a graduate of Newark's Central High in 1923, was a major motion picture director, writer, producer and playwright and my father most have known him from Newark.).*

Back on Avon Ave., Harry was often concerned about me. He disconnected my radio when it was on fire. Another time I awoke screaming in the dark and Harry saw that I was covered with bedbugs and he put me in the tub and washed them off with hot water. All of his doctors said he should go to Hollywood and write. In the year when I was Bar Mitzvahed (about 1945) Harry's brother and sisters put money together for a train ticket to Hollywood. Harry never sold a play. He lived in a small hotel room eating sardines. Then his friend Ben Kaufman invited him to Redondo Beach to run a chicken ranch. When I visited Harry I slept over and we got up early and ran back and forth collecting the eggs. We then "candled" the eggs and put them in boxes (I was about 22 years old, about 1954). I saw Harry only one more time when he flew back east (Dora sent money; she also wrote him monthly and sent cigarette money). Harry stayed only 2 or 3 days (1963-64), cried a lot, and returned to Los Angeles. As I remember more Kal (I am just out of paper) we shall talk. Fondly, Neil.

Neil Simon. 1st cousin, on father's side. Telephone call to his home in New Mexico. His daughter-in-law is Diana, from Puerto Rico. Sept. 1997

KW: Do you have time to talk now, for a few minutes?

Neil: I always have time. I'm retired. No, you're not not interrupting my dinner. I'm very unorganized.

KW: Your letter filled in a lot of blanks for me.

Neil: Morris (your grandfather) wasn't much of a conversationalist. He prayed a lot. At home. He put on his tallis. He didn't go to the schul. He would go out periodically with his big scissors, and work. But don't forget, those years were very bad years for work.

KW: He didn't have a tailor shop?

Neil: Oh, no. I don't think he ever did. He was a tailor, and he worked for other people. He would cut patterns and things for wealthier tailors. They came around the turn of the century. I don't know if they had pogroms or what...

KW: I know that a lot of other Wagenheims left around that time. I ran into various cousins. They all came from Riga and were named Wagenheim.

Neil: I was born in 1932. I came along with the children of the younger Wagenheims, in the depth of the Depression. Times were tough then. That's why everyone got together at Chadwick Avenue. (They were living apart and decided to economize). In most of my time there, lots of people, about eleven, were living together. It's a house, 103 Chadwick. I think it's still standing. I know there was a plum tree in the yard alongside the house. And the older males, Jerry & Bernie, used to climb up and get plums. The only one working at that time was my father. He had lost a business. He had a very big stove and heating business on Springfield Ave. Morris, your grandfather, used to take care of everything. That was his job on Chadwick Avenue. Go down to the cellar, where the coal man dumped the coal and he would get a bucket and put coal in the furnace. He was an older man. He would put coal in the stoves in the kitchen. Most of the cooking was done on coal stoves. I know they had an awful lot of stations for cooking, because I remember my mother was cooking on all burners. (There were 11 people in the house). And they used to heat their wash, you know. In hot water. I guess there weren't any hot water heaters. They would boil the wash. I remember those big pots, with the steaming sheets inside, cooking on the range. They used to sit me on the kitchen table, to watch.

KW: I remember years ago visiting you...

Neil: On the campus at Rutgers...I remember you sitting by the window there. I was trying to get a doctorate in chemistry. That's where my life exploded. That is the site of the explosion. I'm not normal. I got very sick. I was in the hospital for a month. After that,...that's why you lost track of me... everyone lost track. I had a breakdown. (My wife) was going to undergraduate school. Alex was in the crib, and I used to babysit because I did my homework at night, I would teach, and take classes, and I was working on my thesis, and my lab work, and one night she came home...the library was open until 2 am. She took night school. So it turned out she was seeing this guy, who she later married, as her second husband, and it just blew my mind, completely. And I ran away. It's a long story. We finally wound up divorced. We like one another till today. She had a breakdown later. Then I was never good after that, in terms of....There's a sickness called bipolar illness. I had it since the age of thirty. That's when it usually appears. It's manic depression, they called it originally.

KW: Do you still take medication?

Neil: Yeah. I have to take it until I die. Before lithium, there was nothing for it. It goes way back. Thirty-five years. All they had was thorazine. When I broke down , in Texas, I had traveled a little, first they checked me to see if I was a drug addict, and then they took me to the hospital. The only drug they had was thorazine. I said please, I can't sleep, give me something to sleep. They gave me a shot of thorazine. I was on 700 milligrams of thorazine for several years until they started developing new drugs. I proceeded to take every drug that was invented, right up until lithium. Lithium aggravated psoriasis, which I had developed also. It's an ion. It goes through the blood stream, like potassium and sodium. Therefore I couldn't take lithium. But I already had this very good doctor...I had 24 psychiatrists ...that's where all my money went...that's why I'm living where I'm living...I had good jobs, but no one would hire me...I eventually worked for 25 years with this one company; he was the only one who would hire me. And underpay me. I took every medication that was discovered, up until the present. And the doctor found a good combination that works.

KW: Does this thing run in families?

Neil: It's hereditary. Allan had a tragic marriage. Really tragic. She was very demanding. Then she got a little strange. She had like 20 cats in the house. He wanted to move away. I know she had girlfriends. She didn't like boys after that....

KW: The boy, Stephen, he's kind of eccentric, but thank God had the great good luck to meet a math teacher from Irvington High School and this girl really straightened him out. They have a cute little daughter. They live in a house in Roselle Park. They have a supportive family.

Neil: That's wonderful. I didn't know what happened to him. Harriet used to call me to try to sell me her father's photography business.

KW: Everyone told me my father had some kind of emotional problems. How would you diagnose them?

Neil: I don't think Harry was ever manic. I think Greta was. And I think she killed herself with cigarettes. They had heart problems in their family. I have a problem of congestive heart failure, that's what my brother died from. I got it double-barreled. I was more of an optimist. Somehow I had gotten enough of an education on my own. I had read so many books, I was a walking encyclopedia when I was young....of course, my mental problems have taken a lot of that away...especially shock therapy and all that, which blows your mind. Twenty of them. Before they invented anasthesia. I have seen worse than the snakepit. I am glad that I didn't die when I was about 35. The crisis with my wife triggered it. It appears in boys around that age. I wasn't in touch with reality from the moment she talked to me. After some of my treatment she came down and flew me back to Marlboro, which is really a snakepit. We couldn't afford anything. I was there for four months. I get a lot of *deja vu* of that place. Harry, your father, was in the hospital a number of times. I don't know if they had medicine in those days. I used to visit him with my mother. Up in Essex County Hospital. Roseland, I think. It was after we moved to Avon Avenue. We used to take a bus downtown. Then we'd take the bus up there. To Fairview Street. It was called Overbrook. Now they call it New Jersey Hospital Center.

KW: When my father died, they mailed me a bunch of papers that he had. Among the things, there was a letter from the Board of Education in Newark, and it said that, my mother died in May 1937, and it said that from September 1937 on, he no longer was teaching. So he must have had some kind of breakdown in that summer... Then it said he got a leave of absence, and retired for personal illness in 1942.

Neil: That's probably when he moved into Chadwick Avenue. I remember him in that little front room on the second floor. He had this typewriter that went clackety-clack, and I used to wander in and watch him type away at the keys.

KW: I know that he and my mother were separated at least once, and that at the time of her death they were separated. But I wasn't sure how long, or what had happened.

Neil: I think he was home with his parents when she died.

KW: That probably contributed to his breakdown. It must have been a feeling of great ...

Neil: Guilt. He could never forgive himself for her death.

KW: Did he actually say anything?

Neil: He cried a lot. He cried a lot. Dora, his sister, knew an awful lot about Harry, but she died, and her children died, and I was the one who talked to Dora and she made me promise not to talk about anything she told me...she had spoken about her own personal relationships...she lost her husband when she was very young...I saw him cry a lot. He would cry anywhere. He would cry at the table when...see, his mother used to sit...he had his own egg cup at breakfast. I always wished that I could have an egg cup when I got older!

KW: (laughs) She used to make the egg for him?

Neil: Yeah, his mother made the egg, and the toast and the coffee. And he always got dressed up nicely, because he was gonna look for work, or something of that sort. And I wandered the house. I was eight or nine then, this was around 1940. . He would burst into tears many times. His mother she used to...mothers get kind of repetitious. Harry..or Harrele..go out and get yourself a job....I guess the repetition would get to him...It wasn't right that she would sit there while he was eating breakfast...or maybe he wanted her there! So I don't know. I was a kid.

KW: I got a different view. I was raised by my mother's family.

Neil: I think your mother's family was very healthy.

KW: They were very bitter. They felt, they sort of blamed...from a distance they might not have known. They felt that Harry's family , more like his mother, interfered in the marriage. But I have no idea if that's true or not. They used to tell me things. Oh, he was such a bright guy, but he was a mama's boy, but his mother would even buy his own suits for him. .

Neil: There was a lot of hostility. Like I said, I got to see you once, when I was a kid.

KW: They would say things like, his family mixed in...contributed to the thing.

Neil: I think he felt responsible for his wife's death! And he wanted to blame himself... He would always say that she was a beautiful, wonderful person. He was very much, as your family said, a mother's boy. He was like Allan. If you knew Allan, it was almost like knowing Harry. Allan didn't have a breakdown. I think his marriage was somewhat destructive.

KW: Allan, in some ways, had the same disappointments in life as my father. He never had much success with his writing, and he's been very frustrated by that. I don't know how many novels Allan's written, I've read literary criticism of his which I think is very perceptive,

Neil: Writers have to be aggressive. They have to be salesmen, too. Harry had good plays, in the Y, but that was amateur.

KW: I read some of his work. It's not commercial. They're very lovely, very idealistic...

Neil: He was self-effacing, too. He would disappear..He wouldn't go out when people were applauding. He would disappear.

KW: .I've run into people, and Allan has too, who when they hear the name Wagenheim they say, oh, he was a great teacher..Once I was in a bank. And the teller sees my name and says I had this teacher, he was wonderful... that's a gift...He had a gift of being a great teacher...from the little I read of his creative work, it was competently done, but it didn't have a commercial twist to it that would make it a big hit on Broadway...

Neil: He was gonna get a push. I remember that night. I was 13 (year of my bar-mitzvah). He went off to the train, to take him to California. Everyone sat up, waiting that he might come back. They figured he wouldn't have the nerve to go. To try to get his plays produced. He had an appointment with Dore Schary (big Hollywood producer; he knew him from Newark). He met some woman out there, and he wanted to promote her, because he thought she was a good writer. And he had this appointment with Dore Schary, who came from Newark! He used to direct at the Y. Harry went there when he was pretty high up already. And he got this one interview. And my mother keeps saying it over and over, why did he bring that woman along? Oh, God. Life is so tragic.

KW: So after that he just remained in California.

Neil: I don't think he had enough money to come back.

KW: The whole idea was to go out there and present his work. So he wound up on the chicken farm.

Neil:Yeah. I know he lived in a hotel for a long time. In a small room. He didn't have to pay much rent. Dora was constantly helping him.

KW: I know she sent him checks from time to time.

Neil: Yeah, for cigarettes and everything. I remember the words, she would read them to me. Dear Dora, received your letter, contents noted. I knew exactly what that meant.

KW: She was a really devoted sister.

Neil: Yeah. She had lost her husband. She got a job with this guy Black on Central Ave in Newark. It was an auto company. She worked as a secretary for many years....Dora was the sufferer in the family. She suffered for Harry, and my mother, for anyone else that was sick. And Dora, by the way, kept her health so well, kept her weight down, always thin.

KW: I visited her once. All she would eat was steamed broccoli and a baked potato.

Neil: That's all she would make. I used to go up and have dinner with her. She would make me a baked potato.

KW: She had this perfect complexion, because she never ate anything bad! You said you went to see my father in California when you were in your twenties?

Neil: Yeah. I had been in service. I had gotten back from Europe. When everyone else went to Korea, I went to Europe. And I got out around the age of 21, or 22. I was waiting for school to start the following September. I hadn't finished my bachelor's degree because I was going to night school. So when I got out, I had the GI bill which paid me a certain amount. I didn't know what to do so I said to my friend, you know someone dared to me hitchhike across the country, so the next morning I'm out on Route 22 West, that's before any other routes were built. I hitchhiked. I saw my friend Ralph, who was at the University of Illinois. He had gotten his bachelors and was working on his masters and doctorate. In Urbana. I proceeded out to Los Angeles and I ...I think I looked up Wagenheim, and I found Charlie. Charlie was living over a garage at that time. And he was separated from his wife, I forget her name. She was a wonderful person.

KW: Lillian. She was a psychologist. Someone told me that Charlie once separated from her, and he shared an apartment with Paul Muni. He and Muni used to act together in Yiddish Theatre in the Lower East Side.

Neil: Charlie was a fast talker. The manic thing.

KW: Apparently both Charlie and Paul Muni had broken up with their wives, and they lived together for a while, like the Odd Couple. At some point he went back to Lillian.

Neil: I'll tell you what year. In 54, 55, the summer, he was above a garage. I went up the side steps and knocked, and there he was. He had an extra bed, like on a rised section there. He was going out. He said: if the phone rings, you can answer it if you want, but if they sound drunk, don't talk to em. (*laughs*). He had all these girls.

KW: Charlie?

Neil: It was so much fun. Oh, sure, if you're an actor, it doesn't matter how old you are. And I kept answering the phone. They'd say, how are you? Different women. No man ever called there. That's where I lived while I was wrecking houses. I saw these guys burning wood, wrecking houses. They hired me. You're the fireman.

KW: Was Charlie working regularly as an actor at the time?

Neil: He was always into something. I don't know what he did. He always was off somewhere.

KW: When I saw him...he and Lillian were together, and they lived in a six or eight unit apartment building in Hollywood that they owned. They lived in one apartment and rented the rest. They were doing very well at the time.

Neil: Was he gray?

KW: He was older, but what amazed me is that I was already wearing glasses, I was about 33, and he drove me in a car, took me to a restaurant, owned by an old buddy of his, Alan Hale, Jr., the guy from Gilligan's Island, and he didn't wear any glasses at all. He took me to lunch there. He was very spry. Must have been in his 60s. Animated.

Neil: He never had an ounce of fat. He was short and thin. I saw him in a lot of pictures. He played small parts.

KW: So did I. I always show friends, there's that one classic Hitchcock film, Foreign Correspondent, he plays the assassin. It's a famous film. Almost anyone you mention that film to, Oh yeah, Hitchcock. Immediate recognition.

Neil: I was watching a film once with my friend Jerry, and I said, it was a western, that looks like my cousin Charlie. If he gets shot when he walks through the door, that's probably him. And he walked through, they shot him and he fell dead.

KW: I saw him once in a Charlie Chan movie. Charlie Chan and his Number One Son walk into this vacant apartment...

Neil: That goes back a ways...

KW: The son opens up a closet, and out falls a cadaver. And it was Charlie. You had to look very fast! (laughs) But anyway, while you were out there, did my father see much of Charlie?

Neil: No.

KW: They were first cousins.

Neil: Charlie was on his own wavelength. And your father...

KW: They were so unlike each other...

Neil: Yeah, he was more withdrawn. But you know, he didn't cry at the chicken ranch at all. I remember we got up early....

KW: Was it out in the countryside somewhere?

Neil: It was like a suburb. Redondo Beach was a suburb.

KW: This guy Kauffman, or whatever his name...

Neil: Ben Kauffman. I think he was a writer, or producer, or something. He owned a lot of property out there, and he gave part of it to build a synagogue. Across the street. He was an old friend of Harry's from Newark. Harry went out to see him, and he said: You wanna take care of chickens?

KW: This was after the fiasco with Dore Schary.

Neil: Oh yeah, it was when I was there. I remember him getting up in the morning. C'mon, lets go, the air is wonderful. Bracing, it's good for your health. I was in good shape, just out of the army.

KW: He wasn't wearing suits out there, was he?

Neil: No. Plain chino pants, a sweater or a jacket. It was cold early in the morning, and the chickens were yelling. Especially when you take their eggs away. He went like a shot, one chicken after another. He did this in the morning, and he fed them later.

KW: How long were you there?

Neil: About two days.

KW: Was he trying to write at the time?

Neil: We didn't talk much about it. I let him talk about what he wanted to talk about. Chickens. And how nice Ben was. And how well she cooked. We both ate dinner with the family inside the main house. He had a converted ...I guess it was a garage. He had his own bedroom. The air was good. I don't know if he paid him a salary.

KW: I remember he sent a letter, saying the years have passed, and I'm leaving the ranch, and he went to work with the May Company, a department store, out there. In Los Angeles.

Neil: I saw him only once more when he came East. I think it was... between my marriages. After my breakdown. I was trying to work. It had to be around '63 or '64. My parents were still alive. I think he stayed with them. Maybe Nat. I was out of work. He was older. It was colder. He was wearing a coat, I remembered. And wasn't dressed elegantly. He cried a lot. And I think he came by plane, and returned by plane. Dora paid for his trip.

KW: Do you know why he came?

Neil: I think he was trying to make amends with his family. And at the same time maybe something financial. He came back to the same poor family he left. They were older, that's all.

KW: Had there been some kind of rupture with the family?

Neil: No. He didn't really know what to say to anyone. And he came back to the land of all his original problems. He shouldn't be back there, and he shouldn't be bothering his sisters and brothers. I tried to cheer him up. I drove him around. I told him, look I was sick for a while, look at me, I'm a has-been. You gotta just keep your chin up. Eventually I took him back to a hotel in Newark. He took a room. it was never much of a hotel. It was on the right side of Military Park. There was a Public Service Building on the corner. If you go to the end of that building, there's a narrow street that goes in there. If you make a right turn. That narrow street goes down towards Mulberry Street. There's a hotel in there. It's right in back of the main hotel you probably know. I think its the Military Park Hotel. It was a respectable hotel, probably a little cheaper. He came out on a tight budget. I think Dora sent him tickets. He might have even borrowed money to come out.

KW: In your letter you talk about when you were younger. "I gradually learned that Harry was in constant turmoil and depression. He bore lifelong responsibility for the death of his wife and not knowing his daughter. By this time I believe he was not allowed to visit Kal." It's a mystery to me. My family, I'm sure they were kind of bitter, but I don't know to what extent they ...

Neil: I think they wanted to protect you from a very chronic father.

KW: I don't know to what extent he tried to see me.

Neil: I don't think he put up any fantastic fights or anything. I would have heard about it. I think he was withdrawn, and at times he was hospitalized. I very seldom saw him smile. He had a nice smile.

KW: I was told he met my mother when he was in his early 30s, when he was directing plays at the Y. That my mother...she died when she was 22.. I was born when she was 20. I was two when she died. So they must've been married when she was roughly 19.

Neil: So he was much older. That could explain a lot of things. I'm trying to remember your mother's name.

KW: Rozlon.

Neil: He used to mention her beauty.

KW: It was a tragedy. Compounded by the fact that medicine in those days...and if you were poor you probably didn't get the best medical attention. Routine things today were a big problem in those days. I don't know anything about her funeral, or who attended. I don't know where the wedding took place. I don't even know when they were married. I never saw a picture of their wedding. It's like it never happened. I wonder whether maybe parents on both sides didn't approve.

Neil: His mother never said anything against your mother. She did say that it was a shame that she died. And that Harry was losing his mind over it, or something to that effect.

KW: Where did they live? Did they ever live together in their own apartment? Or with parents on one side or the other? There's a lot of little blank spots. Just simple things. It's like a mystery. Was there a ceremony? Was it before a judge? I should have asked when my grandparents were around. It didn't occur to me. But I never saw a photo. A picture of a wedding!

Neil: I never saw a picture. I always heard how beautiful Rozlon was, but I never saw her face.

KW: Now that I'm teaching creative writing at Columbia...it gave me chills...must be in the genes...I'm teaching, just like my father. He was a very fine teacher. My son Jeff writes at the Boston Globe, and at New Age magazine. It's sort of funny. When they offered me this course, I said, my god, history is repeating itself here. My father used to teach literature and English. It's coming around again. I really appreciate your taking the time to do this.

Neil: This is...I never spoke this long on the telephone.

KW: I'm toying around with the idea of writing something. I'm not sure what. But I'm at the point of just gathering information about my mother, my father, I also had this woman, Rose Hoffman, very remarkable, she was my maternal grandmother's cousin, a psychic....she really was...somewhere along the line I wanted to write about her, too...part of a family saga...we've had our share of eccentrics on both sides...Rosie was one of them. I was named after her father. Kalman Hoffman. He came to America around the same time as Morris Wagenheim. He came and opened up a little store on the Lower East Side in New York, and he died in 1929, late 60s, early 70s. I came along six years later, in 1935. Apparently my great-grandmother, this was her beloved brother who had died, she asked my parents to name me after him.

Neil: Oh, my God, you have a whole history...

KW Of abandonment and separation...

Neil: I felt that I was like a poor relative.

KW: I'm sorry you did. We would have liked seeing you more often.

Neil: Maybe my kids will. They have a lot more self-esteem. Alex is 37. Diana is a few years younger. The kids are two and three.

(*Note: My Cousin Neil Simon passed away in 2001 in New Mexico.)*

Growing up in Newark

Mine was not an unhappy childhood, growing up in the South Ward of Newark, New Jersey, during the Great Depression. The earliest years are, to me, enveloped in mystery. I have no recollection of the grief caused by my mother's death. I can only speculate how, at the age of two, I must have wondered where she was, and how my family must have struggled to deal with her death, and the sudden responsibility of caring for a small child. Also a mystery is why my father and mother were separated. I am told that my mother was "artistic" -- she liked to draw--and was also an excellent dancer. Latin music was all the rage in the 1930s, and I am told that she won a tango dance contest in Newark. (I wonder now, if as an infant I heard her play tango music, because many years later, living in Puerto Rico, when I was exposed to the tango songs of Carlos Gardel I became an instant devotee.)

Grandma and Nanny told me, years later, that my father's family was largely responsible for the tensions in the marriage. They said the Wagenheims, as German Jews, thought themselves to be superior to the Russian Jews. They said that Harold's mother was so domineering that she even accompanied him to the men's store to buy his suits. I found no photo recording their marriage. Not a single photo of them together. When I grew up, I had virtually no contact with my father's family, although they lived just a flew blocks away. I can only assume that, since they were separated at the time of my mother's death, Rozlon's family felt a certain bitterness towards the Wagenheims. I recall an occasional visit to a sister of his. And once, when I must have been about ten years old, I was told that my father's cousin, Charles Wagenheim, a Hollywood actor, was visiting the family from California, and I was taken to see him. I enjoyed my brief meeting with Cousin Charlie, and his Hollywood career would become part of my family folklore, as I will explain later.

After my mother's death, we continued to live in the same neighborhood. When I say "we", I refer to Grandma, Grandpa, and a floating ensemble of great uncles (Murrey, Davey, Carl), who came and went. Funds to support us must have come from Nanny, my grandmother, who was married (for the second time) to a retired businessman (some say bootlegger) named Harry Krantz. A small check also arrived each month from Anna, Grandma's eldest daughter, who lived on Chicago's elegant Lakeshore Drive, and was married to a wealthy apparel manufacturer, a Mister Kronenberger.

Nanny's first husband, Abe Heller, my maternal grandfather, had been a pioneer in the movie business in Fort Lee, New Jersey. Long before my birth, when his two daughters, Rozlon and Lucille were young, Abe Heller ran off with another woman to Hollywood, and worked in the unit at Warner Brothers that produced the short coming attraction features. Abe Heller, I was told, lived in a grand house in Hollywood, and was a prominent donor to Jewish charities. He seemed to love humanity in the abstract, because I was told that he never sent a penny to Lillian to support her or their two daughters.

When my mother --- his daughter --- died, Abe Heller didn't even bother to come east to attend her funeral. *(Several years ago I wrote a comic play about Adolph Hitler, and imagined that he had escaped from Germany, and settled in America, pretending to be a Jewish survivor of a concentration camp. When I tried to think up an appropriate pseudonym for Hitler, with the "A.H." initials, "Abe Heller" seemed like a natural.)*

At some point, we moved a few blocks from Peshine Avenue to a different apartment, on Jelliff Avenue. My most vivid recollection of that house is a moment when I was sitting on the wooden front porch, surrounded by dozens of lead toy soldiers, arrayed for battle. Grandpa (my great-grandfather), then in his late seventies, stopped and watched me playing, and smiled. I never heard Grandpa utter a word of English. We communicated with smiles and gestures. Grandpa was a short,wiry man, with rimless spectacles, who usually wore a gray suit, with a vest, shirt open at the collar, and a homburg-style hat. With his short-cropped gray beard and moustache, he bore a striking resemblance to "Gabby" Hayes, the actor who played Roy Rogers' sidekick in the Western films. He loved Grandma's tomato soup, and I remember him at the kitchen table, slurping away, his beard and moustache flaming red from the soup.

Nanny worked on her own for years as a bookkeeper. Somewhere in the late 1930s, she married Harry Krantz, a widower, a colorful character with a great sense of humor. They lived in his three-family house at 510 Belmont Ave, near the corner of West Runyon Street, in Newark's South Ward. I lived with my great-grandparents a few blocks away, in a small apartment, and we were supported by family members.

1940 Census: The U.S. Census showed us living at 441 Jelliff Ave. Occupants listed were: Head, Isaac Shamberg, 75; Wife, Ida Shamberg, 72; Son, David Shamberg, 43; Son, Carl Shamberg, 31; Great Grandson, Kalman Wagenheim,4.

The 1940 U.S. Census also showed the Wagenheim family living nearby at 186 Avon Ave. My father, Harold, then 36, lived there with his father, Morris Wagenheim (75), mother Ada Wagenheim (66), Sister Frieda Simon (45), her husband Samuel Simon (44), and their sons Bernard (18) and Neil (7).

Summer of 1941: Grandma and I occasionally walked several blocks south to visit Nanny, my grandmother, who lived at 510 Belmont Avenue, with her second husband, Harry Krantz.. I particularly recall one of those walks, which I later described in a poem (*published in the Metropolitan Diary column of The NY Times on Dec. 8, 2008).*

"December 7, 1941"
I was six, going on seven,
when early one latesummer evening,
autumn's chill insinuating itself,
Grandma and I walked along
Newark's Belmont Avenue,
a large empty lot to our left.
There on the horizon was
a red moon --
the size of a Jersey tomato
six inches from your nose -- as big
and gory a moon as
I'd ever seen, and have since.
"That means war," Grandma said.
"What does."
"Red moon means war," she said,
tightening the kerchief 'round
her yellowing white hair.
She quickened her step,
scuttering along in her blue wool
sweater on bandaged bumpy
legs, looking every inch the
Besssarabian peasant, retired East Side
butcher's wife she was.
That winter,
we were having supper at Aunt Lucille's
when in burst Uncle Sam from work,
his round face a circle of concern.
"The Japs attacked Pearl Harbor," he said.
Lucille took Sam's supper off the stove.
I kept scooping at my chocolate pudding.
Grandma, who was dipping a puff of
seeded roll into her weak coffee,

made a windsucking sound
with her gums and darted a look
at me over her eyeglasses.

In the early 1940s, Grandma, Grandpa and I moved a few blocks west to Bergen Street, an apartment behind a butcher store. We were in the midst of World War II, and when the sirens sounded, everyone had to darken their lights for air raid exercises. We stood at the door of our apartment, peering out into the darkened street, looking across the street to the shuttered candy store, where Grandma would occasionally spend a nickel to play a number, hoping to win a few dollars. Then the sirens sounded again, and all the lights began to pop on.

1941: At around age six I began elementary school, and I believe I started at Peshine Ave. School. Sometime later, when we moved to Belmont Ave. (around 1942 or so) I enrolled in Bergen St. School, which was several blocks west of our home. I have little memory of that time, but do recall one funny incident. There was a red-haired, freckle-faced kid in our class, Stanley Schwartz, who simply couldn't sit still. Back in those days no one knew of the term ADD (Attention Deficit Disorder) but I suspect he had it. Every few minutes, it seemed, Stanley would raise his hand, asking to go to the boy's room, or somewhere. One afternoon, it was time for our little snack, which usually consisted of a small container of milk and a few Graham crackers (the latter were stored in a closet behind the teacher's desk). Stanley was not in his seat, and when the teacher opened the closet to take out the crackers, there he was! He stood there, shocked, his hand inside the cracker box, and the classroom roared with laughter! *(Years later, in 2001, Stanley somehow obtained my Email address, and sent me a note. I responded, and he replied: "Hi Kal, Thanks for getting back to me. It was great hearing from you. I am the kid with the freckles. I am living down here for the last five years. All of my children and grandchildren live here. I was wondering if you knew anyone else who lived here? Do you know where Abe Schwartz lives? My address is 4781 S. Citation Drive, Delray Beach, Fla. 33445. If you get down here to visit your son please let me know and we will get together. Stay well Stan." I responded with Emails and addresses of Abe Schwartz and Arlene Oberst, two Newark friends who live in Florida.)*

HAPPINESS AT 510 BELMONT AVENUE

Around 1944, when I was nine, Harry Krantz, Nanny's second husband, died. He was a short, dynamic, cigar-smoker, with a great sense of humor. It was whispered that he was a liquor bootlegger during the period of Prohibition, which lasted from 1920 to the early 1930s. I have no idea how or where they met, but he was apparently very good to Nanny, and left her with the three-family house at 510 Belmont Avenue, several blocks from where I lived with Grandma and Grandpa. (*Note: some years ago, in the late 1960s or early 1970s, I believe, Belmont Avenue was renamed Irvine Turner Boulevard.*)

Nanny, then in her early fifties, occupied the spacious second floor of the house, and rented out the top and bottom floors. Now that she was alone, she invited Grandma, Grandpa and me to come live with her. It was there that I grew up, and truly enjoyed life. The "bootlegger rumor" was strengthened after we moved in; down in the basement I found a desk, with a telephone! Someone (can't remember who) told me that the house next door, during Prohibition, was a secret warehouse for illegal liquor and the phone was used to warn the occupants if a police raid was imminent. By the time we moved there, of course, Prohibition was long behind us, and the house next door had been sold to neighbors, who lived there quietly, and legally!

I attended school and Grandma (my great-grandmother), then in her mid-70s, cooked and cleaned the house. Nanny still had to work. Each weekday morning, nicely dressed, she would walk to the nearby corner of Belmont Ave. and West Runyon St, and take the Number 8 or 48 bus to downtown Newark, where she worked as a bookkeeper in a wholesale candy and tobacco company. During World War II, chocolate was rationed, and unavailable to most people. But at her job Nanny was able to purchase a box of 24 five-cent Hershey chocolate bars every so often, and bring them home. I felt very privileged.

The years spent at 510 Belmont Avenue--from the time I was nine until I graduated from high school in Jan. 1953 (I was 18) -- are among the happiest and most vivid of my life. Despite her modest resources, Nanny did her best to make my childhood a happy one. I will never forget, for example, the time she took me, aboard the bus, to New York to see a Christmas show at Radio City Musical Hall and another time we sat enthralled in the audience for the broadcast of a New York radio show.

As an adult, I read a book by the anthropologist Margaret Mead, about primitive peoples who lived in remote corners of the world, disconnected from everything. Today, in retrospect, I realize that in many ways my childhood, spent less than twenty miles southwest of Manhattan, was similar. The world surrounding my house on 510 Belmont Avenue was almost as small, remote, and insulated, as the Brazilian jungle, or tiny Polynesian island inhabited by the people described by Doctor Mead and other anthropologists. Our tribe -- the people in the neighborhood -- might be divided into five groups. First, there was my family. Second were the tribal elders, the adult neighbors. Then there were three groups of youngsters: The Guys (my contemporaries), the few Girls of my age, and The Big Guys (a group of older young men). More about all of them later.

Most of the time was spent walking, or running, in a few blocks square area near the intersection of Belmont Avenue and Runyon Street, a stone's throw from my home, which was located four buildings from the northwest corner of the intersection of Belmont and Runyon. I loved our house at 510 Belmont Avenue. We occupied the entire second floor, a long railroad-style apartment. In the front was an open porch and enclosed sunparlor. Adjacent to the sunparlor was a small (and seldom-used) formal parlor, off of which was my small bedroom. The parlor was adjacent to the dining room, which had the front entrance, leading downstairs to the street. Continuing on through the dining room was a hallway. On the left were a large pantry, and the bathroom. To the right were three bedrooms, one occupied by Grandpa, a spare bedroom (where visiting family occasionally stayed), and the last bedroom, at the rear of the house, where Grandma and Nanny shared a bed.

At the end of the hallway was the kitchen, which had a backdoor leading down to the rear yard.

On Friday nights, Nanny played cards with several of her girlfriends. About once a month, it was her turn to have the card party at home. I looked forward to those nights. Nanny's friends (one of whose names, I recall, was Blanche) were formidable middle-aged women, with hoarse, "cigarette voices" (Nanny, an exception, did not smoke). After playing cards for a few hours, they would take a break, and Nanny brought out coffee, pastry, and candies. There were always some sweets left over for Kalman.

1945: Grandpa and FDR

Isaac Shamberg, my great-grandfather, (I called him Grandpa) was a wiry, energetic old man. During the winters, he would shovel the ashes from the coal furnace in the basement into large metal garbage cans, and drag the garbage cans the entire length of the driveway out the the street. I also remember, as a very young boy, eagerly awaiting the arrival of the big noisy garbage trucks. I would watch from my window as the huge men, muscles bulging like Superman, would lift up the garbage cans and heave the contents into the trucks. In the morning, when I walked out on my way to school, I would find Grandpa sitting atop the large green wooden box outside the corner grocery store, where the milk crates were stored. Grandpa—wearing his usual gray suit, with a vest, but no tie-- would be smoking a cigarette. Grandma didn't allow him to smoke in the house. As I passed, he would raise a finger to his lips, indicating that we should keep this secret between us. I would nod and smile. I remember when Grandpa died, I was just ten, because around the same time President Franklin Delano Roosevelt died, and the entire country (including our home) was plunged into mourning. Grandma, like so many others who lived through the Depression, revered FDR. She had a way, however, of making everyone sound Jewish. She constantly referred to him as "President Rosenfeld." As to his successor, Vice President Harry S. Truman, she asked Nanny, "This man, Harry Schulman...Is he Jewish?" Grandpa died in his sleep. I don't recall him ever being sick. Early one morning, Grandma woke me and said "come into Grandpa's room." They had slept apart for years. I went in, and the shades were drawn. The room was orange and sepia, and Grandpa lay quietly on the bed, his white beard up in the air. "He's dead," Grandma said.

"I wanted you to see him. He lived a long life, and he didn't suffer. He died in his sleep." I went out to play that morning, and everyone was sad about Roosevelt. I missed not seeing Grandpa atop the big green wooden box outside the corner grocery store, putting his finger to his mouth, motioning to me not to tell Grandma he was smoking. Grandpa's death had been painless, but his funeral was traumatic for me. He was buried in a Jewish cemetery way out in Long Island, and I became violently carsick during the entire journey. All I remember of that day is the acrid smell of vomit in my nostrils, and the flavor of Coca-Cola that I kept swigging, to settle my stomach.

My Great-Uncles

My four great-uncles (brothers of my maternal grandmother) were in and out of my life from my early childhood onward, but I have fond memories of them. Each of them was a real character!

Uncle Carlie

The end of World War II brought the troops home from Europe and the Pacific. Among them was Grandma's youngest son, Carl Shamberg. I called him Uncle Carlie. Carlie, who had spent three years in high school, and later worked as an electrician, at age 35, entered the US Army on December 16, 1942. He had slogged through Italy with General Patton, whom he derisively referred to as "Old Blood and Guts ... Yeah, our blood and his guts." Upon his return, he sat in the kitchen for six months, smoking Camel cigarettes, drinking black coffee, and muttering about his bad luck, while Grandma fretted over her youngest boy. Finally, Carlie snapped out of it and found a job. Carlie, like me, was a lefthander, and in his youth was said to have been a fine baseball pitcher. So good, in fact, that he aspired to a professional career. I believe Carlie was injured and had a goiter operation at one critical moment of his youth, which affected his plans to try out for professional baseball. Carlie was not a big talker. But we did communicate on one level: baseball. We played catch several times, and he imparted to me a few valuable secrets about throwing a screwball (just like the fabulous Carl Hubbell of the New York Giants), and a forkball. Very late one cold winter night, when I was gravely ill with fever, and the buses had stopped running, Carlie walked a few miles to Peddie's, the all-night pharmacy on

Broad Street, downtown Newark, to have a prescription filled for me . This heroic act---and it was---became part of our modest family mythology. I recall, as a young man, helping Carlie to get his driver's license. He must have been in his 40s. Not long after that he married Jeane, a New Yorker, and a very sociable lady. Am not sure how or where they met. I was best man at Carl's wedding in Brooklyn. A funny memory. Towards the end of the ceremony the rabbi wrapped the wineglass in cloth and placed it on the floor for Carl to step on and squash. He stepped and *squish!* It squirted away! Carl chased the glass as though it was a stray cockroach, and after a few stomps finally squashed it. I had a difficult time stifling my laughter. Once, in the early 1960s, thanks to Jeane, they took a Caribbean cruise and visited us in our house in Old San Juan, Puerto Rico. Jeane told us that on the cruise ship the chef was distraught, because Carl would only eat his usual baloney sandwich. Carl and Jeane lived in Brooklyn. He had a job in a store somewhere. By then Olga and I were living in Maplewood. Carl and Jeane visited rarely. Years passed. Once, in the 1980s, Cousin Rose, who resided in Brooklyn, tried to find him. She went to his Brooklyn apartment, knocked, and he would not let her in. "I don't want to talk to anyone in the family!" he said. "Why?" Rose called through the door. "Because nobody came to Jeane's funeral." Carl neglected to mention one "minor" detail. He never told anyone that she had died! We never heard from him again. **Note:** On Feb. 3, 2012 I received a fundraising letter from the planned World War II Museum, asking for a donation, and in return I could have a relative's name placed in the museum. I sent them $25 and wrote in "Carl Shamberg", to honor Uncle Carlie. Then, on a hunch, I went on Google and wrote "Carl Shamberg+Obituary." I found that a Carl Shamberg, born Nov. 29, 1907, Social Security #145-05-0691, had died on Oct. 1, 1985 (age 77 years, 10 months), and that his last known address was a home for the elderly in Woodmere NY 11598. I called them (516 374-9300) with the hope they could tell me more about him and am waiting to hear from them. A website called "Find A Grave" lists Carl Shamberg, died Oct. 19, 1985, showing him buried in Mount Carmel Cemetery, Flushing, Queens County, NY. Plot 1-E-54-5-4. The same day, I went on the Internet and looked for "Jeane Shamberg." I found that she was born in Sept. 1906 and died in Brooklyn in March 1976. So if these are the same people I think they are, Uncle Carlie lived alone, without Jeane, for about eight years.

Uncle Murrey

Uncle Murrey, Grandma's eldest son, born Sept. 9, 1891, was almost the complete opposite of his younger brother Carlie. Murrey had served with the U.S. Army in France during World War I. He received a Purple Heart because of a leg wound, which caused him great pain, and periodic stays in Army hospitals throughout his lifetime, but he never complained. Murrey proudly displayed the medal. Often, in a matter of fact way, he told a chilling tale of the night he was wounded on the battlefield. He crawled into a large shell crater, as bombs exploded overhead. In the darkness he spotted another human form a few feet away in the crater. It was a wounded German soldier, a young man, shivering with cold, and fear. For hours they remained awake, each holding a rifle nearby, each afraid that the other might attack. At some point, Murrey tossed a cigarette to the enemy soldier. A few hours later, the German made a sudden move, and Murrey shot him dead. He said that he always wondered whether the German was trying to kill him. *(I later wrote about this event in a short play, "Purple Heart," which was produced in Nov. 2009 as part of a short play theatre festival at the Union County College in Cranford NJ. I then converted the play into a short story.)* But Murrey, unlike Carlie, was not a brooder. He was a tall, slender man with silvery gray hair. A dapper dresser. A gregarious fellow, who liked to sing vaudeville tunes. He smoked big cigars. Walked with a limp, due to this injury on the battlefields of France. Murrey supported himself as bartender in downtown Newark. He was full of wisecracks. I always recall his comment: "Houseguests are like fish. After three days they start to stink!" He once told us of walking down Broad Street, the main street in downtown Newark, and seeing his younger brother, Carlie. Chomping on his cigar, speaking out of one side of his mouth, Murrey chuckled and recalled: "Carlie walked right past me. Didn't even say hello. The guy's a nut!" But he said it with affection. During World War II, Murrey, already in his 50s, met Lily, a lovely lady from Wilkes Barre PA who had come east to work in factories, due to the shortage of male workers. They married and lived for years in a small apartment on East Kinney Street in Newark. We visited them every so often and enjoyed his wisecracking good humor. When Murrey grew older, Lily persuaded him to move to senior housing in Wilkes Barre PA. At first he resisted, but once they were settled in, he was happy. A few times we drove from New Jersey to Wilkes Barre, stayed at a local hotel, and visited them. Had some good times. Lily, born Aug. 27, 1902, died in August 1977, age 74. Murrey died four months later, December 1977, at age 86.

Uncle Eddie

My great-uncle Eddie Shanberg was born and raised in New York's Lower East Side, along with his brothers. But somewhere between World War I and II, he entered the U.S. Army, wound up in North Carolina, and met Aunt Elizabeth. They married and had two sons, Larry and Jerry, and also a daughter Barbara, who was severely retarded and died at a young age. During my childhood, Eddie, Elizabeth and the kids came to Newark (he was looking for better work opportunities) and they lived near us. But after a year or so, they returned to Greensboro NC, where Eddie found regular work (I think with a local utility company). At one point Eddie retired, but was bored (he was a gregarious fellow), and to keep busy worked at a local supermarket, filling customers' bags at the checkout line, and chatting with them. To us, Eddie, after so many years in Greensboro, spoke with a pronounced southern accent. But I recall his son Jerry saying, "Nope. Daddy still talks like y'all up north!" Every few years, Eddie would take a Greyhound bus up from NC to visit us in Newark. I recall driving him once to Newark Penn Station to catch the bus back to Greensboro. When we arrived, I noticed that the bus wasn't scheduled to leave for another hour and a half. "I don't like to be late," Eddie explained. So we sat in the waiting room and chatted until it was time. When dear Aunt Elizabeth passed away, Eddie came to visit us in NJ. I asked him, "Would you like to see the place where you were born and raised?" He responded with a big smile. We drove through the Holland Tunnel, into lower Manhattan, and arrived near the South Street Seaport on the Lower East Side. We drove a bit north from the Seaport along the shoreline to his old neighborhood. The tenements had been replaced by big high-rise apartments. We got out of the car. Eddie inhaled, smiled. He pointed at the East River and said, "when we were kids, we used to go swimming in there!" A few years later, on April 20, 1984, Uncle Eddie passed away. I was recently in touch with Jerry, who is a retired fireman, and is married, with two grown children. I learned that he sees little of his older brother Larry, who, in keeping with family tradition, is quite eccentric, unmarried, and amuses himself, I'm told, by creating huge plastic figurines of Disney cartoon characters, which he places on his front lawn.

Uncle Davey

My Great-Uncle David Schanberg was born about 1897 in New York. Davey was a very shy, quiet man, with eyeglasses, which probably exempted him from military service. During WWII, I believe he worked preparing blueprints of ships, either for the government or for some private firm. He loved the water. My most vivid memory of him is the day (I must have been five or six years old) when Uncle Davey took me on a canoe trip in the lake at Newark's Weequahic Park. I don't recall us exchanging a single word. He just sat there, enjoying the sun, and the water. And so did I. When he was around 50 years old, Uncle Davey met and married a woman named Gertrude. A few years later, Davey told her he was going out for a newspaper, and disappeared. He never contacted the family. His mom (my great-grandma) was distraught. Rose Hoffman (my grandmother's pychic cousin) came to the house one night. . She read the cards and said Davey was OK, and was somewhere "in the southwest." Not long afterwards, we got a phone call from Gertrude. She said that she and Davey co-owned a property somewhere and she needed his signature in order to sell it. She hired a private detective to track him down and he found Davey in Texas. Decades passed without word of Davey. In the 1980s, I got a call from Uncle Eddie in Greensboro NC. He said, "Kalman, you'll never guess who's here!" He explained that Davey was retired, probably from The Merchant Marine (he was in his 80s) and living in a furnished room in New Orleans LA. He'd suffered a stroke. The landlady went through his things, and found a notebook with Eddie's address (possibly phone number too). She contacted Eddie, who drove with his wife Elizabeth and eldest son Larry (a trip like Ma & Pa Kettle) from Greensboro to New Orleans, and took him to their home. I was living in Maplewood NJ at the time, and decided I had to see Davey. I flew down and visited Eddie and Elizabeth in their modest home in a rural area outside Greensboro. There in the living room, lying in a hospital bed facing the TV set, was Davey. He was bedridden but, according to Elizabeth, still had a healthy appetite. I walked in, shook his hand. "Uncle Davey!" I exclaimed. "Where have you been all these years?" He smiled and responded, *"Around."* His Greensboro relatives took good care of him. He even outlived his younger brother Eddie (who died in 1984) and Aunt Elizabeth. But Larry, the eldest son, continued to care for Davey until he died on March 26, 1988 (age 91).

The Steltzers

Aunt Lucille, my mother's younger sister (and only sibling), was born April 30, 1919, and married Sam Steltzer , whose family had come from Pennsylvania some years earlier. Sam was a stocky man, with black hair, swarthy compexion, and a brash sense of humor. Sam and Lucille had four children, my first cousins: Kay (born June 9, 1940), Lynn (born March 8, 1942), Benny (born 1948), and Robin (born July 12, 1957). Sam passed away in the 1960s, and Lucille died on Feb. 28, 2009, a couple of months short of her 90th birthday. Kay's first marriage ended in divorce. She had two children from that marriage: Daniel and Renee, both of whom live in New Jersey. Kay later remarried Sal Del Preore a detective. They remained married for many years. Sal passed away in 2007 and she died a year later. Lynn, divorced, lived in south Jersey (close to her married daughter Shari and three grandsons), until she passed away in 2009. Benny (who lived in Israel for several years) is married to Nelly. They live in Belmar NJ and have three children (Elah, Yaniv and Avital). Robin, who is Sam & Lucille's youngest child, is married to Stan Glogocheski. They live in Highland Park NJ and have two children (Jeff, single, a championship bowler!) and Jamie (married to Minor, from Costa Rica). Recently (2009) Jamie had a baby boy, Jacob, and then a little girl, Jadda Lucia (2011).

Uncle Sam's sister Rose was a lively, heavyset woman with a foghorn voice. Her husband Clarence, a mild-mannered fellow, had a hearing aid. When Rose spoke extra loud to communicate with Clarence, I sometimes wanted to cover my ears, but that would have been rude. Sam had a brother, Irving, whose nickname, Beef, was an apt description of his physique. Sam and Beef made a living buying and selling junk in the winter months, and selling fruit and vegetables in the summer, first from a horse-drawn wagon, and later from a truck. During World War II, Sam and Beef made piles of money driving up and down the East Coast buying used sewing machines, because none were being manufactured at the time. They resold them, at a handsome profit, to dealers who rebuilt them. The legend in our family was that Sam had accumulated $50,000 (a fabulous sum at the time), and then quickly blew it on slow racehorses. Sometime after the end of World War II, Sam and Lucille and their two eldest children (Benny and Robin were not yet born) came to live in the first floor of our house at 510 Belmont Ave.

In 1947, Sam still had some of that money left, and was the first in the neighborhood to buy a television set. It was a $1,000 Dumont, an impressive piece of furniture, with radio, and record player, and a ten-inch black and white screen. I spent many nights downstairs watching Milton Berle and the Texaco Theatre. Ed Sullivan. The Arthur Godfrey Show (Grandma--in her constant tendency to make everyone sound Jewish, referred to them as 'Ed Solomon' and 'Arthur Garfield'!). Children from all over the neighborhood would flock to the Steltzer household to watch television. Among them was a chubby young girl, Connie Franconero, a friend of my cousin Kay's, who later sang and played the accordion and appeared on national TV (I believe it was the Ted Mack Amateur Hour). A few years later, she put aside the accordion, shed quite a few pounds, and changed her name to Connie Francis. The rest is history. And then there were the New York Yankees. I was crazy about baseball, and soon converted my Aunt Lucille, who became even more of a Yankee fanatic than I was. I remember the precise year -- 1947 -- that Sam and Lucille bought the big Dumont television set, because it was the first year I saw a baseball World Series on television. The Yankees played, with a powerful team starring Joe DiMaggio, Charley "King Kong" Keller, Phil Rizzuto, Tommy Henrich, and a rookie catcher by the name of "Yogi" Berra. It was such a thrill seeing these players, after having only been able to hear about them on the radio. The next year, 1948, the Steltzers' third child (and first son), Benny, was born. About a year later, they decided to head west to try life in California.

Grandpa Abe Heller, perhaps out of guilt for his neglect in previous years, had provided encouragement to his daughter, Lucille, and promised to help. Uncle Sam reasoned that California might be an improvement, since he could sell fruit and vegetables from his truck all twelve months of the year (his junk business, in the winter, was not as lucrative as it had been during the war years). So Uncle Sam bought an enormous black automobile (I think it was a Packard or Buick), about ten years old, but very impressive. It had a roll-up window between the driver's seat and the rear passenger section. It had very thick windows, which we neighborhood children thought were bullet-proof. Soon, we were calling it "the gangster car." One day, Sam, Lucille and the three kids, with suitcases and boxes of personal belongings filling every available space, drove off on the three-thousand mile journey to California. They were back in about a year. Uncle Sam had a mordant wit.

Downstairs in the Steltzer kitchen, where I was a frequent visitor, he would sit at the head of the table (always laden with food and several large bottles of soda), and regale the family with tales of California, which he explained was very different from New Jersey. "Here in New Jersey," he explained, you go down the street with a truck full of fruit and vegetables, and the people come out of their houses and buy. In California, you drive your truck through all those fancy suburbs. Weather's beautiful, but not a soul on the street. So you go up and knock. They don't even open the door! So you look through this tiny peephole in the middle of the door, and you see eyes staring back out at you! Strange place. Guy can't make a living."

The Greenbergs

The Greenbergs were our " wealthy" relatives, who lived in their own one-family home on Osborne Terrace in the Weequahic section, a short distance from Beth Israel Hospital, where I was born, and where, later, I had my tonsils removed. *In those days, anyone who owned a house was "wealthy"!* We visited them on occasional Sundays, taking the Number 8 or 48 bus westward for perhaps 20 minutes, leaving us on Lyons Avenue a short distance from their home. Morris Greenberg, who owned a small supermarket in the nearby upscale small town of Maplewood, was married to Dora, a first cousin of my maternal grandmother, Lillian. Also living with them was Dora's elderly mom, Molly, a very sweet white-haired lady who was my great-grandmother's Ida's sister. One of the main reasons we visited was for Molly and Ida to get together. But the Greenbergs were good, generous folks, and provided a tasty Sunday lunch and enjoyable family gossip. And, I was told, when my mother passed away in May 1937, it was Morris Greenberg who kindly supplied the money to pay for the funeral and burial.

A memorable time with Rose Hoffman

1945. My first memory of Rose Hoffman is when I was 10 years old. One Sunday afternoon, we took the bus to visit the Greenbergs, and were sitting in their dining room, when there was a knock at the door. It was Rose Hoffman. She had taken the bus or train (or both) all the way from her apartment in Brooklyn to visit the family. The family regarded Rose as a lovable eccentric, but they also knew (or suspected) that she possessed certain psychic powers. Someone pulled out a deck of cards, placed it in front of Rosie and asked her to read the cards. Rosie spread a few cards on the table, looked at them, and said: "Your son Buddy is coming home..." Buddy Greenberg, the son of Dora and Morris, was in the US Army, and serving in the Pacific, where World War II was raging Rosie's comment elicited a happy sigh from his parents. But when she continued with "...and he is coming home on a hospital ship" this evoked a shocked response. Then Rosie continued, "...but Buddy is fine." Everyone around the table was puzzled. How could Buddy be fine, if he was coming home on a hospital ship? The answer came two weeks later when the phone rang in the Greenberg household. It was Buddy Greenberg calling from San Francisco.

"Mom? It's me, Buddy!"

"Buddy! Are you alright?"

"Sure, mom!"

"You're not wounded?"

"Nah. My two years were up, Mom, so they shipped me first to Australia, to return home. There was this big hospital ship filled with wounded GI's. So they asked a bunch of us, guys who were OK, to go home on the ship and help take care of the wounded."

Over the years, until her death in 1983, Rosie often demonstrated her psychic powers, but that was the first I personally witnessed. Rosie came to visit us in New Jersey every few months. She adored Grandma, her aunt, and she always made a fuss over me, since I was named after her father, Kalman Wagenheim. When she arrived on the bus, Grandma would put a kettle on the stove to heat water for tea. We would sit at the kitchen table and chat, and sometimes Grandma would take a deck of cards from a kitchen drawer, place them in front of Rosie, and invite her to peer into the future. In subsequent years I learned that Rosie adored live theatre, and she knew many people involved in the entertainment world. She casually mentioned a promising director (not yet famous), José Quintero. And she left me a postcard with a photo of a Columbia Recording Artist, the then young singer Tony Bennett, who wrote: *"To Rose, With admiration. Tony Bennett. April 11, 52"*.

Growing up Jewish

I grew up in a neighborhood where many (but not all) of the neighbors were Jewish, but I didn't have a strict Jewish upbringing. My childhood pals were a mixture of Jews and Christians (Irish, Polish, Italian, Hispanic), a real Melting Pot of children and grandchildren of immigrants.

At home, since Grandma did the cooking. Grandma shopped at a kosher butcher, and kept separate dishes for meat and dairy meals. She was also an avid reader of the Yiddish-language *Jewish Daily Forward.* Little did I suspect then that some of the fiction tales published in *The Forward* would later be translated and published in *The New Yorker*, and in books, making their author, Isaac Bashevis Singer, world-famous, and earning a Nobel Prize for Literature. Grandma and the other readers of the *The Forward* were way ahead of the literati. Grandma made delicious chicken soup, and borscht, and kreplach (dumplings), as well as potato latkes with apple sauce, and stuffed cabbage. And most Saturdays she gave me a couple of boiled kosher hotdogs, and a generous helping of Heinz canned baked beans (mmmmmmmmm!), which I washed down with a glass of Hoffman Cream Soda, bottled at a large Newark plant a few miles north of us.

On the Sabbath, Grandma and Grandpa attended the small Orthodox Jewish synagogue a few blocks south of us. They never pressured me to attend, but I went with them on the High Holidays, and, like many of the young Jewish boys in the neighborhood undertook to fast on Yom Kippur because it seemed like an interesting challenge. "Did you eat yet?" we kids would ask each other at various times of the day, as though we were engaged in some form of marathon competition. They also sent me to Hebrew School at the synagogue, which was somewhat of a waste of time. We learned virtually nothing about religion, or even about the Hebrew language. We were forced to memorize the phonetic pronunciation of the Hebrew alphabet, and could soon read the prayers rather quickly, but we had no idea what we were reading! If there was a Hebrew-English dictionary, I didn't know about it. When the time came for my Bar Mitzvah, at my thirteenth birthday, I became terrified by the idea of standing up at the altar in front of all those people, and I was sure that I could never memorize all the prayers. I stubbornly refused to go through with the Bar Mitzvah. Grandma and Nanny were, I'm sure, saddened by my refusal, but I never heard a word of complaint from them later. In some ways, I believe, the fact that I was without a father or mother caused relatives to be lenient with me, and it is a wonder that I didn't turn out to be more spoiled than I was.

The Belmont Avenue Neighbors

Next door, to our left, at 512 Belmont, was a nearly identical three-family house owned by a friendly Italian family, who had a grape arbor in their back yard. We had a polite, nodding acquaintance, but since they had no children my age I had little contact with them. I was told that years earlier, during Prohibition, Harry Krantz (Nanny's late second husband) had also owned that house, used it as a warehouse for illegal liquor, while he entertained visiting policemen in our building.

Next door, to our right, at 508 Belmont, was another three-family house. The Stukalin family lived on the top floor. Their son Lou, a few years older than me, went into the advertising business, and once actually paid me a few dollars to write the text for a furniture store ad, which was probably my first writing gig. On the second floor were the Rudowskys. There was Arlene, a cute girl my age, a good pal, who also attended South Side High. Years later, Arlene married, had a son, and divorced. She moved to Florida, in the North Miami area, and we remain in touch to this day via email. Her son is married, is a lawyer living in California, and Arlene not long ago wrote to me that she is now a grandmother. Arlene has an older brother, Jack, who also lives in Florida. All three of his children were afflicted with an hereditary disease (often found, I'm told, among descendants of Ashkenaze Jews) and died young. *(Then, I believe Jack's wife passed away. Years later, Jack remarried and seems to have found happiness after so much suffering. He came to New Jersey around 2009 for his 60th high school reunion, and I met him for lunch at a diner in Union NJ.)*

On the bottom floor of 508 Belmont lived the Scheps family. Mr. Scheps, a small, dark-haired man, ran a butcher shop nearby. His son Miltie was my age. They had a younger son, and I have a vivid memory when the kid was in his infancy. We heard a terrible scream. People rushed in to the apartment and found the little kid seated on the family's elegant new living room sofa. The kid's diaper had somehow fallen (or slipped off) and he had shit all over the sofa. A major catastrophe!

Two houses down, further to our right, the Friedmans lived at 506 Belmont. Rabbi Friedman was an Orthodox Rabbi. *(The January 6, 1950 issue of The Jewish News published a Synagogue Directory, which included Bnai Israel at 608 Belmont Ave., a few blocks south of our home, with a Rabbi*

Herman Friedman.) He had at least three (possibly four) sons. The youngest, Philip, was my age. The rabbi had given all of them Hebrew names, and Philip was called "Feifl" or (by the guys) "Fifie". HE loved sports, and wanted to attend the Saturday afternoon high school football games at Untermann Field, adjacent to Weequahic High School, a few miles southwest of our neighborhood. From the corner of Belmont and Runyon we would take the Number 8 or 48 bus, which left us in front of the football field. But Rabbi Friedman didn't allow his children to handle money or ride on buses during the Sabbath. So the day before, Fifie would give one of us the few cents to buy the ticket. And, a few minutes before game time, we would stand at the entrance to Untermann Field, cheering Fifie on, as he walked all the way up from our neighborhood! We also played lots of games in the neighborhood. I recall one summer evening when we were playing "Ringaleevio," a kind of tag. Fifie came running down an alleyway near his house; Freddie Plaksy, came running from an opposite direction, and they collided. Freddie, who was taller than Fifie, was sucking on a peach pit at the time. When they collided, the peach pit tore a big hole in Freddie's upper lip, and dug a big scar into Fifie's forehead. For a while, we called Fifie "Peachpit."

The owners of the candy store on the corner were a young couple, Morty and his wife. We (the young guys) loved it in the summer when Mrs. Morty bent down to get a scoop of ice cream and we got a glimpse of her enormous breasts. Living above the candy store, on second floor, was the family of Marlin "Buddy" Hasher, one of the older guys, who had a fabulous throwing arm. He could fling a football 50 to 75 yards! On the top floor was Alan Berlin, also older, a tall guy who I believe played end on the high school football team.

On the same side of Belmont Ave., but to the left of us (northward, perhaps halfway up the block) lived Johnny Mengel (nickname "Puggy") a blonde kid, the star pitcher of The Comets, our neighborhood baseball team, who had a great curveball. I believe his dad was a bus driver. (Johnny later joined the U.S. Navy, and after that became a tugboat captain, working out of Staten Island. I reconnected with Johnny in 2006 at a reunion organized by Gordon Keister, another neighborhood buddy. Johnny was not in good health; he was driven there from his home in lower New York State by his son.)

Directly across street, on the ground floor, were the Schwartzes. The dad was a house painter. The eldest son Abe (my age) is now a retired air conditioning engineer in Florida, with a large family. I was reunited with Abe several years ago when we went to Florida to visit our son David. He told me that in the 1960s he had an air conditioning business on Newark's Springfield Avenue. After the 1967 riots, his business virtually disappeared. He was given good advice to relocate to Florida where air conditioning is a necessity. He did so, and prospered. I believe the business is now run by his children or son-in-law. Younger brother Ken became a pharmacist and worked, I think, in nearby Elizabeth NJ. I saw him a few years ago at a 50th anniversary high school reunion. There were also two daughters, Faye and Rhea.

Living above the Schwartz family were the Visotskis, Polish Catholics, who had come some years earlier from Pennsylvania. Very nice people. The oldest brother's nickname was "Penn" (probably because he came from Pennsylvania). Next was Joe (my age) a very good athlete, who became a history teacher at South Side High School, and was also active in the Newark Teachers Union. Joe and his wife live in central New Jersey. I have a funny memory about Joe's older brother Penn. One summer evening, a few of the older guys in the neighborhood ganged up on Penn, stripped off his pants, and tied the pants to the back of the Number 48 bus. I still recall that vivid image of Penn, in his underwear, running up Runyon Street, behind the bus, desperately reaching out to recover his pants!

To the right of the Visotski-Schwartz house were the Van Poznaks. Marvin was slightly older than me. There was also a daughter (can't recall her name). Ours was a working class neighborhood. Most adults wore a suit and tie only on special occasions (a wedding, or a funeral). But almost every evening, the head of the family, Mr. Van Poznak, a tall, silver haired, distinguished man, would emerge from his house, wearing an immaculate tuxedo, and look around, with disdain, at us "peasants." Turns out Mr. Van Poznak was the maitre d' at the upscale Tavern Restaurant, at the corner of Elizabeth and Meeker Avenues, near Weequahic Park, a few blocks to the southeast of us. *Note: Some years ago on the Internet I found copy of a 1941 dinner menu of The Tavern. A complete meal included tomato juice or fruit cup, soup, entrée, main course (beef, chicken, lobster), vegetables, salads, coffee, tea or milk, and dessert (coconut cream pie, angel food cake ala mode, apple pie). The price for the entire dinner ranged from $1.50 to $2.00!*

Willie was the little old wizened super/handyman in a nearby corner apartment building. Once, as we young kids huddled around him, he taught us about the birds and the bees. In a whisper, he explained, indicating with his fingers that children were born after men stuck their penis into a women. I was shocked!

The Guys

You were one of "The Guys" if you lived in our area, hung out on the corner of Belmont & Runyon, and played ball across the street on the big empty lot next to the Pryrene Fire Extinguisher factory. While one never knows how others perceive you, I always felt that I was different, perhaps even a little bit odd. Why? Because no one else I knew had neither a mother nor a father. No one else I knew was being raised by his great-grandmother. And no one else I knew was named Kalman.

Our neighborhood was all white, and multi-ethnic, with Jews and Christians of Polish, Irish, Italian and Hispanic descent. We guys often enjoyed ribbing each other, with"insults" calling our buddies "Kike! Polack! Mick! Wop! Spic!"

Other "guys" from the neighborhood included: Marty Amster (who died quite young, of diabetes, I believe, but whose older cousin Sonny Amster still runs, with his family, a large successful chain of bagel bakeries); Mel Berger (a tall bespectacled guy who I saw at our 50th high school reunion, is retired, and I think worked for the Social Security Administration); Billy Capodanno (whose dad owned an oil truck, also retired); Jack Haiken (a bespectacled guy who, while standing around the corner at night, was always spitting on the sidewalk); Jerry Kirschbaum (a short, very muscular guy) who, I learned later, died when he was hit by a car while standing in the street; Larry Simon, a big muscular guy who later became a professional wrestler; Burt & Don Weinstein are twins, and both great guys. They've been involved in businesses; are retired, and when I saw them at a HS reunion in 2005, they looked the same as 50 years earlier, except for silver hair. Burt lives in Pennsylvania. Don lived for many years in New Jersey but recently moved with his wife to Delaware, where she has family; Bob Kundin. I think his dad had a fish store; Bob later became a lawyer, married Sheila Peck, a gal from the neighborhood, and they moved to North Carolina. Sheila died of cancer around 2006, and Bob suffered a stroke and in 2009 was residing in a senior citizens' home in Montgomery NY. (In Oct. 2009 I drove up to visit him with three childhood pals: Don & Burt Weinstein and Bernie

Strauss); Irwin Lomozoff (who had a huge comic book collection in his basement, and who I believe died quite young from heart failure); Peewee (a tiny guy who hung out with us, ran errands, was assigned to right field in baseball games, was often the butt of jokes, and seems not to have had a last name); Danny Rodgers (see anecdote below); Marty Slavin (son of another butcher, I think he grew up and got into the wholesale meat business, I see Slavin trucks driving around all the time); Dave Straus (one of my closest pals, very bright and funny, had serious mental problems after serving in the the US Army, was a substitute teacher a while, later became homeless, was confined to Lyons Veterans Hospital in final years, and died around 2002); Davey Posner (Harvey's younger brother, who I think became a stock broker).

Once, I recall Larry Simon and Jerry Kirschbaum lifted a small Volkswagen Beetle auto from its parking space and deposited it on the nearby sidewalk! In the 1960s, while Olga and I were living in Puerto Rico, we somehow connected for lunch with Larry Simon, who had come to the island to appear in a wrestling match. At the time he was known as "Diamond Simon" because the blond hair on the top of his head was trimmed into a diamond shape. A few years ago I looked up Larry on the Internet and was astounded to learn about his long, successful career. Born Lawrence J. Simon in 1933, he began professional wrestling in 1957, retired in 1972, moved to Florida and opened a gym and training center. He died of leukemia on August 27, 1994. According to the website "Onlineworldof wrestling.com" Larry gained fame as Boris Malenko, and also was known as The Masked Muscovite, Mr. Miami, Crusher Duggan, and Otto Von Krupp.

Another colorful character from my Newark childhood was Charlie Pate, who later frequently changed jobs and states where he lived. Burt Weinstein recently shared with me this funny memory. "A few of us drove to Coney Island. We went to Nathan's to get hot dogs and French fries. Kirsch said if Charlie (who was supposed to be well endowed) would put his pecker in a hot dog roll and then step up to the condiment station and mustard up his pecker in front of several girls, he (Kirsch) would pay for his hot dog and fries. Charlie did it and I have to admit I will never forget the look on the girls' eyes. I am not sure how he got the mustard off of his pecker. But he did it."

A memorable evening down the Jersey shore (early 1950s)

I have fond memories of my teen years. I particularly recall one summer evening when we decided it would be fun to take a ride down the Jersey Shore. A problem: none of us owned a car! However, Billy Capodanno's dad owned an oil truck. I think there were five of us. Luckily, I grabbed a seat up front by the passenger window; Danny Rodgers (I think his original family surname was Rodriguez) sat squeezed in the middle, and Billy was at the wheel. Two of the guys (can't recall who) hung tightly to the rear exterior of the truck. We drove for more than an hour south down Route 1-9. A favorite summer spot was Bradley Beach. In those days, shore towns were quite divided by ethnic group. Spring Lake was almost 100% Irish, and continues to have a large Irish population. Most folks who spent summers at Bradley Beach were from the heavily Jewish Weequahic neighborhood in Newark. There were so many that Syd's Hot Dog place, which ran a business opposite Weequahic High School in Newark, operated a similar place during the summer at Bradley Beach. We got there after sundown, left the truck, took off our shoes, and walked around on the sandy beach. Then we felt hungry, so we strolled into Syd's, which was crowded with teenagers, and we sat at a table of the open-air hot dog place. Danny Rodgers was a mischievous sort. He rested his bare, sandy feet up on the formica table, looked around, and shouted, at the top of his lungs: *"Jews! Jews! All I see around me is Jews!"* The large room fell silent. Everyone gazed at Danny, who was quite tough looking, but no one said a word. I wanted to sink to the floor and hide under my table. In a few minutes, talk in the room resumed. We had our hot dog & Coke, and as we drove back north to Newark we laughed. *P.S. Half a century later, around 2005, I reconnected with Danny at our high school reunion and learned that this mischievous, funny trouble maker was now a retired detective! Unbelievable!*

Another time, sometime later, one of the guys (I don't recall who) had a car and we decided to have some fun. We looked upon the kids in the adjacent Weequahic neighborhood as "enemies." One night we sneaked up to a truck in the driveway of the nearby Mrs. Mac bakery. We found the truck door open, and pulled out a bunch of pies. Then we drove up to the Weequahic neighborhood and spotted a bunch of guys our age (members of the enemy camp) hanging out on a sidewalk. Our car pulled up close to the sidewalk and we tossed a bunch of the pies at their heads, like a non-lethal mob "hit." Then, laughing out loud, we drove away!

JE96F

Another summer evening, years before the Bradley Beach trip, we were hanging out in the neighborhood when two automobiles collided near the intersection of Belmont Ave. and Runyon St. One of us, I can't recall who, looked at the license plate of the nearest car, which read "JE96F" and said, "Let's see who can remember that the longest!" For a few years, those of us who witnessed the collision would test each other's memory. That must have happened when I was about 12 years old, in 1947, and for some weird reason, while I don't recall the license plate of the car I currently own, I still remember: "JE96F"!

The Older Guys

The "Older Guys" were really older...most of them married with kids. Often on Sunday afternoons they would meet for a softball game at the nearby Pyrene Lot: Sammy Klinger (short, baseball catcher); Lou Stukalin (next door neighbor, involved in advertising business); the Gordetsky Brothers (tough guys, maybe mob-linked); Kizzy (a fabulous softball pitcher, often earned money to pitch in games). Another "Older Guy" was Jerry Schwartz, a short, very athletic guy who helped us kids get uniforms for The Comets, our neighborhood baseball team. Am not sure, but I think Jerry did a bit of boxing. *Note: Many years later, in the late 1970s, I happened to be in a diner in Manhattan and I spotted him, hair gray, but looking almost the same, and wearing a suit and tie. He remembered me as "the good field, no hit" first baseman on The Comets. I asked him what he was up to and he said he was active in public relations. He handed me his business card, which said "Bermuda Schwartz." He explained: "There are lots of Jerry Schwartzes out there. This gets clients' attention!"*

The Pyrene Lot

The entire southwest corner of the intersection of Belmont Ave. and Runyon St. was occupied by a long, rectangular open field, known as The Pyrene Lot, which was the playground and social center for neighborhood males of all ages. The place had that name, because immediately adjacent to it, a few yards south, was the huge Pyrene Factory, which manufactured fire extinguishers. Some years later, the city erected a metal fence around the lot, and also a small concrete building at one corner, where a city employee (a heavyset Italian-American fellow) sat in an office, and dispensed sporting equipment on occasion. During my entire youth, we played baseball, softball and football on the Pyrene Lot. And often on Sunday mornings older, married men organized softball games. Those days I would watch them play and, sometimes, at their request, run over to the nearby candy store to buy them coffee. *The factory closed years ago, but to this day the building remains, and is easily visible when one drives westward on Route 78. It remained empty for decades, but recently I learned that a company has fixed it up and uses it as an archive for works of art.*

I am left-handed, and played first base on The Comets, our neighborhood baseball team. Some older fellow (not sure, but I think it was Jerry Schwartz) organized us to buy uniforms, and I still have a photo of little me, crouching next to Burt and Don Weinstein, in our uniforms. I was a pretty fair but inconsistent hitter, and an even better fielder. My idol was George Vico, a fabulous fielding first baseman for the Detroit Tigers.

In the late 1940s, the Newark Bears were the farm team for the New York Yankees in the Triple A International League and played at Ruppert Stadium, down along Wilson Ave. in the Ironbound section of east Newark. We baseball fans would take a bus to see the games. I recall one particular visit to the stadium (I think it was around 1946-47, when I was 11 or 12). The Montreal Royals (then a farm team of the Brooklyn Dodgers) had come to play against the Newark Bears. Everyone was abuzz, because the Royals were introducing—for the first time!—an African-American player. His name was Jackie Robinson, who soon after became the first member of his race to play in the major leagues; he went on to stardom, opening the door for many more African-Americans. I still recall that moment when he first came to bat.

We had no automobile--few people in our neighborhood did. On rare occasions we took the Public Service bus-- Number 8 Lyons, or 48 Maple—which came eastward down Runyon Street, continued a few blocks downhill to Elizabeth Avenue, turned left, and proceeded to downtown Newark, a twenty-minute ride, to shop at Bamberger's, or catch a first-run film at the Paramount, the RKO Proctor's, or the Branford Theatres. It was not until age nineteen, after I joined the U.S. Army that I took my first ride on an airplane. The longest walk was about six blocks to Bergen Street Elementary School (we called it "grammar school" in those days). In those early years I wore knickers, and long itchy wool stockings held up by rubber bands. Some Saturday afternoons we walked four blocks eastward, down to Elizabeth Avenue and a few blocks north to the Cameo Theatre, the closest movie house. The Cameo gave out free dishes to moviegoers. We enjoyed cliffhanger serials, such as *Don Winslow of the Navy*, and comedy films starring Abbott & Costello, or The Three Stooges, or The Bowery Boys.

Dad's Cousin Charles Wagenheim

One Saturday the Cameo was showing a "*Don Winslow of the Navy*" episode. The place: hilly San Francisco. Don Winslow was inside a taxicab. The tax driver, unbeknownst to Don Winslow, was a Nazi spy, a short, wiry man with a black mustache and shifty eyes. As I sat there in the dark, thoroughly enjoying my box of Good & Plenty candy, I realized that the Nazi spy cab driver, a shifty-eyed little mustachioed guy, was my father's cousin, Charles Wagenheim, who was a busy Hollywood character actor. I blurted out to my pals: "The driver is my Cousin Charlie!" They all knew about my "famous" relative from Hollywood. Just then, Cousin Charlie let go of the wheel, turned, and tried to strangle Don Winslow, who was in the back seat. As the two men wrestled in the cab, which hurtled down the streets of San Francisco without a driver, all the kids in the movie house were yelling, rooting for Don Winslow, except for our group. We were screaming our lungs out for the spy: "Get him Charlie, kill him!"

I was told by someone in the family that Charles Wagenheim began his acting careeer in the Yiddish theatre on New York's Lower East Side, together with Paul Muni. They went out to Hollywood, and remained friends. Charles was married to Lillian Wagenheim, who had a Ph.D. and was a clinical psychologist. I have a business card of theirs, showing their residence at 8078 Fareholm Drive, Los Angeles CA 90046. Tel: 876-6771. I was told that when Charlie and Paul Muni first went to California they briefly separated from their wives and spent six months living together. Charlie later returned to his wife and I believe they purchased a small apartment building on the outskirts of Hollywood, where they occupied one apartment and rented out the rest. Charlie worked steadily. Look him up on the website www.imdb.com, which shows him in 114 films between the years 1931 and 1977.. For example, he was a regular as Josh Halligan in the popular TV series *"Gunsmoke"*, which to this day is shown on TV. He was a "passerby" in the film *"A Streetcar Named Desire,"* starring Marlon Brando and Vivien Leigh.

In the late 1960s, I flew out to California and met briefly with Cousin Charlie. He drove me to lunch at a restaurant owned by his friend Alan Hale, Jr., the star of the *"Gilligan's Island"* TV show.

Jan. 27, 1949: A diploma from the Newark Public Schools show that "Kalman Wagenheim" a pupil of the Bergen Street School, having satisfactorily completed the course of study for elementary schools, was hereby recommended for graduation. Signed by Principal Anna O. Keane and Superintendent of Schools John S. Herron.

March 13, 1950 : Letter from Nat Wagenheim, to his brother, Harold, my Dad, who was living in California, about the death of Morris Wagenheim, their father (my paternal grandfather). Dear Brother Harry: You no doubt have been informed about Dad's condition from time to time... For some months he was bed ridden and Mother's task was no easy one, as he needed practically twenty four hour service. It goes without saying that the entire household was under a severe strain. Mom and Frieda did a herculean job in caring for Dad. The attention they showered on him was above monetary value. But then as it must to all men, Dad passed away peacefully on Sunday, March 12, at 1 p.m. The funeral took place on March 13 at 1 pm from Bernheim's. Rabbi Weller, head of the synagogue to which Dad belonged and was quite active in, gave the eulogy. It would have done your heart good to have heard him. We all went away feeling uplifted to know that our Dad was so well thought of. A religious, upright and honorable person. So today at the ripe old age of 83, Dad went to a well-deserved rest. The clan gathers in full force at the house to keep Mom cheered up, and when Spring comes we will see to it that she gets some fresh air and sunshine which she so sorely needs. I do hope that you will take his passing in a philosophical rather than in an emotional manner for Dad lived out a full life and left a heritage of goodness behind him. We here at home are well and hope you are too. Do write soon and let us know how you are doing. Best regards to Charlie, Lil and all the friends we know. Kindest regards from Bess, Allan, Harriet. Always your, *Nat. (Note: I was 15 at the time, don't recall ever meeting Morris Wagenheim, and was not told.)*

SOUTH SIDE HIGH & NEW PALS

In January 1949, shortly after finishing Bergen Street Elementary School, I began a four-year stay at South Side High School, which was several blocks northeast of our immediate neighborhood. I have fond memories of those days. I was a better than average student, but—most important of all—during my junior and senior years I was on the baseball team (in the summer of 1952 we were city and state champions). As mentioned earlier, we lived in an all-white neighborhood. On the northeast border of South Side High School was a predominantly black neighborhood. During my four years at South Side I don't recall a single incident of racial friction at the school. At 3 p.m., when classes ended, the white kids walked south and west to their neighborhoods and the black kids walked north and east to theirs; there was little interracial mixing after school. However, if one belonged to an athletic team or a club (chess, etc.), the students from both neighborhoods and races did mix, and often formed wonderful friendships.

In my case, I was on the baseball team, which was about half white, half black. We practiced together, played together, traveled together, and sometimes partied together.

In the 1951 season, as a junior, I was the second-string first baseman, backing up a tall Italian-American guy named Rubinetti. By 1952, he had graduated, and I—now a senior—was the first-string first baseman.

We beat "Whitey" Ford!

One of my closest friends during that period (and for years afterwards) was Ralph Fortson, African-American, who was a star pitcher, and largely responsible for South Side's team being named state champion in 1952. Ralph later was offered a $15,000 bonus by the Cleveland Indians. However, he developed a sore arm, and his major league career was ended. Ralph was such a fine batter, that he did play for a while in the high minor leagues, and later, for several years, played in the Negro Leagues. I wrote a play, "We Beat Whitey Ford", about my friendship with Ralph. It has been performed off-off Broadway several times, and I later converted it to a prose fiction format. It was published by www.jerseyworks.com.

At the end of our 1952 year baseball season, someone on the team decided we should form a semi-pro team. Somehow they booked a game with the Fort Monmouth US Army team at Newark's West Side Park. At the time, many pro players were in the Army. In the bottom of the 9th inning, they were beating us 3-1. Their pitcher lost control and walked a few guys, so the bases were loaded. They brought in a relief pitcher, a short fellow named "Whitey" Ford, who had played briefly for the New York Yankees and would later enjoy a long career with them. It was my turn to bat. "Whitey" threw a slow curve ball, and I hit a pop-up to their third baseman. Two outs. Ralph, our pitcher and fourth in the lineup, came up to bat, swung, and hit a triple over the rightfielder's head, driving in three runs. We won the game, 4-3! For many years afterwards, we would happily exclaim "We beat Whitey Ford!"

Among my African-American schoolmates (some of whom went on to study at Howard University in Washington DC) were: Phil Strothers, a fabulous athlete in several sports, who later joined the U.S. Secret Service and was part of the team protecting President Lyndon Johnson. Phil passed away several years ago; Earl Phillips, a fine athlete, who later, I am told, directed the Newark Housing Authority; Lonnie Jackson, a slick fielding second baseman. Elegant, aloof; James Young, a huge guy, also a fine athlete, who became involved in New Jersey politics. His friends nicknamed him "Pig" Young, because he had large, prominent nostrils; J.B. Bracken, the catcher on our championship baseball team in 1952. A very funny character. I was told that he later became a supervisor of taxi drivers at Newark Airport, and he passed away a few years ago; Calvin West, an infielder on the baseball team who later owned a bakery in Newark's central ward, went on to become a city councilman, and I believe remains quite influential in Essex County politics; Malcolm Hunter, the shortstop on our baseball team. One of the nicest, most sweet-natured people I've ever met; Charlie Lowe was a tall, quiet, gaunt guy who resembled an African-American version of Frankenstein. Since he wasn't on our baseball team (I believe he played on the basketball and football teams), I never caught a glimpse of him in the shower, but those who did gave him the nickname "One Hung Lowe", a reference to what they claim was the enormous length of his penis.

Among the white guys on the team, those I remember best were:"Tink" Young, the catcher on our 1951 team, who had a cannon-shot throwing arm; Rod Cocetti, a hard-hitttting outfielder on our 1952 team, who originally came from Nutley NJ.

1952 baseball team. That's me, front row, third from right, holding a bat.

Although we were champions in baseball, South Side High at the time had perhaps the worst football team in the City League. This was frustrating, because the athletes yearned to celebrate a "victory party" on the night after a Saturday game. Finally, several of the guys decided: "The Hell with it! Win or lose, let's have victory parties!" I recall one Saturday night in particular. The football team had lost, but a big party was scheduled in the black neighborhood. Athletes of all sports were invited. It was a rhythm and blues "belly rub," slow dancing in the dark with cute girls, the first time I'd ever experienced it. When we left, a group of us (black and white) were walking along a dark street when someone, from an alleyway hurled a brick at us. Fortunately, it didn't hit anyone. I think it was Phil Strothers (a black athlete) who was walking with us, and he yelled out "hey motherf-----!" And no more bricks were thrown.

Learning to Type

During my senior year at South Side, we had already completed all the basic requirements for graduation, and a friend suggested "Let's sign up for cooking. Then typing." Why? I asked. "Because they're easy. And there's lotsa girls in both of them!" I shrugged and said OK. When we walked into the cooking class the girls began to giggle; I think we were the only two guys. The same thing happened in typing. Back in those days, long before computers, virtually no males typed; this was a job for secretaries, clacking away on manual Underwoods or Smith-Coronas in an office. But my pal and and I sat down and learned to touch type: a-s-d-f with the left hand, and j-k-l-; with the right hand. I got all the way up to about 20 words per minute, not much, but later, this skill would come in handy and affected my life in a very positive way.

Around the time of our senior year in high school some of the students had purchased automobiles. The legal drinking age in New Jersey was 21, but only 18 in nearby New York. Many a weekend we piled in cars, drove across the Goethals Bridge connecting Elizabeth NJ and Staten Island, and crowded the bars along Victory Boulevard, which featured live music and plenty to drink. It was a fun time, but one sad memory remains. Among our pals was little Augie Cicatelli, who owned a huge older car. One night, with too much to drink, he took off for his home in Newark, speeding alone in the car, and as he approached the Goethals Bridge he slammed into one of the concrete walls, and died. We were so young. No one we knew until that time had died. It was so shocking and sad. Today, I treasure my high school graduation yearbook, and little Augie's photo is there. He never lived to graduate.

Pain, Itch, Pus!

On a lighter note, I recall a class in Personal Hygiene taught by Mr. Cavallero, a very strict athletic instructor, feared by all. This was an all guys class. "Cavvy" (as we called him), holding a piece of chalk in front of the blackboard, said: "Fellas, it's time that you all learned something about venereal disease." He wrote large letters "P.I.P" on the blackboard and drew a huge penis, a long cylinder,with two large testicles. Then he asked: "Does anyone know what the symptoms of venereal diseases are?" He pointed at the letters "P.I.P." and said "these letters stand for Pain, Itch, Pus, which are the symptoms of venereal disease. Remember them!" Just then a young female student entered the class, holding a note, apparently from the principal's office. She glanced at the blackboard with the huge drawing of the penis and testicles. Mr. Cavallero, a quick thinker, pointed to the drawing. "As I was saying, during the Napoleonic Wars, they had these huge cannons..." The guys in the class burst into laughter. The girl was puzzled, shrugged, and left.

On an even sillier note, I recall a moment with my pal Dave Straus, a big dark-haired, funny guy who lived on Johnson Ave., a few blocks from our school. In some classrooms, students were seated in the alphabetical order of their surnames. Being a Wagenheim, I sat in the rear, and a few seats in front of me was Dave. Seated next to him was Grace (can't recall her surname), a painfully shy young lady. Dave leaned over to her, extended his hand, and whispered, "Grace, pull my finger." Poor innocent Grace did as she was told. Dave unleashed a near-deafening fart, which prompted laughter in the class, as Grace turned pale, and looked desperately around, seeking a place to escape.

My favorite teacher at South Side was Miss Emory, a middle-aged single woman, very refined, exceedingly kind, and so sweet that everyone adored her. She taught Latin, one of the required languages in those days. It was our senior year. The class was being taught on the second floor. A nice day, and the window was open. Suddenly, James "Pig" Young rose from his desk, strode to the window and, apparently, prepared to jump. Miss Emory, alarmed, said: "Mister Young! What are you doing?" He replied: "Miss Emory, I'm supposed to graduate soon, and go on to Howard University. I'm not doin' well in Latin class, and if I fail, I won't be able to continue my studies. Life won't be worth livin'!" "Don't jump, Mister Young! You'll be fine!" she said. So he passed Latin.

Another memorable moment from 1952. A singer named King Pleasure (real name Clarence Beeks) came out with a tune called "Moody's Mood For Love" and as soon as it was broadcast on the radio it was banned. By today's standards it would be quite tame, but back then it was rumored to be too sexual. This triggered a mad rush to the stores to buy a 78 rpm record of the song; I was part of the crowd of eager buyers. More than half a century later it is considered a classic and is available on CD. I love that song and included it in my autobiographical play "We Beat Whitey Ford", later converted to a short story, based on my friendship with Ralph Fortson, the pitcher on our baseball team, at South Side High, Newark. The names are slightly changed;

Ralph is "Mitch" and I am "Hal". The names of the girls have also been changed. The play, inspired by a memorable New Year's Eve that Ralph and I "survived," has been performed several times Off-Off Broadway. The short story was published by www.jerseyworks.com, an online literary magazine.

Note: In the year 2000, when the play was going to be presented in Manhattan for a third time, I decided to try and find my old buddy Ralph ("Mitch" in my play); I hadn't seen him for many years. I went on the Internet and searched for "Ralph Fortson". No luck. But I did find a "Mitchell Fortson" , the name of Ralph's younger brother who—unlike Ralph—had gone to college. This "Mitchell Fortson" was living in Texas. I called the listed number and a woman answered. I asked her if Mitchell Fortson was the same one I knew from Newark nearly half a century earlier. Yes! She put him on the line, and Mitchell told me that Ralph was living in Newark and gave me his phone number. I also learned that Mitchell had done quite well; he was a Vice President for Human Resources with Continental Airlines. I called Ralph and we had a great dinner at an Italian restaurant in in Newark. After playing for 10 years in the Negro Leagues he retired from baseball, and later reached out to Earl Phillips, a high-school teammate, who was now running the Newark Housing Authority. Earl helped Ralph find work, first as an electrician's assistant, and later a nice desk job, where for 20 years he assigned repairmen to fix electrical and plumbing problems in the city's public schools. He was living in a nice apartment building in Newark. I invited Ralph to see the play, and we had a wonderful time. In the final moments, when Hal tells Mitch how much he loved him, Ralph's eyes brimmed with tears. After the show, Ralph (dressed in a flashy red sport jacket) walked around the theatre, proudly telling people that one of the lead characters was based on him. In 2003, Ralph attended our 50th anniversary high school reunion. His health was declining, and not long afterwards he passed away.

My first job

While in high school, thanks to Nanny (my grandmother), I got my first job, part-time work at New Jersey Candy & Tobaco Co., 39 Ferry St., Newark, one block east of Pennyslvania Station, at the entrance to the neighborhood known as The Ironbound, and also by locals as "Down Neck." Nanny worked as a bookkeeper for Mr. and Mrs. Spritzer, and got me a job in the stock room. Every pack of cigarettes had to have a tax stamp. A co-worker and I would cut open the big cardboard cases containing cartons of cigarettes. One of us would shove the cartons through a slicer, that tore open the upper lid of the carton, which would then pass through a machine that stamped the tax in ink on the upper surface of the pack. The carton would then continue along a path on the machine, to where the raised carton lid received some glue, and the carton was resealed. The guy at the other end retrieved each carton and threw it back into the large cardboard case. This went on for hours. I worked a few afternoons after school and on Saturdays. Nanny took the Number 8 or 48 bus from our home on Belmont Ave. down to her job. At some point, with a bit of financial help from Nanny, I was able to buy my first automobile, a snazzy 1947 blue Mercury convertible! I think it cost a few hundred dollars. A few times, on payday (a Friday), Nanny would treat me to a nice dinner at a local diner. After working for The Spritzers for a year or two, Mr. Spritzer approached me with an offer where I could earn "lots" of extra money. The Spritzers sold their cigarettes and cigars to bars and other establishments all over Newark and nearby suburbs, where in many cases they were stored in coin operated machines. I didn't realize it at the time, but the bars and other stores where the machines were located did not own them. They were owned by certain "people", namely the Mob, who took most of the profits. Mr. Spritzer learned that a company in Canada manufactured cigarette and cigar machines. He showed me the brochures. "Kal," he said, "if you can sell these machines to the owners of bars and other stores, they could earn much higher profits." Each machine, he told me, cost about $150, and I could earn a $50 commission for each one I sold. At the time, I was earning about $1 an hour; $50 was lotsa dough! So, armed with the brochures, I drove around Newark in my blue Mercury, dropping in at bars, giving them my sales pitch. No one seemed interested! I was discouraged, but one day while driving out on Route 22 near Springfield NJ, I spotted the Echo Lanes Bowling Alley complex (that has since disappeared and later became a multiplex cinema, which also disappeared, and the space is now occupied by auto dealerships). I go in, and am amazed to see several dozen vending machines for cigarettes and other products. This could be a gold mine, I said to myself. I approached a man, and made my sales pitch, showing him how he could increase his profits by hundreds of dollars a week, and to sweeten the deal I was willing to drop my commission from $50 to $25 per machine. The man seemed interested. "I'll talk to my partner. Come back tomorrow." Well, I drove off, and was already counting the money! Possibly a few hundred dollars in commissions! A fortune! The next day I returned. "I talked to my partner," the man said, and then shook his head no. "Why not?" I asked. "Certain people might...get upset," he said. "Upset? What could they do?" "Well, for starters, on a Sunday afternoon, which is Family Day, they could send in a few guys who pretend to be drunk, and start a fight, and scare off our customers. It that don't work, things could get rougher..." That was the end of my effort to sell cigarette machines. Years later, I learned that the vending machines and gambling and almost everything illegal in New Jersey were controlled by Abner "Longy" Zwillman, a major Mob figure. Not long after that, Mob members were being grilled on national TV as part of the Kefauver Congressional Hearings investigating organized crime.

My First Time

When I was still in high school my grandmother changed jobs from the candy and tobacco place on Ferry Street to a similar business elsewhere in Newark. She got me a job there as well, working in the back room, packing orders for delivery to clients, while she worked out front in the office. The owner was a really nice old man. Very kind. He had a son, Morty, who also worked there. Morty, maybe late 20s, always looked tired, or bored. Morty's wife, I don't recall her name, but I'll never forget her! Long brown hair, with tight dresses, high heels and big breasts. I don't know if she worked there, but she often came into the back room, and she would give me the eye, and smile. I was rather shy, and smiled back, I played sports in high school, so I guess I looked pretty tall and strong. One afternoon, Morty's wife came up to me and asked where I lived. I told her, and she said, in a whisper, "stand outside tonight, around 8 o'clock." That night, I was waiting outside, and she pulled up in a big new Chevy. She was wearing a little fur stole around her shoulders. She got out of the car, opened the back door, and jumped into the back. Then she waved for me to get into the back seat next to her. So I did. She reached over to my crotch, opened my fly, and pulled out my penis, which suddenly jumped to attention. Next thing I knew, she climbed onto my lap, facing me. She pulled up her skirt; I don't think she was wearing panties! She sat on top of me, pumping away, groaning, moaning. All the while still wearing the fur stole on her shoulders. Up and down, up and down, and the fur stole was tickling my nose! Before I knew it, it was over! She kissed me on the cheek and got out of the car. I got out, too. She waved, smiled, got into the driver's seat, turned the key, and drove off. I waved back, and got into my house. I changed jobs soon afterwards and never saw her again. Thinking back, I wonder, I wasn't wearing a condom. Did I make her pregnant? If so, the child she bore would now be a senior citizen.!*(Many years later I wrote a one-act play, "My First Time" loosely based on that memorable encounter.)*

Buy, Buy Kirby

Also, while in high school, seeking to earn some money with part-time work, I somehow came across the Kirby Vacuum Cleaner Company (it is still in business today), which then sold its product through door-to-door salesman. I decided to give it a try. We learned how to knock on doors, talk our way into a potential customer's home, and even spread some dirt on the carpet and demonstrate how the Kirby cleaned it up in no time! Our sales meetings, in East Orange NJ, were quite memorable. A bunch of us gathered in what looked like a classroom with a blackboard. The leader gave us an enthusiasistic pep talk, and would write on the board the names of salesmen who had closed deals in recent days. They even gave us a 32-page Kirby Song Book (I still keep a copy), with popular old tunes, but with the lyrics "Kirby-ized" by Kirby folks from all parts of the USA. At the conclusion of each meeting, we would sing favorites such as "Beer Barrel Polka," "Old Man River," "Pack Up Your Troubles" and "Yankee Doodle." I still recall one song, modified from the old favorite "Bye-Bye Blackbirds" by a Corwin Riley of Cleveland, Ohio. The lyrics went as follows:

Listen to the doorbells ring,
You walk right in and everything—
Buy, buy Kirby.
Lady meets you at the door.
Maybe she's a little sore.
Buy, buy Kirby.
Isn't it a wonderful sensation
When you've made the perfect demonstration?
Never worry, take your time
Get her on the dotted line
As Kirbys we sell!

After our meetings, a couple of sales guys bragged to me that, in addition to sales, they had made love to several lonely housewives they met. I lasted a few weeks with Kirby and had success with neither sales nor seductions.

1951-1968. Between those years, Harold Wagenheim (my Dad), living in California, registered a series of scripts: Feb. 27, 1951. *"How Did It Start?"* $1.50 to Screen Writers' Guild. Dec. 14, 1951. *"The Hodgson Girl and Mr. Dnoyeb."* $1.50 to Screen Writers Guild.Jan. 21, 1952. *The Hodgson Girl And Mr. Dnoyeb.* $1.50 to Screen Writers Guild. Nov. 24, 1959. *10-20-30 or Ye Old Time Theaytere.* $4.00 to Writers Guild of America West. Nov. 24, 1959. *"Sailors Snug Harbor"* (TV filmed series), $4.00 to Writers Guild of America West. March 21, 1961. *"Moments of Greatness"*. Harold E. Wagenheim and Patrick Dennis-Leigh. $4 to Writers Guild of America West. June 7, 1961. *"Babel Busters."* $4 to Writers Guild of America West. Dec. 22, 1961. *Two Chance Word Game (or) Two Way Word Game.* $4 to Writers Guild of America West. Nov. 6, 1962. *The Wastrel and Mr. Dnoyeb.* $3.50 to Writers Guild of America West..April 7, 1965. *The Questing Cinquain.* $4 to Writers Guild of America West. Dec. 4, 1967. *Juan's People (or) The Many Lives of Juan Rodriguez* (1st draft).

$3.50 to Writers Guild of America West. July 2, 1968. *The Case of the Changing Habit (or) Box of Sweet Memories.* $5 to Writers Guild of America West. (Unfortunately, I've never been able to find any of those scripts except for *The Wastrel and Mr. Dnoyeb.* The Writers Guild only holds copies of the scripts for ten years, and when he died, his body was sent to New Jersey for burial. All other items (including possibly the scripts) were left behind.)

1952: City Champs at South Side High

In my senior year at South Side High School, our baseball team won the Newark city championship and the New Jersey state championship. My buddy Ralph Fortson was the star pitcher, and I was their first baseman. Below a few brief excerpts from the local daily:

May 6, 1952. "South Side High baseball team beats East Side 3-2. South Side had to come from behind with a pair of runs in the fifth inning to win. Two passes to Varlee Goolsby and John Perdek, followed by Kalmen (sic) Wagenheim's double to right center accounted for the runs." *Newark Star-Ledger.*

May 15, 1952. "South Side High beat Arts High, 8-5 at West Side Park, raising its record to 4-1-1. South Side scored four runs in the first inning aided by Kalmen (sic) Wagenheim's three-run homer over the centerfielder's head." *Newark Star-Ledger*.

May 17, 1952. "South Side High defeated Barringer 6-4 yesterday at Schools Stadium to move into undisputed possession of first place in the City League standings. South Side built up a three-run edge in the first when Cal Wagonheim (sic) tripled with two on and Art Smallwood singled him home." *Newark Star-Ledger.*

May 1952 (exact date uncertain). "Central High broke open one of the tightest pitching duels in the history of the City League with three runs in the eighth inning yesterday to defeat South Side 3-0 at Untermann Field...Herb Benner gave up a single hit, to Cal Waggenheim (sic) in the fourth with two out, and fanned 18 South Side hitters." *Newark Star-Ledger.*

May 20, 1952. "South Side High maintained its slim lead in the City League yesterday when rubber-armed Ralph Fortson hurled the Streaks to a 4-3 10-inning victory over West Side at Untermann Field...Two errors by John Egnatuk, West Side catcher, gave South Side the winning run in the third extra inning. Kalmen (sic) Wagenheim opened the frame by drawing a walk. He stole second and continued to third on Egnatuk's wild throw. The catcher then tried a pickoff play and threw into left field, Wagenheim coming across." *Newark Star-Ledger*.

June 7, 1952. "Ralph Fortson, one of the standout hurlers in the state came up with the BIG victory yesterday when he shut out Central at Schools Stadium to give South Side High the City League crown. Fortson tossed a three-hitter as the Streaks won 4-0. The victory gave South Side an eight and two mark." *Newark Star-Ledger.*

***June 8, 1952**. *The Newark Star-Ledger* newspaper publishes the all-city high school baseball teams selections. Ralph Fortson of South Side, pitcher, was on the first team. Rod Coccetti, South Side, third baseman, was on the second team. Kal Wagenheim, first baseman, was on the third team.

Jan. 28, 1953. Diploma certifying that Kalman Wagenheim has completed the four-year curriculum for graduation from South Side High School, Newark NJ. Signed by Fred Randolphi, Principal. I was the sixth-ranking student in a graduating class of 95. I received a Bausch & Lomb Science Award, and an Art Award.

COLLEGE DAYS

•

Another divine intervention? Thanks to one of my teachers at South Side High I was able to obtain a tuition-free State Scholarship to Rutgers University-Newark Campus. I am ashamed to say I'm not sure of her name (I believe it was Mrs. Gersh, who taught French and also doubled as an adviser). She called me to her office, explained to me that I was a well above-average student and a varsity baseball player, and she urged me to apply. I did, and began classes at Rutgers-Newark in early 1953. *Note: Today, there are more than 10,000 students on the sprawling Newark campus, and many of them reside in dormitories in downtown Newark. When I attended, I don't think the student body exceeded 500, and classes were held in one modest sized building on Rector Street (between Broad St. and Route 21), and the Business School near Washington St.*

Feb. 9, 1953: To me at 510 Belmont Ave., Newark NJ. Dear Mr. Wagenheim: The Scholarship Committee has asked me to inform you that you have been awarded a special scholarship for the semester from January to June 1953 in the Newark College of Arts and Sciences. This scholarship covers tuition and registration fees. It does not cover any other fee or charge. This award is contingent upon your admission to the University. Your application for a State Scholarship will be considered this spring....Sincerely yours, Edwin M. Durand, Dean of Students.

Feb. 9, 1953. To me at 510 Belmont Ave., Newark NJ, Dear Mr. Wagenheim, We are pleased to notify you that your application for admission to the College of Arts and Sciences has been accepted for the term beginning February 1953. Very truly yours, Guy M. Fenstermacher, Asst. Director of Admissions.

Goodbye to Belmont Ave.

1953: Nanny sold the 3-family house at 510 Belmont Ave., where I had lived since 1945, and we (Nanny, Grandma and I) moved to a small one-bedroom apartment at 503 W. 13th St, in Newark, near West Side Park. From there I commuted to study at Rutgers in downtown Newark, and to my after-school jobs. The new apartment was comfortable. Nanny and Grandma slept in the bedroom (as they had done on Belmont Ave., and I slept on a convertible sofa bed in the living room. I have a funny, touching memory of those times. One Friday night Nanny went out to play cards with her lady friends, and I also planned to go out and meet with my pals. Since Grandma didn't know how to operate the TV in the living room, I invited her to sit on the sofa, and I set the TV to the channel for Arthur Godfrey's show (she called him "Arthur Gah-field"). When I returned home hours later, Nanny was still out. And there was Grandma watching TV, smiling. The Arthur Godfrey show was long, long over, and she was watching .... professional wrestling! "Grandma!" I said. "Do you like that?" She shrugged, smiled. That's how she was, so sweet, so accepting of everything.

March 17,1953. Postcard showing a photo of actress Irene Dunne and her home, from Dad (in Los Angeles) to Kal, at 503 S. 13th St., Newark NJ. "Dear Kalman. This is a hurried note. I am sending you a money order and you should get it Saturday or Monday. Keep up the good work. Hope to have good news soon...I hope. Your dad, Harold."

May 14, 1953. To me at 503 South 13th St, Newark. Dear Mr. Wagenheim: The State University Scholarship Committee has asked me to inform you that you have been awarded a State University Scholarship for the year 1953-1954. Provided that you maintain a satisfactory record and that, as we confidently anticipate, the Legislature continues annually to appropriate the necessary funds, this scholarship may be retained for the full four years of your undergraduate course...Sincerely yours, Edwin M. Durand, Dean of Students.

June 4, 1953. To me at 510 Belmont Ave. Newark NJ. Dear Kal: This is to confirm that you have been accepted for the fall quarter at Elon. Everything is ready and we're looking forward to having you on campus...Write or come to see us this summer. We're anxious to meet you. Your very truly, Roger Gibbs, Field Secretary, Elon College, North Carolina. *(I was recommended* *for an athletic scholarship to Elon by a man I knew in Newark, but I decided not to switch from Rutgers).*

Baseball: At Newark-Rutgers Univ. I played first base on the baseball team in Spring of 1953 and 1954. We were not champions, but we had a fairly good club. I particularly recall a fine lefthanded pitcher, Don Cameron, from Kearny. Another pitcher on the club was Irv Rubinoff (surname later changed to Roberts). Both Don & Irv also played basketball. *(Not long afterwards, Irv married Roz Annunziata, who also studied at Rutgers; I met her when she was on the staff of The Rutgers Observer. We remain good friends to this day. Irv and Roz have two daughters and a son, and grandchildren. They lived for years in West Orange NJ, and later moved to a beautiful house in Madison NJ. Roz is a great party organizer, sort of The Elsa Maxwell of our circle. Each Christmas she throws a marvelous party at her home, attended by Rutgers friends from the 1950s and their spouses.)*

Stumbling into journalism

In 1953, at age 18, I had no career plans, but was vaguely interested in being a Liberal Arts major at Rutgers. Without thinking of the consequences, I selected an "Introduction To Journalism" course. I have no idea why. In high school I hadn't worked on the school newspaper, and harbored no conscious desire to pursue a career in writing. The professor in the course was a Dr. Louis R. Zocca, who had what appeared to be a large dueling scar across one cheek. Dr. Zocca explained that his was a lecture course, but that in order to pass the course we also had to gain some "practical" experience by joining the staff of *The Observer*, the weekly newspaper of the Newark campus. *This turned out to be a life-changing move.* I reluctantly entered the office of the *The Rutgers-Observer* weekly paper on Rector Street. The editor was an upper classman, Dave Miller, who years later went on to big jobs in journalism, traveling the world for major newspapers and NBC-TV. Dave asked me about my interests. I shrugged and told him that I had joined the Rutgers baseball team. "You can write for our sports section," Dave said. I nodded okay, and began writing a few articles. Several weeks later, the sports editor of *The Observer* resigned and suddenly I, the novice, was promoted to sports editor! Second in command was Herb Jaffe, another upperclassman, who later became one of the top writers for *The Star-Ledger*, New Jersey's largest daily paper, with 400,000 Sunday circulation *(Herb and his wife Fran are now retired, living in Las Vegas. Dave, also retired, lives with his wife in New Jersey).*

Getting paid to write! I must have had some innate talent for journalism. Dave and Herb, to earn some money, worked a few evenings a week for Sid Dorfman, covering scholastic sports at *The Star-Ledger.* After a few weeks they asked me if I would like to try working there. So I, the novice, was suddenly writing short sports stories for New Jersey's largest daily newspaper. It worked like this. Mr. Dorfman had a small office, Dorf Features, on Court St. in downtown Newark. He arranged for students at the various high schools and colleges in New Jersey to watch the games (baseball, basketball, football), take notes, and when a game was over to call us. On a typical evening, around 6 p.m. several of us would be seated at desks, with headphones, facing large loud manual typewriters. When a student called, we would type out the box score on one sheet of paper, then briefly take notes on a separate paper, identifying the highlights of the game. With that information we would type out a 3 or 4 paragraph story, focusing on "who, what, when, where and why", the basics of reporting. After a few weeks I became quite good at it. (Among my assignments was covering an exhibition series in local gyms between the New York Knickerbockers and Syracuse Nationals of the National Basketball Association.)

Rutgers baseball. Excerpts from stories in the *Star-Ledger* about my brief career as a baseball player. I have the clips, but not the exact dates.

"Fairleigh Dickinson College of Rutherford scored 10 runs in the first inning yesterday—but Newark Rutgers won the ball game, 12-10 in Rodgers Stadium, Harrison....Rutgers got back into contention, scoring twice in the second and third innings, one in the fourth and four in the sixth with the help of an outfield error on Kal Wagenheim's deep fly ball that allowed three runs to score. That reduced the deficit to 10-9."

"Newark Rutgers hopped on Bloomfield pitcher Gene Lieberman for three runs in the first inning and went on to a 4-3 victory yesterday in a rain-soaked contest at Rodgers Stadium, Harrison…Egnatuk drove in the decisive run in the third on a single which tallied Kal Wagenheim, who had walked and stolen second."

Dec. 12, 1953. Handwritten letter from me, in Newark, to Dad. Dear Dad, I received both envelopes. Thanks very much for the money order. You said you wanted a frank appraisal of the film treatment you sent me. Well here is my opinion. Technically it is well written but there are flaws or lackings in some parts of it of the qualities of human interest and originality. This type story has been overdone on TV and radio. I realize that the viewing public is, in the main, unreceptive to a truly artistic work, but they do not wish to see something they have seen before either. The story can be simple but the problem is to get that little spark of creativeness and originality into it so that the audience will sit up and take notice. I must admit though, that the majority of the shows on TV are no better than this treatment and for that reason alone I think that with a few changes it should sell. The part about the auction of the Gettysburg address was more like what they probably want. It had emotional appeal. Cut out some of the trite introductory material and I think that the Big Auction will prove to be as worthy a work as 90% of the 1/2 hr. or 1 hr. shows presently on the air. I think the story editor would rather see an overabundance of really artistic material than a paucity of it. It is easier for him to cut than to create. So don't lean over backwards to make things too pulpy and simple. What type of children's shows were you referring to in your letter? Enclosed is a small sketch which I might incorporate into a short story. I got the idea for that particular incident from waiting in my neighborhood barbershop for a haircut and inserted myself as the present but non-participant Nemo. It has no dramatic climax but is an attempt to develop characters and portray a small relatively unimportant event faithfully. Please send me a criticism of whatever you find wrong with it. I also write a sports column for my school paper. I am the sports editor and the camaraderie and participation in something livens up an otherwise dreary urban school life. Enclosed is my column for last week's paper. It starts with an incident told me by our Editor in Chief. Nothing else, Keep Well, *Kal*

A Fond, Funny Memory

The article below appeared on the front page of the Jan. 15, 1954 issue of the *Rutgers Observer*, the weekly paper at Newark-Rutgers University. But first, some background: Dave Miller, assigned me to interview a burlesque dancer at Minsky's, the burlesque house in nearby downtown Newark. I went there, asked to talk with one of the dancers, and was introduced to Kay Hanna, a lovely blonde woman. I was so nervous as she spoke, and as I stared at her, that I scribbled a bunch of unintelligible notes. After school I worked part-time for Sid Dorfman, covering scholastic sports for the *Newark Star-Ledger* in a tiny office on Court St. At age 19, I was the youngest guy on the staff, so it was my job at the end of the evening to hand carry the typed stories to the main office, a few blocks away on Halsey St, to Willie Klein, the sports editor. Mr. Klein noticed my rather glum expression and asked why. I explained my frustration. I had been assigned to interview a burlesque dancer, and was so nervous that I didn't know how to write the article. He invited me to sit down, and began asking me questions about her and other details, typing notes all the time on his manual typewriter. A few minutes later, Mr. Klein handed me an article, which I delivered the next day to the folks at the *Rutgers Observer*, and it was published with a photo of the lovely Ms. Hanna. I felt obliged to confess that while some of the details came from my memory, the piece was written by Mr. Willie Klein. It was published without a byline. I look back and chuckle at the experience, and continue to be amazed at Mr. Klein's talent for humor. Enjoy!

Kay Hanna

"I Spent 40 Minutes With A Burlesque Cutie"

Dear Mom: Throw away the nature magazines. I've been backstage at Minsky's, a burlesque house here in Newark, but don't get excited. I went there to work, not merely to gander, though I must admit I saw things that I hadn't seen since I was a baby. You see, the editor of our college paper sent me over to Branford Place to interview some of the exotic dancers in the show. I fought against it, fought so vigorously that I was as limp as a rag as I walked to the theater. Surprisingly, as I walked in I was as alert as ever. I guess it was that newspaperman's blood in me. I had a story to do. They picked Kay Hanna for me to interview and I doubt if I'll ever have a better subject on my hands. Remember that day the churn toppled over and the butter spilled out? That was how her honey blonde hair spilled down over her shoulders. She stood about 5'4" in her bare feet and gee, Mom, she was barefoot almost up to her neck (Remember, Mom, this was work, no pleasure). You know, I might change my mind about being I surveyor. I might become a stagehand...but don't get mad, my training in surveying will come in handy. There's plenty of landscape to survey backstage. I found out that blue-eyed Kay was at Niagara Falls twenty-nine years ago—not on her honeymoon—but she happened to be born there. I felt sorry for the poor girl. She never had the advantage of a college education, but she's no dummy. She went to high school in Rochester and Buffalo, New York, and shortly afterwards fell under the spell of l'amour and got married. She wound up in Minsky's just like I did..by accident. She started as a model in Philadelphia, then one day was signed by an agent and started working club dates…and with her clothes on, too. She never expected to shed her apparel. She was double-crossed, Mom, into taking her clothes off. She was billed into a Baltimore date and, when she got there, discovered that she had been billed as the leading "exotic dancer" of the troupe. She turned her big eye lashes at me and asked: "Who ever heard of an exotic dancer with clothes on?" There she was in Baltimore with clothes on and billing as an exotic dancer. If she kept her clothes on the date was off; if she took her clothes off the date was on. Well, gee, Mom, what was the poor girl to do. She barely got on the stage that night. Kay (she told me to call her by her first name) doesn't consider burlesque immoral. She said she wouldn't be doing it if she did, but that she regards it as "adult entertainment." How about the current banning of movies like "The Moon Is Blue" and "French Line"? "Ridiculous, there should be no censorship. The little children who attend these pictures don't understand them anyway, so they're not being harmed, and adults certainly enjoy them." "Sex," Kay says, is an important thing in life and a little of it in theater makes for a balanced show." She invited me to stay and see the performance and, Mom, do you know, she was right. I have never seen a better balanced show in my life. Everything was well planned, and nothing fell off…a few things were taken off but nothing fell off. Kay had a spot in the show about midway through. She came onstage in a strapless salmon and brown sarong and a sparkling ring. She must think a lot of that ring, Mom. You know it was the only thing she had on when she left the stage. I got a lot of ideas in my forty minutes backstage, Mom, and I think you will like one of them. I am going to try to get the cold remedy concession. Gee, I could make a fortune and it's a wonderful place to set up a stand. The scenery is wonderful. Yessir, Mom, there's no business like show business and no show business like burlesque. Your loving son, An Observer Staffer.

Meeting Carolyn Smith, my first wife

Sometime in 1954 (not sure of the date) I went with some friends to a nightclub on Victory Boulevard in Staten Island. At the time, the legal drinking age in New Jersey was 21, but in New York it was 18. So many young Jerseyans from Newark drove across the Goethals Bridge to Staten Island, where we could drink. There, we met a few girls. Among them was Carolyn Smith, a cute young lady who would later become my first wife. Carolyn, an only child, worked with the Singer Sewing Machine Co. in Elizabeth NJ, lived with her parents, first in Elizabeth NJ, and later in nearby Roselle NJ. We saw a lot of each other. She became my first steady girlfriend.

YOU'RE IN THE ARMY NOW

My dear departed friend Robert Bletter (on left) and me as we edited the "Rock of The Marne" weekly paper for the 3rd Infantry Division in Fort Benning, Georgia around 1955.

In the summer of 1954, my sophomore year at Rutgers, a fellow student spread the word that it might be wise to join the military. There was a universal military draft. He said the Federal Government had announced that Jan. 31, 1955 was the official end of the Korean War (hostilities had ceased months earlier). Anyone who entered the military before that date would only have to serve two years. After that date, draftees, in addition to two years of active service, would have to enroll in the National Guard, attending exercises each summer for several years. I (along with several classmates) notified the Draft Board, to put my name at the top of the draft list. Soon after I was notified to report for duty on December 7, 1954, a few months shy of my 20th birthday..

Nov. 23,1954. Selective Service System. Order for Induction. The President of the United States, to Kalman Wagenheim v. 28-18-35-134 (Selective Service No.), 503 South 13th St., Newark NJ. Greeting: Having submitted yourself to a Local Board composed of your neighbors for the purpose of determining your availability for service in the Armed Forces of the United States, you are hereby ordered to report to the Local Board at 69 Academy St, Newark NJ at 8:00 am on the 7th of Dec. 1954 for forwarding to an induction station. Signed Martha Dale (clerk of local board)

I said goodbye to my girlfriend Carolyn, and we promised to write to each other, which we did for my entire time in the U.S. Army. I spent the first eight weeks in basic training at Fort Dix NJ, where I learned how to march, shoot a rifle, and wash dishes while on KP (Kitchen Police). While there, I received at least a couple of visits from my grandmother and great-grandmother, who must have made the long trip on bus, and brought me a special gift: homemade chocolate pudding. Yummy!

Feb. 19, 1955: Training Certificate. This is to certify that Kalman Wagenheim has successfully completed the eight week Basic Training Course under Army Training Program 21-114 with Co. I, 272d Infantry Regiment at Fort Dix, New Jersey. For the Commanding Officer, Kenneth C. Carmichael, Companyy Commander.

"Second Eight," the next eight weeks offered more advanced training, either more infantry techniques, or some other specialized skill. When we lined up for assignment, a sergeant asked: "does anyone know how to type?" This was my lucky moment! I was one of just a handful of soldiers to raise a hand. For the next eight weeks, all I did was sit at desk, learn how to become a company clerk, and type, type, type. At the end of that period, I was all the way up to 70 words per minute!

By the spring of 1955, after completing 16 weeks of basic training, I was assigned to Headquarters Company of the 3rd Infantry Division in Fort Benning, Georgia, where I would remain until my discharge from the military in September 1956. The 17 months spent at Fort Benning were a life-changing experience for me. I was just 20 years old and had spent my entire life living with family in Newark NJ. Now I was far from home, in a different world. Several of my fellow soldiers were a bit older, with far more experience in terms of life and education. Among my companions were: Robert Bletter, a New Yorker, graduate of Williams College, extremely intelligent, and funny as hell. (*We would remain close pals for many years afterward.*) Larry Secrist, from Akron, Ohio. Night after night, once the lights went out, as we tried to drop off to sleep, Larry, in his bunk, would sing the same sad song. Why is it, I ask myself today, I've forgotten so many important facts in my life, and yet—more than half a century later—I still recall the words to that song! *"Why-o, Why-o, Why-o, Why did I ever leave Ohio...why did I wander, why did I roam...why did I ever leave O-H-I-O...why did I ever leave home?"* John Ward, a dignified, bespectacled blond fellow from Knoxville, Tenn. who was the radio voice of the University of Tennessee football team, had a huge brand-new Buick, which he drove us around in on weekends, and was pissed at having to earn just $125 a month as a GI, when he was earning far, far more in civilian life. After hours, John almost always wore a dressy jacket, neatly ironed trousers, and two-toned shoes. John Ward was assigned to the base radio station. John had a fine sense of humor, and with his "radio voice" he often provided comic sketches imitating Wally Ballou, of Bob & Ray radio fame.

Also on the radio station was Pedro Encarnación, a friendly, easy going guy of Puerto Rican origin, who lived off base with his wife, and prior to joining the military lived in St. Croix, U.S. Virgin Islands. *(My friendship would Pedro would later represent another turning point in my life.)*

When I first arrived at Fort Benning, in the Spring of 1955, I thought of trying out for first base on the baseball team, but I soon learned that this wouldn't be easy. The commander of Fort Benning viewed the team as a symbol of prestige for the base, and recruited only the best players. Since there was a universal military draft, many young major league ballplayers were required to serve their two years. I visited the ballfield one afternoon, and observed batting practice. There was a muscular left-handed hitter, slugging long, long, long balls, one after another, way out of sight. I asked who he was, and learned that this was Fort Benning's first baseman, Tito Francona, who later became a major league homerun slugger for the Cleveland Indians. So I decided to stick to reporting.

Somehow I wound up becoming sports editor of "*The Rock of the Marne,*" the weekly paper of the 3rd Infantry Division. Bob Bletter was editor in chief, and we spent most weekdays in a tiny office, near each other at adjacent desks. We were even close at night, since Bob occupied the bunk right next to mine! Although we wrote and edited the weekly paper on the base, we had no printing plant. We depended upon a privately owned printer in nearby Columbus GA. In those days, copy was typeset using a monstrous, complicated Mergenthaler Typsetting machine, where the operator typed one line at a time, and the result was a single thin piece of lead that started out from molten lead in a pot. The guys who knew how to operate these huge machines were highly skilled and proudly possessed ID cards that would allow them to travel and work virtually anywhere in the USA. I would come to the printing plant at least once a week, to deliver the text, and proofread the stories, so I spent hours there on a typical visit. I became friends with two of the guys (I think their names were John and Reuben). When they spoke among themselves, their Deep South accents were so pronounced that I had a hard time understanding them. They had the same problem with me, because one day John took me aside (I'm still not sure if he was serious), looked me in the eye, and said "Y'all talk funny." While there I also got a nice taste of Southern hospitality. One weekend afternoon John and Reuben arranged to take me (the Yankee visitor) out to a little lake, in a canoe, where we fished and relaxed. Back in those days, Columbus GA was part of a "dry" county. People liked to drink, and licensed liquor stores that satisfied their thirst. However, there no bars were allowed. But just across the river was Phenix City, Alabama, where there were plenty of bars and nightlife "action." Phenix City at the time was described as "The Sin City of the South." College football was (and continues to be) very big in the South. When our barrack mate John Ward learned that the University of Tennessee would be playing against the University of Alabama the coming weekend, he invited a few of us to get into his big new Buick and drive over to Alabama. "Where will we stay, John?" "Don't you worry," John replied. When we pulled up to a big hotel and went in, that is when I understood what a VIP John Ward was in Southeastern Conference football. Prior to being drafted, he was The Voice of Sports in Knoxville. John guided us up to a huge suite in the hotel, and several middle-aged men (apparently alumni of U-Tenn), holding glasses of bourbon, smiled and offered a warm welcome to John. "Y'all can stay right here, tonight!" one man said, pointing to the sofas in the suite. So we saw the game (attended by a roaring crowd of thousands), partied, slept on the sofas, and were chauffeured back to Fort Benning by our generous pal and guide, John Ward, who early on taught me that a glass of bourbon and water was a marvelous way to relax. Another time, John suggested that he and I escape for an overnight down in Florida. We got into his big Buick and traveled south along a country highway. Up ahead I saw some huge, dark rainclouds. "Uh-oh," I said. "Not to worry," said John; he was proud of his new car, which had ultra-modern buttons to raise and lower the windows. As we came close to the rainstorm, John casually pressed the button next to him and the driver side window rose, but then it came back down, and continued going up and down, up and down, as what seemed like buckets of rainwater splashed in to John's head. As usual, John maintained his dignity, driving along without saying a word, while I struggled to stifle my laughter. We did eventually get past the rain and spent a fun night at a bar-nightclub in Florida. Years later, I looked up John Ward on the Internet. It described him as "a former radio broadcaster at the University of Tennessee from 1965 until 1999. Ward received a law degree in 1954 at the University's main campus in Knoxville. Shortly after, he decided to go into radio and advertising. After serving in the US Army, he returned to Knoxville and went to work at an advertising agency. In 1964 he began handling the duties as announcer-host-coordinator for UT coaches television shows in football and basketball. His broadcasting career blossomed when he became the Vols radio play-by-play voice, first, for basketball in 1965 and three years later for football (1968). In addition to his duties with the Vol Network, he covered events for ABC-TV and ESPN. Ward is a member of the Tennessee Sports Hall of Fame. He was known as the 'Voice of the Vols' for 31 years on the air. Ward and Bill Anderson, his color commentator for the entire 31 years, became the longest-running broadcasting partnership in college football. His trademarks include: his introduction to each game, "It's football time in Tennessee!;" his touchdown call, "Give ... him ... SIX! ... TOUCHDOWN, TENNESSEE!;" asking, "Did he make it?", and answering, "HE MADE IT!," after a made field goal; enthusiastically saying, "BOTTOM!" after a made basket in basketball; and wearing a light blue towel around his neck while broadcasting. After the 1998-99 football and basketball seasons, in which the Volunteers won the National Championship in football, Ward retired and was replaced by Bob Kesling. The University of Tennessee named the fourth level of the press box at Neyland Stadium The John Ward Broadcast Center in Ward's honor in 1995. His final broadcast for the Vols came in the second round of the 1999 NCAA men's basketball tournament, with Tennessee's loss to Southwest Missouri State University."

* * *

"Operation Sagebrush" was the name of what the US Army described as the first nuclear maneuver. The idea was to see how Army troops managed during a nuclear war. The entire 3rd Infantry Division drove hours westward from Columbus, Georgia to the Kisatchie National Forest in northwest Louisiana. After the comfort of our barracks, we now slept on the ground in tiny tents in the middle of the woods, and we were told to point flashlights into our sleeping bags to make sure that no scorpions had crawled in. As reporters for the base newspaper, Bob Bletter and I roamed about the woods of the national forest, checking on the movements of the troops, taking notes. One day, the Powers That Be decided that an entire company of troops had been "obliterated" by a nuclear weapon. This gave the medical corps an opportunity to move in, check on the "wounded", prepare to carry off the "dead", etc. However, a high-ranking officer (a general, I believe) happened to be visiting the area when it was announced that the nuclear bomb had struck. He was furious! "I will not be dead!" he yelled. "Anyone who says I was here will be asking for trouble!" He jumped into the passenger side of his Jeep, nodded to his driver, and was off. Another day, late in the afternoon, Bletter and I were driving around the national forest in our own Jeep, and somehow we (two "hicks" from Newark and Manhattan) got lost. After about an hour of wandering around, we saw a sign: "Welcome to Texas." My God! Driving along a country road, we spotted a farmer and asked for directions back to the Kisatchie National Forest in Northwest Lousiana. His reply sounds like a nightclub comic's gag, but I swear he actually said: "Hmmmm, Ah don't believe you kin' get thar from here." We thanked him, drove away, and I then came up with a "brilliant" idea. "Blet," I said, "since the sun sets in the west, and Louisana is to the east of us, why don't we just turn around, keep the sun at our back?" After a couple of hours we found our way back to camp.

Converting to Catholicism

I can't explain exactly how or why I, born Jewish, became a Catholic. I met Father Downey, a young Catholic priest, who was assigned to the 3rd Infantry Division in Ft. Benning. He was such a bright, kind, holy man that I somehow wanted to be like him; not become a priest, but to enjoy the wonder of worshipping God, as he did. I told him that I wanted to convert to Catholicism. He gently tried to dissuade me, explaining that this was not a decision to be taken lightly. But I am a Taurus, a stubborn fellow, and I persisted. Finally, he assented, and assigned me to study the catechism, which I did with great enthusiasm. I became a Catholic, and for many months, while in the Army, Father Downey heard my confession.

Aug. 21, 1955. Certificate. Kalman Victor Wagenheim, child of Harold Wagenheim and Rozlon Heller. Received First Holy Communion according to the Rite of the Roman Cathoic Church on Aug. 21, 1955 at Chapel #4, Sand Hill, Fort Benning, Georgia. Signed Sept. 14, 1955. John E. Downey.

Sept. 7, 1955. Certificate of Baptism. Kalman Victor Wagenheim, child of Harold Wagenheim and Rozlon Heller, born April 21, 1935, was baptized August 20, 1955 according to the Rite of the Roman Catholic Church at Chapel #4, Sand Hill, Ft. Benning GA by the Reverend John T. Hayes, Chaplain USA. Sponsors: Thomas McNiff. Signed John E. Downey.

The Kippered Herring at Reuben's Joke

Nov. 6, 1955. For the longest time at Fort Benning Bob Bletter and other sophisticated pals kept kidding me along, debating among themselves in front of me if they should tell me the highly confidential "Kippered Herring at Reuben's Joke". But each time they were about to tell me the gag they would suddenly—despite my pleas--decide "no, it's not time." They drove me crazy! Finally, as my time in the Army approached an end, they relented. Bletter, Charlie Shaffron and a couple of other fellow GIs sat with me and agreed to tell me the gag. I sat there anxiously, and Bletter at last told me: "This guy," Bletter began, "every day for lunch he went to the same place, Reuben's, and he ate a kippered herring sandwich. He did this for years! Finally, one day, he says to himself 'I'm in a rut!' So instead of going to Reuben's, he walks out of the office, and wanders about, looking for somewhere else to eat. He looks and looks, and every restaurant looks full. Finally, he spots one place that is half-empty, and he goes in. He takes a seat, and looks at his watch. He has only 20 minutes left for his lunch hour. He glances at the menu, desperate. He is so accustomed to eating a kippered herring sandwich he doesn't know what to order, and there is so little time! He spots 'kippered herring sandwich' on the menu. So he decides 'well, today I'll have that. At least I'm in a new place. Tomorrow I'll come back here, with plenty of time, and order something else.' When the waiter comes, he points to the kippered herring sandwich, and says 'Can you please hurry? I don't have much time.' Three minutes later, the waiter brings the sandwich. The guy is pleased. He reaches down and opens the sandwich. There is the little kippered herring. It looks up at the guy and asks, 'What's the matter? Aren't ya eating at Reuben's any more?'" *Oy vey.* After nearly two years, I'd been waiting for this gag? And to top things off, Bletter gave me a small card, which I keep in my wallet to this day. It says:

This is to certify that

Kalman Wagenheim

is a member in good standing of the

S.P.C.K.H.R.J.

Society for the Preservation and Containment

of the Kippered Herring at Reuben's Joke.

Sealed in brine on this *6th* day of *November 1955*

Charles Shaffron Robert P. Bletter

Kipper Keeper Herring Holder

Letter from my father, Harold Wagenheim. Jan. 11, 1956 from Los Angeles. Dear Kal: It was nice hearing from you and hope the New Year brings you good health and that before long, you will be in your right place in civilian life. I was also pleased to read that all with you is not the routine of drill; rather, an opportunity here and there to use some of your creative talents such as with your camp paper. I am no longer at the ranch. In July I decided to try my wings in Los Angeles; I felt the years beginning to crowd me. However, I worked at the department store in Los Angeles (May Company) for the Christmas Rush; now, I am looking around again. I do hope to get a job by the end of this week. In the meantime, I rewrote one of my stories and sent copies out to RKO and Twentieth-Century Fox. An independent producer (Aldrich) has a third copy. This ends my writing spree for the moment. I may come back to it in the event I sell or make enough money at a job to take off a few months. Do keep well. Write soon. And send me a copy of your paper. Do hope to have good news when I write you next. Sincerely, your dad, Harold…

Blood donor…May 18, 1956. *Letter to Kal V. Wagenheim, PIO, 3rd Inf. Div. Ft. Benning, Georgia, from Thomas L. Linn, MD, Director Laboratories, Columbus City Hospital, Columbus, Georgia.* "Dear Mr. Wagenheim, On behalf of Columbus City Hospital blood bank we wish to thank you for the very prompt way in which your responded to our call for blood donors. Because of this kindness on your part, and others who also gave, three patients in the hospital are very grateful."

Here's the story behind the above "thank you" letter. My dear buddy

Robert Bletter heard about the need for blood donors and insisted that I go with him to the Columbus Hospital. I had no intention of donating blood, but I agreed to accompany him. We got there, went into a laboratory, Bletter laid down on the bed, ready to donate, and suddenly, he fainted! *Oy vey!* The nurse looked at me, sadly, pleading. Could I help? What could I do? I was trapped! I shrugged, laid down on the cot next to the semi-conscious Bletter, rolled up my sleeve, and in a few minutes the blood was donated. Life is unpredictable, no?

Sept. 6, 1956: I was discharged from the U.S. Army with the rank of Specialist 3rd (equivalent of corporal), 90 days earlier than the normal 24 month period, in order to return to college studies at Rutgers-Newark. .

Sept. 24, 1956: Veterans Administration Certificate For Education and Training. Approved program of Education and Training: 1. B.A. Degree, 2. Masters, 3. Ph.D. Name and address of School or Establishment. Rutgers, The State University, 40 Rector St., Newark NJ. Issuing office, Regional Office, 20 Washington Place, Newark 2, NJ.

CIVILIAN LIFE & MARRIAGE

Back home, living with my grandmother and great-grandmother, I began work as Sales Promotion Copywriter for The Prudential Life Insurance Co. in Newark NJ (am not sure how I found the job, probably in the newspaper classifieds), and continued night studies at Newark-Rutgers. I resumed my close relationship with Carolyn, and we were engaged to be married.

Oct. 24, 1956. From Dad in Los Angeles to me. Dear Kal: Pardon the delay in answering your letter. I was in the midst of polishing a script and it was just plain stupid not answering you immediately. I was quite happy to hear that you are back in civilian life, and from what I gather you wasted no time in getting back to school, your part time job, and preparing to get married. As to your coming marriage, I take it from the tone of your letter that your feet are pretty firmly planted on the ground, that you and Carol are aware of the many adjustments to be made, not only in this "particular" marriage, but in any marriage, and that you look forward with confidence and joy in marrying Carol. It was pleasant to hear that Carol's folks are giving you and Carol a helping hand in preparing for the wedding...I think you should consider yourself fortunate since...you are marrying a girl you love, you are not bound by old customs and traditions such as we older...people are; you will have a compatibility you may realize never existed; the welcoming glad hands of Carol's folks. All these are blessings. Added to these, my blessings to you, Carol, her folks. Kal, I wish you and Carol all the good things of life; health for both of you and your children (a good-paying job for you and Carol if she expected to work), a warm, friendly home, and the happiness that comes from children in a house. May yours and Carol's days be filled with the 'eternal strivings for the Good Life'. Keep well and give my best to Carol. Sincerely, your dad, Harold…P.S. Enclosed is something for the wedded life. I really don't know what I could have sent you in the form of a gift. This way, Carol might suggest something for the home. H. P.P.S. Am trying to work out a deal with Lew Ayres and Warner Brothers. Part, the lead, was written with Ayres in mind. Wish me luck! H.

Dec. 22, 1956. Married Carolyn A. Smith at St. Joseph's Roman Catholic Church in Roselle NJ by Rev. John Dowling. Witnesses: Rodney Coccetti and Joan Busch.

April 8, 1957. From Kal, at 1040B Monroe Ave., Elizabeth NJ to Dad in LA. Dear Dad: With the honeymoon over a few months ago we are firmly entrenched in a nice 3-room apartment in Elizabeth and are lucky indeed because it is completely and beautifully furnished. We were married on Dec. 22 (and thanks for the nice telegram). We spent two weeks on a wonderful tour of the southern part of our fair country. Spending Xmas in luxurious Sea Isle, Ga…a few more days in various parts of Florida and the New Year's Holiday in enchanting New Orleans, where we saw the Sugar Bowl Football game and had a terrific time. We got back on January 7. I acquired a job in the Public Relations and Advertising Dept. of the Prudential Ins. Co. in downtown Newark as an expediting clerk and after 3 months have been promoted. I'm now a sales promotion writer. I'm making about $80 per week now, plus approx. $20 a week for nights as a part-time scholastic sports writer for the *Newark Star-Ledger*…my wife is holding down her office job…so we're paying our bills easily and are doing quite well. We got the apartment on Dec. 1 and in three weeks both of us completely repainted the joint and refinished the floors. After we returned from the honeymoon we ordered a living room set, complete with rugs, lamps, and end tables and received those more than a month ago. A new TV set was a present from my in-laws. The new kitchen set was a gift at one of Carol's three wedding showers and the refrigerator and range were included in the apartment. The bedroom set is Carol's old one, which is in excellent shape and we plan to keep it until the time comes when we can afford to buy a home of our own…I would guess two or three years of frugal living would allow us to provide a substantial down payment and we could become suburbanites in a comfortable ranch home. We're in a nice place and have good friends living just next door and my folks have taken Carol in well (disregarding the difference in religion) as

I had hoped, so I just couldn't ask for more. All I need now is a winning ticket for the Sweepstakes and I would be the picture of joy supreme. By the way, about two months ago we visited Greta and her husband in their apartment in Maplewood. They were very nice and gifted us with a beautiful decanter set. As soon as my raise here at the Prudential comes through (in about six months I would guess) I'll be able to abandon my part-time job and then will resume college on an evening basis...probably in Jan. 1958. I have a year and a half left for my degree. That's all for me...now, what's new with you? How's your writing coming along? I know so little of your activities that I hardly know what type of questioning to employ, so if you'll fill me in with a prompt reply I'd appreciate it. And how about a recent photo of yourself? You know you've never come through with my request for one. I'll trade you...one of us for one of you. Deal? I've only been here as a writer for two weeks so I'm still feeling my way around and doing only simple projects. When I get a few samples of my stuff I'll send it along. I'm afraid it's nothing in an artistic vein but I don't think I have sufficient talent to make a go of it in the serious creative field so I'll try and succeed in the commercial aspect. I'm rather rushed for time now Dad, being at the office, so I must close now...please write soon...and I'll supply a lengthier letter shortly afterwards. Hope to hear from you soon. Carol and I send our love. Your son...Kal

May 11, 1957. From Dad to Kal. Dear Kal: It felt good receiving your letter, chock full of good thoughts and tidings. I had understood that you were in the thick of things, what with setting up house, getting into your job, and numerous other details, part of the new life for you and Carol. At this point, allow me to again wish you the best that life offers young people. The compatibilities are there and can be met with desire on each part to compromise; the challenges still possess elements of the mystery; the goals and aspirations can be met by those who think in terms of courage and heart and confidence. These I know you and Carol possess; thus, I am glad for both of you, and know both of you will prosper in many ways of life. I received a nice, informative note from Greta, so somehow I am "up" on what is happening back home, and when I received your note, this sort of finalized in my mind that things and people were in their place and "all's right with the world." As for myself, my years out here have been somewhat productive, I have developed a philosophical attitude towards the field of writing, and still keep trying for new conquests. This is not easy for one who transplanted himself at a rather late age, came to a place which in itself is beset with heartache and frustration, full of the world's competition, and lacking in warmth. However, somewhere in the Book it is written that one can succeed within oneself. My writings reflect the phantasy, the spiritual, and this, in itself, gives me two strikes against me, Yet, I persist in this literary form and someday I hope it will pay off. My activities, if you call going to social teas, or dances, or men's club, is rather negligible. I read a great deal, follow all the movements and changes in the literary and TV and motion picture fields, keep notes on practically all phases of human activity, have my coterie of friends, and work. This may sound like a strict, introspective life; on the contrary, there are enough challenges herein to cover a hundred teas, or any number of "social" functions. Someday, I will send you my last story…I haven't written anything for the market for several years. As for a photo, I have never been one for taking pictures; however, again, I shall try to get one for you. As for your questioning as to my interests, etc. throw them from any angle. I believe, by this time, my interest, and I believe it is genuine, covers all the interplay and strata of human activities. So, loosen up the pitching arm, and whether it be fast ball or curve, possibly a twister, let them ride the breeze. Write as often as the spirit moves you, and please, as freely and intimately as your heart dictates. I really would like to know you and Carol as closely as time and space will permit. Perhaps, someday, the future will chart a course of clearer proximity, and we will all walk it and come together in warmth and closeness. Until then, love to all of you and all my blessings for the good life. Sincerely, your dad, Harry…

July 8, 1957. Mr. Kal Wagenheim, Public Relations & Advertising Dept. I am happy to inform you of your promotion to the position of Junior Staff Writer. In recognition of your new responsibilities, your salary will be increased to $75 a week. I congratulate you on this advancement. Kenneth MacKinnon, Exec. Dir. of Personnel, Prudential.

Life at Prudential

I enjoyed my job at Prudential, working on the 13th floor of the Gibraltar Building in Newark NJ. The work was pleasant, not extremely challenging, but my fellow workers were very friendly. Also surprising was the fact that lunch in the cafeteria was free! Almost every week there was some kind of party, a women's engagement, or baby shower. They also had clubs for bowling, and other activities. The head of Sales Promotion was Ken Brooks, a cheerful fellow who often praised our work. Next in command was Walter Cornish, a bit pompous, but also funny. The manager of our office was John Cawley, a sophisticated fellow who commuted in from Manhattan. It was John who got me hooked on *The New Yorker* magazine, which I continue to read. (Years later he would retire and move with his wife Ardeth to a high rise apt. building in Hoboken NJ. I visited them and we had lunch in Hoboken a couple of times before John passed away). Assisting John were Bill Coffield, who also commuted from Manhattan, and Carol Ann Petrocelli, their secretary. At the desk next to me sat Hal Burbage, originally from North Carolina, who lived in Manhattan and was quite funny and sophisticated. I suspected that Hal was gay, which was a no-no in the 1950s. So when I asked Hal where he lived, he said "I share an apartment with my cousin Jeb." Another funny person was Julie Zinser, a young woman who lived in Union NJ. In the age before computers, all the secretaries tapped away at manual typewriters. To send messages from one department of the building to another, we would type out our notes, and an elderly messenger "boy" named Johnny would come by, pushing a cart, and walk all over, dropping off messages.

Dec. 16, 1957. Mr. Kal V. Wagenheim, Public Relations and Advertising Dept. I am happy to confirm your promotion to the position of Sales Promotion Writer. In recognition of your new responsibilities, your salary will be increased to $91.00 per week. I congratulate you on this advancement. Sincerely, (signature) Executive Director of Personnel, Prudential

Feb. 11, 1958. My son Jeff is born in Elizabeth General Hospital while we are living in an apartment at 1040B Monroe Ave. in Elizabeth NJ.

Sept. 12, 1958. From Abe Heller, my maternal grandfather, on stationery of Warner Bros. Pictures Inc., West Coast Studios, Burbank, Calif. My dear Kal: I am indeed overjoyed that we are again in touch with one another after all these years. Even though we have never seen each other the mere fact that you have sent those wonderful pictures of yourself and your lovely family makes me feel that I would know you anywhere. It is very gratifying to know that you are well situated in a position that you like and that you are happily married...

"Kalman, you have a sister."

1959: "Kalman, I've been meaning to tell you this for a long time...you have a sister." I was 24 in 1959, when my grandmother gave me the stunning news. From early childhood on, I was told that my Mom--her name was Rozlon-- had died of an illness, when she was 22, and I was just two years old. Now they told me my mother died of hemorrhage while giving birth to a little girl. When I asked Nanny where my sister was, all she could tell me was that a childless Jewish couple in Newark had adopted her. *A year later, both Grandma (age 92) and Nanny (age 67) would be dead. I was alone, with no memory of a mother or father. But years later I would find my sister.*

Starting a Diary

In 1959, I wrote brief diary notes in the small pocket-size appointment calendar that I carried in my right rear pocket. Excerpts are included among other writings below.

Books to read: Picasso-His Life & Work, by Roland Penrose, 392 pp, $6; Lady Chatterley's Lover, D.H. Lawrence, 368 pp, Grove Press; Dr. Sax: Faust Part 3, Jack Kerouac, Grove Press, $1.75; John Betjeman's Collected Poems, Houghton Mifflin, $4; Aphrodisiacs, Allan Hull Walton, $7.95; The Sensualists, Ben Hecht, Messner, $3; The Years With Ross, James Thurber, Atlantic-Little Brown, $5; The Loved One, Evelyn Waugh.

Jan. 17, 1959. Joke I heard: "What's black and white, has three legs, and three eyes? Cole Porter and Sammy Davis, Jr."

Jan. 30, 1959. Directions to my friend Bletter's. Port Authority & 8th. Walk to 40th & 7th. Take uptown IRT local. Get in front of car. Get off at 116th & Broadway.

Feb. 11, 1959: My son Jeff's first birthday.

My cartoon idea in The New Yorker magazine!

While working in my pleasant, but somewhat boring job at Prudential Life Ins. Co. in Newark, I had an idea for a cartoon. Virtually everyone in our huge office (including me) watched the clock, waiting for 5 p.m., so that we could go home. Also, many offices had speakers up on the wall, which offered soothing music by Muzak. I had an idea for a cartoon. A secretary is standing by her desk, powdering her nose, ready to go home. The clock says 5 p.m. She looks up, amazed, at the Muzak box up on the wall, where a small door is open, and a band of tiny musicians is climbing down a rope ladder, to call it a day. I asked Bob, one of the guys in the art department, to make a rough sketch of my idea, which he did. I mailed it together with a postpaid postcard to Charles Addams (1912-1988), my hero, the great cartoonist at The New Yorker magazine. *Note: I later learned that Addams was born not far from me, in Westfield NJ and graduated from high school there!*

Feb. 19, 1959. I was amazed when a few weeks later I received a check for $40 signed by Charles S Addams, with note "Muzak idea", on check by The First National City Bank of New York, 42d St. at Madison Ave, NY. And I was further amazed when it was accompanied by a personal letter on New Yorker stationery from Mr. Addams, thanking me. *"Dear Mr Wagenheim, this is for the small Muzak musicians, a very funny idea. The drawing was sold to the New Yorker today. Sincerely, Charles Addams."* At that point I was convinced I had a career as a gag writer for *The New Yorker*. Wrong! Over the next several weeks I submitted more than a dozen ideas to Mr. Addams and other leading cartoonists, and received polite rejections. But I treasure that Addams cartoon and his letter, which are framed and occupy a place near my desk at home (I cashed the check!).

SINGLE AGAIN

March 1959: Sometime in March, I separated from my wife Carol and moved to 242 N. Broad St, Apt. 107 in Newark, where I continued to work with the Prudential. .

April 11, 1959. The New Yorker magazine publishes the Muzak musicians cartoon by Charles Addams, based on my idea.

Life At 59 Spruce Street

I don't recall exactly how I found the small apartment at 59 Spruce Street in Newark. All I know is that it was just a few minutes from my job at the Prudential Insurance Company in downtown Newark. Next to the apartment building was a long driveway, leading to a spacious back yard, here I was able to park my 1956 Chevy. Towards the rear of the yard was a charming little cottage, like a country place in the middle of urban Newark, with the address 53 ½ Spruce St. The occupant of that cottage was Mildred Kaiser (we called her "Mil") a short, blonde, bespectacled middle-aged woman, a talented artist, who taught at Arts High in Newark. Again, I don't recall how we first met, but Mil—a lively, outspoken lady--quickly included me in her large circle of friends, a fascinating bunch. Many Friday nights Mil would organize a sketch group. Each of us would chip in a couple of dollars, enough to pay for a nude model who posed as we made quick charcoal sketches, sipped beer and noshed on potato chips. I also have a vivid memory of a New Year's Eve party at Mil's. At midnight, she lifted her glass of champagne in the direction of an urn atop the fireplace in the living room and said "Happy New Year, Forrest!" Her dad's ashes were in the urn! On Saturdays, Mil would lead me and others in an expedition to the Goodwill stor (several blocks away) where I was able to furnish my apartment for very little money. Mil's cottage was adorned with low-cost relics from the Goodwill, including a number of gorgeous marble-topped tables, antique lamps and other gems.

Among the new friends I met through Mil was one I recall in particular. Mike was his name (I'll leave out his surname for reasons which will soon become apparent). A truly wonderful, funny character, who was openly gay at a time when that could be dangerous. Mike was from a working class family in Harrison, NJ, a small town just east of Newark. I think that one of his brothers was a fireman in Harrison. Mike was a hairdresser in an upscale beauty salon in Morristown NJ, a long train ride westward from his home in Harrison. On the train--just to raise eyebrows I guess--Mike would sometimes sit there knitting a sweater! A few times, after the Friday night sketch group session at Mil's, Mike and I frequented a bar/nightclub in downtown Newark. I particularly recall one night, as we sat at the bar sipping our drinks. On the tiny stage was an "exotic dancer", slowly stripping away her clothes. I said "Gee, she is something else!" And Mike, never at a loss for words, replied, "That's nothing! Look at that gorgeous sailor on the other side of the bar!" I think Mike liked both men and women. One time, I recall that two or three weeks went by without him appearing at Mil's house. When he finally showed up, I asked him how he'd been. "Very worn out," he said. Some of the wealthy housewives that Mike worked with in the Morristown beauty salon confided in him. One in particular, married to the owner of a large Jersey discount store, told him how unhappy and neglected she felt, and soon Mike was "consoling" her in some secluded spot. As if that weren't enough, one night, while Mike was waiting at the Morristown train station to return home to Harrison, a car pulled up and the male driver smiled and offered him "a ride." It was the neglected housewives hubby! So Mike said he "consoled" him too!

Monday, May 11, 1959. Saw *"Room At the Top"*. Terrific. Really moving. Starring Simone Signoret and Laurence Harvey. *(diary entry)*

A Sad Night With Billie Holiday

Some time in early 1959, I reconnected with my high school pal Ralph Fortson. Several nights we went out for drinks and enjoyed recalling the good times back in high school. Ralph knew his way around Newark. One night he took me to a bar in a black neighborhood where a lively young musician played jazz on a small Hammond electric organ. It was Jimmy Smith (1925-2005), who later went on to become a big star. I don't recall the name of the place, but it was jumping, particularly on Wednesday nights, when fried chicken was the special served at the bar.

But the most memorable night of all was when Ralph took me to Fusari's a small bar on Broad Street, opposite Newark's City Hall. Charlie Fusari, a New Jerseyan (1920-2001), had been a welterweight boxer whose main claim to fame was a loss to Sugar Ray Robinson. Like many retired boxers, Charlie decided to open a bar. It was a narrow, dark place, drew few customers, and didn't last long. Ralph and I dropped in on a weekday night. There were perhaps six customers in the place. We sat at the bar, sipping our drinks. Behind the bar was a small, narrow stage. At one point, a black man in suit and tie came out, sat at the piano and began to play a quiet tune. Then a slender, emaciated woman appeared, and began to sing in a sad, heartbreaking way. I could not believe it. Billie Holiday! She looked almost like a concentration camp survivor, and passed away a few months later.

Wed. May 13,1959. Overslept. Got to work at 1 pm, stayed until 8 pm. Bought gray suit. $34.95 at Howard's. *(diary entry).*

Thurs. May 21, 1959. Bought typewriter. $11.00! *(diary entry)*

Fri. May 22, 1959. Sketch group at Mil Kaiser's. Until 4 a.m! *(diary entry)*

May 25, 1959. R. Decker of the *New Yorker* sent me a nice note. He liked my four cartoon ideas! Spent from midnight to 3:30 a.m. thinking of cartoons. Could they be good greeting cards? *(diary entry)*

Wed, June 9: Attended free performance of "*Porgy & Bess*" starring Diahann Carroll at the Newark Museum. *(diary entry)*

Sun. June 21: Went to Village Vanguard in Greenwich Village and saw comedian Irwin Corey, who billed himself as "The World's Foremost Authority," perform until 2:30 a.m. Funny! *(diary entry)*

Fri. June 26: Am turned away from Village Vanguard. No tie. *(diary entry)*

Wed. July 9: Found great rolltop desk at Goodwill for $20! Broke but happy. *(diary entry)*

July 17, 1959: Took Carol and Jeff to the beach. Jeff loved the water. Took him on merry-go-round. Had long talk with Carol on the way home.

July 27, 1959. To: Kal Wagenheim, Public Relations & Advertising Dept. Dear Mr. Wagenheim, I am happy to confirm your promotion to the position of Assistant Sales Promotion Specialist. In recognition of your responsibilities, your salary will be increased to $114.50 a week. I congratulate you on this advancement. P. MacKinnon, Exec. Dir. of Personnel, The Prudential Insurance Co.

Sun. Aug. 23: Saw "*Some Like It Hot*" at Park Theatre in Newark. Funny! "Nobody's perfect!" *(diary entry)*

Sept. 22: Attended Newark-Rutgers class by Dr. Clement Fairweather. "Stimulating!"

Oct. 5: Went with Carol to Father Dowling to sign separation papers. Went to a bar, drank beer and enjoyed talking over old times. A wonderful gal. I got emotional driving home alone.

Oct. 18: Went to great Sunday gospel concert at Ruppert Stadium in Newark with my pals Dave Straus, Bob Bletter, and his good friend Goldie (a magazine editor interested in gospel music). Dave at the time was a bill collector, and worked under a different name, like Mr. Jones. While we were walking along, an African-American lady seated on a blanket on the ground, looked up at him and said "Mister Jones, I didn't know you liked gospel music!" There were many great singers, and among them was Little Richard, the rock and roll star, who became a born again Christian, stood on the stage and wowed the thousands attending.

Oct. 20, 1959. To Dad from Kal, now living at 59 Spruce St., Atp. 302, Newark 2, NJ. Dear Dad: Sorry for the long, long delay in writing to you, but this year has been a rather trying one for me. Since March, I've been separated from my wife Carol and it's permanent. I met her at the age of 18... didn't see her for almost two years while in service and got married almost immediately at my discharge. My views on what I want out of life, and who I want to spend my life with, have changed tremendously. While I'm still anything but fully matured, I've changed drastically in my outlook. She's a wonderful girl. She's done no wrong...she's actually been flawless. But it's just a tragic case of mismatch, so this spring I just had to split. I thought about it continually for months. And finally, despite the fact that the baby is involved and that morally it may be wrong, I made the move. I somehow feel that it's better this way than to exist with her like a vegetable and wait til we're both middle-aged...and then leave when she's too old to do anything about it. At least now, with God's help, she has a decent chance for a new life, being still in her 20s. I don't know what to say about the baby except that I love him...but it's not enough to make me sacrifice my life, living out in a way abhorrent to me. I know it sounds as though I've gone whacky... but really I thought it out quite coolly and took no quick rash steps. We even went back together for a while but it was no go...and we've been permanently separated since mid-March. Soon, we're filing for legal separation...and in March 1961 for a divorce. Since I didn't leave her for someone else, I'm in no hurry and will simply wait out the legal time necessary in New Jersey. The lone unhappiness in my life is that I've left them adrift. But I feel and hope that Carol will find someone...being so young yet. She lives with the baby at her parents'. They are comfortable financially at least...I send her $30 a week. She has a job...and lives practically free with her parents...so at least money is no great problem. Living alone has made me much happier and freer. I've always had a yearning to work creatively. Maybe this sounds like an old story to you...but to me being young it's brand-new. I don't know if I'll every write anything worthwhile. But I'll never be happy unless I give myself the chance. First I have to complete my education. It'll take about 2-3 years at night school. Wish I could go days and finish faster but I don't want to decrease my earnings because my obligation to Carol is something I won't let go. I must, and want to, send her the money. The job at the Prudential is going well. I'm up to about $115 week now and put in considerable overtime. I'm highly regarded there and I know that if I want to stay I'll be pulling in at least $10,000 by the time I'm 30 if just a break or two falls my way. This however is another problem. Advertising, to me, isn't a completely satisfactory way to make a living. While I'm not yet sick of it because I'm learning all the time, I can't see that I want to make a lifetime work of it. Even newspaper work is more attractive. Right now, though, I don't know of a paper which will pay me $115-120 which I need. Maybe, when college is over, more opportunities will present themselves. Even Europe for 2 years sounds attractive. If I could get some sort of connection with an American company I could take a cut in salary even, with the lower living expenses ...and the experience of working overseas would be priceless, I think. All these things are in the future. When I'll move I don't know. Nothing rash though. I do want to keep making the regular salary for Carol and the boy's sake... Right now, I'm busy at work...and am kept even busier with school. Am majoring in English (fascinating stuff I'm studying) and am fairly happy...and would be most uncomplicatedly happy if Carol found someone. Maybe someday. I do like her so much and want her to be happy. But I'm just not the right man for it.

Do write to me...and if you hear of any promotional or writing opportunities in sunny California, let me know. You son, Kal

Oct. 26, 1959. From Dad to Kal Dear Kal: I rather thought it was odd that I hadn't heard from you these many months. Then, your letter. That you find yourself in this particular circumstance is rather normal and human. I offer you whatever understanding and compassion my years of experience can muster at this moment. However, in the last analyses, your decisions are most singular with you, just as my decisions are unique with me. I could proffer you a mountain of clichés, suggesting this way or that manner of living. This would only engender confusion, leading to utter inaction. Yet, in the human soul, there is a part of it which enables one to employ a divine wisdom in making the just and proper choice. In this, I am confident, after examining the entire scene, with its many ramifications,that you are acting soberly, and in good confidence. (I have deferred probing, the offering of specifics. I take it this is what you might have inferred in your letter. However, should you feel I can be of help to you, please feel free to state your mind) For the present, your work should help take the edge off whatever anxiety you may have. You are rather fortunate that you have a good job. As for future plans, "first things first." Yes, I will let you know, should I come across any leads, of such opportunities as may interest you out here. Are there any particular kinds of work you have in mind. So you are majoring in English. I majored in Education, but minored in English and Literature. It is a fascinating subject. Do keep me informed as to your studies. Who knows but what we may yet collaborate on a writing piece of some sort. I'd be glad to see some of your work as you go along. I close this letter, Kal, with a prayer that you find love, with its deep, mystic meaning; a peace of mind transcending all material barriers; an understanding of, and a closeness to God, and what is meant for us to be and do. Understand that you can write me in confidence...Only in this manner can we ever hope to unshackle the chains which keep us from fulfilling our destiny. Keep well and God bless you. Your dad, Harold

* * *

In late 1959, I visited my grandma's Cousin Rose, the psychic, at her place in Brooklyn and told her about my separation from Carol. I also said that I visited my little son Jeff on weekends (with my friend Dave Straus) and it was heartbreaking when I left, because Jeff would cry so much.

Nov. 10, 1959: Rose Hoffman letter to Kal. From 40 Lincoln Road, Brooklyn NY. Dear Kalman: At 24, you have loads ahead of you, and your son Jeffrey also needs a father--just because you got along without one does not mean you should deprive him of one. Your dad, I understand, was *unfortunate* because of circumstances, and it broke your mother's heart, and it did not do her any good when she had to give *birth to a child.* She was beautiful, talented, but destiny, for some reason, had the upper hand... Now Kal, please I am not preaching to you. You have provided for your son *money,* but what is money compared to *something more.* See him, don't worry about him crying, don't let others say, look your father, he is never around--a child needs a man's love and moulding; otherwise later he grows up lacking something and then you *can never put it back*...if your own mother was alive she could not tell you differently I am sure...Now you will say why does that old lady, meaning me, tell me this. I have enough advisors. Well, Kal, really, I am just the daughter of a man you are named after. *You heard that before and you came to see* -- well you *saw.* Great grandma so loved her brother that she gave you his name...I am not binding you by a name, but do make it worthy in the *eyes* of God...Perhaps you don't believe in God, but Kal, there is one-- *that God is in you...* without the creator, you would stop breathing - Sincerely, *Rose.* PS. I really don't know how to sign myself. Perhaps you have a better title. Go see your dad, and grandfather. Also your father's folks. Learn all you can--then decide--*facts*.

Nov 11, 1959 From Kal (in Newark) to Dad in LA. Dear Dad: I'm just now getting around to answering your wonderful letter. Schoolwork (just took my mid-terms) and a busy little period at the Prudential have taken up much of my time. I was wondering about your reaction to the news in my last letter, and I'm so happy to hear that your point of view is one of understanding rather than shock and an immediate reply in didactic tones. I also appreciate the fact that you chose not to "probe" as you put it. Actually, there's very little else that I could tell you about the entire affair. Perhaps I expect too much out of life...but somehow what I had just didn't seem to be what I wanted for the rest of my stay here. I guess I just haven't learned to settle for things as they are...I realize that dissatisfaction with everything can lead to unhappiness eternally, but I am still in that formative stage where I don't seem to have found my "element"...my way of life...and the attitude which I want to adopt towards life. Meanwhile, my job keeps me interested to some extent...and my studies in English are most satisfying. While I don't plan to make any hasty moves, I've had some resumes of my experience run off. I'm going to circulate them about. The mere cost of postage could lead to something worthwhile. I noticed an article in our company newspaper saying there are several job openings in our Los Angeles regional office. I've asked our personnel department to look into the matter and find out whether these openings might be in the Public Relations Department. If they are, perhaps I'll come out. It would mean free transportation for me and my belongings, plus a job with the same, or better, pay. While this switch is still very much in the "if" stage, it could mean a move before mid-1960. Once I'm out West I could then look around for something else. My grandfather had contacted me recently, offering me a job with him at Warner Brothers, a temporary position, while I'm looking. Since I know nothing of the work, I must assume the pay would be commensurate with my experience...quite low. I just couldn't afford to take a cut in pay. So I thanked him and sent him a few copies of the resumes. Perhaps, with any contacts he may have, he may be able to find someone interested in my qualifications, who would be willing to take me at the salary I need. I'm enclosing a copy of the resume. If you should run across anything of interest for me I'd certainly like to hear about it. Just getting out there to see you would be a joy in itself...and I plan to do just that sometime next year with my next vacation. But coming out permanently would be even better, if the right kind of job comes along. I still haven't taken my 1959 vacation. My busy schedule made it impossible...so I will take it at the last minute...from Dec. 21 through Jan. 5...since I can't afford a trip out to the coast I'm doing the next best thing...the Virgin Islands. Sounds enchanting and *warm*. The prospect relaxing on a beach, in the sun, with nothing to do but enjoy a good book, or perhaps work on a short story, sounds too inviting to resist. I have no money for the trip right now...but I'm getting three consecutive checks for $80 apiece quite soon as part of my G.I. Education Benefits. Since I paid for my tuition from my salary...this is clear profit. This $240 plus about $75 out of my vacation salary should be enough for two enjoyable Caribbean weeks The round trip air fare from New York to St. Thomas, Virgin Islands, is only $108 on the economy flight. That leaves me with about $100 a week for a small hotel room, food...and entertainment. I think it should be sufficient. It's my first trip beyond the U.S. mainline border and I'm really looking forward to it. You asked what type of work I would have in mind. Well...I really couldn't pin-point it. In my few years, I've had rather diversified experience...all in some field of communications: advertising, public relations, newspaper work. What really sounds intriguing is some type of creative writing...however, I don't feel that I'm qualified for this. I've had little experience and have nothing to show as a sample in this area. I've have had one minor, but most satisfying "triumph" thus far. I sent a cartoon idea to Charles Addams, the famous cartoonist for The New Yorker. He liked it, bought it for $40 and the New Yorker published his drawing of the gag early this spring. Enclosed is a rough Photostat of the cartoon. I have a copy framed along with a very nice letter of thanks from Mr. Addams. May sound rather juvenile, but it's my first and only "sale" so I'm rather proud of it. Immediately after the sale, I flooded Mr. Addams and several other top cartoonists with gag ideas. More than a dozen were accepted by the cartoonists, but they couldn't make a sale with them to the respective magazines. The humid summer slowed me down in the idea-manufacturing area. Recently, several books have made great hits by publishing photos of famous paintings, pieces of sculpture, or old movie "stills" and putting humorous captions below. I went to the Newark Library, selected some old prints of classical plays, had them photographed, and submitted them to *Playboy* along with humorous captions. Just sent em in last week. If they're sold in a package, it could mean a sale for several hundred dollars which would be most welcome. I think they're as funny as any I've seen published...and several people whose taste I respect agree with me. However, the big publishing markets are flooded with hilarious material... so I must be realistic and not expect too much....however, I'm working on a second batch of captions. Whether or not they *ever* sell, creating these gag ideas has been a tremendous source of enjoyment. I would like to go on and on, just talking to you...but I have some studying to do. By hook or crook, I'll be out to the west coast in less than a year to see you. Tell then, do write to me when you have time. Your son, *Kal*

Nov. 18, 1959: Went with friend Sharon to to NYC to see "*Three Penny Opera,*" made it just one minute before 8 pm curtain. Great show, terrific lyrics.

Wed. Dec.16, 1959. Saw *"Sweet Bird of Youth*" in NYC. Great play. Went to bar on 1st Ave. for drinks. Home at 3 am.

Fri. Dec. 18, 1959. Took schoolmate Janet Foscaldo to Cherry Lane

Theatre in NYC, met friends for drinks later, my place later for grapefruit. Awfully nice gal.

My first visit to the Caribbean

One key reason I chose St. Thomas in the U.S. Virgin Islands for my very first winter vacation in the Caribbean was Pedro Encarnación, a good friend I met while serving in the 3rd Infantry Division at Fort Benning, Ga in 1955-56. Pedro was either born in Puerto Rico or of Puerto Rican origin, and resided in the Virgin Islands. While in the service, he and his wife lived off the base. He was a talented, charismatic fellow who worked on the base radio station. When we parted in 1956, Pedro gave me his mail address in Christianstead, St. Croix, the Virgin Islands, and urged me to come visit. Pedro said he was well known down there, since he performed as an entertainer. Once out of the military, Pedro and I exchanged Christmas cards for a couple of years. In late 1959, I wrote to Pedro telling him that I planned to visit the Virgin Islands during the Christmas-New Year period. I received no reply, but shrugged it off, thinking he was probably busy.

On Dec. 21, 1959, a Monday, I got up at 4 am, arrived at Idlewild at 5:30, and caught a 7:30 a.m. plane. It arrived in San Juan, Puerto Rico at 2:45 pm., and then I switched to a flight to St. Thomas, arriving at 5 p.m. When I arrived in St. Thomas, at the tiny airport terminal, I approached a woman there and asked if she knew Pedro Encarnación. She shook her head sadly and said that poor Pedro had been killed in an auto accident. His small car, she said, had collided with a big truck on a winding mountain road. I was shocked. I barely knew Pedro's wife, so I decided to find inexpensive lodging at The Gate, a small guest house. in Charlotte Amalie, the main city on St. Thomas. It cost only $40 per week. Despite this sad incident, I had a wonderful time, enjoying for the first time in my life tropical weather during the winter. Over the next few days I met a fascinating bunch of new pals: Dick, Co-Co, Axel, Mike McCarthy, and Rita from Tortola. I also met Joan Petlak, who acted in the musical *"Gypsy"* up in New York, and saw her off at the airport. I recall one lovely afternoon (Dec. 25), a beach party at Magens Bay, when Eric Smith, a black man dressed from the waist up as Santa Claus, stood hip deep in the ocean, amidst gentle waves, strumming a guitar, and singing Christmas carols. The next day I enjoyed broiled lobster that Tom, another new pal, had speared. On the night of Dec.29, I also recall sipping drinks at The Pink

Barrel bar, listening until closing to Axel's philosophical gems. On January 1, I saw Co-Co who came in from an all-night binge and after breakfast spent much of the day with her, listening to the story of her life. At one point, she asked me if I liked boys! Sunday, Jan. 3, I went fishing with Tom & Garry. That night we saw the film "*Blue Angel.*" Monday, Jan. 4, got to the beach at 11:30 a.m. and it was empty. I did sit-ups to work off the tummy flab. Since I was leaving the next day, Maria touched me deeply, giving me a present for my little son Jeff. On Tues. Jan. 5, I took an 11:30 am flight to San Juan, and then caught the 2:30 pm Trans-Carib flight to Idlewild in New York, where my good childhood pals Arlene Rudowsky and Annette Gerstl picked me up and drove me back to Jersey. Shortly before I departed from St. Thomas, one new friend, a local man, said "if you like it now, mon, you should come back for April Carnival. That's when we *really* have fun!"

Doctor Clement Fairweather

As an Army veteran, the GI Bill enabled me to return to Newark-Rutgers and take night classes for free, while working at the Prudential in Newark, and later at Keuffel & Esser in Hoboken. I particularly recall one class, taught by Dr. Clement Fairweather. I had only vague ideas about a major, so I pursued a Liberal Arts path. There was a course in Early English Poetry that I remember to this day. The class started around 6 or 7 p.m. Perhaps 15 of us were seated in the room. Most of my classmates were Business or Accounting majors, who had to take a few liberal arts courses in order to graduate. In walked Dr. Fairweather, a tall, thin, fair-haired man in his 40s, wearing a tweedy jacket with leather elbow patches. He smiled, looked around the room, then pointed to one of the young men.

"Who are you?" he asked.

"I'm Melvin..."

"No, no...I mean who *are* you?"

Melvin was a bit confused. He thought for a moment, and then said, "Well, I'm an Accounting major..."

Dr. Fairweather nodded, pointed to a young lady, and asked, "Who are you"?

"I'm married," she said. "I'm raising our little son, and I cook the meals."

"Thank you," Dr. Fairweather said. He asked the same question of three more students. Then, he asked, "Does anyone want to know who I am?"

Puzzled looks. "I," he continued, "am one of the world's foremost authorities on the poetry of Alexander Pope!" More puzzled looks. Then he turned to the Accounting Major and asked, "Is there any reason why you can't be one of the best accountants in the world?" Then, to the young lady, "And can't you be one of the finest cooks, if not in the world, then in the entire USA?"

During the course of the semester, we read just 3 or 4 poems by Alexander Pope. That was all! Nothing else. On a typical evening, we would cover perhaps 3 or 4 stanzas of *"The Rape Of The Lock,"* or "*An Essay On Criticism*." Each evening, Dr. Fairweather had a stack of index cards, offering details on the historical references in each stanza, the music, the choice of words, etc. He drove us crazy with the slow pace, and then he would make us laugh, commenting: "When you are done with this course, you will be able to read and figure out your own Federal income tax forms!" I still treasure the collection of Alexander Pope poems, which was our textbook more than 40 years ago. Almost every other line is underlined and the margins are filled with my scribblings of his comments.

Jan. 3, 1960. Letter from me to Charles Addams, c/o The New Yorker, 25 W. 43rd St., New York NY. Dear Mr. Addams: Several months ago you told me—in a note—that you would be able to give me the original art from the "Muzak Musician's" cartoon as soon as it was free from the printers who were handling your latest book….I was wondering whether it might now be OK to have this artwork. I'm leaving in 3 weeks for a new job in San Juan, Puerto Rico and would love to take this treasure along with me. It will—I promise you—occupy a place of honor in my tropical hut…I'm having the N.Yorker subscription transferred to my Puerto Rico address so I'll be keeping tabs on your latest efforts…if the inspiration hits me (as it seldom does) I'll try to dream up a few gag ideas and send them along.

Jan. 1960 (no exact date) Handwritten reply from Charles Addams. Dear Mr. Wagenheim, I'm depressed to report that the Muzak picture was given to guess who, Muzak Inc. by the advertising department. Hope you're enjoying your new work in Puerto Rico—there isn't a New York citizen who wouldn't envy you. All best, Chas. Addams. **Wed. Feb. 3, 1960.** With Janet Foscaldo, a friend I met while taking night classes at Rutgers, I went to see a very funny production of *"Once Upon A Mattress"*. My diary doesn't mention that it starred a not-yet-famous Carol Burnett, and was produced at the Cherry Lane

Theatre in New York, but that's my recollection. Later that night we went to The Roundtable Club, and enjoyed songs by Mabel Mercer (unforgettable!). I was running short of money, and Janet lent me $5! Got back at 4:30 a.m.

Feb. 11, 1960. Son Jeff's birthday. Got a card and present, visited with him and Carol for about an hour. Have conflicting feelings about future visits. Yes? No?

March 9, 1960. Bill Franklin called with job offer at Keuffel & Esser. More $$$.

March 12, 1960. Helped Nan move to her new place. Uncle Carl & Jean joined us, and we had dinner there.

March 16, 1960. Letter from Leon Mones, Assistant. Superintendent, Department of Personnel, Board of Education, Newark 2, NJ. To whom it may concern: Re: Experience Statement. Mr. Harold Wagenheim was employed as a teacher in the Newark School System from Sept. 1, 1929 to his date of resignation, Oct. 7, 1942. From Sept. 1, 1929 to June 30, 1932 he taught at Montgomery Street Pre-Vocational School; and from Sept. 1, 1932 to June 30, 1935 he taught at Hawthorne Avenue School. On Sept. 1, 1935, he was transferred and assigned to Monmouth Street School at which time he was granted a leave of absence for personal illness until Oct. 7, 1942, when he resigned. Mr. Wagenheim taught in the seventh and eighth grade at the above listed schools, and his services were satisfactory. Very truly yours, Leon Mones

Changing Jobs

April 1960: I resigned from Prudential, and took a job with Keuffel & Esser, located at Adams and Third St. in Hoboken NJ, to begin in May. They produced drafting reproduction, surveying, optical tooling equipment & materials, slide rules and measuring tapes. I found the job through a personnel agency. I was the junior member of a three-man advertising department, headed by Bill Franklin, and seconded by Dick Danzig. I told Bill Franklin that I would report to work after a brief Caribbean vacation *(details below)*.

April 22, 1960. I took a limo from Newark to Idlewild Airport and caught the 11:59 pm Eastern Airlines flight to San Juan, Puerto Rico. From San Juan I caught a 7:30 am flight the next morning on Caribair to St. Thomas in the U.S. Virgin Islands. Last January, when I was departing from my wonderful vacation there, a friend said I would have an even greater time during Carnival, so I decided to come!

A Life-Changing Encounter

April 23, 1960: During the next week in St. Thomas I had a fantastic time enjoying the beach, the Carnival parades and music, the bars, and most of all the fascinating assortment of people. Early one evening, after going to the beach, I dropped into the Pink Barrel, my favorite bar in downtown St. Thomas. It was early and nearly empty. Suddenly, the door opened and in burst about two dozen people. Mr. Krieger, a tall Texan who was the head of General Electric in San Juan, Puerto Rico, was leading a group of his employees; they had come to enjoy Carnival. They sat at nearby tables. Mr. Krieger saw that I was alone. He waved at me and invited me to join the group. He asked me what I thought of St. Thomas. I told him I had been there for a few days, was enjoying it, and then joked that I might become an alcoholic, since there wasn't much to do except swim at the beach, and drink! "You should come to San Juan," he said. "Puerto Rico is booming." He asked me what kind of work I did. I told him I had experience in journalism and writing advertising copy. "Go see Nelson Lavergne, he's the ad manager at *The San Juan Star*, a new English language newspaper. You might find a job there!" This chance encounter with Mr. Krieger and his GE workers proved to be a life-changing moment.

May 2, 1960: I flew from St. Thomas to San Juan, and made the rounds, visiting the McCann-Erickson ad agency, J. Walter Thompson ad agency, and *The San Juan Star*.

K&E and The Spider Lady

May 4, 1960. I reported to my new job at Keuffel & Esser in Hoboken NJ. *(Keuffel & Esser was a drafting company founded in 1867 by German mmigrants, William J.D. Keuffel and Herman Esser. It started out in New York, selling drawing materials and drafting supplies. In 1876, K&E (as it was known) began selling surveying instruments and in 1880 opened a three-story factory in Hoboken. In the 1920, K&E began manufacturing slide rules, but with the advent of the electronic calculator in the 1970s, the slide rule became obsolete. K&E's market share shrank due to other technological changes, and the company finally faded away. It was acquired by Azon Corp. in 1987.)*

Almost all the folks at K&E were engineers, except for Bill Franklin and Dick Danzig, who, like me, were creative ad men. We loved going out for lunch in Hoboken, then a working class town, with prices far lower than Manhattan, where Bill & Dick resided. The Clam Broth House, a few blocks away, at the time did not allow women in the bar, although there was as family dining room with a side entrance (this sexist practice, of course, faded a few years later). Bill & Dick loved their martinis, which they enjoyed during Friday (payday) lunches. And they cost only 90 cents, compared with about $2 in Manhattan. Hoboken was still a cargo port (before containerization moved all the ships to Port Elizabeth and the town was gradually abandoned by its blue-collar, working class residents).

I worked at K&E for less than a year, but have fond memories of a fascinating place. For example, there was The Spider Lady. This sounds unbelievable, but it's a true story. Shortly after joining K&E I took a tour of the old building. And there was one large room, with what resembled a long pool table inside. The Spider Lady kept large, non-poisonous spiders inside wooden boxes. Each day, she would "milk" them. That's right. Wearing gloves, she would take out a spider, which then (apparently frightened) began to emit a sticky web from some part of its body. The Spider Lady would attach the sticky web to a revolving metal cylinder, and let the spider run the length of the table. As it ran, the sticky web was collected on the cylinder. Later in the day, the Spider Lady gave the web to a man in another room, who examined the web on a microscope. He then used small portions of the web for the cross hairs on surveying instruments. I was told that these fine webs were better than any manufactured cross hairs.

At one point K&E, famous for its wooden slide rule, was getting competition from a cheaper plastic one made in Japan. It was decided to boost sales by creating a simple manual, that would show students how to use a slide rule. Engineers, I learned, are for the most part brilliant, but quite inarticulate. So I was chosen to write the manual! I knew nothing about slide rules. So I visited several of the K&E engineers and patiently took notes as they talked me through the operation of a slide rule. I am told that my Slide Rule Manual was a best-seller. Wish I could find a copy! .

May 8, 1960. From Kal to Dad. Dear Dad: Much has happened since my last letter which went to you sometime last November, I think. I'd better list them in chronological order:Dec. 22-Jan. 6, spent two weeks in St. Thomas,

Virgin Islands. Had wonderful time, met many interesting people, got invited to return for spring Carnival week (which is similar to New Orleans Mardi Gras). Day I returned, found a check for $100, sold humor feature to *Rogue* magazine, copy of which is enclosed. Certainly not a high level of art, but I got a real thrill getting into print when this magazine hit the newsstands in mid-March. Same week, I sent another batch of captioned pictures to *Rogue* and voila! Got another $100 check…the next installment will appear in the August 1960 issue with possibly my picture on author's page. Have sent another batch in with no answer yet, have had short interview with Dell Publication and sent them a few for a small satire magazine, with no answer to date.

May 13, 1960: As the semester was coming to a close, I made plans to leave New Jersey and move to Puerto Rico. Late one night, after class, it was Friday, I was standing outside the Weequahic Diner in Newark and I looked across the street at a White Castle. There, through the window, I saw Dr. Fairweather seated at the counter, hands wrapped around a steaming cup of coffee. I went over, entered, and thanked Dr. Fairweather for the class. I told him that I would be leaving soon for Puerto Rico. He looked at me and said, "Puerto Rico? You will, of course, learn Spanish … *thoroughly*!" Those words have stayed with me forever. Dr. Fairweather was such an inspiring teacher! *(Note: Dr. Fairweather's father was a prominent architect. Dr. Fairweather lived in Metuchen NJ. I believe he died on March 24, 2000. Soon after it was announced that he had donated a collection of more than 300 books and manuscripts related to British poets to the Special Collections in the Alexander Library at Rutgers, New Brunswick.)*

May 30, 1960: Saw *"Our Man In Havana"* movie at Newark theatre, subtle British humor. Then went to Puerto Rican bar on Broad St. Home at 2:30 am.

July 1, 1960. Letter from Kal to Dad. Hi Dad: Am in the office with little time to write, but the August issue of *Rogue* magazine just hit the newsstands so I thought I'd speed one on your way…it's enclosed. My picture is on the inside cover, there's a fan letter on the next page about my last story, and page 73 begins my contribution. I'm notorious! Will write again when the time permits. Your 'Roguish' son, *Kal.*

August 1960. *Rogue* magazine published my series of old engravings with funny captions, called "The Classics Revisited." Among the authors in that issue was Lenny Bruce.

Aug. 23, 1960. Dear Mr. Wagenheim, Your application for hospital treatment, VA Form 10-P-10, has been approved. You will be notified as soon as a bed is available...Very truly yours, John F. Southworth, Chief, Registrar Division,Veterans Adminsitration Hospital, East Orange, New Jersey.

Early September 1960: Letter from me to my pal Bob Bletter who was now stationed in Germany with the US Army. Hola amigo: I'm out of the hospital. I got out yestidday, 10 days after they removed a pilonidal cyst from just above my rectum. They left the incision wide open because they say it heals best that way. It's about 4 inches long, 1 inch wide, and about 1 ½ inches deep—a veritable Grand Canyon—in case gory details fascinate you. For the next 3 to 4 weeks I have to keep it packed with a specially treated bandage and take 2 hot-water sit baths a day which sort of restricts my activity a bit. Except for a little pain when I sit down on a hard surface I'm in top shape though...The VA hospital was really tremendous and while I shudder at the thought of my bubulla ever needing medical treatment, I advise you to check with the VA if the need ever arises...top doctors, the most modern facilities...and not a cent does it cost. I'm glad to be home though, because no matter how good they were to me, I just couldn't take the inactivity and the 10 p.m. lights out. Thassit for now...best regards to Rosemary.

Sept. 10, 1960. Letter from my father, Harold Wagenheim (then age 57). From Los Angeles. I (age 25) was living in Newark. Dear Kal: I have just re-read your letter of August 12 (your visit to Greenwich Village) and find it very interesting. It brings back memories of the two summers I visited at Patchen Place, while I was working on my degree. I spent much time at the Square writing a paper on the bootblack situation around the college. I was taking Sociology as one of the courses, and I recall the many interviews I held with the youngsters. For their efforts I gave each an extra coin. I spent many delightful days and evenings sauntering around the quaint places, attended poetry readings (I read, also), saw plays. I hear the Village has changed considerably: Harry Kemp and Maxwell Bodenheim are no longer with us; a few of us still may remember the Provincetown Players, Edna St. Vincent Millay, Floyd Dell. Ah, the Village days...the true Village...the cafeterias where we sat hours on end talking about our hopes and aspirations...the free spirit...the creative spirit...philosophized...and dreamt...and awakened to the sudden reality of life...O'Neill, the sick, lean, hungry O'Neill, with his one-acters tucked under his arm, seeking solace in the theatre. This was not a Beatnik age; the Village of my day produced true artists. They were bohemians, yes; but, they had artistic drives, they produced, they were thought odd, but what is odd about the search for creative expression? As for myself, I work away at the Land Assessor's Office. My evenings are taken up with a myriad of things: A bit of writing, re-writing, visiting with friends, reading: the last was Moss Hart's 'Act I' which I recommend you read. Of course, his background, at least part of it, was mine, when I directed plays at the Newark YMHA. Do write me when you get the time. I hope you are in the best of health. Keep working at the story, and if I can help, let me know. Exercise all your talents; never let them get away from you. In this we must be persistent. Time is a runaway child: gay, unconcerned, frivolous, impersonal. Hold on to it, tame it, make it work for you. Sincerely, your dad, Harold... *Note: On Dec. 30, 2007, I Emailed a copy of the the above letter from my Dad to my cousin, Allan Wagenheim. He responded:* Kal, thanks for the letter. It is so well written (of course!) and so much the man that I knew and heard of. I believe it was about two years later, sometime in '62 or '63 that I saw your father where he was living in that single room in a rooming house. It is, unfortunately, a sad picture that lingers in my memory. Allan

Sept. 28, 1960. From me at 59 Spruce St., Apt. 502, Newark NJ to Director, VA Hospital, East Orange NJ. Dear Sir: Earlier this month I was a patient in the VA Hospital. I had a (pilonidal) cyst removed and stayed on in Ward 4C for several days. I would just like to express my sincere gratitude for the uniformly excellent treatment given me...not only on the part of the doctors, but the nurses, nursing assistants and all those with whom I came in contact. From talking with my fellow patients, I can sense that my personal feelings quite accurately reflect their feelings, too, and I thought you would be gratified to know this. Again, thank you. Very sincerely, *Kal Wagenheim*

Oct. 23, 1960. Letter to Dad from Kal: Dear Dad: I was very happy to receive your letter of the 19th. Let me emphatically say "yes" to your invitation to see the 79-page treatment you've been working on...While I can't promise to be of much help because I've got enough trouble with my own stuff, I'll try to be objective...perhaps the fact that I'll be looking at it for the first time will enable me to ferret out its flaws...where you've probably been living with it and cannot. I want to thank you again (muchos gracias, papa) for your critique of my short story which you sent a few weeks ago...I think I've come up with a much better angle, much along the lines of your suggestion to add a love interest with a gal in the office…and the first 4 or 5 pages of my rewrite have a lot more zip…My regular job…keeps me hopping. I'm studying Español two nites a week and either listen to Spanish records or pore over my textbook at least 5-10 hours per week…Though politics is something I'm completely disinterested in, I just sent off a 5-page letter to Senator Kennedy on how to help enhance America's image abroad…it calls for sending more (and better) people over there as no-strings-attached advisors in all fields. To recruit these people we could start a full-scale campaign in high schools and colleges, creating a desire for working overseas and outlining curricula (including languages) to help the students qualify. There's no doubt that *people* are much better than "CARE" packages…and a combination of *both* in Asia, Africa, the Middle East, etc. could help these people tremendously, increase our own export markets and keep them neutral.

The Peace Corps: Who Invented It?

Oct. 21, 1960. Letter to Sen. John F. Kennedy, Hyannisport, Mass, from Kal Wagenheim, 59 Spruce St., Apt. 302, Newark 2, NJ.

Dear Senator Kennedy: I wholeheartedly agree with one of your most frequently voiced contentions: that America's image abroad is not as great as it once was and that we must launch some type of active program in order to strengthen our image as not only the strongest nation on earth but as the standard bearer of freedom and progress. However, this is far easier said than done…as the present administration has discovered after 8 years of probing in what I feel is the wrong direction. I have a plan in mind which I think is unique. At least, I, personally, have never before heard it proposed. It's a plan to enhance our image abroad which would begin to bear fruit almost immediately, really hit its stride in 2 or 3 years, and continue snowballing from its own momentum in the future. Here it is…

First Premise…First, I believe that we are spending our tremendous foreign aid budget unwisely…we are sending food, machinery and money to the needy nations, but in many areas these tangible aids are being matched or surpassed by the Soviet bloc..True, we should continue to send food, machinery and money…but most important of all, we should send *people… thousands* of people. Think of it this way. If a person were hungry, sick and unemployed, what would he appreciate most? A check in the mail or a man bearing a check, perhaps of a smaller denomination but who could also cure the sickness and provide employment? I think the choice is obvious. We should send such emisarries to Asia, Africa, the Middle East and Central and South America. They should be well-educated specialists in all fields (mining, engineering, chemistry, accounting, marketing, education, medicine, etc) to insure that the funds we do send are used to best advantage. These people will not only lend valuable assistance to nations lacking the know-how to help themselves, but they will also dramatically illustrate that America is not an invisible, distant "uncle" who sends occasional tidbits for minimal subsistence, but America is *people*...people who are young, friendly, energetic and eager to help.

Where do we get our "ambassadors"? The bulk of this "peacetime army" can be found in today's senior high school and freshman and sophomore college classrooms. Very few of these young people are thinking about overseas work. Why? Because they have never been approached. The tremendous features of overseas work and the ways and means of securing such employment have never been outlined to them. For example, in my hometown library, holding perhaps millions of books, I finally found, in a dark corner, a slim portfolio of literature telling how to get a job overseas. What little information that was available painted a rather bleak picture of the chances for employment. But the latent desire for the challenge and stimulation of foreign travel exists in every young person. We must arouse this desire by first creating more job opportunities and second, making these opportunities known to our youth.

Creating job opportunities... If we were to announce the availability of skilled specialists in all fields, who could travel to any point of the globe, we would undoubtedly be swamped with invitations by nations all over the world. The job openings would literally create themselves. Also, if the private U.S. firms currently engaged in overseas commerce were given encouragement by both the U.S. and the country they are working in, they could easily step up their operation; creating more jobs. And U.S. firms not yet engaged in international commerce might well be encouraged by the favorable climate and perhaps initiate ventures abroad. However, the government itself would be the major employer, sending its army of specialists to economic trouble-spots on perhaps a 2 or 3 year contract basis.

The real crux of the matter: people Just as our advertising profession has so successfully sold our industry products through skillful promotion and creation of desire, we must instill a desire among American youth to travel and work abroad. This can be done..and without great expense... Every high school senior, every college freshman and sophomore is a potential "customer" to whom we should sell the idea of working overseas... Today, most college students, unless they have a particular profession in mind (medicine, law, etc) have virtually no career goal. It's usually several years *after* college that they finally move into their life-long job field...if we could *propose* professional goals to these many thousands of undecided youngsters, and make these jobs sound attractive in terms of salary and challenge, I think we would be literally swamped with applicants. So much so that instead of having to search far and wide for capable overseas help, as we do now, we could actually be selective and pick the cream of the crop...

The benefits of the plan...By helping needy nations achieve a better standard of living, we also create a growing marketplace for our goods. This would eventually aid the employment picture at home...When these young "ambassadors" return home after their "tour of duty", they will bring with them a better understanding of foreign countries and people. ..In just a few years' time we could have tens of thousands of Americans bearing living testimony to our way of life..not with "CARE" packages, but with their dynamic presence....Our nation was founded by people from many countries and is actually a distillation of all their cultures. We have the opportunity, in each nation, to distill our knowledge with their intense desire for a decent, free life. The result can only be the creation of a stand-up-on-its-feet neighbor who will be rock-solid for us and our way of life.

Perhaps, because I am only 25 years old, I'm being rather naïve about all of this. Perhaps, because of my admitted lack of experience, my plan is founded on a beautiful, but unworkable, ideal. Perhaps. But it's the kind of daring, forceful undertaking which can do no harm and (understatement of the year) may do a lot of good. I hope so. All good luck in the coming election. Very sincerely, Kal Wagenheim

Nov. 3, 1960. Front page of The New York Times.

Headline: KENNEDY FAVOR U.S. 'PEACE CORPS' TO WORK ABROAD

By HARRISON E. SALISBURY

SAN FRANCISCO, Nov. 2—Senator John F. Kennedy detailed today a proposal to create a "peace corps" of young men who would serve with technical aid missions abroad as an alternative to the military draft....Mr. Kennedy's proposal was made in an address prepared for delivery at San Francisco's Cow Palace...Mr. Kennedy's proposal for a "peace corps" suggested that young men of ability serve abroad for three years. They would be qualified by rigorous examinations and trained in language, special skills and customs needed for the countries in which they would serve. He proposed that the corps work under the direction of the technical aid program of the International Cooperation Agency. "We cannot discontinue training our young men as soldiers of war," Mr. Kennedy said, "but we also need them as ambassadors of peace...volunteers would be sought among talented young women as well—and from every race and walk of life."

* * *

Did my letter to Senator Kennedy, sent October 21, 1960, reach him and have an impact on his proposal for the Peace Corps, made public Nov. 2, 1960? Did he have the same idea at around the same time? I have no idea. But I am amazed at the coincidental timing. Who knows? Perhaps I inherited some of the psychic powers of Rose Hoffman (my maternal grandmother's sweet cousin) and received signals from Senator Kennedy's brain. It shall always remain a fascinating mystery!

Grandma dies

Nov. 13, 1960: My Great-Grandmother, Ida Hoffman-Shamberg, who raised me, and perhaps was the greatest influence in my formation as a child, died, age 92. She died, as she had lived, lucid, sweet-natured to the very end. Grandma had remained active all those years, cooking and cleaning, while her daughter, Nanny, went to work. When I was a little child, she was the one who fed me, clothed me, looked after me. I remember in particular the occasional times she prepared potato pancakes with apple sauce (still a favorite of mine) and most Saturdays she would make me two kosher hotdogs, with Heinz baked beans, washed down with a glass of Hoffman Cream Soda. In part the reason for her longevity was the fact that she remained active. But one day she slipped and fell in the kitchen, and fractured a hip. During the next month, while recovering in bed at a nursing home for the elderly in Newark, it was a slow downhill slide, and finally up to Heaven, where I am sure she resides. Everyone—everyone!—who knew Grandma adored her.

Nov. 16, 1960. Letter from Anna Kronenberger, my grandmother's older sister, then in her 70s, living in Chicago. "Dear Lillian: I received your letter. I was very sorry to learn you are ill. I hope the exrays will be satisfactory. I wonder if your dieting had anything to do with your illness. People are crazy to diet so strenuously, which lowers their resistance and virises get them down. So many people here laid up in the hospital, people I know, with viris, or heart or cancer. One does not hear anything good. I am not well. I lay around day after day all by myself. I had a cold and my nose and upper lip are all sore. My son phoned he is leaving for the south this p.m. Went into a new business. I have not seen him in a month. He said to take care of myself, and he will phone me tomorrow night. You at least have your daughter and grandson nearby, to do for you, and take you places. I am really all alone. I am sorry I am so far away. It's too bad, but I cannot travel like I used to; besides a trip to NY is costly and I must take it easy. Doctors orders. So if I want to live and be well I must listen to my doctor. Let me know how you are, I will be waiting to hear from you. Anyway, don't be nervous & worry. Its easier said than done—what you need is plenty of good food, rest and medication, so let your doctor advise you, and do what he advises. It's raining and very windy. I haven't been out for several days. I keep food in my freezer. I market once a week. I have pot roast from last night and baked a rice pudding, as I don't eat many eggs, so get them this way. One must eat and get the vitamins. A car cannot run without fuel, and the body also cannot function properly without the foods we need: meats, cereal, eggs, vegetables, butter, milk. Write when you can and advise me fully. I hope you will be all right. Try not to worry. It's not easy for the other fellow to say don't worry. Love, Anna."

Nov. 30, 1960. Letter from Ann Kronenberger (in Chicago) to Nanny (in Newark). Dear Lillian: Thinking of you. I hope you are feeling better, and stronger and eating. I called Lucille's apt 4 times last week, to inquire about you, as I did not want to disturb you. We have had terrible weather. Monday, terrible showers and very high winds. Tues. snow and high winds. No wonder this city is called 'The Windy City'. Today it is clear, cold. 20 degrees and winds not as bad. I must go out and get a little meat. I use so little they don't deliver, so have used my can opener, but a person needs the right kind of food to maintain good health, and strength. I told Kay on the phone that I want to go East to see you. I had some papers to sign Mon. but could not make it on account of the weather. Then I have some financial matters to look after. This all takes time. I plan on going to a hotel. I will not fly. Will take the train. Cannot go until the above two matters are taken care of. Noone can do this for me. I imagine I will be able to go about the 15th. Don't want to plan too far ahead. I will advise you when I make my train reservation. It's nice Murray and Lillian are with you. Give them my regards. Hold the right thought. I memorized a little poem that someone sent me, which was found in a cabin in North Mich. and it has helped me. It goes like this: 'Heavenly Father, who are in Heaven,

Who has looked after me yesterday, and today,
And will look after me tomorrow and every day—
Either he will shield me from harm and pain,
Or give me unfailing strength to bear it.
So, I must put my mind at ease.'

Hope you are feeling better, and so close with best wishes for your good health and happiness. Love, Ann. PS. I called Mon. p.m. but Lucille was at your house. I call instead of writing. I will write in a few days. Nothing new here.

* * *

Dec. 14, 1960. While I was in Puerto Rico for a short vacation, Lillian Krantz, my dear grandmother, who supported me in so many ways during my life, died of cancer at age 67, almost exactly one month after the death of her 92-year-old mother.

Late 1960. I resigned from Keuffel & Esser (K&E) and prepared to move to Puerto Rico. This letter was written by my boss, Bill Franklin. "To whom it may concern: If you are considering Mr. Kal Wagenheim for a position in your firm, this will be of interest to you. Kal has worked directly under me in the Advertising Department of Keuffel & Esser Co. for approximately one year. During that time he has impressed me greatly with his competence, and I regret seeing him leave. "

Jan. 9, 1961. From Candido Negron, The Island Times, Puerto Rico

Dear Kal: I received your letter date Dec.20 and have made arrangements in relation to the apartment as follows: The address is: Europa Street #356,

Apt. 5A. The receipt for one month guarantee is being drawn on my name, but that you can fix after your arrival. You will be paying from January the 25th on. As to the air conditioner you talked in your letter I think is perfectly allright. I hope to see you soon. Sincerely, *Candido Negron.*

OFF TO PUERTO RICO

Jan. 4, 1961. Letter from Kal (in Newark) to Dad (in Los Angeles). Dear Dad: Sorry for the long delay in writing, but much has happened recently...some grief...some happy news. Early in November my great-grandmother passed away after a month-long illness, and just a month later my grandmother died from cancer. Almost immediately afterwards I got word of a job opportunity in Puerto Rico while there on a short vacation in mid-December...and I'm taking it. It's as the assistant promotion manager with an English weekly newspaper in San Juan. It seems as though the job opportunity came about as a natural and logical phenomenon preceded by the severings of my bonds with home and family here in the States... as if Destiny or Fate had a hand in it. The new job means a cut in pay...but I'm eager to strike out at something new in a land and culture different to me... and there are several job possibilities which could break in the next few months which would spring me right back to my present pay area...I'm sorry for not getting any comments to you on the treatment you sent me...I promise to do so before I leave and get a letter off to you with my thoughts on it. Meanwhile I'm in the process of trying to select the books, clothes and records dear to my heart...the ones which I'll take along with me to Puerto Rico. Also in my entourage will be my car, phonograph, tape recorder and airconditioner. I've already landed an apartment...I had truly wanted to get out and see you this Xmas, but not enough spare cash. So I did the next best thing; took my available funds, which were enough for a trip to Puerto Rico (and fortunately a new job). I like my present job here in the States *very* much...and I'm well liked by the people...but I have a yearning for different geographical surroundings which will never be satisfied until I do it. That's it for now...write when you can...and I will, too, I send you my best wishes for this young year. Your son, *Kal*

Jan. 17, 1961. Handwritten letter from Dad (in LA) to Kal. Dear Kal: My typewriter broke down. This letter will be short; a longer one to follow. I do wish you the best in Puerto Rico. The job sounds interesting and challenging. I had hoped we would meet but as you explained there were so many things happening. As for the story, could you send it back to me the first chance you get. I am circulating it, and since I have, all told 3 copies, I could use the copy I sent you. For the time being, good fortune to you. Please send me your new address soon. Nothing else. Best of health and peace of mind unto you. Sincerely, Harry.

1961: Moved to San Juan, Puerto Rico and began work with *The Island Times*, a small weekly newspaper run by Luis Muñoz Lee, son of then Gov. Luis Muñoz Marín.

Feb. 22, 1961. Letter from my father in Los Angeles to me. I had moved to San Juan, Puerto Rico in Jan. 1961. Dear Kal: I do hope that by this time you are pretty well set with your apartment, your job. I am told that *Look* Magazine carried quite an extensive piece on Puerto Rico. I suggest you contact the publisher for the article; on the other hand, if you are too busy, I will get the copy for you. How are you feeling? When you write, feel free to write openly. Let me hear of your successes and.....and your problems. How is your social life, etc. How is the language problem coming along? I mean your mastery of Spanish conversation. I must tell you your evaluation of my story was incisive, highly professional, and valid. In the years this literary piece has been making the studio rounds, it has been read and criticized by a dean of literary agents, the office of Stanley Kramer, all the major studios, and not one of these has managed to crystallize my work in the manner you did. I commend you for a fine piece of criticism. As for myself, I go about my way in rather routine fashion, working at the Land Assessor's office, visit my cousin Charlie and his wife Lil (they are going to Europe this summer), write now and then after a fashion, and engage in a few othere trivialities. I have been thinking of returning to teaching: first on a substitute basis, to try my wings; later, for secondary level teaching (I will take courses for my M.A. while substitute teaching). If this doesn't work out, I am formulating plans to enter the literary agency business (I tried this when I first came to California, but with little success). I hope you are well, prospering, and finding things to your liking. Please write and feel free in doing so. The best to you and God's blessings! Sincerely, your dad, Harold."

Sunday, Feb. 26, 1961. Letter from me in San Juan PR to Mil Kaiser, my next door neighbor in Newark NJ, who taught at Arts High and ran the most marvelous Friday night parties at her small cottage. Dearest Millie: Forgive the long gap between my leaving and this letter…I hope you'll say hello to Frank for me in this letter directed to you (personally) and to all other friends in Newark (Frank, Dave, 'Eddie, Howie, Ralph, Germaine, Michael, and I hesitate to go on for fear that I'll leave someone out...so let's make it all-inclusive….including the dogs). In rather quick time I've become acclimated to the environs and must confess that I feel as though I've lived here quite a long time…especially when a bright-eyed tourist comes into sight and I've got to give him or her the lowdown on where to go, etc. I work with the *Island Times*, a small-town weekly which functions on a rather miraculous informal basis…and each issue comes out as if it were the first one…to the surprise of all..and it's all rather delightful….my job, mainly, consists of visiting ad agencies and direct advertisers in the area, giving them the scoop on our distribution, and the value of advertising with us…so I don't really sell ads directly (signing contracts on the spot) but I hope that when scheduling time comes for the next campaign my words have left their impression. I have two bosses…(1) Candido Negron, the business manager who works with me on selling ads; a swarthy latin type who looks like a lecherous Cesar Romero, but who –quite surprisingly—has a terrific knowledge of the function of newspapers…he was a linotyper in NY for years and and I saw—with my own eyes—him roll up his sleeves, take apart and put together a Ludlow typesetting machine when it was on the machine…no delegating of authority around here! (2) the editorial chief is Luis Muñoz Lee—son of the Governor—who is a rather quiet, intellectual type and one of the nicest people you could ever meet…he's not the loud, slap-em-on-the-back type… but likes to visit a nite club practically every nite and sit off in a corner sipping rum and talking. His reluctance to socialize has been quite helpful to me because thus far—in only 3 weeks or so—he has received 5 invitations to various functions (chamber of commerce meeting, press party for a new restaurant, annual get together of local travel agents' assoc., etc) which he has given me…so I've really been "scoffing" the free booze and food, and meeting lots of interesting people during working hours….in addition, Luis has been very kind, inviting me to several weekend beach picnics and other little functions... Just selling ads has sort of put a damper on my copy-writing activity, but things are looking up. Last week I suggested to Luis that I write a business events column for the paper...he was rather reluctant because he didn't want me mixing up the editorial and business sections of the paper (said it could lead to hanky-panky like free plugs in return for ads) but he said to do one on speculation for his look-see. So I did. And he ok'd it and it appeared this past Friday and will be a regular weekly column from now on. Once I pass the word around, enough items should come in so that I won't have to spend my time news-seeking, but one nite a week I'll be able to gather up the tidbits and slap them together. While I plan to be rather strict about free plugs in the column, it can nevertheless provide me with a good excuse to call up an ad agency, ask "what's new" and then proceed to business matters... sneaky, eh? What the hell: all's fair in love and war...(?) Ah yes, the beaches are *so* beautiful and so many are so close to where I live (less than 15 minutes) that it's really been great. Hope I never become accustomed to this heavenly tropical clime and environs...because now, as a relative newcomer, I'm still rather enchanted with it all. Oh yes, I've changed addresses...I was living at 356 Calle Europa, Apt. 6 in Santurce, a more modern section of San Juan... but now I'm right in Old San Juan, only 2 blocks from work and just above a real swinging night club (La Botella) owned by a good friend. The address is: 100 San Sebastian St., San Juan, Puerto Rico. I had a small 3-room apt in Santurce for $85 a month, but it was a 25-minute drive through heavy traffic to and from the office...and Luis took me to this club (La Botella) one night and introduced me to the owner, Chuck New, who also writes a gossip column for our competition, the *San Juan Star* daily paper. Chuck had rooms above the club, one occupied by the piano player (Hal Hester, who's appeared at Bon Soir in NYC and who wrote *"The Sand and the Sea"*, which Nat "King" Cole put on the Hit Parade), another room occupied by a guy who works in one of the tourist shops, another room now empty which was occupied for one week by two actors who were working in "Auntie Mame" when it was showing here as part of the San Juan Drama Festival...and last, and least...me. I have one good-sized room for only $15 a week, including maid service, kitchen privileges and a brand new washing machine to keep my socks clean. Not a bad deal, and the club-restaurant downstairs is a real swinger...Chuck New, the owner, seems to be able to get every big star who comes down here to visit the club at least once, so it's been lots of fun. So far, the roster has included: Marcel Marceau, Mildred Dunnock, Albert Dekker, Paulette Goddard, Montgomery Clift and Gordon McCrae. Next week, Robert Mitchum is coming to town. Chuck worked with Mitchum in some touring acting company years ago…he says he's got a big bundle of "pot" ready for Mitchum as soon as he arrives. Money-wise, I'm still in the low-low income bracket, but these free-load dinners and rather generous tourists (who seem to think of me as an island character because I'm not as tan as they…which seems to be true of all people who live here permanently) have been letting me live well beyond my means. I've knocked out a few free-lance copy things for my buddy who runs an ad agency here…and now the weekly column, but at best it all hovers round the $100 a week mark…not quite what I had at K&E. The ad manager of the *San Juan Star* (the English daily) quit and he called me up and got me an interview with the big shot of the paper who was looking for two young guys to divide the ad manager's job (who was making about $12,000 per year). This big shot is sort of a real shit-head type, not very well liked. We talked and then he said he'd like me to change my job and work with the *Star* (this was last Wednesday). He asked the salary I'd require. I said "$175 a week" and he balked, coming back with "All we can afford is $100." I got up and walked out. Screw him. I figure it this way. I was making fairly good dough in the states…and have full intention of making it here, some day. But this is a small island. I can't go jumping from job to job here, biting off a $10 increase at each new job opportunity. In 3 months I'd get a reputation as an incorrigible job-hopper. So I prefer to wait things out…I truly love this little paper I'm working on…and will change when the big opportunity comes. If I hang around for a few months, it will come. If not, I'm quite happy here at *The Island Times* and have been promised a raise to $100 a week for the the business part of my activities within two months. So that with a little free-lance copy and the weekly column should get me up close to the K&E salary. But truly, the money isn't that important any more...because so many things are free here. Ran out of paper! Must go. Will write again… and again. My very best regards, to all….Kal

Sunday-March 5, 1961. To my father, from me, living at 100 San Sebastian St., San Juan PR. Hi Dad: Please note new address…have moved to a very nice room directly above a night club (La Botella) in Old San Juan…sort of tropical Greenwich Village. Your letter of Feb. 22 was most welcome...and I'm gratified to know that my 'literary criticism' of your work had something to offer...I don't feel very positive about my analytical abilities or literary judgments...but if it proved to be something of value, I'm glad. I'm very glad to hear about your tentative plans of teaching or agency business work...I have the feeling that this is more 'up your alley' than your present line of work...and if the pay were at least equal, you would find it much more gratifying. Here's hoping you pursue one of these avenues...and successfully...I'm working as an advertising sales rep with a small weekly newspaper (*The Island Times*) and my job consists mainly of visiting ad agencies and large direct advertisers...and with a soft-sell approach try to have them keep us in mind when they schedule ad campaigns. I'm not a salesman-sign-on-the-dotted-line-type...but this type of selling is rather pleasant. And the situation here is a real dream compared to the super-efficient Prudential Insurance Company...just a small staff of part-writers...and the editor is Luis Muñoz Lee, son of the Governor, who is a quiet, highly intelligent guy...who has been most kind to me...and has sort of invited me into his little social group which consists—not of politicians and status seeking executives—but of a really interesting concoction of local artists, dancers and characters. Quite often he comes to the nightclub downstairs...and when we're there together I can't even buy myself a drink..."this one is on *The Island Times*" is something he must have said dozens of times in the past few weeks. In addition to the sales rep job, I suggested that the paper needed a business column, sort of a catch-all for all the little news items about the many businesses here...so Luis said OK and I've done 2 already...it's now a regular thing each week and he's paying me $10 extra per week...which comes in handy and is a bargain because the column takes me only about 1 ½ hours to knock out once a week. In addition, there's a chance I might do a 15-minute weekly broadcast of business news on a local English language radio station. Someone heard about my column and said they if they could get a sponsor they'd let me broadcast it...another $20-25 a week if this comes through. I'll get a yes or no on this in about 10 days...the radio station is moving to new quarters and wants to start this new project when they're settled. So, considering that I arrived only about 5 weeks ago, things are moving along rather nicely. I've met lots of people...and already feel as though I'm a native of the place. The one thing I haven't done is really travel around the island...out in the hills...which are supposed to be beautiful. But a few weekends from now, I'll start exploring....just two weeks ago I met Olga, a pretty senorita...she's a charming girl...only 20 years old...and spent the last 5 years in New York... so she knows both languages perfectly...I haven't formulated any long range goals for myself: not domestically or spiritually, or professionally...and I'm not particularly worried about it...I feel that these things will evolve naturally someday and that now I should just be content to drift in any direction which pleases the whim of the moment...Must go now...us working Puerto Ricans can only enjoy the fabulous beach environs on weekends...and I have a date with the gal in about an hour...must shave, shower, etc. My very best wishes...write when you can. I'll send you a sample of the newspaper soon... plus a few photos if I ever get around to taking any. Your son, *Kal*

March 16, 1961: Letter to Bob Bletter in New York. Hi: Haven't heard from ya.. I feel sort of like a settled resident already; gee. I now have 1 room right above a pretty swinging nightclub restaurant right in Old San Juan...and only 2 blocks from my office...The owner of the club is a great guy and rent is only $15 per week, which includes maid service linen and towels. I share the top floor with a few other roomers: the club's piano player (Hal Hester) who is sort of on the skids now after being part of a rather successful musical trio in New York which broke up last year...he played Bon Soir and other good spots...also wrote a pop song called *"The Sand and the Sea"* which Nat Cole made into a hit a few years ago...pretty good guy...and the other room is now occupied by 2 African negroes billed as Prince Onago and Princess Muana (a drums and dance duo) who were out of work and I got them room and board here in return for 1 act per nite downstairs. As their agent for this booking I get 10% of their salary, which is actually 10% of their room and board which is actually nothing. Gee, there are so many things to tell ya...I still visit ad agencies and companies, telling them how the *Island Times* is... and I just put out a little brochure (enclosed) which saves me lots of repetition and seems to be making a favorable impression when I visit media people at agencies because their mouths water when they see statistics and stuff. Just like Jack Webb, they want "only the facts, ma'am." Another thing is a weekly column I've been doing the past 3 weeks which takes only about 1 afternoon a week to write and for which I get $10 extra pay...and is starting to get pretty popular because more things get sent in to me each week...and as a good ad salesmans should, I send clippings to all people mentioned in the column, if they seem like good ad prospects. No startling results have happened yet…like full-page ads…but I've already gotten some nice "thank you" notes from people I've sent clippings to…now I'm awaiting insertion orders for ads. You know, "don't clap; throw money." I'm slowly getting little writing assignments here because I hang around the office late sometimes when Luis is working in the editorial section…had a little story last week about Johnny Mathis getting angry and walking off stage, which was sort of fun…and just finished a rather long feature about a new movie company—the first in Puerto Rico—just being formed. This story will appear in two weeks. I'll send it to you because the whole idea is rather interesting and unique… and I know most of the guys in the group, who hang around "La Botella' at night and also in the place next door which is a cheap restaurant called "Sam's" which serves big hamburgers for only 30 cents and is becoming my regular eatery. I'm not hitting the beach as often as I thought…but I do go at least once a week and it's really fine lolling around..sometimes I combine the beach with a car-washing spree…I take along a bucket of clear water…get in my suit and drive right up to the sand, underneath a shadetree…alternating my waxing with dips in the surf. aaaaah….a mechayah! I've gotten into a rather steady dating arrangement with a pretty gal named Olga who spent several years in the states…she's really a little doll…we've been seeing each other regularly and just letting things develop casually…She's just a 20… the *Island Times* is sort of like putting out the old school paper…and a little of the *Rock of the Marne* thrown in…Thursday nights is publication nite and we all stay up rather late and gab away …sometimes till 3 or 4 in the a.m… not all spent in the office. At about 8 pm all stories are downstairs with the linotypers … and we usually go to La Botella (Luis, me, Charlie Connelly, who is one of the writers and also studying judo and is quite a guy, and other assorted characters who wander into the office) and have drinks til about 11 or 12…return to the office and then finish putting out the paper. So I've sort of found a little home here…I'm just too damn adaptable I guess …because I don't feel as though I've lived anywhere else, unless I really sit and think about it…sort of takes a little of the charm from this place and I hardly know it…but I plan to go exploring the island a bit in future weeks (haven't been more than 30 miles from San Juan yet). This Sunday, I'm going to Aguadilla, which is about 3 hours from here to the west…and there's a beautiful beach called Guajataca…and Monday and Tuesday will be spent selling ads in the area to store owners who sell to members of Ramey Air Force Base which is in that area, and which receives our paper. And in several weeks I may hop over to St. Thomas and sign up some advertisers over there whose contracts are running out. Well, must go now…it's Thursday nite and I've got to OK some ad proofs. Be good and write or talk when you can. By the way, when are ya comin' down? (hi Rosemary) kal

March 18, 1961. Letter from my father, in Los Angeles, to me, in San Juan, Puerto Rico. Dear Kal: I have your letter of March 5th. Well, congratulations on your entering into a series of new experiences: a tropical land, a room over a Greenwich Village type nightclub, a job on a newspaper with the son of the governor as editor, weekends at the beach. I shall look forward to receiving a copy of *The Island Times.* You have made some fine adjustments in the short period you are on the island. You should feel right proud of yourself. And, with a creative approach to the many phases of life in your new environment, I am confident that you will expand and make some worthwhile contributions to your job, the community, and to your personal self. Things with me about the same. I just got off a letter to Rod Serling asking that he read my story, the one you read, with a possible collaboration, if he likes the basic premise. He is committed to make 4 pictures for MGM. I hope I get a favorable reply from him. I am working on a 5 minute TV series with a friend of mine who works in my office. He was in show business at one time, now wants to get out and do things. The format should be completed this week, then I send it to the Writers Guild for registration. Either one of these projects would open the door for me (and my friend), and allow us to work up many ideas I have stored away in envelopes: format, short synopses, outlines for series, etc. By the way, Kal, if there is anything you want from the States, printed matter, material things from the stores, pertinent information relative to your work, etc. etc. just say the word. Keep well and the best to you in all the ways of life. Sincerely, your dad, Harold.

A Fond Memory of Peter Brook

A few weeks after I moved to one of the four rooms above La Botella bar-restaurant, the owner, Chuck New, approached me and said he needed a big favor. "Kal, there's a film director coming here from England with his family. They're going to need a place to stay while they shoot the movie. Would it be terribly inconvenient for you to find some other place to live? I wouldn't ask, but he's offering me a nice price for renting out the whole upstairs and I can use the money." All I had was a suitcase with my clothing, so I said "sure." A few days later, I found a small apartment nearby. Late one afternoon, not long afterward, I passed by La Botella, and Chuck stopped me. He pointed to a man seated at a table inside. "Come," he said. He guided me over to the man, then in his mid-thirties, and said "Mister Brook, this is Kal Wagenheim. He's one of the fellows who gave up his room, so you could stay here with your family. The man he introduced me to was Peter Brook, an Englishman, who was about to film "*Lord of The Flies*" on the nearby island of Vieques, which later became a classic. *(Mr. Brook was in the early stages of a fabulous career as a producer and director of films and plays. In 2008, at age 83, he resigned as director of the Paris-based Bouffes du Nord theatre.)* Mr. Brook smiled, shook my hand, and said "Let me take you to lunch!" We walked next door to Sam's Patio, a casual neighborhood place, and enjoyed hamburgers and drinks, while Mr. Brook politely asked me about my life and plans for Puerto Rico. I will never forget his gracious gesture. A true gentleman!

May 13, 1961. From my father (age 58) at 127 S. Serrano Ave, Los Angeles 4, Calif. Tel: Dunkirk 3-5047. Dear Kal: Are you still living over the "night club"? Has the radio job gone through? What with the young lady you dated when you wrote me last? I'm a bundle of questions. As for myself, I am quite well, considering the way the years are rolling on. I continue with my job at the Assessor's (Land) Office. The pay is insignificant (I started five years ago), the job rather dull and routine, but I hold on; at the same time, plumbing opportunities for betterment. I inquire into substitute teaching on my vacation this summer. If it proves profitable, I will continue, take courses, and try for a permanent teaching job. The literary agency business, which is of greatest interest, such thoughts will have to be abandoned. Cost of licenses, rent for office, incidentals makes such a project prohibitive. Kal, I wish you the best in everything: your personal life, the job, your meetings in the social sphere, and a peace of mind derived from your particular way of life. As I stated in a previous letter, if there is anything you want from the States (some research information, something from the stores, a book of sort) let me know. I live in a metropolitan area, and everything is quite accessible. Regards from my cousin Charlie, and his wife, Lillian. I haven't heard from Neil, but my sister, Frieda, tells me he is doing well at Rutgers College: Teaching, and taking work toward a higher degree. I get nostalgic when I hear about Rutgers. I spent two summers there, working toward my B.S. Yes, Kal, I got around in my younger days: NYU, NJ Teachers College, Rutgers, even a repertory theatre group in NY for several seasons. Some day we'll go over all of this. Write when you can. Sincerely, your dad, Harold....

June 1, 1961. Letter from me to Bob Bletter. Hope this catches you in time, because I wanted to wish you folks a grand "bon voyage" and this letter will look sort of silly if you read it after returning from your tour. Also want to thank you for rounding up all that info about my art cinema project which is sort of stumbling along slowly, but in a forward direction. Thus far, I have received a letter from one major distributor, who could provide me with at least 25% of my good films...and he said he'd let me have them at any minimum rental I feel I can afford...he's being so generous because I told him that the market is limited here, but that there's no competition...and also said that even if I couldn't pay much for each film perhaps it would be worth his while over a year's time, should we do lots of business with each other. Now I'm waiting to hear from 2 or 3 other major distributors of foreign films and if their anwers are favorable I'll be able to talk business with the big movie magnate around here—a Mr. Cobian—and see if he'll rent me the theatre he once promised me. Then there's the problem of getting the necessary capital—about $3,000—to start this thing rolling...but I have a few people interested already and am positive one of them will come in with me if I could assure him that we could get the really top films...so the really important thing is distribution...nothing else can progress without being sure of the product. On another note: I'm at a rather low ebb financially here because the *Island Times* has been hit by a bad advertising slump...very little revenue coming in...there's a slight depression here and the ad dollars are mostly going into *El Mundo*—the big Spanish paper. What's left over usually goes to the *San Juan Star*, which has gained much prestige with its recent winning of the Pulitzer Prize... I've been put on a 3-day basis...taking a 40% pay cut...however I still write the business column...plus have a 15-minute unsponsored as yet radio show which pays me a few bucks...so all in all I'm making a hefty $65-$70 a week...far cry from the stateside salaries...but things will pick up either here at the Times or I'll just move over somewhere else. Opportunities spring up quite unexpectedly, but often enough, down here. When things were rosier here I had turned down job offers—both at $100 a week—which I'd snap up....but as I said, hope! Of course, this art cinema thing can change drastically and provide me with a tidy little living if all goes well...and another possible source of income which may come my way in several months is a movie script that I just wrote...the chief director of a new film company here OK'd a general idea I had about a movie and last nite I handed him a 30-page shooting outline. Of course I have no assurance that they will actually buy this thing but the guy seemed exceptionally interested in the idea and kept begging me for the script...so finally I knocked it out. If it is approved, they have an opening to start filming it in August...they've already started work on a full-length feature this month which will keep them busy until August... but haven't scheduled any films for after that. There is quite a chance for good success on the film...not because yours truly is handling the writing... but because the director, a Puerto Rican named Amilcar Tirado Santiago (nickname Mickey) has already come away with a few European film festival prizes for his documentary stuff. I'll get his opinion on Monday—this is Thursday—and then will either tear the thing up or else start polishing it up into a finished shooting script. So that's it for now...don't forget to send me postcards and pink toilet paper from Chinese restaurants in Germany...and all other kinds of interesting trinkets...and somehow, despite the fact that I *know* I paid you, Rosemary has brainwashed me so well that I feel that for the rest of my life I will have the sneaky suspicion that I owe you $50 dollars for *something*. So be patient, I'll pay you when I can....By the way, another side feature of this art cinema business is that I'll probably be able to take tax-deductible flights to New York a few times a year on the pretext of seeking out likely Wagenheim shows of the week...so I've got my fingers doubly crossed for this project....can't think of another thing so I'll shut up. You're best friend ever....*Kal*

MARRIED AGAIN

Photo of my wife Olga and me in Puerto Rico shortly before our marriage in 1961, taken by our good friend Marvin Schwartz.

June 10, 1961. Olga Jimenez and I married in a civil ceremony in San Juan. Olga, who would be 20 in September, and I met earlier in the year at the Palm Beach Coffee Shop in Old San Juan, where she was working part-time while attending school. She was born September 24, 1961 in Barrio Puertos, Camuy, a rural area in northwestern Puerto Rico. Her father, Santos Jimenez-Hernandez, is a farmer. Her mother, Victoria Mendez-Ramos, died when she was about 14 years old. Olga attended public school in Puerto Rico. She had six siblings on her mother's side, plus four half brothers and sisters from her stepmother. In May 1957, before age 16 she went to live with an aunt at 122nd St. in Manhattan. She studied English during the summer of 1957, in preparation for entering the 10th trade at Washington Irving H.S. then an all girl's school. Olga spent 2 ½ years in Manhattan. She returned to Puerto Rico in December 1959, missing just one semester to complete H.S. She went to live with her cousin Teresa Jimenez in the Miramar section of San Juan and shortly thereafter went to share an apt. with her cousin Nelsa Jimenez, who also found her a job at the New York Dept. Store. She stayed there for a few months before taking a job as a waitress at a cafeteria in Old San Juan (the Palm Beach Coffee Shop), in time to pay for the apartment, being vacated by Nelsa who was getting married. In August 1960 she enrolled at Central High School in Santurce, in order to complete the courses missing and obtain a high school diploma. I was living and working in Old San Juan while Olga was working at the Palm Beach Coffee Shop It was late 1960 or early 1961 when we met, and began dating..Prior to our marriage, Olga thought it would be correct to have me meet her family out there, and to obtain permission for the marriage from her father, Don Santos Jimenez. I agreed, but there was one minor problem. Don Santos, a wonderful man, knew no English, and my Spanish was quite limited. We came up with a solution that years later, in retrospect, made us chuckle. Sergio Burzio was a good friend in San Juan, originally from Trieste. He spoke Spanish, English and several other languages. So we drove out to the countryside with Sergio. Olga introduced me to Don Santos, and—with Sergio serving as interpreter—I asked Don Santos for permission to wed his daughter. He agreed, which was the beginning of a long friendship with her Dad, a truly admirable person. *(I later learned that when we first arrived at the farm Olga's younger sisters and brothers were amazed by... my big gringo feet--size 11-plus...since everyone they knew had size 8 or less!)* After the wedding, Sergio arranged for us to enjoy a free, brief honeymoon at Villa

Firenze, a small guest house in the Miramar section of San Juan run by his mother, Madame Burzio.

The San Juan Diary

My job with the *Island Times* was enjoyable, but my salary of $75 per week began to shrink as the paper's income diminished, since advertising was leaving and going to the emerging *San Juan Star* daily newspaper. Poor Luis Muñoz Lee, the owner of the *Island Times,* was such a decent fellow; he could no longer afford to pay my full salary and asked me to come in three days a week, rather than five, cutting my weekly paycheck to $45. One day, fate happily intervened. Connie Underhill, a friend and coworker, told me that Tony Beacon, publisher of *The San Juan Diary* weekly, needed a production assistant. I learned later that Tony's real name was Herbert Smolen, and he was originally from New Jersey! During pre-Castro Cuba, he published a weekly gossip sheet for tourists in Havana. He fled to San Juan when Fidel rose to power, and soon became known as The Walter Winchell of the Caribbean, with his weekly magazine, covering showbiz in the hotel nightclubs, and gossip about the local VIPs who frequented the hotels along with the tourists.

Tony was constantly trying to attend parties all over San Juan, to gather gossip for his publication. My old pal Chuck Corbett told me a funny anecdote. One night Tony heard about a party at a beachside home in the Isla Verde sector of San Juan. Tony called the house, and according to Chuck a drunk blonde gal picked up the phone and said "Hello? Who is this?"

"I'm Tony Beacon."

"Who?"

"Tony Beacon! I'm the Walter Winchell of the Caribbean!"

"Hey everybody! Walter Winchell is calling!"

"No! I'm Tony Beacon!"

"Gee, put Walter back on!"

I heard that Tony was earning about $50,000 a year, which was a fortune in those days. Tony was a gruff guy, who liked to bark out orders, but he was polite to me. He always sat ringside in the fancy nightclubs, but didn't drink alcohol. He insisted on fresh orange juice, and if there was none available he raised hell. When I began working for Tony, he occupied an apartment in the Darlington building, in the Miramar section of San Juan, facing Fernandez Juncos Avenue, directly across the street from the Castle Club, a well-known bar/restaurant, where US Naval Officers, tourists and wealthy locals found hookers. At first, Tony did all of the writing for the *Diary,* which was published weekly. I spent my time taking the material for typesetting to the printing plant in Puerto Nuevo, about 20 minutes away, and would also handle the proofreading. When the *Diary* was published, Tony would personally drive to the major hotels and restaurants in San Juan and plop stacks of free copies on the counters of each. Tony gradually entrusted me to write brief items. Also, on occasion there were so many nightclub openings that Tony sent me out to cover the shows, and write reviews, hopefully favorable. My wife Olga often joined me as we were given VIP treatment in nightclubs. Later, Tony moved from the Darlington to the wonderful Hotel El Convento in Old San Juan, where—in exchange for an ad in his magazine—he was given a two-room suite, one for sleeping, and the other where he set up an office with two desks, one for him and one for me. Now, rather than drive to Miramar, I could walk from my home in Old San Juan down to the hotel. If I got there a bit early, I could sit in the interior open-air patio of the hotel and enjoy a nice breakfast. My starting salary with Tony was (if memory serves) $125 a week, a big raise from my work at *The Island Times*. By the time I left, about two years later, I was earning $200 weekly. Tony was an eccentric character. He owned a fancy silver gray Karman Ghia automobile (nothing but the best!). He drove the car dealer crazy, because almost every week he called to complain about the color of his seat covers, and often they would change the fabric to please him. Tony always dressed well, but was awkward with women. After we got to know each other well, Tony would open up. One morning he said, "Kal, I don't know. I take out these showgirls all the time. I buy them a great dinner, I even give them nice little pieces of jewelry. But always, around 9 pm they say they had a headache!" I gave a light-hearted response: "Tony, have you ever thought about carrying aspirin with you?" He just shook his head. Tony could also be quite generous, but in strange ways. As Thanksgiving approached one day, Tony came with me to the printing plant where they produced his *San Juan Diary*. Across the highway from the plant was a supermarket. "Come with me," Tony said. We entered the store, and Tony motioned for me to grab a cart and follow him. We walked along the aisles and Tony kept throwing big turkeys into the cart. Then, as Tony led the way, I followed him, pushing the cart full of turkeys, dodging traffic as we returned to the printing plant. We entered the office, and Tony told the manager to call in all the guys from the plant. About eight of them entered. And Tony, in his gruff way picked up a big turkey and gave one to each of the guys. They were stunned. They mumbled thanks. But I heard one guy comment to a fellow worker, "What the hell am I gonna do with this? It don't fit into my tiny oven!"

Around 1961-62: *Undated letter from Hal Burbage, my dear funny pal and one-time co-worker, who sat at the desk next to me at Prudential. Excerpts from 1 ½ page typed letter.* Let me start this note off with a word of congratulations and good wishes. The *Diary* looks like a grand fun publication...and that casual-type writing is also the most fun. Good luck, lad—you'll do well I'm sure. The prime purpose for this epistle is to let you know that Jeb and I are taking your advice and going to spend a two-week vacation in St. Thomas, and will probably stop for a couple of days in San Juan on our way back...we will give you a call sometimes during our short stay and have a long phone chat. I have your office number off the masthead and will use that. If you have a home phone, send it to me—the number, that is, not the phone—so I can try to reach you there. Also, if you have the time, I'd appreciate your suggesting a couple of lively spots for us to visit during our stay. We both realize that August-September is not the ideal time to go "down yonder," but winter vacations are out of the question for Jeb, and I need to get away *now*. I've never needed a complete vacation as much as I do now, and although Mother will faint and fall in it when she hears I'm not coming home, that can't be helped. And we're flying, of course. I don't know why I said *of course*—there's nothing in this world I'd less rather do. Already I'm scared sick and by the time we hit San Juan I'll be stiff as a board and shaking like a leaf. But even Judy Garland is flying now, and I've got to learn, too. So we're taking a Jet (even that word scares me) out of Idlewild on Saturday morning, Aug. 26 at 2:30 am and will arrive in San Juan at 5:30, then leave for St. Thomas at 7:30. We're taking the night flight because I don't want to see all that earth below us. Anyway, we leave San Juan in the middle of the day, Sept. 10, and it's the during the 2-3 days preceding that that we plan to be in your city and it's then that I will try to call you. Things at the office are not different than they were in John Dryden's time—nothing exciting ever happens here. We've had a few more losses in personnel, however. Alan Sapiro left about a month ago and joined Atlas Metals in New York...George Brown retired early—his health wasn't at all good...Sandy Romaine left two weeks ago to drop her child...Dwight Ragle leaves this vale of tears on Friday to join Shearing (Sheeering? Shering?) Pharmaceutical Co.... Carol

Petrozulli and Glady Maude are about the only ones around here who either have twin beds or believe in birth control—all the others are gone. Julie has been every shade of blonde and is now sort of an "ash-brownette," I think she calls it. John Cawley and family returned Sunday from 2 weeks in another town—New Orleans—they went by air, not freedom-bus. The boys in the art department are enjoying the change of seasons—their windows look into the women's dressing room of Kresge's, and they're delighted that women are now trying on bathing suits. I just came by there, and they're clustered around the windows with field glasses. Julie just drifted by, sat and smoked one of my cigarettes, and complained how bitterly she hates everything. I told her I was writing you, and she took your address. Sez she hasn't got anything to do. Everything's fine but quiet with me. I didn't take a house at the beach this summer, and have visited only once, so I have no tan. As a matter of fact, I had a virus in my liver last week, and am now not only white, but really more ecru or saffron colored. And I've been nowhere at all all summer—no theatre, no trips—so there is no news of me. I've heaps of work to do so I'll start that and stop this. Don't worry about trying to to think of kicky places for us to be attend, but *do* be sure to send me your home phone number and let me know whether you work Saturdays, because I do want to talk and hear all about your current, exciting life. Sorry you moved from the hoe house, 'cause I might have run Into you there. By the way…are there *any* blondes in that part of the world? Hal *(Note:Hal never came to visit. I lost touch with him while living in Puerto Rico. Many years later, back in New Jersey, I somehow found his phone number and called. A man answered and tearfully told me that Hal had died. Much later, I went on* www.google.com *and saw a paid notice online from The NY Times: Memorials: Burbage, Hal. Published June 4, 1999. "Burbage-Hal. 6-14-84. Hard to imagine you at 70, though I'm sure you'd have done it very well. Miss you still. Always will. Stu." A similar paid notice appeared in the NY Times on June 14, 2001. "Burbage, Harold P. Jr. June 14, 1984. Oh for the touch of a vanished hand and the sound of a voice that is still. Stu." I miss him, too.)*

The Classics Revisited

In 1961, I decided to have some fun and perhaps earn a few dollars by self-publishing a little paperback book, *"The Classics Revisited,"* which showed more than 60 engravings of historic moments in history and literature, beneath which were hopefully funny captions. Example: on the cover we see a scene from Homer's "The Iliad" with him soaring through the air in the grip of a huge bird, and looking very unhappy. The caption: "This is absolutely the last time I take the Economy Flight." Several of my selections had first appeared in *Rogue Magazine*, a wannabe competitor to *Playboy Magazine*. I found most of the illustrations for the book a few years earlier in the files of the Newark Library. Accompanied by my dear wacky childhood pal Dave Straus, I looked through the files, pulled out an illustration and came up with a screwy caption. If Dave giggled or guffawed, it was a winner; I borrowed the illustration and had a photo copy made for future use. "*The Classics Revisited*" was printed at a small plant, Litografia Guilliani, in Santurce, Puerto Rico. In the prologue, I dedicate the book "to my close friend Johann Gutenberg (1397-1468), who helped make all this possible." The inside front cover shows a photo of me, in my early 20s, being sketched by a woman artist in New York's Greenwich Village. Below it is a short section titled: "Notes About the Author" which reads as follows: "Kal Wagenheim, 26, moved from the States to make his home in Puerto Rico after a tragic injury cut short his fast-moving newspaper career. 'My pants got stuck in the chains of my bike…I fell and broke a leg… and some other lucky stiff took over my delivery route.' Like other members of the school of hard-boiled Social Realism, Wagenheim has toiled as an ordinary laborer. 'I sweated and strained in a factory for exactly 14 minutes when, all of a sudden, I had an insight. A guy must be nuts to break his back for that kind of money.' Next, he slaved to perfect his literary style, writing day in, day out. 'I filled out every magazine coupon I could find. Soon I belonged to the RCA Victor, Capitol and Columbia Record Clubs, Book-of-the-Month Club (3 times), The Rosicrucians, The Charles Atlas School, Famous Artists School and the School For Young Hotel Executives.' This book is an important first for Wagenheim. 'Yes, it's the very first I've ever read. Personally, give me TV any day.' Wagenheim plans to give up writing for a year and devote his time to study. He observes, with a wisdom far beyond his years, 'You can never be too smart. I won't be happy till I've solved the riddle of long division.'" At the book's conclusion, on the inside back cover, I wrote: "DEAR READER…If for some uncanny reason you liked this book, perhaps you have friends with the same demented sense of humor. Or, you might have enemies you'd like to harass! Whatever the case, "Classics Revisited" makes an ideal gift. And the special paper stock is super for wrapping sandwiches, too. If you can't find an extra copy (only 6 were printed), write to the address below, enclosing $1.50 (check or money order) for each copy desired: Noble-Savage Productions, 57 San Jose St., Suite 7A, San Juan, Puerto Rico." Actually I printed 100 or so copies, and left a few dozen on consignment at different shops in the area. I sold a few, but not many! In fact, I still keep a couple of dozen copies in my garages, and inflict them on friends.

.**April 9, 1962.** A small item on page 27 of *Box Office*, a showbusiness newspaper, had the headline: "UJA Drive Cochairmen Appointed by Mirisch:" The article began: "HOLLYWOOD—Walter M. Mirisch, chairman of the entertainment industry section of the United Jewish Welfare Fund campaign, announced the appointment of these co-chairmen:" *The last of the 20 names listed was "Abe Heller, Warner Bros. and WB-TV." (My grandfather)*

The House in Old San Juan

Our son David would be born on May 30, 1962. Before that, it became clear that Olga and I would need larger living quarters. I don't recall how, but somehow we found a lovely old corner house in Old San Juan, at 309 Calle Sebastian, just one block in from the boulevard that encircles the old city. From our windows, and particularly from the roof of the two-storey building, there were spectacular views of the Atlantic Ocean, and directly below it the notorious La Perla seaside slum. The ocean breeze was so steady that we had no need for air conditioning or even an electric fan. In fact, some nights we actually closed the windows facing the sea. A copy of the mortgage shows that we bought the house on May 3, 1962 from Dona Crecencia Santiago Viuda de Nieves for $20,000. We paid up front $4,500 (obtained with a loan), with a mortgage of $13,000, and another $2,500 to be paid to the owner within two years, guaranteed by a second mortgage. We were barely able to cover costs. The two-storey house had tenants! We occupied the top floor, which included a spacious corner kitchen, living room, bathroom and two (or three) small bedrooms. Downstairs was divided into four small rooms, occupied by four gentlemen: one, "Caguitas" was a longshoreman, another, Goyo, did not live there, but had what looked like a barbershop chair, and he installed teeth; another, was rented by a dwarf-like little fellow, Zapata, who used it as a base for a carwash on the street outside, and the corner room was occupied by a kind older gentleman (Don Juan?) who, like "Caguitas" at the other end, slept there. Each of them paid $15 per month, for a grand total of $60 p er month.

My mortage at the time was $150 per month. I met with my four tenants and explained that since they occupied the lower half of the house, perhaps they could each pay me $20 per month, for a total of $80. Three of the men agreed, but "Caguitas" tersely replied that he was not willing to pay more, and he left. For the next few years I would use his room as my downstairs office. We did not move in immediately. Our friend (and handyman) Sergio Burzio, took charge of making some needed improvements in the ancient building, and we moved in some time later in 1962. Around that time we brought Olga's young sister Norma, age seven, to live with us. She had come down with diabetes and good medical care was not available out in the rural area where she lived. Norma was lovely little girl, and later was like an older sister to our two children, David and Maria who would be born soon afterwards.

1961-68: Olga recalls: "The years our family spent in Old San Juan were the most enriching years of our lives. During those years Puerto Rico was very prosperous economically and the government was very supportive of the arts and culture. As a result, artists, writers, film producers and all creative sorts were concentrated in Old San Juan and employed by the Division de Educacion de la Comunidad, an agency created by the Muñoz Marin Administration to mass produce pamphlets, posters and films as a way to reach out to the rural population of Puerto Rico. Many of those artists and writers met daily at Bar Seda or at the nearby Patio de Sam to have a drink after work, to catch up with friends, to discuss world issues, books, art and their own works. Kal and I were often part of those discussions with writers Pedro Juan Soto, René Marques, Emilio Diaz Valcarcel, artists Antonio Maldonado, Rafael Tufino, (occasionally Augusto Marin and Lorenzo Homar joined as well); and filmmaker Amilcar Tirado. From time to time an equally impressive group of talented and urbane norteamericanos such as Andre Dalrymple, Charles "Chuck" Corbett, jazz musician Dale Wales, radio personalities Sally Jessy Rafael, Vic Miles (later of U.S. fame), the sculptor Bonnie Reissman and actress Liz Kennedy dropped in. On occasion journalists Joel Magruder, Robert Friedman, Bob McCoy and photographer Marvin Schwartz joined the group or sent visiting guests from the U.S.

Ocho Puertas

Among the many attractions of Old San Juan was Ocho Puertas, an elegant nightclub at the corner of Calle Fortaleza, the street which leads to the governor's mansion. It was called Ocho Puertas because its walls were decorated with eight doors, four on each side, one of which was the entrance. The owners were a male couple, Bern Zale of Brooklyn, and Tor Boberg of Sweden. It was like an intimate, dimly lit, classy Manhattan nightclub, with a small bar, and a main room with a tiny stage, piano, and comfy chairs. I believe that Ocho Puertas lasted from about 1960 to 1980. A long list of star performers, both from Puerto Rico and beyond performed there. These included Gilberto Monroig (1930-1996), one of the island's greatest singers, and the marvelous singer-comic Raul González. I will always remember his hilarious version of *"On the road to Mandalay"*, with lyrics changed to *"El tapón de Bayamón"*, a reference to the enormous traffic jams (*tapones* in Spanish) on the highway between San Juan and Bayamón. I am told that it was also a popular hang-out for visitors such as Marlene Dietrich, Burt Bacharach and Liza Minelli. I do recall seeing Sylvia Syms at the club. *Note: In 2003 a 90-minute documentary film about Ocho Puertas was released, directed by Paloma and Gabriel Suau, as part of the Banco Popular series on the musical legacy of Puerto Rico. It describes the club as a popular place "where the future musical talents of Puerto Rico were first showcased, and given a chance to succeed." The film was made available in DVD, VHS and CD formats. I was unable to find it on Amazon.com, but note that it is available at the Library of the Center for Puerto Rican Studies, part of CUNY in New York.*

May 8, 1962: This was Mother's Day, and about a week before the birth of our son David. Among our friends and neighbors in Old San Juan were several gay men. The fact that Olga would soon give birth was big news. There were a few other heterosexual couples in our circle, but none with young children. Several of our gay pals organized a Mother's Day Party to honor Olga at a nearby apartment (I think it was Chuck New's, owner of La Botella Bar). It was my task to deliver her there, stay away, and pick her up at the conclusion.

July 1962: Almost every evening after dinner I continued to slave away, with an an English-Spanish dictionary close at hand, translating a page or so of *"La Charca"*, the classic Puerto Rican novel, and I would then show the English version to Olga, who helped polish the translation. I loved doing this. So much so that on the inside back cover of the original Spanish paperback, there is a handwritten note in ink, saying *"Such delicious, torturous hours spent over this this tome! July 1962."*

Early 1960s. While working for Tony Beacon at the *San Juan Diary* (I think) I met with visiting famous author Philip Wylie & his wife, who were staying at a hotel. Can't recall how, but some years earlier I must have bought his book *"An Essay On Morals"* (published in 1947) at a used bookstore or The GoodWill in Newark NJ. After we had a nice chat, I asked Mr. Wylie to sign the book and he wrote something which I treasure: *"For Kal Wagenheim, with the hope and damn near certainty that he, too, will come to know all the rug-chewing vacuity (and the inner rewards) of our profession, because he is honest, full of beans, and (the essential thing) loving. Salud, Philip Wylie."*

I met another famous writer around that time, but only briefly, and it was rather comical. Once a month, Tony Beacon sent me flying from San Juan to the Virgin Islands, where the *San Juan Diary* had several advertisers. It was my job to collect the payments for the ads, and return the same day (it was a short flight). Once. I got on the small plane, took an aisle seat, and looked at the passenger next to me by the window. It was none other than Herman Wouk, the author of "*The Caine Mutiny*" (later made into a film starring Humphrey Bogart)! I believe he was doing research for another novel, *"Don't Stop The Carnival,"* published around 1965, which was set in a small Caribbean Island. I knew who he was. I smiled shyly, and nodded. He nodded back. We didn't say a word to each other. I guess I hadn't had much sleep the day before, because after a few minutes I dozed off, and my head leaned to the right, and I was, asleep on Herman Wouk's shoulder! He was so kind; didn't push me off. When the plane landed, I was jarred awake, looked at him, and shrugged. He grinned and shrugged back! (*As I write this, in Nov. 2008, I see that Mr. Wouk, God bless him, born in 1915, lives in Palm Springs, California)* .

In the 1960s, when Olga & I lived in Old San Juan, we met two wonderful musicians,Hal Hester & Danny Apolinar, who a few years earlier had collaborated on a big hit Broadway musical, *"Your Own Thing."* Hal also wrote the music for *"The Sand & The Sea,"* a big hit tune by Nat King Cole. Danny later moved back to New York, where he was popular at Danny's Skylight Room Cabaret, on W. 46th St. But what I most remember about Danny is when he would sit at the piano on a quiet night in Old San Juan and gently sing a tune originally written back in the 1920s, but which seems so timely today, when many folks are going through hard times. See the lyrics below. The last two lines remain engraved in my memory

In the movie plays of now-a-days,
A romance always must begin in June,
Tales in magazines have all their scenes
Of love laid in a garden 'neath the moon.
But I don't miss, that kind of bliss
What I want is this,
Chorus:
A cup of coffee, a sandwich and you,
A cozy corner, a table for two,
A chance to whisper and cuddle and coo
With lots of huggin' and kissin' in view.
I don't need music, lobster or wine,
Whenever your eyes look into mine.
The things I long for are simple and few;
A cup of coffee, a sandwich and you!

A number of talented American expats were living in Old San Juan at the time. Among them were Liz Sheridan, then a dancer, and later, when she moved back to the USA acted in a number of plays and musicals, and gained fame as the mother of Seinfeld on the hit TV series. While living in New York as a young dancer, she lived with James Dean, and later wrote a book about their short romance. Her long-time companion (and later husband) was William T. "Dale" Wales, a gifted jazz trumpeter (1929-2003). Their good pal and neighbor was Max Frye, a brilliant artist, and quite eccentric and funny.

November 1962: *Letter from me at our new house on 309 San Sebastian, Old San Juan, to John Cawley, at Prudential, Newark NJ.* Dear John: Like my new typewriter? It works in both black and red...the typeface is called "senatorial" according to the salesman and just the authoritative sound of it swept me off my feet and got me groping for my wallet. I am still with Mr. Beacon (the Walter Winchell of the Caribbean) and find the work as breezy as ever. I have become a bit jaded as to receptions and cocktail parties which I never attend anymore. But there are still the "must see" nightclub shows for our weekly entertainment reviews. These, in the main, are mediocre, but every so often we get a good show which makes it all worthwhile. This coming Winter Season, for example, shows promise. Sammy Davis, Jr., Harry Belafonte, Sylvia Syms, Shelly Berman, Miriam Makeba and others of equal drawing power are expected for two-week engagements. Let me interrupt to say I'm delighted over Bob Hart's and Len McCue's promotions. Please relay my congrats. Hart, in particular, with his quiet, efficient manner, seems like real executive material. Back to Beacon. Aside from reviewing the shows one or two evenings a week, I put in a normal 40-hour stint...but this is highly unsupervised since Mr. Beacon is always somewhere in search of "chisme" ("gossip" in Spanish)...I usually knock out the required number of inches (we need about 12 typewritten pages double-spaced to fill a normal 24-page issue and I provide about half of that) and spend the rest of the time reading and goofing around. My latest diversion has been a series of letters under a pseudonym to *The San Juan Star*, the English daily paper. I can't use my own name since Beacon hates the *Star* and would fire me for contributing. My letters have been highly critical of U.S. intervention in Cuban affairs and have caused a minor uproar here. My letters and the angry replies (and a few good ones in support) have virtually monopolized the Letters section for the past few weeks. Next target is local TV, which is even more dismal than the U.S. and has as many as four consecutive commercials at station breaks. Oh, if only I had my own paper. I believe I mentioned in the last letter that I'd bought a home by the sea. It's really fine. Actually needs blankets for protection from the sea breezes. Am slowly trying to reconstruct the house, but funds are limited. Perhaps in a year it will be completed, but it's quite livable now. The rental from the downstairs tenants reduces my monthly payments to $94 so I've got quite a bargain. Especially so, since the Institute of Culture claims the house may double in value during the next ten years. They've got some sort of Williamsburg reconstruction program going here and property values are zooming as the houses are improved, one by one. Mine, in particular, is overlooking a seaside slum called "La Perla" (The Pearl) which, they say, is due for clearance and will be made into a lovely public park. I finished the translation of *"La Charca"*, all grinding 267 pages of it, about a month ago. I sent a couple of chapters to Indiana Univesity (which has a translation program) and the entire text is in the hands of the president of Puerto Rico's Senate, who is also a literary essayist and expressed interest in reading it. If he likes it he may be able to smooth the way for its publication. I spoke to him on the phone yesterday and he said he's three-fourth finished and that it is "a magnificent translation". I hope it was the literary man and not the politician talking. With the translation done I felt at loose ends for a week and started rummaging around for something. I came upon a draft of a short entitled *"The Home Office"* which is about a man who lives in his office. I believe you read it. Looking at it now I see its many, many faults and am attempting a new version. Perhaps in a month I'll have something. I'll shoot you a carbon for your opinion which, I begrudgingly admit, I respect. Hate to get cruel, but I can't resist mentioning that the temperature here is in the low 80's and it's been delightfully sunny all week. This is indeed a scenic island. I've yet to see many of the best spots but the new house has tied me up of late. I am planning a few weekend jaunts in the near future to the eastern tip of the island (about 40 miles away) where a new hotel (El Conquistador) has been constructed on a rocky cliff with a magnificent view of the sea and the far-off Virgin Islands. This is close to Luquillo Beach which is the island's most famous watering spot and is often featured in magazine articles and ads. I remember your kidding me in a letter long ago about La Botella Bar when I lived above it. I still go there, but my most frequent haunt is a little place called El Burrito where all sorts of expatriates gather to talk and drink. It's also the favorite spot for the governor's son (my ex-boss at *The Island Times*) who is a wonderful fellow and whose last thought on earth would be to enter politics. He hates being in public so much that he never even goes to the movies. His amour of long-standing is the prima ballerina of the local company (which opened last night) and he restricted himself to seeing the dress rehearsals. There are other interesting ones in the group: (1) an atheist who paints exquisite little saints on driftwood and sells them for $10-$75 each. This fellow's work just came to the attention of America House in N.Y. and they've contracted his next two month's supply. (2) the bartender, a fellow with a crewcut and VanDyke beard who maintains an apartment in Greenwich Village, speaks with a delightful Harvard accent, was married to an Oklahoma heiress and lived La Dolce Vita on the Spanish Riviera and then tried to sue her for alimony. These are the two of the most interesting, and charming, fellows, but there are others who provide flashes of enjoyment. This may sound as though I spend all my time in some joyous state of euphoria. Far from it, but I do much prefer the life here. San Juan is a big town and very noisy and very crowded. But if a fellow's careful he can avoid these things and control his life to a much greater extent than in New York. For example, I'm only 10 minutes from my office; a pleasant non-congested drive along a modern road. Lunch is spent in a quiet restaurant where I can relax and read nearly the entire *NY Times* if I'm not obligated to talk to someone during the meal. At night, sports shirt and slacks gain admission to almost all places except the supper clubs of the major hotels which I don't go to anyway except when I'm reviewing a show. There are several good book shops and there is the library of the University of Puerto Rico which is quite adequate. There is at least one good movie a week, sometimes many more. I saw *"Phaedra"* two nights ago and will see *"Hiroshima Mon Amour"* this weekend. The ballet opened its eight day season last night (there were 2 guest artists from the New York ballet company) and I'll be getting tickets from friends for as many times as I care to go. Then there is the wide, wide world of Spanish culture and I'm nibbling at the edge of it with the delight of a mouse who's stumbled upon a mountain of cheese. If *"La Charca"* proves to be a good translation, I may continue and do the author's last novel before his death. It's entitled *Redentores* (Redeemers) and concerns the U.S. takeover of Puerto Rico after the Spanish-American War. Quite a biting satire, I'm told. Also brewing is a series of short stories by Pedro Juan Soto, a young Puerto Rican author whom I know and who lived in New York for several years under very bitter circumstances. He's had three full-length novels published thus far; none of which have made any money because the Spanish-language market suffers from a great lack of promotion. One of his earlier books (the short stories and sketches) is entitled *Spiks* and is quite powerful and pessimistic. He speaks English fluently and could translate them himself but is too busy with Novel #4. So I may take a crack at it and with his help come up with something salable. In this case of course the book is his and I would earn some percentage, where in *La Charca* it's all mine since the book (written in 1894) is in the public domain. I'll leave you now Jonathan. My fondest regards to you and Ardeth and the kiddies. And please say "hello" to all those at the Pru, especially dear old Bill Coffield, and dear getting-older Hal Burbage, and others who may or may not still be there, such as Jim Blue, Ken Brooks, Walt Cornish, Dick George, Roy Cohen, Carol Ann Petrocelli, etc. I'd love to pay a visit but savings accounts have always baffled me so up until now I've avoided them. Someday though, I'll be bursting in on you . P.S. Almost forgot! I met *Playboy* publisher Hugh Hefner's secretary a few months ago while she was vacationing here. She told me that ideas for Playboy's Teevee Jeebies (movie stills and funny captions) pay $50 apiece. So I sent a few up to Chicago and voila, just got $100 for 2 sold. Am now scouring the local film distributors for more stills which I can convert into dinero.

Meeting Pedro Juan Soto

Pedro Juan Soto and I met in a rather accidental way. When I completed my translation of *"La Charca,"* the 19th century Puerto Rican novel, I reached out to Professor Manrique Cabrera at the University of Puerto Rico, who was a familiar with that novel. I asked him if he could evaluate my translation. Don Manrique told me that his English was somewhat limited, but he knew a young professor recently returned from the United States, who was bilingual. He put me in touch with Pedro Juan Soto, who came to my house, picked up the manuscript, and left. Two weeks later, Pedro Juan returned with the manuscript, was marked up with dozens of corrections. I was so grateful for the hard work he'd devoted to correcting my translation. This was the beginning of a wonderful friendship that lasted until Pedro Juan's death in 2002.

The Perils of Translation

In the early 1960s, while living in Old San Juan, I became friends with Augusto Font, a young man who had recently returned from college in the US, and was working with Publicidad Badillo, then the largest ad agency in Puerto Rico. Later, Augusto and I would co-found a monthly magazine, *The San Juan Review,* which lasted for three exciting years (1964-1966). But before that I recall a truly funny moment. The ad agency asked Augusto to write the text for a film commercial that would be shown in local movie theatres. The topic: a brand new office skyscraper was going to be built in the Santurce business sector of San Juan. The idea: to show an architectural rendering of the office skyscraper, while an announcer proclaimed something in Spanish. Since Augusto had spent the previous four years at the US university, he wrote the first draft of the commercial in English: "A huge landmark rises in the center of Santurce." It sounded great! We then sat down together, and looked in a Spanish-English dictionary, for help in translating to Spanish. The dictionary showed that the Spanish word for "landmark" is *"mojón."* In Puerto Rico that word is commonly used in two ways. First, it refers to the cement kilometer markers at the side of rural roads. Second, it refers to a pile of shit!

So, if Augusto had made a literal translation of his English text, moviegoers would be shocked when they saw the image on the screen and heard: *"un gran mojón se levanta en el centro de Santurce!* (A huge shitpile rises in the center of Santurce!)" After laughing uncontrollably for several minutes, Augusto and I agreed that the wording of the commercial needed to be tweaked. Such are the perils of translation.

A Few Hours With James Baldwin

One of my fondest memories from the early 1960s was when I spent a few hours with James Baldwin (1924-1987), the great African-American writer. Old San Juan was a popular winter refuge for writers, actors, artists and other celebrities seeking to escape from the cold, and wanting to enjoy a Caribbean version of Greenwich Village. A good friend of ours was Amilcar Tirado, who produced a number of excellent short films for the government's Community Education Division (one of his best ones, *"El Puente"*, I believe is in several museum collections). Amilcar was eager to produce a full-length film. He made a poor choice, selecting a screenplay from India, and placing it in Puerto Rico, under the title *"Más Allá Del Capitolio (Beyond The Capitol)."* One day, Amilcar approached me, explained he already had a rough cut of the film, and said "James Baldwin is here in Old San Juan with his French friend Lucien."

"And?"

"It would be fabulous if I could get him to see my movie. Maybe he could then recommend it to distributors!."

"Sounds like a good idea," I said.

"But there's one problem," Amilcar said. "The film is in Spanish, and he doesn't understand Spanish?"

"So," I asked, "How can I help?"

"Kal, I already invited Mister Baldwin to see the film in our small studio tomorrow afternoon. You understand Spanish. Could you sit next to him and translate?"

The next afternoon, James Baldwin and I sat side by side in the small dark screening room, watching a mediocre two-hour film. Every time a line of dialogue was spoken, I would lean close to him and whisper the English translation. Baldwin sat there, nodding, and sometimes whispered "Interesting." When the film was finished, Baldwin rose, smiled, shook my hand, said "thank you very much". He then walked over to Amilcar, chatted for a moment, and left. Many other celebrities might have lost patience, and left after a few minutes. Not James Baldwin. I will always remember those few hours with such a kind man.

May 15, 1963. Our daughter Maria Dolores Wagenheim is born in San Juan, Puerto Rico.

Dear Jose

Not long after our daughter Maria was born we realized that, with two young children, and Olga wanting to work outside the house, we would need someone to take care of the kiddies. Someone introduced us to José, a slender, very poor, dark-skinned Dominican man in his early 40s, and he turned out to be a gem. We we not able to pay much, but José came to live with us, eat in our house, and became part of the family. He came to adore David and María, and they adored him. He would take them on walks all around Old San Juan, and a couple of times he even took them on the ferry from Old San Juan across San Juan Bay to Cataño, something that truly excited them. Despite his very very modest salary, José a couple of times went to a local discount store and bought cute little dresses for our daughter. In 1965, when I went to the Dominican Republic to report on the civil war, I was able to make a brief visit to his family, and they lived in extreme poverty, in a tiny shack. José was gay, but very proper and shy about his sexuality. He had a small circle of gay Puerto Rican friends, who a couple of times came by our house to visit him. They made a big fuss over our cute little daughter Maria. I remember one of them, a large black guy who dressed rather elegantly, which is why they called him "La Hilton." José remained with us for two or three years, and later found a better paying full time job preparing food for a company. But he was illegal, and needed to obtain legal residency. Someone came up with a brilliant idea. They arranged for him to marry a Puerto Rican woman, a US citizen. We never attended the wedding or the party afterwards, but I wish I had a photo!

Norma & El Bocón

Norma, Olga's little sister, who lived with us, was such a sweet gal. Old San Juan had a number of very poor areas, but the crime rate prior to the outbreak of drug use (years later) was quite low. However, there were a number of poor drunks who wandered around the neighborhood. One of them we called El Bocón, because he was such a loudmouth, always shouting. One day, El Bocón was standing in front of our house yelling out loud how hungry he was. We were seated at the kitchen table, on the second floor, just above him. I think it was around lunch hour. "I'm hungry!" he kept yelling. "I'm hungry!" Norma, near tears, looked at me, silently pleading with me to give the guy some food. I explained to her that if I went downstairs and handed him some food he would be at our door every day. Impossible. But poor little Norma looked so sad, as El Bocón kept yelling, that I came up with an idea. I told her to wrap up a nice big sandwich, and then stuffed it into a paper bag. I then told Norma to sneak up to the window and drop the bag down next to the man. As he kept yelling, Norma quietly reached out, and dropped the bag, which landed on the sidewalk, next to him. El Bocón picked up the bag, opened it, and suddenly kept quiet, looking around, perhaps wondering if God had heard him. Norma and I smiled. A good deed!

Dec. 5, 1963. Letter from Bess Wagenheim (Uncle Nat's wife) in Irvington NJ to Lill, Charlie Wagenheim's wife in California. Dear Lill: The Wagenheim family is very much concerned and disturbed in regard to the condition of Harry. From my son Allan we have learned that Harry is unable to work and is now receiving public assistance under the Aid to the Totally Disabled program. Knowing that you are well acquainted with Harry's background and are in close touch with him I thought you would be in a position to give us all of the facts concerning his condition, for which we would be very grateful. Harry's sister Dora Seidner telephoned him this week and spoke to him for about an hour. He told her very tearfully that he is very sick and unable to work. She suggested that he come back East, but he is not sure what he wants to do. He told her that he is not on a friendly basis with you anymore, and that he has been seeing a psychiatrist. Lill, we would be very grateful to you if you will take the trouble to write to me and let us know in details facts concerning Harry. Do you think it would be best for him to come back East? Or is he better off to remain where he is. How does he spend his time? Is he physically ill or only emotionally? Should he be hospitalized? Please hold nothing back. Anything you tell us will be carefully considered... Do you think that sending him additional money each month would better his situation? I hope that you will reply very soon, as Dora is beside herself with worry and pity for her brother. She is now convinced that her brother

Harry is friendless, alone, a broken ailing old man. Please set us straight on this score. Thanks ever so much for all you have done, and I know that is considerable. With kindest regards to you and Charlie. Sincerely yours, Bess Wagenheim PS. My son Allan has told us of your hospitality…for which we are very grateful. He too is far from home and has a heavy burden to carry. Your friendship means much to him—and to us. Thank you!

Dec. 8, 1963. Letter from Bess Wagenheim (my aunt) to her son Allan.

Dear Allan: I am writing you about Harry Wagenheim and I would like you to get us the answers to some of these questions. 1. From what you know about Harry, and his present condition, do you think he should be hospitalized? 2. Can you contact his psychiatrist and find out whether the doctor thinks Harry should be in a hospital? 3. Is there a good State or local hospital (not private, too expensive) in your locality? 4. What is the doctor's fee? Do you think the doctor should send us the bills, and the family will get together and pay for them, as we cannot be sure as to whether Harry actually goes for treatments. Lill phoned us Saturday evening, Dec. 7, and said she felt a visit East would do him a lot of good, and that Harry felt abandoned and… had threatened suicide. She said if he had a *round* trip ticket East, his absence from Los Angeles would be considered only temporary and he would not lose his assistance from the State. It seems that Harry phoned his sister Dora Seidner twice last week and sobbingly told her that he is very sick, could not work, hated his friends and had many fears etc etc. Dora was beside herself with worry and insisted that Harry be brought back here for the family to take care of him. Today we had a family conclave with both sisters, Sam and us to discuss the matter. Frieda is very much against having Harry brought back here, as she had her fill of him years ago when he was home, before he went to Calif. Dora says she could not rest unless she knew he was getting adequate care. As for myself and Dad, to be honest, we are reluctant to have him as we know that all we would see would be crying and sobbing, heart rending complaints, etc and I just cannot take it, and we could not really help him. The end result would be to hospitalize him here, and then after a lapse of time his public assistance would cease, and the family would have to take over completely. None of us are in a position to do this. Tonight Harry himself phoned us, and of course wept and said he is full of fears, could not work, hated his friends, and himself. He really is a sad case and we don't know what to do. Dad tried to pacify him and made him promise to see the doctor Tuesday ...things have come to an impasse and we really don't know how to proceed. No doubt from now on Harry will be calling both Dora and us regularly to get some emotional relief...Please call us some evening this week, after 9 o'clock and reverse the charges. We are always up until after 12 midnight. I promised Harry's sisters that I would get in touch with you, so that you could investigate the matter fully and let us know what to do. Thanks dear very much. I really hate to burden you with this task, but before we make such a drastic step such as taking Harry back east, we want to be sure that there is absolutely no other way out. Thanks again...

1963-64: Olga took typing and other secretarial courses at a school in Santurce in preparation for office work. By then her brother Carlos (then 16 years old) had come to live with us. In 1964 she found a secretarial job at La Concha Hotel, to help with home expenses. Carlos graduated middle school within two years and left for the United States as a contract laborer in the Carolinas. His place was quickly filled by Olga's sister Maria, who needed to attend H.S. We enrolled her at Juan José Osuna, a model school in Hato Rey while Norma attended a Catholic school and then the public middle school José Julian Acosta in Old San Juan.

La Concha!

One day in the early 1960s, I was strolling along Ashford Avenue in the Condado section of San Juan. I approached the Hotel La Concha, and saw a group of about five people, laughing, and posing in front of the huge conch sculpture in front of the building. A friend was snapping photos of them while they waved and laughed. Assuming they were tourists, I came up to the photographer and asked him, in English, if he'd like to join the group while I took a picture. He replied in Spanish.

"Ah, where are you from"? I asked.

"Buenos Aires, Argentina," he replied.

Then, laughing, he explained that while everywhere else in the world a "conch shell" is something from the sea, in Buenos Aires it is a slang word for a woman's private parts. So, they were having a great time and looked forward to showing the photo to their friends in Buenos Aires!

THE SAN JUAN REVIEW

Feb. 1964: Together with Augusto Font we launched *The San Juan Review*, a monthly English-language magazine, which continued until Nov. 1966. Augusto, from Puerto Rico, had returned recently from college in the U.S. and was working with Publicidad Badillo, the island's largest ad agency. Through him, we obtained substantial financial backing for the magazine from Marcos Ramírez, a prominent lawyer, who had recently purchased a printing plant, Talleres Gráficos Interamericanos, in the Puerta de Tierra sector of San Juan. I was paid $700 per month salary, not much, but enough in those days to support our family, with a little left over. Our literary editor was our dear friend Pedro Juan Soto, a published author. Each month, Pedro Juan would select two short stories (one by a Puerto Rican author, another by an author from elsewhere in Latin America) and assign them to be translated to English. I look back with amazement at the number of marvelous writers who contributed fiction and articles to the magazine during its three years of existence. A few examples from just the first year: Fiction: Juan Bosch, Emilio Díaz Valcárcel, Ramón Ferreira, René Marqués, José Luis González, Abelardo Díaz González, Pedro Juan Soto, Emilio Belaval, William Kennedy (then a local journalist, who later became a famous US novelist), Dalmiro Saenz, Hal Underhill, Jorge Luis Borges, Antonio Márquez Salas. Articles: Former *Time* music critic Carter Harman, Nathan Leopold, Florangel Cárdenas, Manuel Maldonado-Denis, Thomas Marvel, Leopold Kohr, Jane Alderdice, Carlos Fuentes, Teodoro Moscoso, Robert W. Anderson, Nilita Vientós Gastón, Robert Hamory, George Moberg, Virginia Matters, Irving Peter Pflaum. Great photos by Marvin Schwartz and cartoons by Max Frye also enhanced the magazine. Ernie Potvin, a dear friend, was our art director.

Marvin Schwartz at the time worked for the *San Juan Star*, the island's

English-language daily. In addition to taking photos for the paper, Marvin was active shooting all aspects of Puerto Rican society, urban and rural, rich and poor. Today, his black and white photos of Puerto Rico in the 1960s are valuable pieces of history. Later, Marvin would leave the *Star,* and do quite well as a freelance. Among his major clients was the government's Economic Development Agency (Fomento). They paid him thousands of dollars to take photos of existing factories on the island, to be used in brochures to attract investment to the island. When Marvin collected his thousands, he would pay several months rent for his rent-controlled apartment in Greenwich Village and spend the time in France. He knew how to live the good life, and took many photos while staying in France.

March 9, 1964. Monday, 10 p.m. Letter from Bess Wagenheim to her son Allan Wagenheim. Dear Allan: ...Harry did arrive Friday evening about 8:30 and the next evening I had all the family in our house. Harry is somewhat heavier and quite gray, but his face is the same. I feel very sorry for him, as he has no control over his emotions. Practically everything, no matter how insignificant, makes him weep. Well he has seen the family at long last and now what? We each have our own affairs, work and plans, and cannot give too much of ourselves to him, at least not to the extent that he needs it. He already has said to his sisters that he should not have come out, and I feel that he soon will be going back. He has nothing here. If he could work (which he cannot as he doesn't know what he should do with his life) things would be different. Every human being must have something to keep him occupied if he is to find satisfaction and contentment. One must have a PLAN, a purpose. He is not staying with any of us, but has a room in the Carlton Hotel downtown Newark near the P.S. Elec. & Gas Co. He is trying to get into the Y.M.C.A. but for the time being there are no vacancies. He hates Newark. It has changed a lot in the years he has been away...With all our love, Mother.

March 22, 1964. Letter from Bess Wagenheim to her son Allan Wagenheim.

Here everything is very disturbing because of Harry's situation. It seems that one institution requires a fee of $8.00 *per day*, and even then there is great doubt that they will accept him as a patient. Another place insists on at least one year's residency. As for Harry he is dilly dallying back & forth & we are at a loss to know what to do with him. He hates to go back to L.A. and he can't stay here as who can take care of him? We are meeting again to discuss the matter to-day in Dora's home. Will get in touch with you later on if we can get him to go back to L.A. At least he will be able to get institutional care there, which he desperately needs. The problem is getting him to go. We would be glad to keep him here in the East if an institution would take him in but there seems little hope for that, so what else is there to do but send him back. In such case, we will have to ask you to get in touch with his Dr. Ruskin, who in turn will have to pave the way for his admittance in Camarilla...Love, Mother.

June 1964: *Nugget* magazine published my short story *"The Way It Really Is."* Featured on the cover is a blonde model, and a headline featuring a major article inside: "Mutual Gratification: And The New Uninhibited Petting Techniques" by Dr.Albert Ellis. Also, inside an interview "James Baldwin speaks from Paris."

July 1, 1964. Letter from Kal (in San Juan PR) to Harold Wagenheim, 127 S. Serrano Ave., Los Angeles, Calif. Letter returned, stamped "Moved, left no address." Written on envelope "429 Calle Mayor, Redondo Beach CA" Dear Dad: I shudder to think how long it's been since I've written to you. Forgive me but once I get involved in something I get involved right up to my ears. And, for nearly the past year, I've been busily trying to keep afloat a new monthly magazine—*The San Juan Review*, Puerto Rico's first in English. The six issues to date are sent under separate cover. Am interested in your opinion. It's been so long since we've communicated. First, I'm married (happily, this time). Her name is Olga. Born in Puerto Rico 22 years ago. Spent her high school years in New York. I met her here several months after I arrived. She is lovely, petite, intelligent, delightfully temperamental and a fine mother to our two children (that makes you a 'granpa' thrice over now!) who are named David (2 years old) and Maria Dolores (1 yr. old). Also, about 2 years ago we bought a crumbling old house overlooking the ocean in Old San Juan. It taxed our financial resources to buy the place, but a perpetual sea breeze is ample compensation for the lack of luxurious décor which will come later. As for my fiction, have been too busy with the magazine to spend much time on it. Remember the short story which you evaluated for me? Well, not long after you returned it I began to expand it into a novel (using several of your suggestions) and I think it has possibilities. But it needs a careful polishing (at least a 6-month task) which I hope to be able to begin at the end of the year. Thus far, Puerto Rico agrees with me and I have no desire to return to the mainland except for occasional visits. Haven't been back yet, but I have taken quick vacation hops to St. Martin's, St. Croix, St. Thomas and Aruba. The next order of business would be to book passage for a visit with you in California. I've often dreamt of it, but somehow there are always obstacles—almost always financial. But just you wait—I may surprise you one of these days. How wonderful it would be if you could come here. Do you think it's possible? We can always put you up...it would just be the expense of travel that you'd have to worry about. I promise you a grand tour of the island and heaps of good creole cooking. Please write to me soon. Am anxious to hear from you. Love, *Kal"*

A Shot in the Dark!

In 1964, a very funny Pink Panther film, "*A Shot In The Dark*", starring Peter Sellers, made its debut in Puerto Rico movie theatres. *The San Juan Star,* the island's English-language daily newspaper, had a list of movies playing. Some mischievous member of the *Star* (the rumor is that it was Bob McCoy) made a tiny change in the spelling, so the film was announced as *"A Shit In the Dark"*, which of course prompted enormous laughter among many readers.

Meeting Dick Friedman

A young man named Dick Friedman came to my office at *San Juan Review* and asked for a job, but with unusual details. Dick said his family from New England planned to buy a small radio station in Puerto Rico, and he would be assigned the task of selling ads for the station. But he was new to Puerto Rico and had no contacts. He proposed working as our ad salesman for a while, and at some point he would leave and take charge of ad sales for the radio station. Dick did a fine job and each week would drop by to give me an update on his sales. One funny memory. During a gathering of local writers I met Nathan Leopold (1904-1971), part of the infamous Leopold-Loeb case. In 1924 he and Loeb, both young college students, murdered 14-year-old Robert "Bobby" Franks, thinking they could commit the perfect crime. They were arrested and sentenced to life imprisonment. Loeb was killed while in jail. Leopold, in his 60s, was released after many years and allowed to live in Puerto Rico. He sent an article to us about the threat to a pigeon that was native to the island. We published it and later published another thoughtful article of his that explored whether prisons did or did not rehabilitate. Dick was sitting in my office when Nate called me to say he was pleased to see the second article in print. "Thanks, Nate." He then asked when I might send him a check as payment. "I'll be mailing you a check this week, Nate." I hung up the phone. Dick looked at me and asked "Who was that?" "Nathan Leopold," I replied. Dick's eyes opened wide and he said "You owe money to Nathan Leopold?" I nodded yes. *"Pay him! Pay him!"* I remained friends for many years with Dick Friedman, who built the radio station into a huge, successful enterprise. He was a funny, generous guy. And we often laughed over his "Nathan Leopold" moment.

April 4, 1965. *To Mil Kaiser in Newark NJ.* Millie, my love: Howtheheckareya? I can't remember *when* we communicated last, but today's a lazy sort of Sunday and I was sitting around thinking (waxing nostalgic if you must know) and suddenly it came upon me to send you these few lines to ask about you, the dogs, the house, our mutual friends, that status of the old neighborhood, etc.etc. I've been busier than heck the past year or so with the magazine (*San Juan Review*) which I believe I sent you copies of. It's an uphill struggle as all new publications are, but it's slowly catching hold and contract ads are starting to mount up. It occupies every day of the week and even my socializing is usually involved with the mag (opening nights of shows, plays, new products, press conferences) but to tell the truth there is nothing like being on your own with your own business, which depends on your sweat and tears. If I had stayed at the Prudential I will have been a Gray Flannel Zombie by now. It's always mild weather here, but it is a bit chillier in the winter months, and now the warmer climate is starting…It fluctuates perhaps 10 degrees from winter to summer, but after one lives here a while that slight fluctuation seems like the difference between spring and summer. Ever revive the Friday sketch nights? Those were the days. I still keep a couple of my quick charcoal sketches in a dusty corner here and every so often I glance at them and remember the good times. I also have a quickie which you did of Joe the Gardener, which I treasure. Have a cold and feel too fatigued to make this a long letter, so will close with my best, best regards to you and please say hello to any of the others who may drop by (Howard Saltzman? Dave? Is Frank Farah still in town? Mike? Germaine? Jim Earle? Eddie? The Carlsons") Love, Kal P.S. I am, and have been, a happily married man for some time…my wife's name is Olga (beautiful, intelligent and you'd love her—she knows all about you, I so often speak about you) and we have two kiddies: David and Maria. Olga works with us at the magazine and the toddlers (ages 3 and 2) go to nursery school during the day. I've become quite domesticated: my house is full of toys, diapers, cowboy pistols, etc. and I'm quite happy. Olga may soon go to work for a local airline and after 6 months we'll be entitled to generous discounts on flights. If this comes to pass, we'll be dropping in on you. So keep a few of those great hamburgers around in the refrig just in case.

May 22, 1965. *Letter to my father on letterhead of The San Juan Review, Puerto Rico's English-language monthly magazine, PO Box 2689, San Juan PR 00901.* Dear Dad: I hope this letter reaches you. I sent one to you a long while ago to the 127 S. Serrano Ave. address and it was returned, but scribbled on the envelope was 429 Calle Mayor, Redondo Beach...Have all sorts of things to tell you, but will wait to hear from you first. In general things go well, am quite happy (wife, 2 kiddies) and busy (struggling new monthly magazine)...Write soon...Love, Kal

Civil War in the Dominican Republic

June 1965: A civil war erupted in the Dominican Republic, and I flew there to report on the event for the *San Juan Review*. I spent a tense week in Santo Domingo during the truce. One light moment: when I arrived, I took a taxi to the Inter-Continental Hotel, where I would be staying, and the driver, while en route apparently taking me for a horny tourist, said in Spanish: "I am sorry, señor, due to the revolution, all the whorehouses are closed." Not long after my return, I gathered up the wealth of material and sent an article to *The Nation* magazine, which published it on Nov. 21, 1966 and paid me $75. (This would pay off handsomely later, a job offer to work with *The New York Times*!)

Chuck Corbett, Never at a Loss For Words

At some point in the 1960s, Olga enrolled in the university. Some evenings, after dinner, while someone watched our two young kids, David & Maria, we would stroll a few blocks to Corbett's, a small dark bar owned by our good friend Chuck Corbett. One night, as we sat at the bar sipping our drinks, Chuck asked Olga how she was doing with her college studies. Sitting next to us was a fellow who apparently had downed several drinks. He looked over at Olga and asked: "You're going to college?" She nodded yes. He eagerly continued "Gee, I got my bachelor's degree at such-and-such university, my master's degree at such-and-such, and am working on my doctorate…" Chuck interrupted him with: "Dah-ling, you have more degrees than a rectal thermometer!"

July 28, 1965. Letter from Lyle Stuart of Lyle Stuart Inc., 239 Park Ave, New York City 3. Oregon 4-2255. Dear Mr.Wagenheim: Sorry to be tardy in replying to your letter of 7/17. I've been away—we have secretaries on vacation—and things are generally an unholy mess, because instead of the usual summer quiet, things are "booming" here. I happen to be a paid subscriber to the *San Juan Review*…you're publishing a hell of a fine magazine and I hope it is richly rewarding on some levels…Cordially, Lyle Stuart. P.S. I gave the copy of the *Review* you sent me (since I have my own subscription copy) to Dr. Pedro Casals—just here from a junta prison in the Dominican…former Minister of Finance in that country, etc.

Oct. 18-23, 1965. I took part in "The Caribbean In Crisis," a conference at Inter-American University of Puerto Rico, organized by CISCLA (the Caribbean Institute & Study Center for Latin America, in San German). My contribution was *"The Communist menace and the press."* The proceedings were published in a 80-page report.

Jan. 3, 1966: *Letter to Mr. Lester Markel, Editor, NY Times Magazine, Times Square, New York 36, NY.* Dear Mr. Markel: Perhaps you'll be interested in this piece on the Dominican Republic, consisting primarily of two interviews with Juan Bosch several months apart. Some of the things Bosch says might be considered libelous; the reference to Reid Cabral was witnessed by 3 persons, including myself—and the others are on tape in Spanish. If you do find the article usable, here's my bio: 30 yrs old, born in Newark NJ, have lived in Puerto Rico since 1961. Founder-editor of *San Juan Review* (now 2 yrs old). Was in Santo Domingo during the recent mess and have interviewed Bosch several times during his exile in Puerto Rico. Also, if you have any ideas you'd like me to take a crack at, would be delighted to do so—even on "spec". Happy New Year, Kal Wagenheim. P.S. Am enclosing recent piece I did for the *New Republic.*

Jan. 14, 1966. *Typewritten letter to me as Editor of The San Juan Review, PO Box 2689, San Juan PR from former Governor Luis Muñoz Marín, then a member of the Senate of Puerto Rico.* Dear Mr. Wagenheim: Thank you very much for your letter of Dec. 28. I am glad you found my article of the 1920s

"The Sad Case of Porto Rico" of interest. However, as you say, I do not think it should now be published. My job now is to make things clearer and not more complicated for the understanding of our people. I would not have time at present to do the up-dating that you suggest. And even so, I believe it could be more amusing than enlightening. Best wishes for the New Year. Cordially, *LMM* Luis Muñoz Marín *P.S. The Anderson book is good, but it has a few errors. People will learn more from reading it than from not reading it. This is the best review I have time to write. LMM.*

February 1966: *The New Leader* magazine publishes my lengthy interview with Juan Bosch, exiled President of the Dominican Republic.

March 4, 1966: Letter to Travel Editor, New York Times, Times Square, New York NY 10036. "Dear Sir: First, thanks for the $80 check for my article on the forthcoming First InterAmerican Festival of the Arts in Puerto Rico...will you have anyone covering this event here in Puerto Rico? The travel pages may not be interested, but from the news end there may be some good material. If the *Times* isn't sending a man down, or if it doesn't have a 'stringer' down here to handle the event, I could take a crack at it if you could give me some idea of what kind of material you'd want. Could also get photos. Sincerely....Kal Wagenheim."

March 13, 1966. My article, with byline, appears in the Travel & Resorts section of the *New York Times*: Culture Under Sun; Puerto Rico Schedules Festival of the Arts.

April 4, 1966. Letter from Dora Seidner, 81 Union Ave, Irvington NJ 07711.

Addressed to me at 309 San Sebastian, Old San Juan, Puerto Rico. Dear Kalman:

I think it best that I start this letter by telling you I am your father's sister Dora, Greta's mother. I believe you will remember Greta as she told me you visited her one evening a few years ago. I wanted to write to you so many times in the past, but for one reason or another never did so. I feel very guilty for not writing and keeping in touch with you through the years and hope you will forgive me. I never knew your address, however about a week ago a neighbor came across a letter you had written to the editor of the magazine *Ramparts* signed by you and your address was listed as San Juan, Puerto Rico. She knows the Wagenheim family, so she brought this letter in the magazine to our attention. I then contacted Information in San Juan and obtained your street address from them. I do hope I heard her correctly, as the connection was not a clear one. Your father's sisters, that is Frieda, myself, and his brother Nat would be very happy to hear from you. I want you to know we are concerned about you and would like to know how you are doing, and how you are feeling. I am also very sure that your father would like to hear from you. I know, Kalman, that all of us didn't exactly do the right thing by you, but please, let us, in a small measure, try to make amends. I want you to know and feel that you have a family that is concerned about you and would liked to hear from you. I keep in touch with your father by mail regularly. I always ask him if he hears from you and he tells me he hasn't heard from you in a long time. He is ill and I am sure a letter from you now and then would cheer him up quite a bit. I do hope you will do so. This is his address: Harold Wagenheim, c/o The Gilbert Hotel, 1550 North Wilcox Ave., Hollywood, California 90028. Please Kalman, write to me soon and we will all write to you from time to time. Let me know if I can do anything for you. Greta and Bill and everybody here send their best to you. I just received a letter from your father and I am enclosing it herewith. Sincerely, love, Aunt Dora.

April 12, 1966. Letter to my father, from San Juan PR. Dear Dad: It was such a tremendous surprise, and relief, to learn of your whereabouts. I don't know how it happened, but the last letter I have of yours dates back to about 1961...and I never learned of your new address. About a year ago I tried writing to you at the S.Serrano Ave. address and the letter was returned to me. I thought of all the worst sort of things. Yesterday I got your sister Dora's letter explaining where you were. It's almost miraculous that she learned my address from a letter that I wrote to *Ramparts* magazine. That was a letter I almost didn't send; and how happy I am that I did. Well, I guess we two have a lot of catching up to do. So much so that it would take a book to get you right up to date on me. As you know, I came to Puerto Rico in 1960 to work with a weekly paper owned by the son of the governor. Since then the paper folded and I took a job as a reporter for another weekly publication which dealt with tourism and show business in San Juan, which is quite a booming tourist center. The job was excellent (paid over $200 a week for a minimum of work) but it grew extremely boring. About two years ago a friend of mine and I started a monthly magazine, called the *San Juan Review*—a serious magazine dealing with the politics, economics and arts of the Caribbean and Latin America. We've had rocky going, as all liberal magazines do, but it's been immensely rewarding and we've been slowly making our way, gaining lots of respect, little money...and harboring big hopes for the future. In addition to editing the Review, I've also contributed articles to *The New Republic, New Leader* and a few others, have finished a novel which is presently in the hands of an agent (a novel based on a short story I sent you a long time ago and which I expanded, in great part, according to some very fine advice you gave and and I've got my fingers crossed for its success) and have also had a short story or two published. I'm still not a writer in the full artistic sense of the world—I've been sort of dividing my time between fiction and journalism—but I'm groping along and hopefully progressing. I am now very happily married and have been since a year after I arrived to a lovely Puerto Rican girl named Olga. We have two children—David (3) and Maria (2) and are living in an ancient house in Old San Juan (a type of historic zone) and are slowly reconstructing the house as it must have looked a few hundred years ago. Having lived this long in San Juan, and having learned Spanish quite fluently (I also translated a Puerto Rican novel which is in the agent's hands) I've become quite identified with the island—it is "home" to me more so than the United States. I've been back to visit the states only one time in 5 years (that was last summer). But I would like to be able to visit more often (at least twice a year) however up until now, with a growing family and very demanding job it's been impossible to do so. I do hope we'll be able to write to each other frequently. I'll be sending you copies of the Review each month, which I hope will be of interest to you. I'd love to be able to fly up to California and see you, but I don't see how it is possible right now. It's a rather expensive trip and at this point I wouldn't be able to get away from the magazine which is practically a one-man operation. Do you think it would be at all possible for you to come down here some time? Aside from the plane fare, you wouldn't have to worry about a thing. You could stay at our house and all would be provided; it would be just great to have you here—and I know that you would just love your little grandchildren, who are very bright, and real devils. Their other grandfather, Olga's dad, has a farm about 90 miles west of San Juan and he's delighted every time we leave them there for a week-end. He spoils the heck out of them and they don't even want to leave, what with all the chickens, hens, cows, etc out on the farm. I just returned from a trip to the Dominican Republic and have to start working up an article on the political situation there, both for my own magazine and for an article requested by *The Nation.* Arrived last night and haven't even finished unpacking. On the way home from the airport I stopped at the post office and got Aunt Dora's letter—so I didn't want to put off this letter too long. Am enclosing a few photos of us—do write soon and tell me what's happening up there. Keep well, and give some thought to coming down if at all possible, even if it's just a week or so. Would be wonderful. Love, your son, *Kal* P.S. and love too from Olga and the kiddies. *We'll send more photos later. Do you have one of yourself?*

April 19, 1966: Letter from Harold Wagenheim (my Dad, age 63) to Kal, from the Gilbert Hotel in Hollywood. Dear Kal: I was equally surprised at receiving your letter until I read that my sister Dora had written you, although I didn't know that she did. She did mention that she saw a letter you had sent to a magazine. It was a complete surprise her writing to you. In fact, I don't know what she told you about myself. First, I want to wish you the best of everything in your married life, with the children, Olga's father, and in your work which shows much promise, and does keep you pretty well occupied. I, too, go back to about 1960-61, when we had corresponded. I was going along pretty good with work, and routine, then a series of reverses entered the scene. A year ago, I took ill with diabetes, spent a couple of months at the hospital, and am slowly regaining my strength. Don't discuss these details with Olga, and should you write back home to Dora or the others of if they write you, just say you hear from me and I am working. In fact, I just started a week ago, and am trying to take it in my stride. At 62 years of age, I must take things in stride. I do hope your *San Juan Review* goes into big circulation. Your literary properties interest me, and these, too, I hope find a market. Olga must be kept pretty busy with 2 young children and the house. Is her father's farm large? Does he farm for himself, or for the market? Kal, I do wish you the best, good health, peace of mind, the continuing development of your talents (you do have many ...guard them preciously and express them fully), the most harmonious relations with Olga, the children, Olga's father, and those about you. Give my fondest regards and love to Olga, the children, and Olga's father. Love...your dad, *Harold.*

April 22, 1966. Letter to my father on stationery of San Juan Review. Dear Dad: How good to hear from you after all this time. Am sorry to hear about the health problems. I know what diabetes can be. My wife's 10-year-old sister Norma, who lives with us, is a diabetic and although she keeps it pretty well under control we've had a few scares with her, and she must watch her diet closely. I hope that you are feeling better. You mentioned that you are working, which at least means, I hope, that you are up and around. So you're 62 years old now. That puts us in a peculiar position. Just yesterday I celebrated my 31st birthday; exactly half your age. Am putting on a bit of a paunch and a few strands of grey are coming out at the temples. So I guess we're both getting on in age. Thanks for the nice comments about the *San Juan Review*. It's been quite a struggle, but having my own magazine gives me the kind of independence that so few people these days can have. I don't know whether I would ever be able to work *for* someone anymore; for the past 2 ½ years I've been just about on my own and I like it that way. If I do anything poorly, or haphazardly, I know that I have just myself to blame. I've come to learn that working on one's own can be dangerous, because a person can become quite lethargic or complacent, and the biggest challenge is to exercise self-criticism continuously. You asked about Olga's father, and his farm. He has a very tiny farm, just a few acres. But he is a wonderful man. Olga comes from a big family. Most of her uncles and aunts left the countryside years ago and came to San Juan or went to the states and most of them are you might say "comfortable upper middle class." But her dad always stayed back on the farm and he seems quite happy there. He drops into the city occasionally, but getting him to stay overnight is quite a chore. We go out to visit him from time to time, and staying overnight there—in the chilly, dark countryside, being lulled to sleep by the chirping of the *coquí* (a tiny local frog which "sings" like a tenor cricket) is a lovely experience; a real tonic after the cacophony of the city. As for Olga, I don't think I could have made a better marriage. She is quite beautiful and—even more important—an intelligent, generous person. She treats me like a king, is good with the children, and is now working as a teacher in the local private school and seems quite happy with this new job which gives her an important feeling of doing something useful and significant. She is teaching Spanish (she is perfectly bilingual) and Puerto Rican history. Our two children, David and Maria, are handsome and precocious and give us a great deal of joy. Also living with us are Olga's two sisters: Norma (10) and Maria (16), both of whom are studying in school, are very fine girls and, rather than being any burden to us, are a great asset because they help with the housework, care for the children, etc, which gives Olga and me complete freedom to go out in the evenings or on weekends whenever we wish. Thus far, fortune has smiled upon me. We are by no means wealthy, because to start the magazine I had to take a substantial cut in pay, but my work is quite satisfying, we eat well and we get along without depriving ourselves of anything important. Being a member of the press, I get invited to a number of thing *gratis*—occasional nightclub openings, art gallery exhibits, movies, etc.—so a number of the things which we couldn't ordinarily afford are free to us. Last year my trusty old Volkswagen was stolen after 4 years of good service (it was about ready for the junkyard anyways, so no great tragedy) and next month we plan to buy another small car. I really don't need the car urgently for work as the bus system is good and takes me from home right to the office door, but on the weekends with the beaches so near, it's quite convenient to have a car so that we can go on family excursions. Loading our entire family onto a bus, with beach blankets, sandwiches, books, etc is rather difficult. That's what we do now, but having a car once more will be a help. A friend of mine, a sociology professor at the University of Puerto Rico, is heading back to the States for the summer so he's selling me his 1961 Anglia for $400; a reasonable price, and a bargain I won't pass up. Also, as you may know, we live in an ancient house in Old San Juan and we plan to restore the house, which will cost several thousand dollars, which we don't have. However, I'll soon be applying to the Government Bank here to see whether I can get a loan on a 20-year mortgage basis, so if they approve it we'll be able to restore the house at not great financial sacrifice...just a few dollars extra monthly, in addition to our present mortgage payments. Hopefully, we'll have the house finished by year end. If you can ever see your way clear to visit us, please do. You can stay with us. It will be wonderful to have you here with us, and you can brush up your Spanish with your grandchildren (who speak more *español* than English). Think it over. I had been hoping to go to see you in California, but I just don't know how or when, what with my job, family, etc. Do you ever see Charles Wagenheim? If you do, please give him my best regards. I met him just once many years ago; perhaps he'll recall. Must go now. Keep well, and write a few lines when you get a chance. Love, your son, *Kal*

May 1, 1966. From Dad. Dear Kal: Congratulations on your 31st birthday. I hope and pray that all your years will be filled with good health, peace of mind, closeness to your family, and productivity in your work. As for a visit, I feel for the present that with the money involved going and coming back, it would be too much. I do not want to dwell on the subject of my illness, but I did have a two month bout with it in the hospital and it took quite a bit out of me. You are very fortunate in having a wonderful family, and having found happiness in so many areas. As for wealth, this is really of no matter when you have love in your life, children about your house, and a healthy integrated family. I pray that as the years go on, you maintain all these wonderful qualities and spirit. Wealth is ephemeral. It is here today, gone tomorrow. What you have cannot be bought. I hardly visit Charlie although I speak with him on the phone. He is well, on in years, but still does TV work. I admire him for his drive…love, your dad…Harold.

May 23, 1966. *The New Leader* magazine publishes my 5-page article, "Puerto Rico: Kinship or Colony."

May 25, 1966. From Dad. Dear Kal: I do hope that you and the family are in good health, and that you are continuing to make progress with your magazine. I went through all the magazines you sent, and you are to be commended for the job you are doing. Your trips to other locales do sound very interesting, and your reporting "in depth" is quite revealing. You are also to be commended for your tireless effort in bringing such a publication to the people of Puerto Rico, and, I suppose, outside the island. Kal, it is my hope that some day when conditions avail themselves, we will see each other. I think of you and Olga, David and Maria, and know that you will have a long, fruitful life…I look forward to hearing from you…Love, your dad, *Harold.*

May 30, 1966. Dear Dad: Good to hear from you, and am glad you enjoyed the magazines I sent you…if I'm a bit remiss in writing from time to time you can depend upon hearing from me at least each 30 days via the *Review*, which occupies a great deal of my time and is, in a way, a pretty accurate "diary" of my activities. Have also done a bit of free-lancing with U.S. news magazines. Have sold two pieces to *The New Leader* and one to *The New Republic* and am now working on articles for *The Nation* and *Ramparts*. Also, have an idea for a book dealing with the election campaign of Dominican President Juan Bosch (if he wins, that is. I go to Santo Domingo on June 1 to see the elections). So, as you can see, your son is a busy boy; what with the magazine, the free-lancing, and at the same time running a household. Olga and I will have a bit of peace starting next week; we're sending our little ones, David and Maria, off to the country with Grandad for part of the summer at least. We'll probably go nuts with so much silence in the house; right now silence is a rarity because both David and Maria are, to put it mildly, rather loquacious. Must leave now. Have to prepare for Santo Domingo trip, which will be a two-day "quickie"...By the way, got a letter from Alan Wagenheim, who's teaching out in the Midwest and we've begun a correspondence...Keep well, and write when you can. And if you can ever manage to make it down here... the welcome mat is always out. Love...your son, *Kal*

July 18, 1966. From Dad to Kal: Dear Kal: I just got your two issues of *San Juan Review* and...I will say that you are managing to keep up the format and standard of your previous issues. I did read your editorial and didn't realize there were so many ramifications to the "U.S.-Puerto Rico dilemma." I do hope you and family are well...I suppose David and Maria are at the farm. I also suppose Olga might be teaching this summer...I am feeling all right physically, trying to control my diabetes through diet. But, the problem is to keep occupied since I have not worked for a month when the Registrar of Voters dismissed all of us. I have been trying to write and am developing a sort of fill-in for a newspaper. It is a hassle, and if anything worthwhile turned up, I would take it, and drop all this intensive, introspective writing. I haven't spoken with Lil and Charlie for some time. I have gotten out of the swim and must get back. My sister Dora wrote me, and tells me she got a copy of your magazine, and likes your work. Love and fondest regards, *Harold*

July 26, 1966. From Kal to Dad: Dear Dad: Got your letter of July 18 and am glad that the *Review* had some interest for you...Just got back from a 3-day weekend in the countryside; which is always welcome. Olga's father's place is really isolated; about 3 hours from San Juan, and well in from the main highway. So at night it's pitch black; the stars stand out like spotlights, and the only sound is that of the *coqui,* a tiny frog which has a soprano call just like it's name: *co-kee! co-kee!* Within walking distance of Olga's dad's house—where we all stay when we're there—is a brand new small concrete home put up by the family, atop a breezy hill, and unoccupied, just for visitors. I "confiscated" it day before yesterday and sat down with my typewriter and spent the whole day there trying to work up an article on Santo Domingo for *The Nation*. The work went well, and it was quite pleasant up there... eating bananas picked from a nearby tree, sipping lemonade (lemons also from nearby tree)...that fellow Thoreau knew what he was talking about. I haven't the vaguest idea whether *The Nation* will adopt the piece, but writing it under those circumstances was certainly great fun. Although my work at the magazine keeps me very busy, I am hunting around for something extra to provide more money and perhaps I will go to New York in the new few weeks to see whether I can pick up some free-lance work (either journalistic, or maybe translating some literary work from Spanish). If I do go up, I'll be sure to visit the family in New Jersey. That's all for now. Keep well, and write when you can. Also, keep in mind that whenever you can make it down here, you're more than welcome. Love, your son.

August 1966: Among the articles in the August issue of *The San Juan Review* was "Spiritualism in Puerto Rico" by Nathan Leopold. We published three of his articles during the three-year life of the magazine. At the time he worked for the Commonwealth Dept. of Health's Social Sciences Program.

Sept. 26, 1966. *Letter from me to Caribbean Editor, The New York Times, Times Square, New York NY 10036.* Dear Sir: I have been editor of the enclosed magazine since Feb. 1964 and have also contributed articles on the Caribbean to *The New Republic* (copy enclosed), *New Leader*, and will have one in *The Nation* published sometime in October. Perhaps my sources are wrong, but I have heard that the *Times* is not wholly satisfied with its stringer in Puerto Rico, and if this is so I would like to inquire about the possibility of my filling the post. I have lived in Puerto Rico since 1961 (I am a permanent resident, my wife is Puerto Rican and my children were born here). I am bilingual and I have had journalistic experience dating back to 1955, when I worked on the scholastic sports desk of the Newark (NJ) *Star Ledger*. Should you be interested in discussing this further, please drop me a line. Or, better yet, I plan to visit New York for a week in late October, and if you think it worthwhile for me to drop in at your office, please let me know via letter. Very sincerely yours, Kal Wagenheim, Editor

Oct. 1, 1966. *Letter from me, in San Juan, to Editorial Director, Nugget Magazine, 545 Fifth Ave., New York 17, NY.* Dear Sir: In your March 1964 issue, you printed a story of mine, "The Way It Really Is." Not only did you change my original title; not only did you make some editorial cuts; not only did you spell my name wrong; you never paid me the $100 for the piece. On Jan. 1, 1964 I received a letter from Seymour Krim telling me that *Nugget* had accepted the article, and that "payment will be between one and three months after publication." I think you'll agree that I've been patient---more than two years have passed. I know the kind of financial problems which magazines suffer. My own is now closing down after nearly three years of operation due to economic reasons. Which is another reason why I'd like my $100. Please? Even in installments of $5 a week? Hopefully, Kal Wagenheim, Box 2689, San Juan PR 00903 PS. I hate to be nasty, but so much time has passed without any word from you that I have little other choice. I plan to fly to New York on Oct. 9. If my check isn't here by then I promise you that I will enter your office and carry off $100 worth of merchandise. My typewriter is getting a bit rusty, and I imagine that one of yours might do as a replacement. I'm not looking forward to seeing you, but unless that check is in the mail I'm afraid we will be seeing each other. Batten down the typewriters—and the secretaries! ***Note:*** *When I flew to New York, I went to the office of Nugget, and saw that the entrance was enclosed with an iron gate. An employee, behind the gate, reached out, and handed me a check. Finally!*

Oct. 24, 1966. Letter from me to Lyle Stuart, 239 Park Avenue South, New York NY 10003. Dear Mr. Stuart: Just got back to San Juan and wanted to thank you for taking the time to see me at your office. I enjoyed meeting you and was, quite frankly, flattered that you should consider me employable. I'm in no position to relocate in the immediate future, but the idea *definitely* interests me and I hope that we can keep in touch so that maybe something can come of it when I'm more mobile. In the meantime, I'll hope to hear from you about translations and any other work you think I might be capable of from sunny Porto Rico. Oh yes. I also appreciate your negative (and frank) comments about a few book ideas I have. Sometimes things which appear important from a Caribbean-LatinAmerican viewpoint have little interest among N. American readers, as you point out. Question: what do you think the chances would be for a documentary-type book (with plenty of gory photos which are available) about the Puerto Rican Nationalist revolt. This would include the time the Nationalists shot up the U.S. Congress, when they tried to kill Truman at Blair House, when they invade the governor's palace at San Juan, when they took over the town of Jayuya in Puerto Rico and declared it the center of an independent public—all on Amercan soil. All this, which occurred in the 1950s, would be surrounded by a brief history of Puerto Rico, a brief bio of Nationalist leader Albizu Campos (who died last year) and other pertinent stuff. It might have some interest at universities and also among NY Puerto Ricans, I think. Best wishes, Kal Wagenheim.

Oct. 25, 1966. Letter from Kal on San Juan Review stationery to Dad: Dear Dad: Last week I went to New York on a business trip, and although my free time was disappointingly limited I did manage to spend part of one day with a branch of my family that I haven't seen in a long time. First I dropped in on Dora, who took me over to see Frieda and her husband, and then Dora and I had a wonderful supper at Nat and Bess' house, where we also spent some time with Greta and her husband. The visit was short…but we did manage to take advantage of the few hours and catch up on past years. Also, my wife Olga and I hope to take a strictly-pleasure vacation trip sometime next year and then we can enjoy a more extended visit. Business-wise my New York trip was also a success (or at least promises success). Our monthly magazine will cease publication this month and probably go into a quarterly because it was too great a financial struggle to keep it alive. I have already lined up a few part-time jobs which will pay me a good deal more than my work with the magazine; and perhaps also leave me free to do some free-lance work for US magazines and publishers. I visited a number of editors, people with whom I've corresponded before, and further cemented my relationship with them. Also sold a piece to *The Nation*, and was assigned 3 book reviews by them. Also, *Harper's* suggested a few articles I might do and it's now just a question of my giving them a detailed outline of any piece I want to do for them. As I said, the trip certainly paid off in terms of my making invaluable contacts in the magazine field. And if I ever "connect" with an article in a major magazine the pay will be good enough to perhaps allow me to zoom out to California one of these days and finally see you; something I've looked forward to for a long time. Must go now. Ten days away from my office has caused a lot of work to pile up and I must get at it, as well as dash off a number of thank-you letters to people who were kind to me during my visit. Write when you get a chance, and keep well…and remember, anytime you feel up to a flight to Puerto Rico just say so and you're more than welcome. Love, your son, *Kal* P.S. Your 4-year-old grandson David, who is quite fluent in Spanish, is just now beginning to learn English. The words he knows best are: "I don't know" and "Shaddap!" which, believe me, have caused us some amusing, and embarrassing, moments.

Nov. 1966: *The San Juan Review* was a critical success, but advertising revenue was scarce (our paid circulation was just about 7,000). Each month, in addition to articles on culture and politics, we published two short stories translated from Spanish to English. I translated a few of them as my Spanish became more proficient. Among the authors whose work appeared in the magazine was the great Argentine writer Jorge Luis Borges, and Juan Bosch, former President of the Dominican Republic and an accomplished writer as well. Our final issue appeared in November 1966, and we had to seek work elsewhere. I began searching for freelance assignments to help pay the bills.

Nov. 21, 1966. *The Nation* magazine published my 4-page article, "Dominican Republic: Burden of the Past", together with an article "Haiti: Chaotic and Corrupt," by Gerard L. LaTortue. This article discusses the effect of civil war of 1965 that took place in Dominican Republic on its present socio-political conditions. Although, President Joaquín Balaguer is back in power after a military coup, his victorious Reform Party shares legislative responsibility with Bosch's Partido Revolucionario Democratico (PRD)

However, the mere existence of a legally elected President and a loyal opposition does not solve the problems of the Dominican Republic. The roots of its dark and tragic past still live and threaten to strangle what is as yet only a promise of social, economic and political progress. One of the biggest threats is the army, heavily influenced by a clique of ruthless, corrupt officers who long for "the good old days."

Working For Oscar Lewis

After *The San Juan Review* closed down, I had the good fortune to do freelance work with the anthropologist Oscar Lewis, who achieved considerable fame for his book about Mexico's poor, "*The Children of Sanchez*." It all happened by chance. Dr. Lewis, affiliated with the University of Illinois, received grant support to continue his work with a study of "the culture of poverty" in Puerto Rico. He was putting the finishing touches on his book, "*La Vida*", which became a best-seller. He wrote to us at *The San Juan Review* asking to what extent writers of fiction in Puerto Rico had written on the subject of urban poverty. I consulted with Pedro Juan Soto, a friend who was also our fiction editor, and we sent a reply to Dr. Lewis, who graciously acknowledged our cooperation in the introduction to the book. Later, with "*La Vida*" in the bookstores, Dr. Lewis came to Puerto Rico and, offered me a job as a translator! He planned to do a sequel to "*La Vida*", focusing on the lives of six women in poverty-stricken communities. He would spend many, many hours doing tape recorded interviews, in Spanish. He then paid someone on the island to transcribe the interviews, which added up to hundreds upon hundreds of pages. Then he hired me, and Muna Lee (daughter of Governor

Luis Muñoz Marín) to translate these interviews into English. He would then incorporate the material into a book. This was an active part-time job which paid reasonably well over a period of more than a year. Also, Dr. Lewis visited my wife Olga and me several times, and I recall a couple of dinners with him at local restaurants. In addition to translating the interviews, Dr. Lewis gave me a fascinating assignment. I was to go down to La Perla, the seaside slum in Old San Juan, and tape record interviews with Toña, to learn the history of every object in her tiny wooden shack. As she explained where and how she obtained each item, from silverware, to cups & saucers (many of which were from dead relatives or friends), to the small TV set that sat on her kitchen table (purchased on credit from a local appliance store). In doing so, one learned a great deal about the person's life and socio-economic status. It was fascinating. One of my fondest memories is the time I sat talking with Toña in her tiny kitchen. She had the TV on the table, facing out the open window to a small shack right next door, a few feet away. In that shack was an elderly woman, who could not afford her own TV, and she was enjoying the afternoon soap opera on Toña's TV! During that time, there was talk that Hollywood wanted to make a film of *"La Vida"*. I was told that famous director Elia Kazan was quite interested and would be coming to the island. His key script writer for the planned project was Budd Schulberg (who passed away in August 2009), author of the script for *"On The Waterfront"* and well-known novels such as *"What Makes Sammy Run."* I recall meeting briefly with Mr. Schulberg a couple of times during his visit to San Juan; he was a nice fellow. A few years later, with the "six women" book virtually complete, Dr. Lewis decided to travel to Cuba, where he planned to examine how a socialist society coped with severe poverty. Around that time, he died on December 16, 1970 at age 56. The book on "six women" was never published, although it is discussed in some detail in a book called *"The Culture Façade"* by a scholar named Susan Rigdon.

Dec. 5, 1966. My review of the book *"No David In Sight"* by Juan Bosch appears in *The Nation* magazine.

Dec. 14, 1966 Letter to Kal from Cousin Allan Wagenheim. I'm glad that you and my parents were able to meet, and they spoke with delight about your visit. Your father is darker in coloring than mine, but in general appearance and in gentleness of nature they are very much alike. I wish that I could write freely about your father, based on my few visits with him, but it is rather painful, and I know that it will not make happy reading for you. In 1963-4, when I saw him, he seemed to be a man who was either forsaken by life, or had forsaken life. Perhaps both. Which is very sad, because there is so much greatness and understanding in him. When I taught in high school, some of my colleagues had studied under your father, and they recalled him with true adoration and admiration. He must have been a fine and unusual teacher with a real devotion to people and to his work. As a writer and director, he was a real force behind the WPA and community theater projects during the 1930s and 40s, doing the work for which other men usually took credit. But these are some of the sad details. I'm sure that you have inherited many of his fine qualities, and this legacy is perhaps all that you can be concerned with now. Your father is unwilling or unable to accept help from anyone. I know this because I have spoken with people, in California, who have tried."

Jan. 2, 1967: My review of the book *"My Fourteen Months With Castro"* by Rufo Lopez Fresquet appears in *The Nation* magazine.

Working for Mike Segarra

Jan. 10, 1967. Letter on stationery of El San Juan hotel, from me to pal Bob Bletter in New York. "No, I am not writing this from a hotel room, bubulluh, the el san juan hotel is one of my clients. Since none of my part-time job offers have yet jelled I've accepted a nice little spot with a fellow named Mike Segarra, who has a public relations firm which handles the El San Juan Hotel, Trans Caribbean Airways (maybe discount flights to New York) and a few others. The pay is $175 weekly to start, which is nice, and thus far I've had time to also work on Oscar Lewis translations (I made $12 yesterday) ...and some of the part-time job possibilities are still pending...I don't see how I can accept them all, but some of them might be weaved into Mike's operation on a profit-sharing basis. He's a nice guy, very low pressure, whom I've dealt with over the years when I was with the press. He's hosted me to many free dinners at the hotel...and now I'm hosting the press as his assistant. Last week we saw Paul Anka, and I got an album of his! Zoweee! And the night before last it was Peggy Lee...who was very good...and the filet mignon was just right. So how's your leg, gimpy? Have you thought over that idea for a film I sketched out, about your dramatic rehabilitation. If you like it, I'll send it in outline form to my grandpa at Warner Bros. I was thinking of Rocky Graziano for the lead, with Vincent Price as Louie the Vegetable Man. Must go now...but just wanted to say hello and send our love before I get involved today in the fascinating trivia of my new *trabajo.* Kal and fambly PS. Psychologically I'm rather confused. I have lunch at an elegant restaurant in the el san juan hotel (or sometimes dinner) then I go home and translate the testimony of slum dwellers for oscar lewis...then the next day I mull over my idea for a book on the Nationalist revolution and the next minute I type out a press release for Trans Caribbean Airlines...then I receive a copy of my book review on the Cuban book from *The Nation* ...then I drive a reporter out to the hotel to interview sun-tanned VIP at poolside ... my reality these days is, to put it mildly, rather kaleidoscopic and confusing. Politics, social conscience and just plain intellectual hunger keep interweaving themselves with Rum punches, rock n roll music and the lapping of the waves against the sun-bleached sands of the El San Juan Hotel beach. *Must* go now. Schizophrenically yours.

Looking back on my work with Mike Segarra. My job with Mike Segarra was also kind of accidental. Mike had a small public relations company, specializing in tourism. He had an account with the El San Juan Hotel in the Isla Verde section, between San Juan and Carolina. This big hotel was first built in 1955, and was gradually expanded over the years. It was the only large hotel in the area. Also in 1961,the San Juan Hotel Corp. parceled off five acres west of its property and sold it to the Loews Corp, owned by the Tisch brothers, who built a brand-new hotel, the Americana. (a few years earlier they had built the Hotel Americana in Bal Harbour, Florida). They wanted Mike to handle their public relations also. So Mike hired me and we worked together on both hotels. I recall how Mike and I sometimes went to report to Mr. Louis Puro, who in 1961 acquired more than 50% of the hotel's shares and became the company chairman. Here is a brief excerpt from an article by Robert H. Boyle in the January 13, 1969 issue of *Sports Illustrated* magazine, explaining Puro's role in the growth of tourism on the island: "The boom is due, in fair part, to the efforts of a onetime New York feather merchant, Louis Puro ... Puro has more visions of splendor than the Great Gatsby, and he has spent money on hotels with such a lavish hand that even the people at the Rockefeller-owned Dorado Beach have had to gasp. Short, dapper and white-haired, Puro is a strong family man (three daughters, six grandchildren) who likes to mix with the fancy show-biz crowd. Euphoric by nature, he peppers his conversation with such superlatives as 'fantastic,' 'wonderful' and 'beautiful.' Now 54, Puro was born and raised on the Lower East Side (which was not beautiful), and when he was 16 went to work with his father in the feather and down business...In time, business grew as he and his father expanded into pillows and comforters, and Purofied Down Products is now the biggest pillow company in the world...In 1960 Puro and his wife went to San Juan on a vacation. 'I fell in love with it,' he says. 'I thought the future of Puerto Rico was fantastic.' Castro had closed down Cuba, and Puerto Rico was starting to get a tourist trade...'Even if Cuba did open up tomorrow, Puerto Rico wouldn't have to worry.' A bit of a wheeler-dealer in suburban real estate in The States, Puro was approached by some business associates who wanted to buy the El San Juan Hotel. Puro joined in and became chairman of the board of the San Juan Hotel Corp. which bought the hotel from a subsidiary of Pan Am. 'The hotel wasn't doing too well,' Puro says, 'The hotel didn't have a dramatic flair.' To give it that flair, Puro called in Alan Jonathan Lanigan, a young decorator who had done the Puro home in Forest Hills, and let him have his head. Ten million dollars later, an expanded, redecorated and very loud El San Juan was hopping. It would sprain eyeballs even in Miami Beach, but in San Juan it has been a hit both with tourists and Puerto Rican society. Puro broke with tradition by bringing in star entertainment. Victor Borge, Sammy Davis Jr. and Eddie Fisher perform regularly at El San Juan, and, after other hotels followed suit, Puerto Rico soon ranked immediately after Vegas in big-name entertainment." Mr. Puro would be lying almost naked beneath a towel in a steam room, and Mike and I would enter, fully dressed, to report to him. He was a nice man, and spoke with a lisp. The El San Juan attracted Vegas-style headliners who appeared in the huge Club Tropicoro (designed to resemble the famed Tropicana Club of Havana). These included Frank Sinatra, Sammy Davis Jr., Nat King Cole, Milton Berle, Louis Armstrong, Johnny Mathis, Ray Bolger, Sophie Tucker, Eddie Fisher, Carol Channing, José Greco, The Supremes, Betty Grable, Paul Anka, Xavier Cougat, Maurice Chevalier, and Liza Minelli. One time, Jimmy Durante, the great comedian, was going to open at the next door Americana. I went there with a photographer, to snap some shots for the local press. Mr. Durante came down from his room and met me by poolside. I brought with me my little son David, around age 5 at the time, and Jimmy made a big fuss over him, then smiled and posed for the photos.

HIRED BY THE NEW YORK TIMES!

March 21, 1967. Letter from Kal to Dad. Dear Dad: How are you? Some good news. I've been appointed local correspondent for the *New York Times*—just a part-time job, but am flattered that they chose me, and the small payment is ample reward for the small amount of time required to handle the assignment, not to speak of the satisfaction of working with such a fine paper … practically the only real newspaper in the U.S., to my mind. Must go now. Our love to you, and best wishes. Your son, Kal

March 21, 1967. Dear Blet: Not much time, but received some nice news today and thought I'd let you know…I've been named the Puerto Rico "stringer" for the *New York Times.* Not much dough, but I'm up to my ass in prestige, as they say. Probably no byline stuff, but any short pieces you see saying "Special to the New York Times" with a San Juan dateline will probably be mine…I'd estimate that they want me to file about one story a week, and maybe I can make $100 a month on this job…which is fine providing I don't have to dedicate too much time to it…and who knows, maybe it'll lead to something bigger in the future; like editing Tony Beacon's San Juan Diary. Also, Oscar Lewis may employ me full time starting next week, for a few months, and part time after that…am awaiting confirmation from him…and also am thinking of maybe opening a bookstore…so as you can see I'm not exactly happy in public relations. Love to you and Rosemarie from me and the family and our "Motengator," which is our favorite paperweight of all time. Kal Your man in San Juan (and the *Times*)

* * *

I look back with amazement. In 1965, when a civil war broke out in the Dominican Republic, I flew there and spent a week, during a tense truce, gathering information. I wrote a long piece for my magazine, the *San Juan Review.* Then I sent a long article to *The Nation*, which paid me about $75, and published it, featuring it on its front page. On Sept. 26, 1966 I wrote to the *NY Times* offering my services as their Caribbean correspondent, but had received no reply and assumed they'd forgotten about me. In early 1967, I got a call from Henry Giniger, who at the time was based in Mexico and covered both Latin America and the Caribbean for the *Times*, and was staying at a local hotel. He invited me for coffee and explained that Miguel Santín, a top writer for *El Mundo* daily, was also the *Times* "stringer" (part time correspondent) but was so busy he rarely sent any stories to New York. Henry offered me the job. "How did you decide to offer this to me?" I asked. "I saw your piece in *The Nation*," he replied. Thus began a three-year relationship with *The Times*. It worked as follows: Henry Giniger traveled throughout the Caribbean, but couldn't be everywhere. *The Times* had a "stringer" in every major place: Dominican Republic, Cuba, Haiti, etc. Between March 1967 and July 1970, I wrote more than 50 articles for the *Times*. On occasion, I would hear from Irv Horowitz, the Assistant National News Editor at the *Times* office on W. 43rd St. in Manhattan who asked me to write a particular story. More often, I would call Irv and suggest a story. Most of the time he agreed. In those days, before Email, I would type out the story, call *The Times* collect, and be connected to someone there who listened while I dictated the story, word by word. It was fascinating work, and each story provided me with a decent day's pay. The job would also help me to find work in Buffalo when Olga and I moved there a few years later.

The first story I did for *The Times,* dated March 24, 1967 was a short piece starting "The Rev. Billy Graham, whose week-long religious crusade closes here Easter Sunday, denied knowledge yesterday of Central Intelligence Agency financial support for his recent trip to Latin America." Articles included Puerto Rico's political status plebiscite, protests against the U.S. military draft, the sale of a hotel, the retirement of long time political leader Luis Munoz Marin at age 70, a major oil spill by a tanker, the death of pro-independence leader Dr. Gilberto Concepcion de Gracia, a controversy over payments to casino gamblers, terrorist bombings, a rise in narcotics addiction, the banning of a Jesuit priest who wrote a book critical of the Roman Catholic church, a violent student protest at the University of Puerto Rico, the 93rd birthday of the famous musician Pablo Casals, the introduction of compulsory auto insurance, an overview of the island's economic growth, a major art show, and the slaying of a Nassau County Judge.

The bombings of the hotels

On the night of Dec. 12, 1969, while at home in Hato Rey's El Monte Apartments, I was watching the TV news, which reported a series of terrorist bombings by radical pro-independence groups between 10 pm. and 10:30 pm. at five local hotels, and a bar frequented by U.S. sailors. Also, two men armed with pistols broke into a local radio station and forced a disc jockey to play a tape announcing: "A revolution against Yankee imperialism begins tonight." Despite the blasts, only one tourist was slightly injured, and there were no deaths. As the *N.Y. Times* stringer, I felt compelled to cover this story. I went downstairs, and drove the 15 minutes to the Condado section of San Juan. I stopped at all five hotels, which were only several blocks apart: the San Geronimo Hilton, the Sheraton, the Racquet Club, the Americana, and the Howard Johnson. At the latter, I recall seeing that the blast had damaged a front wall of an ice cream parlor at the front of the hotel. I then headed home, driving out of the Condado section a few minutes inland along Fernandez Juncos Avenue in the Miramar section. Many police were gathered in front of The Big Bamboo Bar, a popular spot for locals and U.S. sailors from the nearby U.S. Naval Station. I walked around for a bit, asked questions, and discovered that police found a small explosive device which had not gone off. Next door was The Castle Club, a bar/nightclub, known for the lovely ladies who were "available" to local business executives as well as Naval officers. Was a bomb planted there, too? I had to find out. I walked over, entered the dark vestibule which had just a few tables. Sitting alone at one of the tables was a well-known Puerto Rican artist (name excluded), who was known for his aggressive support of the island's independence. I nodded to him, walked into the main room, and stood at the long, rectangular shaped bar. A number of Naval officers, American tourists and local executives were among the clientele. Lively music was playing. I ordered a rum and water. Immediately, a couple of beautiful women, scantily clad, approached me, smiling, and asked if I was interested in "company." I smiled politely, sipped my drink, and shook my head "no." Moments later, the lonely artist entered from the vestibule and walked into the men's room, which was directly across from me, on the other side of the bar. I wondered: was this pro-independence activist planting a bomb in the men's room? Moments later, the artist exited the men's room and walked outside. Would a bomb explode in a moment or two and kill, or maim, us all? As the sexy women kept chattering in my ear, I stared at the men's room door, and wondered: if there was a blast from inside there, would I be able to duck down in time to avoid death? I stood there for several minutes, tense, frightened, numb. How could I leave and miss the explosion? I was there on behalf of *The Times*! But nothing happened. After a while, I shrugged, paid my tab, said buenas noches to the ladies, exited the Castle Club and drove home.

Pablo Casals' 93rd birthday

In late December of 1969, I received word from the *Times* office in New York that Pablo Casals, the great Catalonian cellist, would be celebrating his 93rd birthday. The maestro had lived in Puerto Rico for years, an exile from the Franco dictatorship in Spain. Thanks to his presence, Puerto Rico created the Casals Festival, an annual event of classical music which attracts admirers worldwide. Don Pablo and his 33-year-old wife Martita lived in a seaside villa in the Isla Verde section of San Juan (it is no longer there). I called ahead, and received permission to observe the birthday party. I arrived shortly after Don Pablo, Martita and an entourage of 50 friends returned from a nearby church where a special mass was celebrated for him. Cider and hors d'ouvres were served as Don Pablo, wearing a gray suit and blue tie, sat in the airy living room as friends filed by to congratulate him. A large birthday cake with one candle was placed before him, as Jesus María Sanromá, the Puerto Rican concert pianist, broke into a grandiose "happy birthday" and the friends sang the lyrics in English and Spanish. With mock sobriety and a glint in his blue eyes, Casals directed the chorus with a large silver cake knife. Mr. Sanromá then played a lilting 19th century Puerto Rican danza titled "Laura y Georgina", and was joined by Olga Iglesias, the Puerto Rican soprano. As she reached the line "Bella es la vida"(Life is beautiful), Casals sat with his eyes closed, puffing his pipe, his head nodding gently to the music. As Mr. Sanromá began a solo of another nostalgic danza, Don Pablo hushed some whispering ladies across the room and sat back to enjoy it, eyes closed. The only somber note of the day was struck during our interview after the party, when Casals expressed his concern about the war in Vietnam. "I feel happy today over all my friends have done for me but very sad for what is happening in the world," he said. "I try to talk to get my ideas about peace across. Is it possible to stop the war? Armaments are so ugly. Why the arms? We are all humans, all the same, children of God and nature." His final comment to me: "We are all the same, like the leaves of a single tree." Don Pablo died on October 23, 1973, at the age of 97. I shall always cherish the memory of that magical day with the immortal Pablo Casals, the lovely music, and his concern for all of humanity.

May 5, 1967: Letter to Kal (in San Juan PR) from Cousin Allan Wagenheim, (in Denver, Colo.) To answer your question about your father and (a possible) trip to Puerto Rico: from my brief contact with him in California I don't think there is much to gain from pressing the issue. I think he is suffering from a peculiar form of mental illness which leaves his intellect perfectly lucid and sharp but affects his emotions. He seems to be absolutely trapped by his fears. He is also terribly humiliated by his own position, what he considers his abject failure in life, and he was embarrassed and apologetic when I came to see him in the boarding house where he lived. He also did a bit of moaning and crying about his fate. I think he is too ashamed to face you directly, and would rather maintain the relationship by mail, a medium which leaves him at a considerable advantage. My analysis could be quite wrong, but this is how I see it.

June 14,1967. Letter from Kal (in San Juan PR) to Harold Wagenheim (in Los Angeles). Dear Dad: As always it is good to hear from you. I was a bit disturbed, tho, by your June 5 letter, which mentioned your trouble with diabetes. I also felt a bit upset when, in reply to my invitation to you to come to San Juan, you suggested that you might be interfering with my *modus operandi* by coming here; or even by my *worryng* about you! On the contrary, I think it would contribute to it greatly—the opportunity to see you and talk with you. How can I, as you request, not 'feel concerned' about you? Since we have been apart for so many long years, only God knows how far apart we may be in our respective ways of life, our respective problems, etc. And I certainly don't want to meddle in areas of your life which you feel you can work out best alone. But please don't ever feel—as your letter seems to imply—that you would in any way be an imposition on me. I may be wrong, but perhaps the fact that you didn't raise me causes some sort of guilt feelings on your part—some sort of feeling of 'not coming through.' This is a touchy subject for both of us, but we're now both adults and I think we can discuss it. I, frankly, don't feel in any way that I was neglected by anyone. I still don't quite understand exactly what happened when I was a young child and my mother died; no one really ever told me the whole story. But despite that, I was brought up by Grandma and the family with a great deal of love and affection and care, and in no way during my youth did I feel 'deprived' of anything. In fact, in retrospect, I feel I had a rather privileged childhood because as you know Grandma was a rather exceptional person whose guiding spirit—even at that advanced age—was responsible for many of the motivations and values which I now share, and which have contributed to all the positive aspects of my life. So, if you should at all feel that you are in my debt, there is no debt. It's now—as an adult—that I feel I need you. Now, as a father myself, I feel a certain loneliness and yearning for 'family'. Now that my grandmother and great-grandmother are gone, and most of the rest of the family, I'm in the position of so many 'grown-ups', a feeling of isolation from 'roots' and—while I admit that this is not a problem that plagues me daily—it is responsible for a nagging malaise which manifests itself occasionally; a desire to be with and communicate with 'one's own.' And you *are* one of my own. Judging from your letters, I suspect that the last few years haven't been particularly happy ones for you. If it's any help at all, I want you to know that you have a son here in San Juan, Puerto Rico who cares about you and who is willing to make your problems his if that will in any way alleviate them... and you also have a daughter-in-law, and two fine grandchildren...all of them yours. So whether or not you feel you can come—please don't ever feel that it would be any kind of imposition. It would be a joy for me, for us. There is so little we know about each other; and it is this, now as an adult, which nags at me and makes me want so much to know you better.) I am, at least, heartened by your statement that 'all will eventually be well' with you. I hope so. And remember, you are always welcome in my life; whether in person or via the mails. Must go now. Oscar Lewis is a hard taskmaster and keeps me up to my ears in work. Love from all of us, Kal

Nov. 22, 1967. From Kal to Dad. Dear Dad: Haven't heard from you since back in June when I sent you what may have been a rather unsettling letter...I've been busy as the proverbial beaver. And have also corresponded occasionally with Bess and Nat, and with my newly discovered cousin Allan, with whom I have a great deal in common. How are you? You got me worried in the last letter, the diabetes problem…my little sister-in-law Norma is a diabetic and I know how serious it can get when out of control. I shudder at the idea of becoming a diabetic myself someday because I love sweets so. I admire little Norma a great deal for the way she controls herself in that respect; we buy her the artificially sweetened canned desserts, and she also eats fresh fruits, etc. Has your diet been curtailed very severely because of the illness? In the past few months I've had more work than I could humanly do. Am just now completing a 2-month project for the Dept. of Education here; an 80-page booklet about Public Education in Puerto Rico. I think it's ironic that they should choose me, a college "drop-out" for the assignment. (I promised the Secretary of Education a discount for the job if he would also grant me an honorary degree, but aside from breaking up with laughter, I doubt whether he'll come through). Am also translating for Oscar Lewis, doing occasional pieces for the *New York Times* (may also break into their Sunday travel section with some luck). Next year I may work part-time as editor of a small tourism monthly magazine run by my ex-partner from the *San Juan Review*. If I'm lucky enough to get "employee" status with the airline which sponsors the magazine, I'll be eligible for grand discounts on air travel. If so (all these if's!) you may see your son for a brief visit. My wife Olga is busy at the university, and your grandchildren David and Maria are busy discovering the marvels of learning to read and write at kindergarten, so it's a studious family here…Love from all, *Kal*

Dec. 18, 1967: *The San Juan Star*, Puerto Rico's English-language daily paper, publishes a full-page ad, **"A Warrant For the Arrest of Lyndon B. Johnson"** and other U.S. government leaders **"instrumental in directing the Vietnam War."** I helped to organize the ad, which was signed, and supported by, dozens of people, including my wife Olga. The newspaper at first hesitated to publish the ad, but finally relented, and it caused quite a controversy.

Jan. 10, 1968. Letter from Harold Wagenheim (age 65, at Gilbert Hotel in LA) to Kal in San Juan PR. Dear Kal: First, take note of change in address. When I came out of the hospital the last time, it was felt that I should try to convalesce at a home. After a while I came back to the hotel. Thanks for your letter and the Christmas card. I do hope you and Olga and the children are in the best of health, and enjoying the good life. I have not written you much nor in detail because I truly have little to write since I have been concerned with things which persist to bother me, such as diabetes (I came from the doctor yesterday) and my drive to adjust myself to the world about me. Many things bother me, and I still can't get around to talk about them. It is not only the diabetes, but a host of things, past and present, which still plague me. I have tried to get help, but this is difficult. When I have gotten over the hurdles, you will know about it, and I will be free to talk and act,without prompting of any kind. I must have more time to make further adjustments, and your coming out to see me at the present time, with conditions the way they are, keeps adding pressure on me. I should like to have certain areas in my life become more tolerant, and this will take time. I do want to see you, and possibly try to get closer, but presently I am struggling with my own personal adjustment. I have noted your activities and I must admit tolerant towards mankind, and liberal, etc. I also must admit that I worry somewhat that the stand you take about the U.S., President Johnson, the Vietnam War, may hurt you in some way as far as cutting yourself off from future needed outlets. You see how I talk: I was a school teacher, and acquiesced in all things; possibly this did me more harm than good, for I hid under the umbrella of self-righteousness, and feared the outside world. The outside world looms large and hostile. But, please, I say all this for your welfare and do please examine all you do, and all you advocate. I realize this sounds like a tired, old man, and accept it in that light. As for your shuddering at the idea of diabetes I suggest that you don't. Like all humans, we neglect those yearly or semi-yearly examinations. Whole families should get check-ups on cancer, tuberculosis, and all the other ailments and diseases that visit mankind. You have a lovely family, and health is the most important factor: emotional, mental, spiritual and physical. All other things pale in insignificance. One of the things that has been bugging me is my exaggeration of things which ordinarily I would pass over, and not give a second thought to. I had tried making certain contacts in the way of liaison, trying to help people make contacts in business, etc. Before I realized what I was doing, I became involved in matters of a speculative nature and have been worrying about these things. After two years of this sort of thing, I suddenly realized I was dealing with sources I knew little or nothing about, spending much time and not getting a penny for my work. It is nothing serious, and am presently crystallizing my position so that I will know what actually must be done to make a living in a realistic way. Add to all this unwise friendships made, and one can find onself fearful and alone. I will write more later, and now love and the best to you and Olga and David and Maria. Please write and feel free to ask anything that is on your mind, past or present, however sensitive. Love, your dad, *Harold."*

Jan. 12, 1968. From Kal to Dad: Dear Dad: How good to hear from you after several months! Don't interpret my rapid reply as the setting up of ground rules where you must ping-pong another letter right back at me. I just wanted to let you know how welcome your letters are and I hope we can correspond more frequently. (Sometimes I'm the one to blame, because work pressures the last couple of years have been tremendous.) I appreciate your letting me know at some length about some of the things which are "bugging" you, and I respect your desire to be no more explicit than you were in describing them. When you say, of the "things" that bother you, "I still can't get around to talk about them," I understand completely. To a lesser degree, I'm sure, I have inner problems of my own which sometimes torment me, and trying to articulate them, even with one's most intimate friends or relatives, is just about impossible. Since I am, after all, part of you, I think that in a vague way I understand some of the things which trouble you. I'll pry no further, but just let you know that if ever you feel that it is helpful to *you* to discuss it further, you have a sympathetic ear here in San Juan. We had a hustle-bustle Christmas holiday season. Xmas down here begins Dec. 25 and stretches through January 6, Three King's Day. Visits to friends, visits from them. We also had a huge New Year's Eve party, about 75 people, which was much fun, but I'll think twice before throwing another because of all those cigarettes, paper cups, etc. we had to clean up the morning after. Next New Year's I think we'll be more "bourgeois" and go to one of the hotel supper clubs for our champagne and noise-making. The house has also been rather lively because of school vacations, and our two children, as well as my sisters-in-law Norma and Maria have been home. Also, we had a house guest from Washington, a girl who used to live here and is a friend of Olga's and mine. Also, another young girl who is Olga's classmate at the university had a serious problem with her parents ("boyfriend" trouble), ran away from home, and is staying with us for a few days. I'm thinking of putting up a "hotel" sign at the front door! Actually, though it's made life more hectic, I haven't minded, because both guests are nice folks. In a week or so, though, things will be back to normal. Everyone at school and me here in the first floor office, pecking away at my typewriter. Oh, before I forget, I've been doing a little experimenting with poetry of late and I enclose one which evokes a vague childhood memory of mine. Let me know what you think. I also enclose another in a (I hope) humorous vein. I just got a letter from Aunt Lucille who tells me that her 19 year old son Benny (your nephew) has all of a sudden sprouted literary interests, and is writing poetry, and devouring Shakespeare, etc. I guess it runs in the family! Re: the anti-Vietnam War ad which I authored and co-signed, that may have been my last gasp politically; I've recently lost interest in politics. I don't know how permanent my attitude is, but politics seems less sensible every day, which I think is why my mind turned to poetry at just about the time my attitude changed. I doubt whether I'll remain permanently apolitical, but I have a feeling that when I swing back towards that area of interest, it will be with a different outlook. As for the ad hurting me personally, I don't think so. Just recently the local Department of Education has assigned me some contracts for free-lance writing (they even asked me to be a permanent part-time editorial consultant)...and I was just named a member of the board of directors of the Community Development Foundation here, which handles anti-poverty funds out of the Office of Economic Opportunity. It's a no-salary, advisory post, where we participate in policy-making at once-a-month meetings. I was just named, along with a few local educators, politicians, etc. and haven't begun yet, but I'll give it a try to see whether I can offer anything useful to the program, and vice versa. That's all for now. I am arm- and mind-weary at this point since I just finished a batch of translations for Oscar Lewis. I've been working with him for about a year now, and have been translating close to 10,000 words a *week!* I wonder what he's going to do with all that material! Much love from all of us here in San Juan, Your son, *Kal*

1968. We sold the house in Old San Juan, for about $19,000 and moved to El Monte Apartments in Hato Rey, where the kids would attend public school, and enjoy a large swimming pool in the back yard. Rent was about $230 a month. I freelanced, for NY Times, and also Puerto Rico Nuclear Center. Hato Rey, a suburb of San Juan, was closer to the to Inter American University for Olga. The fact that she did not yet drive was part of the reason for the move. And the nearby public schools for kids were said to be better than those in Old San Juan. Olga's sisters Maria (about 19) and Norma (15) continued to live with us and also attended nearby schools.

1968-1970: Olga recalls: The best things that happened to us in Hato

Rey was cementing our friendship with the journalist Joel Magruder and his wife Teresa Ortiz then our neighbors at the El Monte Apts. Theirs and our children spent most days playing and swimming after school while we, the adults worked on our projects and shared many enriching experiences.

Dec. 17, 1968. From Dad (age 65) to Kal: Dear Kal: Enclosed a bit of Christmas cheer for David and Maria. You might get them something of your and Olga's choice, knowing better than I what they really would like. I have both your articles in front of me, and I do know that in time you will be a regular contributor to *The New York Times*. Do you get *The Wall Street Journal*? I pick it up once in a while, not so much for the business information, as for the 3 main articles which appear on the front page. They are delightful, informative, and although stereotyped, make for interesting reading. Have you ever approached the *Journal*? How is Olga? What kind of teaching is she doing? It must be wonderful for both you and Olga to be engaged in work of such interest. I do hope the monetary returns are sufficient to make everything run smoothly. However, do not press the work too hard: things will right themselves., and you will find in time that once creativity has been discovered and made to work for you, it will bring untold, priceless results. Again, don't push too hard, but seek the creative approach, and nurture it wisely. As for the children, I do hope they are in the best of health. I pray that they are getting on well with their playmates, friends and at school. Coming to myself, I had worked for several months until election day (Nov. 5) when the job terminated. I am looking around, and probably will get something soon. I have my fingers in several projects, but nothing of a financial nature has yet materialized. I keep checking with my doctor as far as the diabetes is concerned. The condition is controlled, and for this I am thankful. Well-being is most important, and where we fail in this area is not being cognizant and alert to preventive medicine: the taking of medical tests on a periodical bases, engaging in healthful routines of eating, exercising, sleeping, etc... and, however difficult at times, a positive and healthy attitude toward people and life in general. Keep well. Much joy and health to you and Olga and David and Maria in the Christmas Season and the many years ahead. Love and greetings, *Your dad, Harold*

Feb. 19, 1969. From Dad in LA to Kal in San Juan. Dear Kal:I got your letter containing the clipping of your newspaper work, with the note, and was pleased to hear from you. First off, I notice that Budd Schulberg will write a screenplay based on Oscar Lewis' two works: *La Vida* and *Down these mean streets* (did I get the second title right?). He also produces, so I suppose he will produce, and probably do it down your way. I do know he is due in San Juan, or by this time, he is there. I have been trying to get back to work, and am taking an examination for a civil service job. In the meantime, I keep puttering with a number of projects, somewhat long-ranged, but take little stock in them: if one works out, fine; if not, will keep trying. As for my health, I try to adhere to a sensible diet, although I do indulge which I shouldn't, like a piece of cake, chocolate, etc...However, I believe I can do without all this added stuff which only does us more harm than good. It is really a matter of slight discipline, and one can adhere to most any kind of regimen. I do hope you and Olga and David and Maria are in good health. If I receive good news concerning the projects I am working on, I will let you know immediately. In the meantime, take care of your health (and the family's), keep a steady pace in your work, enjoy the simple things around you, meditate on good fortune and deeds, and be at peace with yourself. Love...your dad...*Harold*

1968: The Puerto Rico Nuclear Center

Another chance meeting, this time in an elevator, lands me a job when I need it!

Hugh Barton was a leading economist who worked with Fomento, the Economic Development Administration, in Puerto Rico. His wife Marie Barton was Executive Asst. to the Director of the Puerto Rico Nuclear Center, part of the Eisenhower Atoms For Peace Program, affiliated with the University of Puerto Rico. By chance, I met her in the elevator of an office building in Santurce, Puerto Rico. She asked me how I was doing, and I told her I was looking for work. The PRNC had a number of scientists there, receiving generous Federal funding for research projects, who were required to submit quarterly update reports. They were not very articulate, so Dr. Henry Gomberg, the head of the PRNC hired me to put together their reports to funding sources. It was a fun assignment. I met a number of brilliant, eccentric scientists. Among them: Dr. Jorge Chiriboga, whose field was Pathology and Biochemistry, a brilliant man who was equally inarticulate (in writing) in Spanish and English. Amador Cobas, head of the Physical Sciences Division; Victor Marcial, the Associate Director; Fred Rushford, Technical Asst. to the Director (a really nice guy); One man (not sure of his name) researched the possible radiation of the sugar cane borer, to reduce its population in the sugar cane fields. One day, I saw him in the PRNC cafeteria, and he looked ecstatic. I asked him why. He said he was being transferred to Southeast Asia, to study the rice borer. 'They've given me a new insect!" he exclaimed.

The Caribbean Review

With the *San Juan Review* magazine closed, I was still interested in some form of publishing. My good friend Barry Levine (a professor at the University of Puerto Rico) and I joined forces and we launched the *Caribbean Review*, a quarterly journal. This enabled us to continue our regular work and also publish something of value. In the late 1960s, Peruvian writer Mario Vargas Llosa (born 1936) spent some time as an invited professor at the University of Puerto Rico. Then in his early 30s, he had recently published his first novel, *"La Ciudad y los Perros"* and his second novel, *"Casa Verde"* was coming out. I went to interview him on the UPR campus. When I commented that I knew he had worked as a journalist prior to writing fiction, he nodded his head and said "Nosotros los periodistas somos como los buitres, nos nutrimos de la carroña de la historia" (I translate): "We journalists are like vultures; we feed off the carrion of history." *(Note: in October 2010 it was announced that Vargas Llosa was awarded the Nobel Prize for Literature. The announcement brought back a vivid memory of the time, four decades earlier,when I interviewed him).* My two-page interview with Vargas Llosa appeared in Vol. 1, 1969, the first issue of *Caribbean Review*. Recently through Florida Intl University (where Barry Levine worked for years), they digitized all issues of *Caribbean Review* and it is now available online.

June 4, 1969. Letter from novelist Norman Mailer, 142 Columbia Heights, Brooklyn NY. Dear Kal: Thank you for your letter, good wishes and contribution. I've seen the ASPIRA people a couple of times, and I'll make it a point to contact you when and if we need some more information or help regarding the Puerto Rican community. Best regards for now. Sincerely, *Norman Mailer.* P.S. Pete Hamill is supporting Badillo.

June 26,1969. Letter to Dad. Dear Dad, sometime in early July I have to go on a business trip to the Western U.S. as part of my job for the Nuclear Center. I was planning at first to simply drop in on you...a surprise visit. But I think this unfair, and have decided instead to write to you in advance. I don't know the exact date yet, but it would probably be around the 12th of July. Dad,

I am sure that *both* of us will be nervous about such an encounter after all this time, but I'm also sure that both of us want very much to see each other, and this seems like such an ideal time. After the initial difficulty of those first few moments, I look forward to a couple of delightful days of really getting to know each other. I'm sure there is so much that we'll have to say to each other about all the years that have passed by, each of us going our separate way. It is often said that youngsters are cruel, unsentimental, to say the least. And I must confess that while a youngster, although I always kept in mind the hope of meeting with you, I never felt "sentimental" enough to really make the effort; it was never a case of not wanting to go, simply not wanting *hard enough* to go. But now, as an "oldster," in my 30s, and with a family of my own, the idea of family and old friends, etc. seems to increase in importance to me, and I've come to realize how "incomplete" my life will have been if we let time pass on and on and never get together, when it would have been so easy such a long time ago. As evidence of how little we really know each other, I must confess that I don't really know how you feel about my planned visit. And out of respect to you, I wanted to let you know in advance, to find out. There is another purpose in my trip. In one year Olga finishes her bachelor's degree and wants to take graduate work in Latin American History and we have been told that either Stanford or the Univ. of California have excellent programs in that field., so I thought it would be wise to inquire there, get catalogues, etc. on the possibility that we might relocate to California for at least 2 years while Olga gets her Master's, and I of course would have to get a new job, but I'm not too worried about finding something decent. Would very much appreciate hearing from you, with respect to my visit. And I look forward to mid-July when we can get together, at long last. With love from me and all the family, *Kal* P.S. I enclose a couple of snapshots taken recently, with identification on the back.

July 3, 1969 letter to Kal from Dad. Dear Kal: Thanks for your last letter, and the pictures enclosed. You are the busy man, and do hope that all of you are in the best of health. As for myself, things have been rather rough. I have had some dental x-rays made (I have an upper plate) but the bottom six teeth, with a partial plate, have been causing me much concern. I will know on Monday what the results of the x-ray will be. The possibility is that the teeth may have to be withdrawn; at best, one tooth may have to be taken out, and a new bridge made. I say all this to let you know that the time you expect to be in Los Angeles may be a rough time for me. On the other hand, I may need one extraction. Added to this, I have the precaution to take, being diabetic, not to run too high a risk of infection. I know all this is very depressing, and wish to God I were in a better, more comfortable physical and mental state of mind. I have worked only 4 to 5 months each in the last two years, and barely get by with my allotment. Now, I have been trying in many ways to get research work; sent one or two things to the studios, but months have gone by, and nothing has resulted. Once my teetha are taken care of, I may get back to the County work again. Kal, I know how eager you are to meet with me. I once stated in a letter that this can't be forced...But there must someday be a propitious time, when all conditions are much more favorable than now. I don't know what the folks back East have been telling you about me; I must be the judge of my situation in the final analysis. This I know: conditions for me can only go upward now. I believe I have weathered the most difficult times. Please be patient with yourself and with me. There have been many pressures on both sides, and I am solely concerned with everyone's welfare. As for seeing me for the present, please consider all the details I have stated in this letter. Keep well, and my love to all. Love, your dad, *Harold*

July 5, 1969 letter to Kal from Dad. Dear Kal: I felt very bad after I realized the kind of letter I sent you. I felt that by unburdening myself I could get you to see the picture as realistically as it exists. My whole concern has been to become productive, self sufficient without becoming a burden to myself and those I care for, and who care for me. Decisions have been difficult for me to make: the years have slipped away, and before one knows it, the obstacles become larger. I have tried my best, in earnest, and now must leave things to the creative power that invests us all. I will keep trying, however, toward the work goals I have been pursuing, and do feel the law of averages will see me through. Please don't fret through all of this. You are very young, have good spirit, a fine family, and I know things will work out eventually. Please bear with these situations. Who knows but what the coming weeks will bring good things to all of us. Again, in the light of all that I have said, I will leave the decision making as far as the trip is concerned with you. I do have dental visits to make, and will not know until the middle of the week what has to be done. As you surmise, I would rather have you come under conditions much bright, but for the present, such is the picture. With love to all, Your dad, *Harold*

July 19, 1969. Letter from Kal to my Dad, Harold Wagenheim, after seeing him during brief visit to Los Angeles. Dear Dad: Just got back last night, and am still savoring the good feeling of our long-delayed reunion. I can't quite articulate how I feel having had the chance at last to meet you, and talk with you, but somehow I feel more 'complete,' if you know what I mean…I hope by now that the case worker has come up with some definite news as to the dental work. I know how important this is to you for your peace of mind. Have faith. Eventually it will be done, meaning one less obstacle in terms of finding steady work. I understand your discomfort over being dependent upon the relief folks after all these years of fending for yourself and I pray that soon you can work your way out of the situation. As I said when we shook hands and said goodbye, Dad, each person must run his own life, but it makes things a bit easier when there are friends and family around to help smooth over those rough moments. So be assured that you are not alone. Here in Puerto Rico you have a family of people who care a great deal for you, and whom you can call upon whenever necessary. I must get busy now with job resumes and other tasks that have been piling up. Please write whenever you can. In the meantime, I include a small check to cover that hotel bill which you so kindly covered for me, plus a little something extra which I think will come in handy at this particular time until the dental work is done. Love from all of us, *Kal*

1969: At some point during my visit to LA I also met with Charles Wagenheim, my Dad's cousin, who lived there with his wife. Charlie, who had a long career as an actor in Hollywod, took me to lunch at The Lobster Barrel, a restaurant owned by his actor friend Alan Hale, Jr, who was well known for the show *"Gilligan's Island."* It was fun seeing Charlie and I was amazed that at age 73 he drove his car without the need of eyeglasses, while I (age 35) needed glasses to drive!

1969: Letter from Kal to his dear friend Bob Bletter in New York, after Kal has brief re meeting with Dad in California. I flew to LA and had a very emotional reunion with my father. Not really emotional in the teary sense, because neither of us, it turns out, are that way, but it was quite an experience. My dad was quite active in theatre back in the '30s, and knew many of the people who are today fairly big names on Broadway, or in some cases, Hollywood, and we spent a good amount of time just sitting and talking about his youth. He is a very sweet, surprisingly innocent, and very vulnerable man; he has been through a lot and he feels rather beaten, rather resigned, and he is not in very good health. It felt so good knowing him; I can't tell you, I somehow feel more 'complete,' if you know what I mean.

Dec. 18, 1969. Letter from Dad to Kal: Dear Kal: I had intended writing you this evening when I got your Christmas card and the money enclosure. Thanks so much for the remembrance. Thus this immediate reply this morning…I have your *Caribbean Review* before me, and it is quite a job I imagine getting it out. Your translation work must have proved exciting (and I hope financially worthwhile.) I had the extractions of my teeth finally taken care of about 6 weeks ago; however the requisition of the making of the plates got fouled up, and finally it was ironed out. I go for a fitting December 23. So what started in June is slowly coming to a finalization. In the meantime, my diet is pretty well distorted. When the plates will finally be made is anyone's guess. The thing that hurts is the "hanging around" with no work and no income. However, I am patient and live within the public assistance budget. Now, you can understand why I keep harping on: (1) maintaining your health and the health of the family, (2) working and earning a good amount, and providing for the family, and saving as much as is realistically feasible. Thus, one has a grand chance of entering "age" and living comfortably. Give my love to all: Olga, David, Maria, and the others. I will write more often, and pray that all our lives are filled with good thoughts, peace of mind, well being, and the joys from a family and close ones. Enclosed 5 dollars for gifts for the kids. Keep well and joyous, and the best to all into the Christmas and New Years seasons. Love…your dad, *Harold*

My first published book, and meeting my dear pal Leon King (1925-2000). Around 1969, while living in San Juan, I had submitted a proposal to Praeger Publishers in New York for a book on Puerto Rico's Nationalist movement. They were not interested, but since there was a growing interest in ethnic studies at U.S. colleges, they counter-proposed that I write a "survey" of Puerto Rico, a snapshot of the island as it was at the time, with background on its history, culture, economy, etc. It would form part of a series of "profiles" of different countries worldwide. We signed a contract, and I began writing the book; my first ever. Several months later, still in San Juan, I received a letter from a Leon King, informing me that he had recently joined Praeger, and had "inherited" my book from the previous editor, whose name I don't recall. The book, *"Puerto Rico: A Profile"* was published in late 1970 or 1971. It was around then that I first met Leon face to face. Praeger at the time was located on Fourth Avenue in New York's Greenwich Village. I think our first meeting was at the nearby Cedar Tavern, a popular spot for many writers and artists, and we met there a number of times afterwards. Leon was a fascinating fellow. His father, an African-American lawyer from Philadelphia, had moved to France early in the 20th century, and met and married a white French woman from a prominent family. Leon was born, and resembled his dark-skinned father. When Leon was about six years old, his parents died in an automobile accident. Leon, the orphan, received a classical education in France, thanks to his maternal grandmother. Some years later, Leon moved to Canada to pursue university studies. He then moved to the Midwestern U.S., became involved in the publishing world, and eventually moved to New York City, where he joined Praeger and became my editor. Leon spoke both fluent French and English, and also was quite proficient in Spanish since he had spent part of his childhood in Spain. Thus began a three-decade relationship, which blossomed into a close friendship. Leon, 10 years my senior, in some ways became my older (and only) brother. We met frequently, and he also became a good friend of my wife Olga.

I become a stamp collector!

After finishing the book *"Puerto Rico: A Profile"* I was so hyper from all that intense work that I found it hard to relax. One day while driving through Santurce (a borough of San Juan) I spotted a tiny store that had a sign saying *"Sellos Para Collecionistas"* ("Stamps For Collectors"). For some reason I parked, went in and met Don Carlos, a Spaniard in his 60s, who had lived in Cuba and came to Puerto Rico after the Castro Revolution. He was a friendly man who owned the shop. I had collected postage stamp as a young child, and for some strange reason I decided to take on the hobby as an adult. I bought a few stamps from him, as well as an album, and a catalogue that lists stamps and their current value. Working with the stamps tended to calm me down after the hectic work schedule to complete the book. This time I decided to take a more sophisticated approach and decided to collect the earliest stamps from all nations worldwide. While living in the US later on, I even attended a few rare stamp auctions in New York. As I learned more, I bought more rare stamps that grew in value over the years. This led to my writing a book, *"Paper Gold: How to Make Money and Hedge Against Inflation by Investing in Postage Stamps,"* published in 1976. In the 1990s, my interest in stamps waned, I delivered my collection to an auction house and was pleased when it sold for several thousand dollars.

May 4, 1970. Letter to Kal from Dad. Dear Kal: I got your two photostatic copies and congratulate you for the fine writing you are doing, and for the honor the Overseas Press Club has bestowed on you. I know you are capable of further good, creative work, and this will come in time. I received some back social security money; and enclosed please find check with which you might get a gift for Olga for Mother's Day, and something for the children and yourself. I do pray that all of you are in good health; that you continue to prosper in your work; that Olga is content; that Maria and David are blessings to you and Olga. Do not overwork. Be relaxed. There is little "to prove" except to be at peace. Love to all, *Harold*

April 1970. Covering Culebra for the NY Times. Another fond memory is the time I traveled to the tiny island offshore municipality of Culebra, 22 miles from Puerto Rico's east coast, which at the time had about 900 inhabitants. For decades, Culebra had been partly occupied by the US Navy, which owned one third of the island's 10 square miles, carried out Naval-Marine maneuvers, including aerial bombardments, and maintained a small base. When the Navy sought to evict the islanders and expand its operation, the locals refused, and mounted a protest, led by Mayor Ramón Feliciano, who said Culebra had a promising future as a tourism destination if the Navy was gone. On March 15, the people of Culebra voted for the Navy to leave. This seemed like a natural for *The N.Y. Times*, so I went to the Isla Grande airport, reserved a seat on a small plane and was flown to Culebra, just a short flight away. Other than the pilot, my only companion was a fellow passenger, who held next to him a cage of pigeons! When we reached the Culebra airport, my fellow passenger got out, placed the cage on the ground, opened it, and to my astonishment the pigeons flew away. The man then explained to me that these were carrier pigeons, and he was conducting an experiment to see if they returned home safely to the main island of Puerto Rico!

Not long afterwards, I booked a room in a tiny guest house and began to wander about Dewey, the island's town. While there, I met a young American couple who told me they swam in the local waters, trapped occasional tropical fish, and shipped them north to a store in the USA that paid them enough to continue their idyllic life. The island's only factory breeded bacteria-free rats for scientific laboratories and employed 40 persons. During a protest rally that I attended, a handful of folks seemed to be on the verge of violence. The Mayor calmed them down, saying: "We want the Navy to leave, but let us remember, a daughter of Culebra is married to one of the young Navy sailors."

Note: The people of Culebra continued to press the issue and finally, by 1975, the US Navy had transferred its operations to neighboring Vieques island, where it had a much large presence, and later became a target for more protests. Today, Culebra has about 1,800 residents, and there is a small, thriving tourism industry.

On June 30, 1970, I wrote to Dr. Henry J. Gomberg, Director of the Puerto Rico Nuclear Center, explaining that "a combination of rather unexpected circumstances makes it necessary for me to resign from PRNC, and to request a terminal leave, beginning Aug. 1, 1970." I explained that Olga graduated with honors from Inter-American University and received a letter from the State University of New York at Buffalo, "which not only granted her entrance to their graduate program, but also offered a quite generous fellowship stipend, to teach in their new Puerto Rican Studies Program...Although I have not yet investigated employment situations for myself in Buffalo, our needs have now been substantially reduced, and I plan to make the move. We expect that we will be in Buffalo for about three years." I have fond memories of my two years at the PRNC, earning decent money, and dealing with a group of brilliant, eccentric scientists.

July 22, 1970. *From Elwood M. Wardlow, Office of the Managing Editor, Buffalo Evenings News.* Dear Mr. Wagenheim: As time goes by, it becomes increasingly likely that we will have interesting openings—and are looking ahead to seeing you in that regard.

BUFFALO DAYS

Aug. 1970: We moved with family to Buffalo NY, where my wife Olga, who graduated with her B.A. from Inter-American University, began graduate studies at State Univ. of NY. Thanks to a referral/recommendation by Irv Horowitz, Assistant National News Editor at the *NY Times*, I was able to find work as a reporter and rewrite editor for *The Buffalo Evening News,* the city's largest daily. I had free time, so I also began graduate studies in American Studies at SUNY-Buffalo (I didn't have a bachelor's degree, but they admitted me to the graduate program on the basis of "life experience.") My first book, *"Puerto Rico: A Profile"*, was published by Praeger Publishers (hardcover) and Washington Square Press (paperback) of NYC. As a thesis for the SUNY graduate program, I also researched a book *"A Survey of Puerto Ricans On the U.S. Mainland,"* based largely on a detailed analysis of census data. The Erie County Library was excellent and facilitated our research. The trip to Buffalo was quite memorable. We flew up with our children, David and Maria (then about 8 and 7, respectively), Olga's teen-age sister Norma, and our tiny cat, Chiquita. We shipped our auto, a tiny Anglia, and drove from New Jersey to Buffalo. For the first week or so, while looking for permanent housing, we stayed at a "colorful" place called The Sundown Motel, which should have been called The Rundown Motel. Soon we were fortunate to find a reasonably priced house (about $15,000 or $18,000) at 358 Minnesota Ave, a quiet working class neighborhood a short walk from the SUNY campus. The neighbors were friendly, and little David and Maria soon found nearby playmates their age. It was August, and we thought to ourselves, "hey, this isn't bad." Little did we know that Buffalo winters were....memorable!

Soon after arriving, I went to a used car dealer and decided to change my small Anglia for a more spacious car. I saw a big 1968 Pontiac, decided to buy it, and asked the dealer what he might give me for the Anglia. He looked it over, opened the hood, his eyes widened, and he yelled to his partner, "Hey, Charlie, c'mere!" I wondered what was up. He pointed inside and said, "This car ain't got no heater!" It never occurred to me, living in tropical Puerto Rico, that the car did—or did not—have a heater. "That's okay," Charlie said, "we can sell it to some college kid!" So now I had a big Pontiac.

Now we were fine. The cost of living in Buffalo was quite reasonable. Food prices in particular were low, given the many farms in the region. My salary at the Buffalo Evening News wasn't bad, and Olga earned something as a graduate assistant, studying at SUNY, and also teaching part-time.

Olga adds some good details: "I had graduated with honors from Inter American University, which in turn had granted a graduate scholarship to attend any school in the U.S. of my choice. Pedro Juan Soto, who had then been hired to teach Latin American Literature at the newly created Puerto Rican Studies Dept. at SUNY-Buffalo encouraged me to apply to that institution. I did and was quickly accepted by SUNY Buffalo's History Dept, and given a T.A. line at the PRSD by its director Francisco Pabon. With the graduate fellowship from IAU and the T.A. line from PRSD I had enough economic support to pursue a graduate degree up to the Ph.D. The T.A. line required me to teach one course per semester at the PRSD. I was one of seven TAs from Puerto Rico and New York City some of whom are still my friends. Among the best known of that group was the great poet Pedro Pietri. Although Suny-Buffalo proved to be a fine university, with a wonderful research library, Kal and I could not wait to leave Buffalo. In Buffalo Kal and I unearthed a lot of documents on Puerto Rican history and began to edit them (later published as *The Puerto Ricans: A Documentary History,* which was meant as a companion to Kal's book, *Puerto Rico: A Profile,* being published that year by Praeger)."

"I'm not dead!"

One vivid memory of my time at the *Buffalo Evening News*. In late 1970 or early 1971, I was sitting at my desk in the City Room when the phone rang. The reporter next to me picked it up, listened for a moment, then said "we'll fix it...I said, we'll fix it!" He shook his head, hung up the phone and chuckled.

"What's up?" I asked.

"Some guy just called, all upset. Say's he's not dead!"

"What?"

"He says his name appeared in today's obituary section, but he's not dead, and he sounded scared shitless!"

My coworker flipped through that day's paper, scanned the obit section, and pointed. It said that so-and-so (I don't recall his name) had died and that the funeral was being held at the Magaddino Memorial Chapel, a funeral home in nearby Niagara Falls. The funeral home was owned by Stefano Maggadino (1891-1974), a notorious mobster, the boss of the Buffalo crime family in Western New York, and a charter member of Charles "Lucky" Luciano's Mafia Commission. *(Don Stefano had his share of enemies and survived several assassination attempts. In 1936, rival gangsters tried to kill him with a bomb, and killed his sister instead. In 1958, someone tossed a hand grenade through a kitchen window, which failed to explode. He outlived most of his rivals, and died of heart attack on July 19, 1974 at age 82.)* Was the death notice a simple mistake? Or was it don Stefano's "subtle" way of warning the guy away from something? We'll never know, but it certainly made for an "interesting" episode that day.

Some days at the *Buffalo Evening News* we were extremely busy. Other days, there were a few hours of "dead time" and we fiddled around at our typewriters to amuse ourselves, tapping out silly stories, to be hidden from Bud Wacker, the City Editor, and distributed among our Inner Circle. Below is an example of my contribution to the fun, referring to a small town nearby:

"State police at Athol Springs reported today that 'things are very quiet.' This makes the 1,396th day in a row that nothing has happened at Athol Springs.'"

And another: "Buffalo's Indonesian community will celebrate the Year of the Bore, with a long yawn at midnight."

And another: Twas the day before Christmas and all through the News,

not a person was stirring, they were groggy from booze. There in the corner, his nose all aglow, Ray Hill was composing an ode to the snow.

And another: Hysteria, a radical, anti-pollution group, picketed the White House today, demanding a federal ruling that all pencils be imprinted with: "Warning, this pencil contains lead."

Aug. 19, 1970. From Dad to Kal. Dear Kal: I got your postcards and when I got your letter I was elated to hear that in one swoop you got yourself a job, a place for the family and most of all that you were quite spirited about the whole thing. I believe this will be the beginning for a bright future for you,

Olga and David and Maria...Enclosed are several items which you no doubt will find stimulating, although I presume you cover a number of newspapers and magazine in connection with your work...I am still involved with the trials and tribulations of a lower plate. I came from a dentist a few days ago and all he can say is: You must learn to live with it. In the meantime, he files the plate, I try wearing the darn thing, and wind up with sores on my gum...I accept the situation until such time when I have gotten rid of the adjustment period. Otherwise I still check my sugar level with the doctor and after several months it has lowered...I have been trying to get research assignments, but so far no luck. I seek out leads in the newspapers where I feel someone might want such a service. Possibly, I am trying too hard to get work...I pray the children make a good adjustment to school, and fine expert teachers. As for Olga, I pray she gets suitable situations in her studies. And for you, the same in your work and in your family life. Remember what I said in a previous letter...there is nothing to prove but to be at peace with yourself, to build and maintain a family life. Oh yes, a good, healthy sense of humor...Love... Harold...

Sept. 16, 1970. From Kal in Buffalo NY to Dad in LA. Dear Dad: All is well here. Olga starts studying and teaching this week, the kids are in school, and since Aug. 15 I have been busy with my job at the *Buffalo Evening News,* which is a pretty good paper, and has thus far treated me well. I enclose a few clips of my work...Am also especially busy this week because I am preparing the index for my book on Puerto Rico, which appears in December, God willing. Am also working on the next issue of *Caribbean Review* quarterly, and have also registered for some graduate level courses at the university, but I won't have to attend classes. They've accepted me in their master's degree program in American Studies, on the basis of research and field work, with the end product in a couple of years to be the equivalent of a thesis. Must go now. Hope you're well, and hope to hear from you soon. We send you all our love, Kal

Sept. 23, 1970. ***Article in the Buffalo Evening News. 'Valley of the Dials': The Plot Rings a Bell. By Kal Wagenheim.*** Quick now, what do Frank Sinatra, Charlie Brown, Richard Burton, Enrico Caruso and John J. Zywinski have in common? They're all in the new 1970-71 edition of the Buffalo Metropolitan Area Telephone Directory, that's what. Starting this week, 450,000 copies of the hefty, 1548-page best-seller will be distributed in the area to phone subscribers...If you're a celebrity hunter, you'll be pleased to know that Buffalo has a Garbo, a Gable, an Einstein and eight Huntleys and five Brinkleys. Literary fans who enjoy browsing will find a James Joyce, a Jack London, a James Baldwin, a Hemingway, and a Shakespeare. Presidents? Look up Abraham Lincoln, George Washington, J. F. Kennedy and L.B. Johnson. There are also six Trumans, and six Agnews (not a Spiro among them). (Local politicians are harder to find. No residential numbers are listed for Mayor Sedita or County Executive Tutuska.) If you like sports, wet your thumb and look for Tyrus Cobb, George Ruth, J. Dempsey, John L Sullivan, J. Louis, a Dimaggio, a Mantle, a Graziano, and (for you old timers) a Tinker, an Evers, and a Chance. Children will find a Hansel but, alas, no Gretel. There are also Blacks, Whites, Grays, Greens, Browns, a Redd, and even a Mr. Pink. There is a Mr. Sharp and a Mr. Blunt. A few Apples, and Pears, a Mr. Peachey, and a Mr. Plumb. You'll find no Sun, but at least one Starr and 14 Moons. Four Uppers and a Lower, plus a Meek, a Strong, and a Wild. A More and Less. A Chan, a Holmes and a James Bond. If you enjoy the book, just wait until they make the movie!

Oct. 27, 1970. Handwritten letter from Dad to Kal. Dear Kal: Enclosed a couple of dollars for the children for Halloween goodies. I dislike kids going out on "trick or treat." We had some unfortunate situations out here last year when youngsters were given drugged apples, etc. by sadistic minded people. Too sad such things go on. I know you and Olga will supervise closely, or make festivities an indoor affair. I am about the same. Am looking for research assignments where I can work at a library, and avoid pressures such as I worked under for the county. Do write when you get the chance. Take things in stride. Give my love to all: Olga, Maria and David. Love, your dad, *Harold*

Jan. 18, 1971. Praeger publishes my first book, *"Puerto Rico: A Profile."* (My second book, an anthology of historical writings on Puerto Rico, contracted with Praeger, is scheduled for 1972 publication.)

Feb. 19, 1971: *I wrote many, many articles for The Buffalo Evening News in the brief time there. One of my favorite moments was a brief interview with a then-young but already famous musical director. A small excerpt from my article follows:* "Michael Tilson Thomas came to Buffalo today to sign a memorandum of agreement and confirm his coming next season as musical director of the Buffalo Philharmonic. He appeared in black bell bottoms, an Edwardian corduroy jacket, light blue glasses with silver frames, a burgundy shirt and a tie blending lavender with electric blue. Tall and thin, with a generous shock of black hair, he looked very much like the recent national magazine description of him: 'Like a big bird, impersonating an adolescent.' He also came with a soft-spoken good humor, cracking jokes as the photographers snapped away in the green carpeted, wood-paneled room of the Philharmonic House, 26 Richmond Ave..The young director said 'I am interested in music, period.' Among his extra-curricular favorites are James Brown, the Rolling Stones, early blues, and—leaping several light years in time and geography—Asiatic music ."

March 12, 1971. From Kal to Dad: Dear Dad: We here are OK, and are just recovering from a flu that was going around. I missed a couple days' work, but am back in action now…the winter weather is loosening up, which is a relief. Two weeks ago I was invited to Syracuse U. to speak about my book before a Puerto Rican Studies group. I spoke for 10 minutes and spent 2 ½ hours answering questions. It was fun. The publisher has now given me a verbal commitment to go ahead with a second book—this one to be an anthology of historical writings on Puerto Rico, covering from the discovery in 1493 up to today. I guess it will take me 9 months to 1 year to finish it. So I'm on my way to my second book, and I enjoy doing it. Olga may finish her M.A. at the end of the summer and our plans are indefinite. She may want to continue studying here, or perhaps take a job at the university here, or perhaps we'll even move into New York City for a while, where she could work with some Puerto Rican Studies program at one of the universities, and, as for me, I'm sure that job opportunities wouldn't be lacking…will make a decision this summer. Must go now. We all send our love, Your son…*Kal*

April 26, 1971. *From Kal to Dad:* Dear Dad: Time flies…sorry I haven't written sooner…Spring season seems to be arriving at last, although we've had a few minor snow flurries this week, last little gasps of winter. My time's filled to bursting with the job at the newspaper and my extra-curricular work on a second book…an anthology of historical documents about Puerto Rico. I spend much time at the library, reading through old magazine articles and newsclips, Xeroxing some, editing them down, etc. Olga is busy with her studies and with teaching her class to seven Puerto Rican girls here, and is very proud because the girls organized a convention of Puerto Rican young women from different part of the Eastern Seaboard. The convention this past weekend was quite a success. The children are fine, and looking forward to the warmer weather since they are already tired of viewing TV. Me, too, because on the few warm days I've enjoyed trying my very amateurish hand at gardening—flowers and a few vegetables—but the frost has made it tough to work the ground. We've done a bit of traveling the past few months...I spoke about my book at Syracuse University in Feb. On May 8 we go back to Syracuse, as observers this time, of another conference on Puerto Rican affaris. We also went to Toronto, a marvelous city just 90 miles away, during March and we hope to go there again in May. We also flew down to NY City (Olga and I, expenses paid) for a job interview at Lehman College up in the Bronx, where it seems that Olga may get a good job offer ($12,000 a year), although this is not for sure. My own job plans aren't yet clear...we're quite comfortable here for the time being. Our eventual career plans will—I'm sure—draw us to New York-New Jersey and later probably to Puerto Rico. In the meantime, Buffalo is quite tolerable, except for the overabundance of snow. Must go...with love from all of us...Kal

May 4, 1971. From Dad to Kal. Dear Kal: Thanks for your letter of April 26 and bringing me up-to-date. I am very happy to hear that you are taking "little vacations". This is as it should be. Tell Olga I wish her a very happy Mother's Day, and many, many years of peace, serenity, prosperity, good health and productivity. As for the second book you are working on, I was down at the library, sort of browsing, and came up with a couple of references which you will find enclosed, together with an item from The Wall Street Journal. Things are about the same with me...I am still trying to get into real activity. I guess I am impatient, so will take things in stride, until things open up. Thanks for the invitation to visit. Right now, must take one things at a time, and in due time, all things will work out. Give my love to Olga, Maria, David and keep well. Don't push too hard. Really, as I have said in the past: There is really nothing to prove except to be at peace and have closeness...Love, Harold...

June 3, 1971. To Dad from Kal. Dear Dad: Am just now able to answer your May 4 letter. First,thank you for sending along the library material for my anthology. I am moving along steadily on it, stealing a few spare hours here and there, and I think I'll have it done by year's end, as planned. The first book appears to be doing well, according to the publisher. They say it's sold about 5,000 and they hope for another spurt this summer, if and when orders come in for schools which may use it this fall. Life here proceeds smoothly enough. My job at *The News* is not exactly challenging, but is pleasant enough, and pays the bills. Olga will probably complete her required classwork for the M.A. degree by the end of June. She seems to have been bitten by the author's bug, too, and this July, together with a girlfriend/classmate, and with our children, will probably fly to Puerto Rico for 3 or 4 weeks, to research an anthology on Puerto Rican women. This will also give her a good opportunity to visit her sister and father…in fact, the kiddies will probably stay on their grandpa's farm for part of the time, while Olga toils away in the university library. In the meantime, during July I will continue working here, but I may take 1 week and go into New York City to see family, friends and also explore the possibility of work. We are still undecided about what to do this fall… Olga has been given a tentative teaching job at Lehman College in the Upper Bronx, working with a Puerto Rican Studies Program. Tentative, because it depends upon final budget considerations at the school. The job pays well, $12,000. But we still aren't sure what we'll do if the offer is confirmed… the decision should be forthcoming this month. If we don't take the Bronx offer, we'll probably stay here at least 1 yr longer, and then think about either relocating to the NYC area, or back to Puerto Rico. Buffalo has turned out to be a nice, friendly enough town, "comfortable" in the sense that a heavy, old overstuffed easy chair is comfortable, and in that sense I prefer it to the hustle-bustle of New York City. On the other hand, the winters here are long and confining, and we have no real "roots" here in the sense of old friends or relatives…so I can't see any long-term commitment. However, if things proceed as they have, I shall look back on Buffalo as a pleasant interlude. For one thing, it's given me the opportunity to plant a small vegetable garden in the spacious yard behind the house. If we're lucky late this summer, we'll be chewing on our own tomatoes, cucumbers, onions, radishes and carrots. Since I don't know one leaf from another, I have had to label the rows of seedlings in order to know what is growing where! This, of course, amuses Olga, whose father is a life-long farmer. I've often dreamt of being able, some day, to have you come to Puerto Rico for a visit…I don't know if you'd like it on a permanent basis, because its takes some adjusting, but having you come out to the countryside, to visit Olga's father on their small farm, would be a marvelous experience. He is a fine man, a modest man, with little formal education, speaks no English, but he is deeply religious, very kind, and has a dignity which I greatly admire. We get along very well, and I think you would, too. Matter of fact, you might even be able to teach him a thing or two about chickens and eggs… Must go now, Dad. I'm at the office and must attend to a few assignments. Oh, by the way, we took the children to Toronto (90 miles north) for their birthday last weekend and they greatly enjoyed it It's a marvelous city, with a good blend of old and new, all in good taste, and planned with…imagination. It is very civilized in the best sense of the word… if it weren't for the winters, I would seriously consider staying there. But those winters! Brrrrrr. We all send you our love. Your son, *Kal*

June 22, 1971. From Kal to Dad: Dear Dad: And a belated, but happy, father's day to you! Thanx for your letter…today am quite busy, but I did want to say hello to you and send our love and warm regards. I'll write again soon, with more details. It's at least 50-50 that we'll be moving to the NYC area. Love, Kal, Olga, the kiddies PS and thanx for the clippings…they make good reading.

The Circus Scandal

July 1, 1971. *Perhaps the biggest, most controversial story I wrote for the Buffalo Evening News fell right into my lap when a troubled, guilt-ridden college student walked into our office and got me started. After interviewing him and several other contacts, I wrote a story that caused a big uproar. A brief excerpt follows…*

"Headline: Badge & Shield Circus to Raise Little Money for Police Programs."

"The Badge & Shield Club has sold thousands of dollars worth or tickets for a circus in August, with proceeds advertised as going for 'drug abuse prevention and law enforcement scholarships.' It was learned, however, that up to 75 percent of the funds donated will go to the circus, to fund-raising salesmen, and to cover operating expenses. The club, an association of Erie County Sheriff's Department employees…has refused to register with the Better Business Bureau of Western New York, a BBB official said Tuesday...A local college student who worked for four weeks as a phone solicitor…calls it 'an unbelievable operation'…after my 15 percent, and the 5 per cent for those who to out to collect the checks, and the sales manager's commission, and what goes to the circus, there's not much left to fight drug abuse or anything,' he said."

July 14, 1971. The *Buffalo Evening News* and I were sued by the Rudy Brothers Circus for the article that appeared on July 1, claiming it was "false and defamatory," and seeking $2 million in damages. On Oct. 7, the plaintiffs agreed to dismiss the lawsuit after refusing to testify in court as to the details of the case.

July 27, 1971. *Handwritten note to myself on small piece of paper.* "Life continues to be a great mystery--& all I know is that it feels good to be kind to people."

Sept. 1, 1971. Letter from Dad to Kal. Dear Kal: Pardon this long lapse in writing...I want to thank you and Olga for the check you sent for Father's Day...a word of explanation for the time lapse; I mentioned to you in the past that I was going to have a check-up. I had not felt well. What was supposed to be a week or 10 days, turned into a month (July 9-Aug. 7). It was pretty rough and after I came out started a convalescence. I am feeling better... but extensive traveling would be out of the question. The past two weeks has been spent going to the library, taking long walks, and beginning to feel my old self. No worrying, now. I am well and looking for research work again. Don't worry. I have been very fortunate. I watch my diet, exercise, and my attitude has changed for the better. How are things going? What are the plans for work for Olga and yourself. And the children? I spoke with Charlie lately. He is well and so is Lil. I hear from home, and as with aged people there are aches and pains. Do keep well...By the way, each year I have to fill out forms for renewing my public assistance. I spent Saturday and today on most of the questions...Now, Kal, I spoke with my case worker this morning (Monday) and explained that I might not get a reply from you within a week. The questionnaire must be in by next Monday. She said not to worry, that if I don't get a reply in time, to put down some word of explanation to the series of questions. Remember, the above questions and statements are addressed to me; I am to get information from you and fill in this part...Let's try to write more often. Again, I am well and eager to do something to get rid of the boredom. Keep well, busy, and my best of everything to all of you. Love... Harold.

Remember The Corn Boil!

One day in early September 1971, at the *Buffalo Evening News,* fellow reporter Ray Hill whispered an invitation to a few of his buddies. Prior to joining the Buffalo newspaper, Ray had worked at a major daily in Toronto, Canada (about 90 miles away) and kept up his contacts there. Each Fall, the bigwigs at Toronto City Hall invited lots of folks, including journalists, to a "Corn Boil," a party featuring lots of drinks and, of course, just harvested corn. Ray was invited to the 10th Great Annual Corn Boil, and he spread the word that the big event was scheduled for Sept. 9, 1971. The problem: how could we all escape from our jobs to attend? We cooked up a plan. Each of us would separately tell Bud Wacker, our City Editor, that we had an appointment that afternoon to interview someone for a feature story. So, about five of us (including Ray, Lee Coppola and me) invented an excuse to be absent. On the morning of September 9, we were all in the office, quietly giggling, and winking, like young schoolkids about to play hooky. Our plan: to leave the office a few minutes apart, around noon, then gather in the parking lot and drive up to Toronto to the fabulous Corn Boil! We couldn't wait! Around 10:30 that morning, the phone rang in the City Room. One of our reporters, Bob Buyer, a quiet, bespectacled fellow who specialized in reporting on the price of farm crops in rural New York, was on the line. He informed us that a riot had broken out in the Attica Prison, roughly 40 miles east of Buffalo, where about 1,000 of the 2,200 inmates had seized control, taking nearly three dozen hostages. Suddenly, everyone on *The News* staff was involved. I stayed pinned to the phone, gathering details, typing away. Three of the reporters ran outside, jumped into cars, and headed up to Attica, to cover a story that would capture national—and world—headlines for days. At the end of that first day of the Attica riot, a few of us sat in a bar near *The News* office, sipping drinks, puffing on cigarettes and cigars, trying to relax after a very stressful day. We were thankful that the riot had erupted at 10:30 a.m., and not two hours later. Had it been later, five of us would have been driving in a car up to Toronto, to attend The Corn Boil. All attempts to reach us (there were no cellphones then) would have been fruitless. By the end of the day, there is a good chance we would all have been fired for being AWOL!

After four days of tense negotiations, Governor Nelson Rockefeller ordered state police to take back control of the prison. When the uprising was over, at least 39 people were dead, including ten corrections officers and civilian employees. *Note: several days later, it was found that while the rioting prisoners had been holding the officers and employees with knives, these hostages were actually killed by gunshot wounds, the result of careless shooting by the state police. At first, angry City Editor Bud Wacker, refused to acknowledge this possibility, but when a trusted medical examiner confirmed the causes of death, he allowed The News to print the results.*

Some time later, when I left *The News*, to live in New Jersey and take a job in Manhattan, the guys at the paper gave me a little going away party. At the end of the party, they handed me a gift which I will always cherish. A ballpoint pen mounted on a beautiful black base, and a gold plate inscribed: "REMEMBER THE CORN BOIL." How can I ever forget it?

Sept. 29, 1971. Letter to Dad from Kal (in Buffalo). Dear Dad: It was, as always, a pleasure talking with you tonight. As I mentioned on the phone, it is almost 99% certain that I will be co-author (with 3 other journalists) of a book about the Attica prison riots. Scott Meredith Literary Agency told me today that already two publishers have offered a $5,000 advance for the hardbound—but he's trying to hold out for more. Split 4 ways that doesn't add up to much, but if the book comes out half as good as our concept of it, it will be eminently satisfying ... and I think readers will respond with more sales, to boost the financial reward. One problem is that we will have to do the book in about a month's time, and will have to focus almost exclusively on the riot itself. If you have the time, could you look through the NY Times Index and other sources, back thru American history, and find brief sketches of other important prison riots? And then send me Xeroxed copies? I'm sure we could weave this into our narrative to give it some historical perspective. Also, if you happen to run across some old book (in the public domain) which gives a good first person narrative of prison life (about 500 words), of say 50, 75 or 100 years ago, that would be useful as a counterpoint to a 1st person narrative that we plan to use of a present day Attica prisoner. Don't feel pressed on this project. If you don't feel well, don't be concerned...whatever you come up with...will be useful.

I'm enclosing a check which I'd planned to send some time ago, for you, and also to cover any Xerox or mailing costs for material you might dig up. Assuming that we get the book published...more $$$ will be forthcoming for all concerned...Keep well, and remember whenever you feel up to the trip we'd love to see you. You son, *Kal*

(Note for the above: The deal on the Attica book fell through. When another publisher announced that N.Y. Times reporter Tom Wicker, who was involved in the negotiations during the riot, had been hired to do a book, our

publishers backed out. Wicker wrote a fine book, "A Time To Die," published in 1975. Our book could have been completed and released well before that, and I think that both would have been successful, but our publishers seemed unwilling to take the risk.)

Another phone call: EPA gets us out of Buffalo

Some time around Sept. 1971 (I don't recall the exact date), while still living in Buffalo, I received a phone call from a complete stranger, Bob Jacobson, head of public affairs for the U.S. Environmental Protection Agency (EPA) regional office in New York City. Bob explained that Region II covered not only New York and New Jersey, but also Puerto Rico and the U.S. Virgin Islands. He needed an assistant to help him with press relations in Puerto Rico who was familiar with the language and culture there. I was puzzled that he should call me. Bob explained that he had first called my good pal Joel Magruder, a journalist living in Puerto Rico who was deeply involved in environmental affairs, and offered him the job. Joel, married to Teresa Ortiz de Magruder, with three young daughters, said he did not want to leave Puerto Rico, but he knew someone (me!) who might also be interested in the job. So Bob offered, I expressed interest, and soon we prepared to move south so that I could take the job in lower Manhattan. I shall always be grateful to President Richard Nixon who (despite his other flaws) was responsible for creating the Environmental Protection Agency, officially inaugurated in December 1970.

Oct.25, 1971. Handwritten letter from Dad to Kal. Dear Kal: Enclosed find 'trick or treat' money for Maria and David, and, of course, you and Olga. I must remind you we have had sad experiences out here with tricking and treating. Sadistic givers have doctored the treats, so take care...Love to all, your dad, *Harold*

Nov. 19, 1971 Handwritten letter from Dad to Olga: Dear Olga: Enclosed are letters for Maria and David...I would like to know the birthdates of Maria and David as well as school grade each is in. Kal informs me of the possibility of moving to New York City. If so, my best to all of you. I hope you are keeping busy but not overworking. With best wishes for good health and happness, and with love, I am...Harold PS. Also Kal's birthdates and yours.

Nov. 19, 1971. Handwritten letter from Dad to our daughter Maria (age 8)

Dear Maria: I feel very good at receiving your letter. I do hope you had a happy Halloween as well as David and all your friends. You write a nice letter, and I know in time you will enjoy writing more and more. With best wishes for good health and happiness, and with love, I am, your grandfather, Harold

Nov. 19, 1971. Handwritten letter from Dad to Kal. Dear Kal...I try keeping occupied with reading,walking, and continuing to send out letters for research assignments. To date, no responses. I did enjoy researching for you. I do hope if you move to NYC you and Olga will find rewarding work and the children compatible situations. Their letter writing is beautiful. Best of health and closeness to all of you and a Happy Thanksgiving. Love, Harold

Dec. 3, 1971: Handwritten letter from Dad to Kal. Dear Kal: I hope you and the family are settled by now. Enclosed clipping was sent to me by my cousin Charlie. He feels that you better hurry with your book. He must think your work might be suitable for the movies. However, since Schulberg will be shooting in P.R. and NYC, you might look into the matter. Anthony Quinn will be doing *"Children of Sanchez."* This has been talked about for some time. If it's your pleasure I will try to keep you informed of both projects. Being consultant on a film is not a bad job. Give my love to Maria, David and Olga. Good health and joy to all. Love, your dad, Harold. Note: attached a check and note ("Christmas cheer for the family") plus clipping from *Hollywood Reporter*, Nov. 26, 71, p. 3, noting that Schulberg has completed a screenplay of his novel "Sanctuary V" and met with prospective agents on another project he has had in the works dealing with the Puerto Rican situation here and in Puerto Rico. He has been working with Elia Kazan on the project.

Dec. 7, 1971. From Kal in Buffalo NY to Dad in LA. Dear Dad: Thanks for sending along the clip about Bud Schulberg doing a film treatment on Puerto Rico. I knew about this, because he is adapting Oscar Lewis' book *La Vida* (the National Book Award winner) and I met him and Kazan very briefly in Puerto Rico before I came here. Schulberg already had some adequate advisors, I think, so I don't know if I'd fit in very well. I have lost touch with Schulberg, and it was news to hear that Tony Quinn is doing *Children of Sanchez*. By all means, yes, I'd love to get clips from you if there are new developments. Now I have news for you. I have been offered a job as public affairs officer with the Environmental Protection Agency of the federal government, with offices in downtown New York City. That salary is a good jump from what I'm making, and the work can't possibly be worse than what I'm doing with this newspaper. We will probably be in New York by Dec. 27. I will head down one week before that to look for a house. You can write to us here, as long as the letter arrives before Xmas Day. The interesting part of the job is that the NYC regional office of this agency covers New York, New Jersey and Puerto Rico. They hired me because I am bi-lingual and they anticipate some work with the Puerto Rican communities in NYC, and on the island, which may mean a nice business trip or two back to the island. After my first year at the new job I'll take stock, see if I really like it. If not, I'll have a number of contacts in NYC, perhaps in publishing. Olga has already received a couple of job offers with Puerto Rican educational agencies in NYC. So it looks quite promising. Main problem now is to sell our house here, and find a comfy place to stay down there, but as usual I'm an optimist. As for my Puerto Rico book, I expect to have it all done sometime in January, and will then move on to other ideas. Must go now. Please give my regards to Cousin Charlie. I'd love to see him. Perhaps once we're in NYC we can manage a trip west. Love from all of us…keep well, your son.

BACK IN NEW JOISEY

Dec. 1971. Tired of two terrible snowy winters, we decide to leave Buffalo. Olga completed an M.A. in History and can pursue a Ph.D. at Rutgers in New Jersey.

Finding the house: another "happy accident."

Through a realtor in Buffalo, who put up our house for sale, I was referred to a realtor in New Jersey. I drove down by myself, while Olga got ready for the move. I was shown a house in Union NJ, with an asking price of about $42,000. I was in a hurry, so I gave him a deposit of several hundred dollars, offered $40,000 and figured that would be acceptable. The realtor said the owner was in the hospital, and he would relay my offer. I would hear back in a couple of days. While waiting, for some strange reason, I decided to drive to Maplewood, where, I recall years earlier Morris Greenberg (the husband of my grandma's cousin Dora) owned a small supermarket, and it sounded like a lovely town. I had never been there. I arrived in the center of the small town, picked up the *Star-Ledger* at the corner candy store, walked half a block to the local coffee shop, The Maple Leaf, sat at the counter, ordered coffee and opened the paper to scan the real estate section. After a few minutes I spotted a small ad, offering a house in Maplewood for $40,000. It said the realtor was "W. Klein." I asked the lady behind the counter where the W. Klein realty office was. She pointed and said "right next door." Fate? After gulping down my coffee, I went to the realtor and a nice woman there took me all of three blocks to a large corner house at 52 Maple Ave. It was right across from the Maplewood Middle School From the large front porch, one could see the nearby golf course of the Maplewood Country Club. One block away was the Maplewood Public Library, and two blocks away was the train station which connected with Hoboken, and the PATH station to New York, where I had landed a job! And, in the front yard was a huge, huge tree, with a trunk at least four or five feet wide! I fell in love with the place, and put a small deposit on the house. I now "owned" three houses: the one in Buffalo, the one in Union, and now the one in Maplewood! I called Olga, all excited, and told her about the house in Maplewood. "How's the kitchen" asked ever-sensible Olga. "Kitchen?" I replied. "I think it has a kitchen." Well, now I had to tell the realtor in Union. I called him and he said the owner wanted $42,000. "I'm sorry," I said, "I won't pay a cent over $40,000." After a pause, he said, "Have you seen another house?" "Yes," I said. "Where?" he asked. "In Maplewood." "Maplewood?" "Yes, and there is a good train connection to my office in New York, better than the one in Union." Then, since he didn't know that I was originally from New Jersey, he said, "You know that Maplewood is really close to Irvington." "And?" "They're coming over the hill." He was referring to the growing African-American population in nearby Irvington. I played dumb and asked, "Who's coming over the hill?" "You know! "No I don't!"

"Look, there are certain things I can't say over the phone...in Union, we have a few of them, but they all live in one neighborhood, that's it." "I'm sorry. I've decided to stick to the place in Maplewood. Please return my deposit." So a few days later, I got my deposit back, and focused on Maplewood.. Thanks to the GI Bill, I had to pay only $1,000 down. We would remain at that house for more than three decades, until Aug. 2003. It all started thanks to Morris Greenberg, who lured me to Maplewood.

The US Environmental Protection Agency

In early 1972, I began my new job with the U.S. Environmental Protection Agency. My routine: Each weekday morning I walked three blocks from our new house to the Maplewood NJ train station. The train took me through Newark and the Oranges to Hoboken NJ. There, I took the PATH under the Hudson River to the World Train Center. From the WTC, it was a few minutes walk to 26 Federal Plaza, the Federal Building, where the Region II office of US-EPA was based. Bob Jacobson was head of Public Affairs, and I worked as his assistant. There were several really nice coworkers. The days passed pleasantly. At the end of each day, together with Bob Jacobson we would hurry out of the office, take the PATH to Hoboken, and most days grab the 5:35 pm. express train, which dropped me off in Maplewood at 6 pm. Bob continued on for a few minutes to his home base in Summit NJ.

January 1972: Olga recalls: "Unsure as to which school to apply to, I looked for and found a part-time teaching job. I was hired by Rutgers-Newark, thanks in part to the efforts of Maria Canino, Maria De Castro Blake and Hilda Hidalgo, three women who would become my mentors and dear friends from that date onward. All three of them were employed at Rutgers and had much clout. Hilda, whose course (Puerto Rican Life Styles) I was to take over, recommended me to Dr. Norman Washburn, Chair of the Sociology Dept. I met Hilda and Maria Blake thanks to Maria Canino, whom I had met in April of 1971 when she attended a Conference on the Puerto Rican Woman I and several others had organized during my stay at Suny-Buffalo. Maria Canino was then the Director of the Puerto Rican Studies Dept. at Rutgers New Brunswick. We had remained in contact ever since the conference. The idea for the conference was born out of a course on the Puerto Rican Woman I and Gloria Isabel Rodriguez were teaching as part of our T.A. work at the PRSD. The persons most instrumental in securing funds and publicizing the conference were the seven women taking the course, chiefly among them Carmen (Margie) Santiago and Noemi Velazquez, both of whom became dear friends and collaborators with me in another of my community ventures."

March 8, 1972. From Kal to Dad: Dear Dad: Thanks for sending along the batch of news clippings; you could run a very fine clipping service if you could ever develop a few clients! Work here goes pretty well, and the weather is improving. Olga and the kids flew to Puerto Rico last night (Tuesday); she will speak at a conference on Puerto Rican Women Wed. night at the Bar Association Auditorium. Unfortunately, I'll miss it, but on Friday night I fly down and we'll spend the weekend together. She returns here on Monday and I stay on for 3-4 days to perform a few chores for EPA, such as editing a bulky report on garbage problems in Puerto Rico. Such is modern life! ... Uncle Nat and Aunt Bess were here for dinner a couple of weeks ago, and we hope to get together again soon, this time with their son Bill...Bill seems to have made quite a success with his business, and it's nice to know that one can get a discount on a TV set from a relative! Must go. Am at the office and trying to wind up many details before the trip. Keep well....Love from all, your son, *Kal*

July 3, 1972. To Dad from Kal. Dear Dad: I'm glad you called me the other day…We are doing well, keeping busy, particularly with our new house, which we enjoy a great deal, but demands lots of attention. After all these years I've finally met Nat's son, Bill, who has a large electronics appliance store in downtown Newark. He seems like a wonderful person. Next Sunday, we plan to invite him over for dinner with his wife Shirley, and I'm hoping that Bess & Nat will be able to make it, too. Have you been able to inquire further about library work on a part-time basis? I am confident that you are more than equipped for such work and I think that if you make inquiries you might find some library whose needs are compatible with your goals. Please pursue this—I have a feeling it will pay off…Love from Olga and me, and your grandchildren …*Kal*

July 1972: Olga is hired as the Assistant to the Director of the EOF (Equal Opportunity Fund) program by the Dean of Arts and Sciences at Rutgers-Newark. She recalls: "In that program I became aware of the great need there was in the areas of education and curriculum development. I was instrumental in securing credits for preparatory courses minority and other poorly prepared students were asked to take as part of the fequirements of being accepted by the university. I had worked briefly in a similar program at Suny-Buffalo. As Kal and the children began to grow roots in Maplewood, I decided to relinquish the job offer I had at Inter American and to start looking into graduate schools for the Ph.D. program. In the process I learned that as a staff member of Rutgers I could apply, and if accepted, would not have to pay tuition at the New Brunswick campus. I applied to both the Depts. of Education and History at that campus because of my work at the EOF program. I was accepted to both programs and had a sleepless week trying to decide which road to take. Eventually I chose the history program and began attending graduate school part-time in Sept. of 1973."

Aug. 19, 1972. After many years, I am reunited with Rose Hoffman, my grandma's psychic cousin. It happened in a typical offbeat way. One Sunday, we received a phone call from Dora Greenberg, my grandmother's cousin, who lived nearby. She explained that they were on their way out to attend a wedding when suddenly Rose Hoffman appeared at their door; she took a bus all the way to NJ from Brooklyn. Dora asked if we could come pick up Rose, and I was delighted! We brought her to our house, and one of the first things she asked was "Have you ever found your sister?" When I said "not yet," she said "you will!" We called her "Cousin Rosie." On this day I gave Rosie a copy of my book, "Puerto Rico: A Profile" and signed it: "To my dear relative, 'Rose Hoffman, on the day of our reunion. May there be many in the future. Love, Kalman."

Oct. 23, 1972. Review in Publishers Weekly. *CUENTOS: An Anthology of Short Stories from Puerto Rico. Edited and with a preface by Kal Wagenheim.* Schocken. $3.95. Hardcover $9.50. Six Puerto Rican writers display very distinct styles and rhythms in this refreshing collection of 12 stories. A variety of settings and time frames make the selections delightfully unpredictable. In Emilio S. Belaval's "Monsona Quintana's Purple Child" the author's tone is direct yet gentle as he depicts a mother's desperate attempt to keep her sickly child—her 17th—alive. In contrast is the fast, free, first-person narrative of "The Night We Became People Again" by José Luis González. A man tells of the night of his first child's birth, when a blackout trapped the anxious father in Manhattan subway. Humor, pathos, poverty and courage are just a few of the recurrent elements in the volume. The English translation of each story appears on the page facing the original Spanish. (*December*)

Oct. 24, 1972 to Dad from Kal: Dear Dad: How are you? Enclosed a little check for you to buy some goodies with. We here are well. The fall colors in Maplewood are gorgeous, and we are enjoying our house, and the season, immensely. As usual, however, we're busy with all sorts of work. We've been seeing Nat & Bess occasionally, and more of their son Bill & his family, and we enjoy our get-togethers. Wish you were able to visit, and join us. My job goes well, although I still can't enjoy commuting very much. I have a project pending which is too premature to discuss, but if I'm lucky I may get a large study-grant which will take me off in another direction for a couple of years, starting next year. I'll keep you informed when there is concrete news. Love from all... Your son, *Kal*

ANOTHER PHONE CALL: CLEMENTE!

Dec. 31,1972: Olga and I were in Puerto Rico, on vacation, visiting her family. On New Year's Eve, Roberto Clemente, the 38-year-old baseball superstar of the Pittsburgh Pirates, got into a small plane at San Juan airport, which was loaded down with goods to relieve earthquake victims in Managua, Nicaragua. The plane took off, and plunged into the deep ocean off Puerto Rico's north coast. Clemente's body was never recovered.

Tuesday, Jan. 2, 1973 was the inauguration of Governor Rafael Hernández-Colón. I attended the ceremony, on the steps of the Capitol Building, facing the ocean where Clemente's plane had disappeared. It was a sad day. Olga and I returned to our home in Maplewood NJ a few days later.

On Friday, Jan. 5, 1973 the phone rang. It was my good friend Leon King, from Praeger Publishers, which had published my book *"Puerto Rico: A Profile"* and *"The Puerto Ricans: A Documentary History"* compiled and co-edited by my wife Olga and me. He invited me to lunch.

On Monday, Jan. 8, 1973 we met for lunch at El Quijote, a restaurant on W. 23rd St. in Manhattan, and Leon surprised me, saying that if I could write a quick biography of Roberto Clemente, he could obtain a good advance for me.

"How quick?" I asked.

"If you could deliver the manuscript in three months, we would beat out any competition, and it could be quite successful." He offered me a generous advance of several thousand dollars.

I asked for a day to reply. I had to check with my boss, Bob Jacobson, at the Environmental Protection Agency, where for the past year I was employed full-time.

I met with Bob, who was also a friend, and explained my dilemma. Bob said: "Look, I'm a baseball fan. Go ahead and write the book. I'll give you a six month leave of absence, and your job will be waiting for you when you come back."

I signed the contract with Praeger dated Jan. 23, 1973. It specified that I would deliver a 240-page book, due no later than April 30, 1973. I would receive $6,250 on signing the agreement, $3,125 on acceptance of half of the manuscript, and $3,125 on acceptance of the completed manuscript. I had only three months (about 12 weeks) to deliver a book, which seemed impossible! I decided that without some kind of structure, I would go crazy. My strategy: I would spend half the time (6 weeks) researching the book and half (6 weeks) to writing it. First, I did some newspaper research, to determine who were the key people in Clemente's life. I then set about to interview them with a tape recorder. I began with Clemente's elderly mother, moved on to his Little League coach, then his Pittsburgh Pirates teammates, his doctor, and some fans and friends. Since I was interviewing them so soon after Clemente's tragic death, they poured out their grief to me, with moving accounts of their time with their beloved Roberto. After six weeks of research, involving trips to Puerto Rico, to the Pirates spring training camp in Florida, and to Pittsburgh for opening day of the baseball season, I headed home and went up to my office in the attic, and began typing on my trusty Underwood manual typewriter. I kept a diary notebook (which I still have), detailing all my trips and interviews.

1973: *"The Puerto Ricans: A Documentary History,"* edited by Kal Wagenheim, with Olga Jimenez de Wagenheim" published by Praeger, NYC. Described as "an essential sourcebook" in *The New York Times*.

March 1973: Dear Dad: Sorry I haven't written sooner but, as you can imagine, the Clemente book has kept me hopping. It's an 80,000-word project and the deadline is short, have to deliver the ms. by end of April. However, I've set a rigorous schedule for myself of 2,000 rough draft words per day, and am ahead of my schedule thus far, with about 50,000 first draft words already accounted for. In late February I spent 2 weeks in Puerto Rico, mainly tape recording interviews; in March I spent one week at Bradenton, Florida, interviewing members of the Pirates team. From April 3-6, I'll be in Pittsburgh, gathering data there, and seeing the opening game of the 1973 season. So it's been a hectic time, but a very enjoyable one. I thrive on work that I like to do. Olga is well, and teaching one class and studying for her doctorate. Next year she won't have to teach and can study full-time because she has been awarded a very prestigious Ford Foundation Fellowship, and we're all very proud of her. David and Maria are fine, as is Norma, up at the University of Buffalo. We see quite a bit of Nat's son Bill and his wife Shirley…we go to movies or eat out every so often and enjoy each other a great deal. Tomorrow p.m. Bill is busy, so I'll be going to Newark Airport to pick up Nat and Bess as they return from their Florida vacation. Must go now. Thanks for the clippings about Roberto Clemente. There were a good anecdotes that will be most helpful. The book is expected to be out in September, and you can be assured of a signed copy. Love from all, *Kal*

April 3-6, 1973. With more than 50,000 words completed, I fly to Pittsburgh for the opening day of the 1973 baseball season and remain a three days.

April 12, 1973. Notebook says "goal: 58,000 words" (I have reached 68,475 words).

April 27, 1973. Notebook says "goal 80,000 words" (I have completed the book with 94,275 words, including a 1,000 word introduction, and deliver two double-spaced typewritten copies by the April 30, 1973 deadline)..

My biography of Babe Ruth

Praeger was mainly a textbook publisher, but, encouraged by the sales of *Clemente!* it decided to venture into the trade book world. Leon King, my editor, invited me to meet him and a senior editor (whose name escapes me) at Bradley's Jazz Club on University Place in Greenwich Village. Over drinks, they said they'd like me to write another baseball biography and invited my suggestions. A few days later, after a bit of research, I suggested a biography of Babe Ruth. Why? Because Hank Aaron was closing in on the Babe's record of 714 career home runs. And. the last book about the Babe was in 1948, when sportswriter Bob Considine collaborated with him on *The Babe Ruth Story.* I presented the idea, and Praeger signed me up.

June 27, 1973. I signed a contract with Praeger linking together both the Clemente book and a new project, a biography of Babe Ruth, that would be about 288 pages. This time, Praeger agreed to pay me $30,000, of which

$12,500 was an advance, and remainder to be paid upon signing the contract, $4,375 upon delivery of the first half of the manuscript, and $4,375 upon payment of the complete manuscript. I was given until March 30, 1974 to deliver the Babe Ruth manuscript.

Initial sales of *"Clemente!"* were strong, and reviews were favorable. For example, *Publishers Weekly* said: "Wagenheim, author of two books about Puerto Rico and ex-ballplayer-sportswriter…is the right man to perform the essentially serious task of bringing the real Roberto Clemente close to the many fans who misunderstood his intense self-pride as arrogance during his magnificent major league career. Wagenheim's glimpses of the boy Roberto growing up in the town of Carolina in Puerto Rico to play in his late teens with stars such as Willie Mays are fresh and revealing…A final chapter on Clemente's last days and his death last New Year's Eve flying aid to Managua's quake victims is moving indeed."

July 9, 1973. Letter to Robert Jacobson, Director, Public Affairs, EPA, Region II, 26 Federal Plaza, Rm 908, New York NY. "Dear Bob: This is to confirm my conversation with you earlier this month. As you know I was granted a 6-month leave of absence from EPA (from Feb. 7, 1973 through Aug. 7, 1973) in order to write a biography of Roberto Clemente. An opportunity has arisen for an even larger book project, and I wish to submit my resignation, effective Aug. 7, 1973…I can say most sincerely that it's been a real pleasure working with you, with Jerry Hansler, and with everyone else in the agency. My sole reason for leaving is that it has always been my personal ambition to become an independent, free-lance writer and the opportunity offered me proved irresistible. Best of luck to all of you in the 'good fight' that EPA is waging to clean up the environment. If, in the future, there is anything I might be able to do for EPA on a free-lance basis, be assured that I'm interested. Cordially, Kal"

1973. Clemente. A biography of the first Latino Hall of Fame baseball star. *American Library Association Selection as One of the Best Books of the Year for Young Readers. "The classic stuff of sports tragedy, the athlete dying young...the man beyond the ball field," Roger Kahn, The Chicago Tribune. Available on-line from E-Reads.com and in paperback from Olmstead Books/ LPC Group.*

July 1973. At some point around this time I went to the Office of Baseball in New York City and met with Monte Irvin, a former major league star who worked there. I knew that many old-time ballplayers attended games and were honored. I asked him if he had contact information for players who knew Babe Ruth. He was kind enough to look through his records and was very helpful. Thanks to Mr. Irvin, I was able to get in touch with Jumpin' Joe Dugan and Whitey Whitt who played with Ruth in the 1920s, Harry Hooper, captain of the Boston Red Sox when Ruth began his major league careeer. Later, on my own, I reached Marshall Hunt, who was a reporter for the *NY Daily News* during Ruth's career and who often traveled with him. I gathered a lot of information about Babe Ruth at libraries in Boston, Newark and Baltimore, but my tape recorded interviews with these men, provided fresh, often highly entertaining, perspectives.

FINDING FAMILY

"Kalman, I've been meaning to tell you this for a long time...you have a sister."

I was 24 in 1959, when my grandmother gave me the stunning news. From early childhood on, I was told that my Mom--her name was Rozlon--had died of an illness, when she was 22, and I was just two years old. My Dad, Harold, who suffered from severe depression, had separated from my Mom and lived with his parents; I was raised by my grandmother (I called her Nanny) and great-grandmother (I called her Grandma). When I asked Nanny where my sister was, all she could tell me was that a childless Jewish couple in Newark had adopted her. A year later, both Grandma (age 92) and Nanny (age 67) were dead. I was alone, with no memory of a mother or father. Not long after their deaths, I moved to Puerto Rico and spent 10 years there, often wondering about her. When Olga and our children moved to New Jersey in 1971, I still thought about my missing sister, but didn't know where to start, and believed it would be an impossible task. Finally in August 1973, after delivering a book to my publisher, I had some spare time. I asked Aunt Lucille, my late Mom's only sibling, where her older sister Rozlon had died. "In the city hospital in Newark," she said. I went to the Martland Hospital Unit on Tuesday, August 21, 1973, explained that my mother had died there many years earlier, but gave birth to a little girl who was adopted. They said they had no records, but to try the Adoption Bureau of the Essex County Hall of Records, a few blocks away.

I entered the building, was directed to Room 213, and told the lady I was trying to find a sister, born in 1937. She said that normally a court order was required to obtain this information, but since so many years had passed, she pulled out a large ledger, written in ink, turned the pages, pointed, and said that a "Dolores Wagenheim" had been adopted, and her name changed to June Lydia Goldman. Her adopted father, Louis Goldman, age 37 at the time, was a schoolteacher at Central High in Newark, and the mother, Frances, age 28 ,was a housewife. They resided at 261 Clinton Place in Newark's Weequahic section, perhaps two minutes away from Beth Israel Hospital, where I was born, and a 15-minute bus ride from 510 Belmont Avenue, where I was raised. The written record made note of an "Essex County Orphans Court", and a "Benjamin L. Winfield, Executive Director of the Jewish Children's Home of Newark." My sister was born on May 30, 1937, and our mother died of a hemorrhage the following day. It is not clear whether the newborn girl remained in the hospital, or at the Children's Home in Newark during the two weeks between her birth and when the Goldman's took her home on June 13, 1937. The formal adoption papers were signed April 13, 1938, when June was nearly a year old.

I was so excited to obtain this information that from a payphone in the lobby I called nearby Central High (733-6897). It was summer vacation, but a Mrs. Celiano answered. I asked about Louis Goldman. Miraculously, she told me she remembered "Lou" fondly, that he had retired some years ago, and had a cute little adopted daughter. "I think she lives up in Massachusetts or Connecticut," she said. I rushed home and called the New Jersey Department of Education in Trenton to see if they had a record of Louis Goldman, who might be receiving a retirement pension. They told me to write a letter. I did, to a Mrs. Severino, Division of Pensions, PO Box 2058, Trenton NJ 08625, expecting it would take forever.

In just one week, I was surprised to get a reply saying "Please be advised that Mr. Goldman died in February 1961, and our files are closed for him. G. Severino." The next day I went to the Newark Public Library, and searched for February 1961 obituaries in old editions of the *Newark Evening News*. One brief death notice said: "Goldman, Louis, of 366 Leslie St. Newark, on Feb. 2, 1961. Husband of Frances, father of Mrs. June Stern, brother of Mrs. Sadie Davis, Mrs. Anna Suskind, Mrs. Louis Krasner, and Charles Goldman. Services at Bernheim Funeral Home, 357 Chancellor Ave. Burial at McLellan St. Cemetery, Newark." A longer obituary said he had been an English teacher at Central High School, died of a heart attack at home, age 59. Born in Austria, he came to the U.S. in 1906, graduated from Central High, and CCNY, and did graduate work at NYU. He taught Hebrew at Temple Bnai Jeshrun for many years, was a member of the Tri-Lumina Lodge, F&AM Israel Verein of Newark, and the Newark Education Association. Surviving him were his wife, Mrs. Frances Sandler Goldman, a daughter June Stern of Cambridge, Mass., a brother, Charles of Melbourne, Fla., sisters Sadie Davis of South Orange NJ, Mrs. Anna Suskind of Hillside, NJ and Mrs. Louis Krasner of Newark NJ. He had been active in community affairs, as well as teaching. It said he had a daughter, June Stern (her married name) living in Mass. He also had 2 sisters living in nearby New Jersey towns.

Although it was 12 years after Mr. Goldman's death, I decided to try my luck, contacting one of his relatives in New Jersey. In the phone directory I found a Milton Suskind, residing at 611 Buchanan St. in Hillside NJ. Tel: 688-8962. I dialed and the call was answered by Mrs. Anna Suskind, Mr. Goldman's sister. When I explained the reason for my call, she surprised me when she said she knew who I was. I told her I was anxious to contact my sister, who, according to the obituary of 1961, was residing up in Massachusetts. "You don't have to go that far," she said, explaining that a few years ago June had moved to Metuchen NJ, just 30 minutes from my home in Maplewood, and gave me the number (201-548-3732).

On Monday, Sept. 10, 1973, after some hesitation, I picked up the phone and called her. She knew she had been adopted, but was never told she had a brother! Twenty-three years later, while vacationing together with my sister and her family in Cape May NJ, I tape recorded the following recollection of that momentous day.

June: "I had just come from school. You said 'hi, this is Kal Wagenheim.' You sounded very nice. You asked 'does the name Wagenheim mean anything to you?' And it did! I had heard the name like in whispered conversations over the years, not to my face. So I said 'go on.' I thought you were going to tell me you were a long-lost relative."

Kal: "Then what did I say?"

June: "You started very gradually, to tell me, well...the whole story. I remember I started out in the kitchen and ended up, with the phone, in the dining room. When you said 'I'm your brother,' I was really shocked. Complete shock."

Kal: "I had the advantage over you. I had known for years that..."

June: "Then you asked 'when can I see you?' It was a Monday, and I said Thursday. I had to digest it. I had to call my mother. I went through the next few days in a daze. I went to work. I called and said 'Mom, I got this phone call from a Kal Wagenheim.' 'Oh yes,' she said. 'We always knew, and we meant to…'"

Kal: "Did they say when they were planning to someday tell you?"

June: "Before they died. (Laughter) When you first called, I felt a little distance. I thought, 'he lives in Maplewood.' I thought you were like another Jewish relative from the suburbs. You know what I mean…"

Kal: "I was a little worried, too…"

June: "A Jewish princess from the Weequahic section…"

Kal: "I said to Olga, 'Some brothers and sisters don't get along…"

June: "But the minute I saw…it all dissolved."

Four days later, on the afternoon of Thurs., Sept. 13, I drove to June's apartment at 265 Newman St. in Metuchen, and met her and her son Lowell (then nine), and daughter Rebecca (then five).

Kal: "The night I came over, I brought a family photo album, which included a photo of our maternal grandmother, Lillian (Nanny), as a young woman. I recall how your eyes widened with astonishment as you stared at that photo."

June: "There was an amazing resemblance between us... We sat for a long, long time. And when I said to Becky and Lowell 'this is Uncle Kal' they acted like nothing had happened!"

Kal: (laughs). "The same with my kids!"

I had grown up on Belmont Avenue in Newark, and attended South Side High. June grew up about a 10-minute auto ride south-westward, and attended Weequahic High, our arch-rival in sports. I later spent two years studying at Newark-Rutgers; she attended Douglas College, a branch of Rutgers in New Brunswick. During college years, I had worked part-time at the *Newark Star-Ledger* morning daily, and she had worked a few blocks away at the *Newark Evening News* afternoon daily.

It seems I arrived at an opportune time. June's husband Larry, a college philosophy professor, six months earlier had separated from the family. June was now on her own, beginning a teaching career, and raising two young children. For months after we first met, June and I talked constantly on the phone, and almost every Sunday we visited at each other's home, connecting with relatives and friends.

June: "My God, the first time I walked in to your home, people said 'she looks just like Lillian.' It was so amazing that a granddaughter could resemble the grandmother."

Another memorable moment was a Sunday when June came to our house in Maplewood with her children, and a few minutes later her step-mother, Frances, arrived. From my taped reminiscence:

Kal: "She walks into the living room, pulls out a photo from her purse, and shows me a picture of this handsome young man with dark hair, and asks me 'do you know who this is?' I didn't have a clue. 'It's your father, Harold. I used to go out with your father.'"

June: "I heard that she was very much in love with Harold. But his mother paid a visit to Frances' mother and said 'my son has a lot of problems; he cannot see your daughter any more.' So they broke it off."

Kal: "So a few years later Frances winds up adopting her former boyfriend's little daughter!"

And then, there was the memorable trip to the Spiritualist church in Hoboken NJ, in May 1974. My wife Olga, through one of her students, had learned of a fascinating Spiritualist church run by a Puerto Rican man, Reverend Sepulveda. We had attended a few sessions, and enjoyed the wholesome, loving environment. We wanted to include June in all aspects of our life, and invited her to come with us one evening. From our tape recorded reminiscence:

Kal: "Do you remember the time we went to see the Spiritualists on Willow Street, in Hoboken? It was shortly before Mother's Day."

June: "Yes. We went up the stairs of a brownstone building and sat in the living room. With all the chairs around. Everyone was Hispanic. There was the older man, the Reverend. And the younger one, he came right over to me and said 'I see two mothers around you, in your aura.' Can you believe that?"

Kal: "Then I recall they invited you to return, because they were going to bring in an English-speaking medium...a guy from the Caribbean. From what you told us later, this guy sat with you in a darkened room upstairs, with other people there. And he asked you, 'do you ever smell flowers in your bedroom when you're going to sleep, and you feel very sad?' And you said 'yes'..."

June: "I remember now...."

Kal: "And he said not to worry, or feel frightened, 'it's just your mother's spirit; she feels regret that she was never able to hold you in her arms.' I recall we were in the car driving away from Hoboken and you remarked, 'I feel like a big burden has been lifted from my shoulders.'"

June: "Yes...they were wonderful, caring people. It was a very searching time in a person's life...that age...35!"

In the ensuing years June and I were amazed at the power of genes. For example, during one of our first visits to a seaside restaurant in Cape May NJ, we both scanned the menu, looked up at each other, and decided on: "crab cakes"! June is an accomplished poet; we learned that my Mom also wrote poetry. June worked for years as a Special Education Teacher in Metuchen. Our Dad was also a teacher. I, too, taught for more than three decades at Columbia University. Following in my Dad's footsteps, I also wrote plays and screenplays.

Six years after we reconnected, on Dec. 22, 1979, June married a wonderful guy, Ed Logue, a music teacher in Metuchen NJ. The joyous wedding reception was held at our house in Maplewood, and they have been together ever since. Ed's three children from a previous marriage (sons Eddie and Jesse, and daughter Effin) have also become part of our family. They are wonderful.

June's son Lowell on Aug. 12, 1989 married Juleen Savarese and they have two boys: Benjamin and Nicholas. Lowell, a lawyer, works with the U.S. Justice Dept. and they live in Arlington, Virginia. Her daughter Becky on Aug. 14, 1994 married Michael McElreath, who is now a college professor. They live in Carrboro, North Carolina and have a son, Caleb; they later adopted Ana, a lovely little girl from Guatemala.

Since 1973, June and I and our families have had a close, loving relationship. For years after we met, each August, we would spend time together in Cape May NJ, where the children (June's, Ed's and ours) bonded and became good friends.

Another time I tape recorded a three-some: my wife Olga, June, and me. It was fun recalling how our children bonded.

Olga: I remember Lowell and David in the back seat of the car, telling all those jokes, competing. We assigned them one joke each.

June: Lowell remembered the whole Monty Python routine.

KW: David could remember an entire show of All In The Family. I'd ask him, so why can't you remember your school work like that? (Laughs)

Thinking back to my early childhood, I recall how at least once a year --it could have been some anniversary—Nanny and Grandma would take me on the bus to visit my mother's grave in the Jewish cemetery off South Orange Ave., in Newark. As a man recited prayers in Hebrew, I would stare at the modest gravestone which had Hebrew lettering and then, in English, read: "Wife and Dear Mother, Rozlon Wagenheim. Died May 31, 1937. Age 22 Years." Nanny and Grandma would stand there and cry, and cry, and cry. Now, in retrospect, I believe they were weeping not only over the loss of my mother, but over their remorse, having been unable to raise the little girl born at the time. If there is a Heaven (and I suspect there is), those two wonderful ladies--and our parents--must now be looking down, smiling, over this happy ending to a tragic beginning.

Shortly after we met, June wrote this poem, which she gave to me, hand-written:

Upon Discovery of a Brother
1973

The game is up,
the time has come
Now we know
where I am from
and my real name.
I liked not knowing who I was,
I could be from anyplace.
I could be anyone.Who needs the "Identity Crisis"
now, full-blown
long past the time of leaving home.
The story, of course
was pure tragedy;
orphaned you, foundling me;
death, betrayal; an agony
I, the foundling, found a father,
and a husband; had a son,
even an analyst.
Learned to name, one by one,
my own dark sides.
Now comes a brother,
sprung, full-grown,

tall, heroic,
You were there all along.
What to make of this?
My Platonic missing half,
At last, a mirrored self?
I never was a sister
I do not know myself
in this role.
If I could throw
away like a ball,
the childhood I spent alone,
I would; and begin again,
whole, not rent;
innocent.

And I, without knowing that June was writing a poem, also wrote one…

Dolores…

Sister, (a thrilling sound
for unpracticed lips to savor):
would it be so sweet now,
would you be sister-mother-child
to me had not our sun been quenched
so long ago, leaving us in darkness?
No. But nevertheless,
I miss
the time of
rough-and-tumble frolic
that veils young sibling love.
Sharing the sun
as we skip and run beneath
Rozlon's radiant eyes.
The milestones, yours and
mine: flickering birthday lights,
beribboned parchments,
wedding bands, solemn vows
to write or call.

I miss
not having missed you then.
I miss
not being when Lowell
and Rebecca came to be.
Three wars, famines, storms,
a billion people dead and born.
One-third a century's laughter,
tears, murmurs, tranquil
shared silences.
Thirty-six voyages around
this earth, solitary voyagers we,
two specks on a vast uncaring globe,
shared blood coursing on
separate uncrossed paths. Now
I look,
throat aching,
into those gentle
eyes—so familiar—and
glance away for fear
I'll cry aloud just how much
I miss. I miss.
-- October 1973

KW: Did your father feel uncomfortable over the fact that you were adopted?

June: I think he may have, at the beginning. As soon as there was a child in the house, he was a like a maniac. He really doted on children. His nieces and nephews. I know he was crazy about them. He became wrapped up. The fact that I was adopted never came up. They gave me as a little child a book about The Chosen Baby. My cousins would talk to me about it sometimes. When they came over. Arlene. "You know that you are..." I never got uncomfortable. I always felt better off than they! There was a lot of sickness in their families. They didn't have as much materially. We didn't either, but we had more...I was treated well to a certain degree. I had piano lessons, nice clothes.

I knew without a doubt that I was going to college. Most of my friends commuted to Rutgers Newark, or NYU. He got into his head that I should go to Douglas, because Janet, his brother Charlie's daughter Janet, went to Douglas. My mother thought, for a girl, that was awful. But I finally got there. He used to walk around, and say, look at this, it's like a country club. It was so pretty.

KW: He mustve been thrilled. You were fulfilling a dream that he had for himself.

June: I had mixed feelings. No, in the middle. I wasn't crazy about it. So made a little attempt to go home. I went to visit my friends at Rutgers Newark. They gathered around me and said, what are you crazy? You want to come here? My father was very unhappy that I was considering leaving. So then I returned, and I won a poetry contest, and the last day of school they came to take me home, and I was crying, and I loved it. I graduated in '59. Then we got married. I think the best thing we ever did for him (my father) was, we were married in August, and that following summer, he came to visit us on a bus, by himself, in Cambridge, and we took him to the Royal Shakespeare, Henry the Fifth, and we took him to a lot of parties, with graduate students, we took him to Lexington & Concord, because he thought that anything to do with American history and New England, and the whole thing, he loved. We moved to Boston in Aug. '59. Larry was in grad school at Harvard. I was looking for a job. And I worked in an office. Then I worked at the Harvard Library.

KW: Is that when you got fired? (laughs) That's so funny, when I tell people my sister got fired, for reading in a library!

June: Yes. I worked there 30 years ago. "We won't be needing your services any more." I was reading old cartoons from *The New Yorker*. It was fascinating. I worked at the *Newark News* while in college. I graduated from high school in January '55. I went to college the following September, so I needed a job. I got a job in downtown Newark near the Essex House in a public relations office. Doing the dittoing, xeroxing. The guy was a great boss. And he was sending stuff to the newspapers. Jefferson Lyons. Became after that a big executive with Blue Cross. He arranged that I should deliver stuff by hand to the Newark News. Press releases. A big envelope. I would go on the bus. All I had to do was see that city room, somehow he arranged that I write a Sunday column about the YMCA. I loved that. It was a terrific thrill. Through him, he told me they needed a copy girl for the summer at the *News*. I worked there other summers, pretty much for the four years. It was a full-time job. They let me do a review of a French movie. My job was the timetables for the theatres. It was fantastic. First I had to get coffee for everybody. And carry the copy. The people were wonderful. Then, that's probably how I got a part time job at Dartmouth with the press bureau. We were in Boston for 5 years. My father died the second year, while I was already teaching. Becky was born in May of '68. And we moved here in '69. Larry didn't get tenure. It wasn't that unusual at Dartmouth. The five year deal. And jobs were plentiful then. He had a pretty wide range of offers. One was in Detroit. One was at Temple, in Philadelphia. There were some others....

KW: And what did Frances remember about Harold Wagenheim?

June: Just this dance that they went to. Good-looking, poetry reading, he liked poetry, he read poetry out loud, his voice was very...this romantic thing. He must've been very attractive to women... Frances was in love, love, love. She was very young, and went to the Y. The love of her life. Then the mother came to see my grandmother. This is the story I got. Harold's mother. She came to visit Ruth and said, your daughter shouldn't see my son, because he's got a lot of problems.

KW: I didn't know that the mother came.

June: Perhaps the story was embellished. I remember hearing the story that the mother paid a visit and said we're going to break this off with the children. My son has problems. He cannot see your daughter any more. She was 16, or 18.

Sept. 13,1973, letter from Kal to his father. Dear Dad: I have some startling news for you; news that has given me a great deal of joy, and I want to share it with you.

Last night, I met and spoke with my sister. We talked for hours. My head is still swimming with thoughts. The whole idea of discovering a sister after all these years is so outrageously wonderful that I really don't know what to make of it, except to feel very, very happy. She is a lovely person. We hit it off well, and I think we'll be seeing lots of each other from now on. How I found her is quite a complicated tale. Until I was in my twenties, I assumed that I was an only child. But then my grandmother told me that when mother died a little girl was born and was adopted by a Jewish couple in Newark. That was all. Once I knew that somewhere in this world I had a sister, the urge to know her became irresistible. Finally, early this month, I began a serious search.

At the hall of records in Newark, I learned of the adoption by a Louis and Frances Goldman, he a teacher at Central High School. I also learned that he died in February 1961. But in the newspaper obituary, I found the names of his sisters, and one of them led me to my sister, your daughter. Her married name is June Lydia Stern. Her husband teaches philosophy at a university in New York City. She has a master's degree and teaches in an elementary school in New Jersey. She has two beautiful children, a boy, Lowell, and a girl, Rebecca. I called her earlier this week, and went to see her last night. It was a marvelous time for the both of us. She, naturally, was full of questions about her mother, about you, about the rest of the family. I tried as best I could to bring her up to date on the whereabouts of the family. I know that all of this must come as quite an emotional shock to you. But June, your daughter felt (and I agreed) that she would like you to know where she is, and that (in the wake of the tragedy so many years ago) it might be of some comfort to you to know that she is well. I can say one thing; she has grown up to be a fine woman and mother. I don't know how you feel about communicating with her—I can understand how complex your thoughts must be at this moment—but she would very much like to hear from you. Her address is: Mrs. June Stern, 265 Newman Street, Metuchen, New Jersey. Her telephone is 201-548-3732. Give it some thought. I know that the idea of contacting her, after all these years, is difficult. But I urge you to consider it. Must go now. We here are all quite well, and quite busy now that school has begun. Have you received the Clemente book that I sent you? Hope so, and hope you like it. I have to go to Pittsburgh on September 28 (publication date) for an autographing party at a big bookstore. Your son, the celebrity! With much love from all, *Kal*"

Connecting with Cousin Bill Wagenheim

All the years I was growing up in Newark I had little or no contact with members of my father's family. At some point, however, around 1971, when Olga and I and the children moved from Buffalo NY to Maplewood NJ, there was a beginning. First I saw my Dad's brother, Nat Wagenheim, and his wife, who lived nearby us, in Union NJ. Then they connected us with Nat's son Bill Wagenheim, his wife Shirley, and their two daughters, Susan and Diane. At the time, Bill—with a partner, Stanley-- owned Parts Unlimited, a thriving store (sale and repair of electronic products) on Washington St. near the corner of Market St. in downtown Newark. We saw each other many times, often in the summer enjoying afternoons at lakes in rural New Jersey. Bill and Stanley sold the building in Newark, and Bill retired. He and Shirley moved to an adult community in central NJ, but later moved up to Delmar NY (near Albany), close to their daughter Susan, and her husband Michael, and two grandchildren. Bill and Shirley have been married for more than half a century. A few years ago, they invited us to a wonderful 50th wedding anniversary celebration at The Nevele, a classic old resort in the Catskills. Bill, born April 7, 1930, is such a wonderful, genuine guy; over the years he's become like an older brother to me.

Bill Wagenheim, my cousin, son of Uncle Nat Wagenheim. Taped phone conversation. Sept. 26, 1997; Bill: My father didn't marry until he was about 35. He always went alone to visit his parents.

KW: You never went to that house?

Bill: He wouldn't take me. My mother wouldn't permit it.

KW: What was the problem?

Bill: She didn't get along with Dora. She didnt get along with Frieda. She didn't get along with the women. My father was the pet of the family. They loved him. I think my mother was very possessive. I think they didn't like my mother, because she could be very aggressive. She provoked a lot of the antagonism.

KW: Your father didn't want to make any trouble, so he went on his own.

Bill: Yeah, my father was that way. A quiet type of guy. Don't make waves. That was the problem I had growing up, with a weak father, and a strong mother. It's cockeyed, its unbalanced.

KW: Neil did say he remembers visiting your house, and you were out playing. But Allan was playing the piano, and your mother would sit on the bench next to him with a handkerchief...

Bill: Crying...

KW: Right. And he said Allan had cats or dogs...

Bill: My father would go out to the back yard on Peshine Avenue and feed the cats. They were wild. I think he brought one in the house. Too bad you couldn't have started a long time ago, when my father was alive. He would have been a fund of information. What do you propose to do with this?

KW: I don't know. I want to put it together for the family. Someday the kids are going to grow up and ask: who did this, and who said that, blah-blah.

B: I thought you were thinking maybe of a Neil Simon play.

KW: Right now, I'm at the point where I just want to fill in a lot of blanks about my own background.

Bill: That's a very good idea.

KW: I know that June is curious. I know that Becky and Lowell are curious. I'm sure that Diane and Susan are curious. I was talking to Lucille the other day. She's 78 years old.

Bill: Is she still lucid?

KW: She doesn't have a good memory, but once in a while some little thing will pop up. Like the other night, I went over there, and suddenly out of nowhere she said she remembered a time when I was a little baby, and my mother sang a funny song to me when she would feed me, and she actually remembered all the lyrics!

Bill: Is that right?

KW: She never told me that before. Lucille was a teenager when my mother died. At some point, when she was feeding me, she would remember the lyrics. I recorded it.

Bill: You went over there with the specific purpose of getting that information.

KW: No. I went over there to visit. Then when I came home, I called her and asked if she would tell it to me again, and I taped it.

Bill: That's really nice that you would have that interest. The fact that you're a journalist makes it even more valuable.

KW: I was asking my Aunt Lucille some basic questions. Like where did they my parents get married. She doesn't know. There's no pictures. Did they get married in a simple ceremony in a house, which is what I think.

Bill: My mother and father had a big wedding in Kruegers Auditorium in Newark.

I think there was a brewery by that name. Kruegers. 1926 or 1927.

KW: Times were better then. When I came along it was the Depression. Neil was telling me his father had a big plumbing business, but he said the business collapsed...

Bill: And he went to work in a factory...Everyone was very poor.

KW: Our grandfather. You never saw him at all.

Bill: I saw him once. Who the hell remembers. I was just a little kid. My mother refused to take me there. I only grew up knowing her mother. On that side. My uncles. Uncle Izzy. Uncle Arthur. They were brought up on Peshine

Avenue. My mother lived on Peshine Avenue. Then we moved four doors down, so I saw my grandmother, and my uncles. I didn't know anything about the other side of the family. It was like they didn't exist. When you're a kid, you don't ask questions.

KW: I don't know of any picture of a wedding. It's amazing. You think, a wedding! Not even a snapshot. Unless it was something people didn't approve of. Maybe they went off and got married with a judge.

Bill: My father never talked about his family, or anybody.

KW: Your brother Allan, years ago, wrote to me, how he had visited my father in California, and saw how fragile he was emotionally. He said he described it in a novel. I wrote to Allan, saying I found his old letter, and that I wonder if he still has that novel, and I would love to read it. To learn what was going at the time. It would give an insight into what my father was like at the time. He was in pretty sad shape, he was very depressed, didnt have any money.

Bill: It seems that people who are disconnected from parents for one reason or another have that insatiable desire to put the pieces together in their lives.

KW: Yeah, I think so. He was a very sad case. The more I learn about it... sometimes people will say to me, oh don't you resent your father because...the more I learn about him, the less I resent him. You can resent someone who for reasons of malice tries to hurt you. But he ...

Bill: Had no control.

KW: He was just a poor soul. The more I see...

Bill: The tragedy of it all is that he was a brilliant man. He had everything. He was a handsome man, too. I had pictures of him.

KW: I see him as a very sad figure. And I feel sorry for him. I don't think he ever did anything out of meanness, or selfishness. He was emotionally unstable.

Bill: That's right. I remember my father used to say that he was not well. My father used to send 5 dollars in an envelope to California.

KW: Have you been in touch with Allan at all?

Bill: I try to call him often...I have the emotional feeling towards him, but I can't share it with him. It was about three months ago we last spoke. He has this intellectual snobbery about him. He can't imagine...He said to me one time that you and I were close, and he asked, what could Kalman have in common with you?

KW: (laughs)

Bill: That is the most insulting thing I ever heard. I said Allan, he may be a lot smarter than I am, but I love the guy, and he cares about me. That's all you need. He doesn't understand that. It doesn't make any sense to him. He's like my mother. My mother adored you if you had something to offer. If you were very personable, if you were an artist, you could write, you were a musician. That you could converse about books, the opera, then she loved you. But a shlub like me, who was uneducated, who played football in the streets, broke windows? I was like the black sheep in the family. He grew up thinking the same thing. He really is a snob. My father wasn't like that.

KW: Just a regular guy.

Bill: My mother wasn't. So only in the latter years, when she became older, and I was more mature, I was able to love her, and forgive her....

KW: (tells Bill about finding June...gets to point, finds phone number)

Bill: Oh, God. I'll bet you didn't dial it right away.

KW: I stopped, and said to Olga, what's if she's some spoiled Weequahic girl? Some snotty JAP (Jewish American Princess)? I hesitated for about an hour or so. It was Monday. Finally, in the evening I called her...

Bill: What did you say?

KW: I explained to her how I found her. I went there on a Thursday. I brought a photo album. She'd never seen anybody in our family. she was a dead ringer for my grandmother. it was amazing. Like twins. Very clear resemblance. About a week later, she brings her mother, you know, she called her her mother, Frances, to our house...we started visiting back and forth, back and forth, and so Frances comes over, and pulls a picture out of her wallet. and she shows me a photo of this handsome guy, with dark hair. she asks, do you know who this is? It's your father. I used to date your father.

Bill: Holy...

KW: Yeah, they were dating before he met my mother. A few years before. My father had had serious emotional problems over the years, and our grandmother said to Frances`mother: it's not good for him to go out with your daughter, or something like that. She mixed in, rightly or wrongly. Frances had saved his picture all these years, she'd had a crush on him. and by sheer chance, my father marries, has a child, and Frances was unable to *have children, something like peritonitis. They'd been married for 7 years, and were looking to adopt a child. and by accident.*

Bill: By accident...her ex-boyfriend's child...

KW: The Jewish community of Newark was like a big small town. Lots of people knew each other, went to the same synagogue...lots went to Bnai Jeshrun on High Street. They used to go to the Y over there, that's where my father directed plays....

Bill: That's fascinating. And you could add to it your son Jeff, for the years in between there was nothing there, and all of a sudden you resumed your relationship. That's a heartwarming thing. People would cry over that! *KW: Me getting together with June and my somehow getting together with Jeff is kinda trying to put the pieces back together. The family was kinda destroyed by my mother's death. The whole thing collapsed. In some ways, either consciously or unconsciously we try to put the pieces back together. ...I got a joke for you. I heard it on the radio. It's so bad it's good. Why doesn't a seagull fly over the bay?*

Bill: Why?

KW: Because if a seagull flew over the bay, that would make it a bagel.

(both laugh)

Bill: I like that dumb stuff. So long bubulluh.

Dec. 3, 1973. Flew to Seattle WA to interview Marshall Hunt for the Babe Ruth biography. Hilarious anecdotes!

Dec. 5, 1973. Flew to Los Angeles, to visit my father, and his cousin, Charles Wagenheim, the actor. Cousin Charlie picked me up in his car. I was 38 years old at the time, and needed eyeglasses for distance, when I drove. But Charlie, age 77, was merrily zipping along in the car, without glasses! He took me for lunch at the The Lobster Barrel, a Hollywood restaurant run by Alan Hale, Jr., his pal who starred in *"Gilligan's Island."*.

Dec. 6, 1973. Traveled to San Jose CA and interviewed Harry Hooper, the elderly, long-retired Boston Red Sox star when Babe Ruth played with Boston. Returned home to New Jersey.

Dec. 11, 1973. From Kal to Charles Wagenheim & his wife Lil after my visit to see them: Dear Lil & Charlie: What a fine sparkling time it was, first at the Lobster Barrel and later at your home. I hope we can do it again sometime. If you do venture east sometime, please be sure to call us at 201-762-1565. My wife and children would love to meet the "Cousin Charlie" that they've seen so often on the screen. As for the pictures by Babe Ruth, he made one picture in 1920 (in New Jersey I believe) and its title was "Headin' Home." Then, in 1927, he made a film in California, titled "Babe Comes Home", a 6-reeler, by First National Pictures, co-starring Anna Q. Nilsson. If you could track down one or both of these, and find out about their availability for possible screening at a later date, I would be most indebted to you. I haven't yet had a chance to talk with my editor about the idea of Charlie's reminiscences of his times with all the Hollywood greats, but as soon as he returns to New York next week I have to have lunch with him and will bring it up. If there's a glimmer of interest, I'll let you know. I, personally, think it could be a real winner, and it could be done "painlessly" with occasional tape recording sessions—I think if we all sat together with the recorder and a big bottle of Scotch the memories would fly fast, furious—and hilarious! Must go now. Warmest greetings of the season to you both from all of us…Love, Kal

March 19, 1974. Drove to Cooperstown, NY to attend the Baseball Hall of Fame ceremony honoring Roberto Clemente. While there, met a number of retired major league stars, who autographed a baseball for me.

About Rose Hoffman: Taped conversation with my sister June, Cape May. 8/19/97:

KW: Your first memories of Cousin Rose. Was she there the first time you came to the house in 1973?

June: There were so many people there...I didn't realize her role in the thing, until a little later on. I was always struck by her elfin quality, her youthfullness, something childlike, elfin...and blue eyes. And I remember her very well in my house and we had a party , a Xmas party, and she talked to Kurt and to us...and at our wedding we had asked her to make a toast, and it was really beautiful. Remember that honey? I thought it was really appropriate, because we were married in your house. What I mostly remember about her, altho I think she's responsible for the whole thing, really, is she was so kind to the children. The sweet fortunes she would tell the little kids. They would take it very seriously. I'm sure she had it....A young couple stole my house plants, and they were found in Englishtown. My plants were stolen from the porch, and they were really gorgeous, I'd spent a lot on them, and that summer the plants had disappeared, and they were stolen by a couple who had taken them to Englishtown.

KW: What did Rosie say to you?

June: She said she saw a man and a woman, with the plants in the car, and they were heading south. (laughter)

She predicted about Larry. Larry is gonna be in Alaska, she said. She met him at a party, one Xmas, and she said I see Alaska. He wound up in Tacoma, Washington. She could pick out places. She had it. Whatever it was. I never believed it before.

KW: She told me that I was going to find you...

June: Before you even...Before the search.

KW: Yeah... That year, I had reconnected with her, the Greenbergs, I was driving with her, and she said, If my brother Moe had met someone like Olga, he wouldn't be dead today. (laughs). Then, she would call me, and say have you found your sister, I know you're gonna find your sister.

June: She felt that I wasn't far away. How would she know that? And the other thing she said, I'll never forget really, your kids and Ed's kids are gonna get along fine. I had no idea what that meant. How serious and important it was. This is before he and I were married. It never occurred me to what an important thing that was, because look at how many families..In fact, its very true. More than most. They're good friends. I always thought that was amazing. It wasn't a conscious concern of mine. It should have been. I just didn't think about it. My kids with you, they were very matter of fact. Lowell, Uncle Kal, Uncle Kal...here's Uncle Kal. Now we have Uncle Kal. Like a given. He just right away. You were like...it was instant. David, I remember... we went on Sunday to your house, first you came, the whole day, it was a big wonderful day. I'm walking to the car, it was time to leave, and David walks me to the car. And David said, "Bye, Aunt June." He's the first person who ever said that.

KW: David loved the idea of a big family, because in Puerto Rico there's a big family.

June: My mother wasn't there the first week. That first Sunday.

KW: That was another Sunday then? When she pulled out of her wallet a picture of Harold Wagenheim?

June: She had that picture, which I never knew about, and she carried it for 40 something years.

KW: Did she know our mother, Rozlon?

June: No. Sylvia did. Sylvia's the same age.

KW: When I first came over to see you that Thursday, you were going to start school...

June: I had started. I started on Monday. I had had Thursday and Friday. Monday was the first Monday of the school year. How I ever started that job, I was in a daze, didn't know what I was doing...new kids, new town, I didn't know one person.

KW: How long had you been there?

June: Five years, in Metuchen. I had taught part-time in Plainfield, and at the Yeshiva. And I got my masters degree. But I hadn't worked in Metuchen. I didn't know anybody. My friends...I was really busy. Larry was in City College, and then he had just moved to Maryland, College. Park. We had been separated six months, in January. By September, he started the Maryland job. Toby's the first close friend I made.

KW: I remember when I first came over. I was nervous, in a daze. I brought an album with me. I thought there was a strong resemblance to our grand mother.

June: I know. I really look like her more than anyone else, wouldn't you say? I could see it...my God, when I walked in, they said, she looks just like Lillian...they followed me. It was so amazing that a granddaughter could resemble the grandmother...

KW: (re Grandpa Heller). He invited me to this dinner, in a downtown hotel, near Military Park. They were going to be heading back. I don't know why he came. Mainly to see Lucille and his grandkids. I was working it Newark, I had been separated from Carol, and living downtown, and he said to me, if you ever want to come to Hollywood I can get you a job as an apprentice film editor at Warner Brothers. I guess he was trying to make amends. I thanked him, but at the time I believe I was planning to go to Puerto Rico. Otherwise, I might have gone, because I wasn't attracted to my job.

Kay went out there. He was trying. There was a lot of bitterness towards him. They said, he was good to all the Jews, except to his own family. I don't know when he died.

Reconnecting with my Son Jeff .Feb. 1, 1974. From Kal (age 39) to Jeff (age 16)

Dear Jeff: I don't know how to begin this letter, after so many years. I don't know, for example, how you feel about me—a father who hasn't been in touch with his son for such a long time. Guess I couldn't blame you if you wanted nothing to do with me. I wouldn't dare ask you to forgive me, because all these years apart can't be erased by a simple "I forgive you." All I can hope is that—as you grow older—you'll come to understand that people are far from perfect, that although they *try* to do the right thing, they don't always.

Your mother may have told you about my childhood. When I was two years old, my mother (your grandmother) died. My father became sick and went off to California. I was raised by my grandparents. I never saw my father until I was 33 years old. He is now an old man, quite ill. Somehow, I found it in myself to understand him, to care for him. He is, after all, my own flesh and blood. we've been writing to each other for the past few years. Nothing will ever replace those lonely years I spent as a child without a father or a mother, but at least now I have a father, we keep in touch, and it's a good feeling. Just a few months ago, I found that when my mother died (in 1937) she gave birth to a little girl, who was then adopted by another family. I found that girl, who is my sister (and your aunt)—she is married, has two children and lives in Metuchen NJ. We had never seen each other for 36 years, and now we do, often, and that's a very good feeling. It would give me a great deal of joy to hear from you in a letter. I'd like very much to see a picture of you, and to learn how you're doing in school, and what plans you have for your future. Please think about this. Talk it over with your mother. She has raised you all these years and I'm sure you love each other very much. I wouldn't want to do anything that would upset her. But I would very much like to hear from you. Your father, *Kal W* P.S. I am enclosing a little extra birthday gift with this letter. Also, in a separate package, am sending you a copy of a book I wrote. Hope you're as much of a baseball fan as I was when I was a kid, and that you'll enjoy it.

Feb. 28, 1974. From son Jeff to Dad, Kal: Hi—I would have written sooner but I wanted to look at your book. I read a few short parts, and from what I read I think it is very good. Also, before I forget, thanks for the book and the money for my birthday. I really like sports and have read about 100 sports books, the best being BALL FOUR, by Jim Bouton. Jim is my favorite writer. I write for the school newspaper and I submitted my first article a few weeks ago. I like writing and my most probable career will be either a writer or a photographer. Those are my scholastic interests. I attend Roselle Catholic High School and I am averaging about 82, far below my capabilities. The reason for the 82 is my lack of interest in Biology, thus bringing a low mark.

My favorite activity at school is playing soccer. I started on the J.V. team this year as goalie. We finished with a 8-4-2 mark, going undefeated in our last 8 games (6 wins, 2 ties). My goals against average was 1.28 and I had 2 shutouts. I don't have any recent pictures of myself but if I get one I'll try to send it to you. Just to tell about my interests, I like all sports, especially professional wrestling. I like rock music, and I go to the movies a lot. Well, that's about it. Your son, *Jeff*

March 30, 1974. Through Leon King I met an agent, Charles Neighbors, 240 Waverly Place, New York NY 10014. Tel: 212-924-8296. I proposed to him a book about investing in rare postage stamps. *"Paper Gold: An investor's guide to profits in the stamp market."* As mentioned earlier, I had been a stamp collector as a young boy, then gave it up. In subsequent years I became quite active, attending stamp auctions, bidding on older stamps. I started a collection of the first stamps issued in every country worldwide. Later, on a train from New York to NJ, I met Howard Stuewe, who was also interested in rare stamps. Howard had recently retired, and together we started a small stamp auction house. I later dropped out, but Howard mounted a quite successful auction house, which he ran for several years. Howard and his wife Shirley lived in Summit NJ; we became good friends and met quite often for dinner. More recently they moved to Pennsylvania, close to their married son Jeff, who is an executive with a major radio station in Philadelphia.

June 24, 1974. To Dad from Kal. Dear Dad: It was good talking with you, and receiving your letter shortly afterwards. Sorry I haven't written more often, but in the past few monthsI've been quite busy finishing up the Babe Ruth biography. It's already in page proofs and I feel some optimism...the Playboy Book Club has already chosen it as one of its selections for members, which should help sales, and also enhance the possibility of a paperback. Also, Washington Square Books (a division of Pocket Books) has come out with a paperback of my Clemente book, and Anchor Books will soon come out with a paperback of my anthology *The Puerto Ricans*. These are for small sums (they're not mass market paperbacks, most for the for the school and library market) but every little bit helps. I'm not 100% sure about book assignments this fall, but there are a few possibilities, and I feel generally optimistic. Because of this, we're going to spend one month in Europe (England, Spain, Portugal) during July (we leave July 1). Olga has been dying to go for so many years now, I figured that we shouldn't let the opportunity go by. We do have the time, and we have a little bit of $$$, and I figured that with the current inflation it will never get any cheaper. So we're off in a few days. We'll be sending our son David to Puerto Rico, to stay with his grandpa there; and our daughter Maria will go to Indiana, to stay with her aunt Maria (Olga's sister) who is married and has a new baby. We'll all meet back here in August, and we're looking forward to a nice summer. We've been seeing a lot of my sister June and her two children, Lowell (10) and Becky (6). They're wonderful, and we've established a warm, fine relationship that has enriched my life immeasurably...Have also been seeing my cousin Bill (Nat's son) and his wife Shirley now and then, and they're wonderful folks. As I mentioned, also saw Neil Simon after many years (he came over for coffee) and I look forward to seeing more of him since he lives nearby in South Orange. Dad, I'm concerned about you and your diabetes, but I know that it's something controllable if you take care of yourself. Any ailment, however, gets aggravated if your mental outlook is negative. I know that it's not easy, but you must *try* to seek some kind of serenity and peace with yourself; you can make a start in this direction by not dwelling so heavily on the past, which is inalterable. Must go now, Dad. Have to start thinking about what to pack for Europe. I'll keep in touch with postcards, etc. Love from all of us...*Kalb*

Cousin Rose Moves to New Jersey

1974. When Rose Hoffman's sister Lillian passed away, she was left alone, without family, in Brooklyn. We helped her move, first to Maplewood NJ and soon afterwards to a small comfortable apartment at 17 Myrtle Ave. in nearby Irvington NJ. But Rosie, now 77 years old, remained an enthusiastic New Yorker, who loved theatre and film. She often took the 107 bus, which passed near her apartment, and ended up in the Port Authority in midtown New York. From there, she would walk up to the Theatre District and get low-priced tickets for seniors or attend a film. I recall, in particular, one weekday in the winter. There was an enormous snowfall, so bad, so deep, that I was unable to get my car out of the driveway at our Maplewood NJ home. I was concerned that Rosie might need some food, or some assistance. I called her in the morning. No answer. I called again in the early afternoon, again no answer. Much later in the day, I called again, and finally Rosie responded:

"Hello?"

"Rosie! How are you?"

"I'm fine."

"We were so worried. We called you all day. What happened?"

"Oh, nothing. I took the bus into New York."

"You what?"

"I went to New York. And with all that snow, it took forever. But I saw a great movie!"

With Rosie living nearby, we enjoyed picking her up on Sunday afternoons, and riding around to visit family, or just see the sights. I recall one Sunday in particular.

Olga and I had been going to a spiritualist church in Hoboken NJ, run by a fascinating Puerto Rican man, Reverend Sepulveda, who truly possessed psychic powers. The Reverend did not have a solid grasp of English. He was planning to move to Florida at some time in the future and had received some brochures about a location there. He asked me to come by some Sunday and help translate the content of the brochures. That Sunday, we picked up Rosie to take her on a ride, and then I mentioned, "Oh, Rosie, we just have to make a brief stop in Hoboken, okay?" I didn't mention who Reverend Sepulveda was, and made no comment about his special powers.

"Sure, sweetheart. Whatever you like!"

When we reached the brownstone building in Hoboken, I rang the bell, and Reverend Sepulveda's head appeared outside the second floor. "Hello! Come up, please!" We walked upstairs, entered the kitchen and were seated at a rectangular table, while the reverend's wife began pouring coffee. Rosie sat at one end of the table, facing Reverend Sepulveda. Olga and I sat at either side of the table facing each other.

Suddenly Rosie's eyes opened wide. She appeared shocked. "Oh, my!" she exclaimed, as she stared at the reverend.

"What is it?" he asked.

"Who is that Indian standing behind you, with that big feathered headdress?"

I stared above his head and saw nothing! But the reverend smiled and replied, "That is my ally…I see you have powers."

Rosie said, "Oh, sometimes at night, I try to sleep, but I keep seeing so many things flashing by me, like ribbons of light!"

Then the reverend gave her some friendly advice. "It just takes practice.

Me? I can turn it on and off." He raised his hand and gestured. "Just like a faucet!"

More About Cousin Rosie

Lowell Stern (Kal's nephew). Taped conversation. Also with my wife Olga. Cape May NJ 8-1997. Lowell: This is a remembrance about Rosie. Something she said to my father, Larry Stern. A number of years ago, in the 70s. She told him that he would find a job at some point 20 miles south of Baltimore. She met him at your house, when he came over. At the time he was working at CCNY. I didn't even know that he was looking for a job. And I don't think he wanted to be far way from us. We were living in NJ. She said I see you 20 miles south of Baltimore. My dad ended in a job in College Park, Western Maryland, 20 miles south of Baltimore. (laughs). She also said something, when she first met him, something to do with Atlanta. Several months later, the Philosophers Convention was held in Atlanta, which was very unsual, because it was the first year they held it there. It was usually in Boston, or New York, or Washington. In high school, I was involved in musicals, and I was talking to her about ....I really liked acting, and maybe I'd become an actor. And she said, no, I see the law, the law for you.

KW: (laughs) She did say that?

Lowell: Yeah. You're gonna be a lawyer. I said, well, that can be a little boring, and I really like this acting...and she says, no, no, no, the law.

KW: And you didn't go right into the law.

Lowell: No, not right away. I worked on Capitol Hill for a few years after college.

Olga: When everyone was telling Norma (my little sister) that she couldn't have a child, because Norma was diabetic, and the doctor saying no you shouldn't have a baby, it's too complicated, and Norma decided she would check with Rosie, and Rosie said you will have a child, it's gonna be a little boy, it'll be fine, and don't let anyone discourage you..and Norma went ahead and got pregnant.

KW: She was in frail health. it was risky.

Olga: Logic said she shouldn't have a child. But Rosie said OK, and Norma went ahead, and she's very happy. It's her only child. A very healthy, wonderful person.

More about Rose Hoffman. Taped an interview with Ed Logue, June's husband. On the beach at Cape May. Cape May NJ 8-17-97.

KW: When did you remember meeting Rose?

Ed: It wasn't too long after June and I started going out. 1977, '78. I think it was the first time I came to your house. She was a character. She got me aside and started telling me about her plays. And also her trip to Israel, where she said ...somebody frightened her, and she stabbed him with a big hat pin. She told me this on a number of occasions after that, too. It was one of her favorite themes for a while. I guess she thought he was going to abduct her or assault her, and she took care of it very quickly.

All the trips to the city. Every week, or every day, was it?

KW: I think she chose the garden apartment near us because there was a 107 bus at the corner that took her right to the Port Authority in New York..

Ed: I took her home one time. Junie and I dropped her off. I walked her into her apartment. It was a pretty spartan apartment. Everything she needed to carry on her activities, but no too much in the way of luxury items.

KW: Rosie never cooked. She would eat out all the time.

Ed: She did on two occasions mention things to me that afterwards I realized that something has been said that was more meaningful than someone merely talking. She said something about long, long hallways, she saw me in this long hallway. I never thought of it. Suddenly, in my building at school where I work, my room was at the end of a wing, and that wing stretched out and went to another wing, and if you looked down the hallway it was quite a distance. Every day for a year after that I thought of Rosie every time I walked out the door. The other one was...this time I thought she'd really slipped. Junie and I were married, and we moved into a little house on Jonesdale Street. And my house, the one that I lived in with Carol, had been sold. So we had a lot of stuff to store. One back room had stuff, that we had to keep until we bought a place of our own. Rosie said to me something about what are you going to do with that harp in your attic? And I thought: this is it, she's really winged out. But later on, a week or so afterwards, I was working in the back room, trying to move some stuff around, and here was my baby grand piano, standing on its side...and um, it was a strange feeling, because it did look like a harp, standing in the corner.

KW: It used to amaze me...she seemed to have two separate talents. One to look at someone and see something about them that's either happening or is in the past. But once in a while she would see things that haven't happened yet. Both are rather astounding. But they're two separate powers.

Ed: I've heard that Rosie predicted something with Olga's sister and who she would marry.

KW: Yeah, Norma. She even predicted his name (Alfredo) and where they would meet.

Ed: She was a singular personality. Not what you'd call, at all concerned with wordly things, except her writing of plays, and going to shows, not much else, except her love for the family. This is one of Kurt Schwartz's favorite stories. He met her perhaps only once. And she said something about her son becoming a doctor. I think he was in dental school at the time.

More about Rose Hoffman. Taped interview with Becky Stern. June's daughter. Cape May. 8/19/97

Becky: Then there's the story about my dad..

Michael (her husband): I heard this about 20 times...

Becky: This is marriage, part of marriage, hearing the same story over and over...

KW: (sings) Tradition! Tradition!

Becky: My first memory of Rosie is when I was ...when she said something really relevant to me is when I was in second grade. So I was about seven. I know this will sound very strange, and very, not like it was a big deal, but there was a boy, his name was Kyle Cleric, and he liked me very, very much. He liked me so much that he was very mean and possessive. He would browbeat me a lot. And I was very meek. So for example, I had a very good friend named Jill and he'd pull me aside at recess and say, why do you always have to be with Jill? why do ya always have to be with her? Your giant giant. She was very very tall. And I (falsetto) I don't always have to be with her. You always are! And he walked away and he and his little friend did a high five. They were glad they had just made me feel bad. This tormented me. I hated him! I hated having to go to school every day and face him. But everyone knew that Kyle likes Becky so I had to hang out with him. It's not the kinda thing you'll tell your mom. So, Rosie sits down with me at your house one Saturday afternoon or evening and she looks at me very intently and she did that thing where her eyes look up into the sky and her eyes move back and forth...

KW: Was she reading cards?

Becky: No…and she said to me, somebody likes you, a boy likes you, and I said yes! then she said, too much. he likes you too much. you don't like it. Aaaah! To me, it was so...validating! I had not told a single adult that this was the condition of my second grade existence. I hated having to face this boy every day who ordered me around. And she sat me down and said a boy likes you too much, and it's not good. There's no way she could have known that. I didn't tell it to mom. Second grade it was uppermost in my mind. So that's my personal Rosie story.

Visiting Spain

July 1, 1974. Olga and I departed for a wonderful one-month visit to Europe. We first flew to London and spent a week traveling around England, partly to visit with our good friend Irma Rodriguez, who was living there. We then crossed the English Channel (by train!) to Paris, spent one day there, and spent about three weeks in Spain. We adored Spain, rented a small car and spent marvelous times in Madrid, Barcelona, and a bunch of smaller towns along the east and south coast of the country. We didn't reserve rooms in advance. We simply drove from town to town, and late every afternoon found reasonably priced *paradores* (country inns), thanks in part to Spain's tourism office in every town. Among the highlights were Peñiscola, a small town on the south coast, where we feasted on gazpacho, paella and other delicacies. Another paradise was the hotel El Morosco in Mojacar. One night in Granada, at our hotel we actually saw the "Colombo" TV detective series, in Spanish! Other places we visited were Málaga and Sevilla. On a typical day, for lunch, I feasted on the tasty potato omelette, available everywhere. The vegetable soup, gazpacho, was also marvelous. We then returned to Madrid, which was where we were supposed to fly back to the US. But one day on a tour bus we met two young Portuguese ladies who insisted that our trip would not be complete without a visit to neighboring Portugual. So we changed our plans, took a short flight from Madrid to Lisbon, and spent four wonderful days in Portugal. I particularly recall time spent at Estoril, an exquisite seaside resort a short train commute from Lisbon, and also a visit to a nearby seaside town, Cascais, where we heard Rodrigo, a great singer, perform Fado, Portugal's classic traditional music.

July 9, 1974. Review in Publishers Weekly: "*Babe Ruth: His Life & Legend.* Kal Wagenheim. Praeger, $8.95. There can always be too much of a good thing, but even this fourth Babe Ruth biography of the year makes grand reading for the clubhouse and bleacher set. Veteran sportswriter Kal Wagenheim, like Smith in *Babe Ruth's America* (PW, June 17) and Creamer in *Babe* (PW, June 24) seems implicitly to view the Babe as an elemental force, a 'bad boy', an 'animal' and a secretly pathetic overgrown child whose gusto and achievements were so awesome that his blemishes fade in the afterglow of his legend...Wagenheim's richly detailed narrative (some marvelous new Ruth stories crop up along with the oldies) still has the power to touch off both guffaws and tears. 24 pages of photos." *Playboy Book Club selection.* (Published September 16)

PHONE CALLS OUT OF THE BLUE

Four Babe Ruth biographies, including mine, were published in 1974, so neither one became a best seller. By 1974, my money from the Babe Ruth book began to run out, and I had to find some way to pay the bills. For the next decade or so, phone calls out of the blue came to the rescue. Here's how it happened. Back in the 1960s, when I co-edited *The San Juan Review* magazine, Marcos Ramírez, the wealthy lawyer who bankrolled the magazine, suggested that we devote an entire issue to the question of education in Puerto Rico. A good idea. He arranged for us to "escape" to a little island off Puerto Rico's south coast, where we would do in-depth interviews with Angel Quintero, the Secretary of Education, a wonderful, devoted man. While there, I also met with Dr. Quintero's key assistants: Rafael Torregrosa, Mario Anglada and Arcilio Alvarado Jr. These three men would, in later years, come to my rescue, in the period between 1974 and 1985, when I was struggling to make a living. .

First I received a call from Rafael Torregrosa, who had recently arrived in New York to direct the Migration Division, a branch of the Puerto Rico Labor Dept., with an office on W. 45th St in NYC. On July 31, 1974, Torregrosa sent a note to my home in Maplewood, saying he wanted to get in touch with me. On Nov. 8, 1974, I sent a letter to Rafael (in Spanish) with my resume. Soon after I received, and signed, a contract, effective Dec. 1, 1974 through June 30, 1975, to work as a consultant, 20 hours weekly, with the Puerto Rico Labor Dept. Migration Division in New York, for $1,250 monthly for "professional services", mainly reaching out with information to the Puerto

Rican and other Hispanic communities in the United States, and advising on studies and reports, speeches, etc.

Sept. 1974: Olga recalls: "After a year of struggle with work and graduate school, while also trying to be best mother I could to my kids, I decided to apply for a Ford Graduate Fellowship. I received it (Sept. 1974) and quit my job in order to become a full-time student. That year a book Kal and I had edited, *The Puerto Ricans: A Documentary History* was published to great reviews, including an extensive one in the *New York Times* book review section.

Oct. 13, 1974. *A page and a half review in the NY Times Book Review by Roger Angell comments on four Babe Ruth biographies, "Babe" by Robert W. Creamer, "Babe Ruth's America" by Robert Smith, "Babe Ruth And The American Dream" by Ken Sobol, and mine, "Babe Ruth: His Life & Legend." A brief excerpt:*"Kal Wagenheim's book is especially rich in press-box yarns...Pleasure is permitted in the Wagenheim and Creamer books. The loud Ruthian jokes, the famous malapropisms, the preposterousness of 'the big baboon' come bursting through... Wagenheim's 'Babe Ruth' is graceful and anecdotal and uncommonly readable (and the only one of the four books to include the almost essential lifetime records), but it is clear that Babe Ruth has at last found the biographer he deserves in Robert Creamer."

Oct. 14, 1974. Handwritten letter from Dad to Kal. Dear Kal: Thanks to you and Olga for the check. I got the book and it sure is a monumental job. Incidentally, if there is a second printing, please check the following typographical errors: (1) page 19, end of line 27 (sp); (2) Page 256, Line 17, MacPhail. Otherwise a sterling effort. As for my health, still have acute anxiety with physical effects. I keep praying that things will improve. I also pray that you line up some productive projects. Don't force it. Relax. Write out all your ideas and try to visualize each idea and project in its entirety. Don't worry. Don't fret. Have fun and be joyous and thankful...Keep well and be at peace. Love to Olga and the children, Your dad, Harry.

Oct. 17, 1974. Leon King called me to say that Mrs. Ruth (the Babe's wife or daughter) told him that my biography of Babe Ruth was "the best" of the lot.

Nov. 22, 1974. *Letter to me c/o Praeger Publishers, 111 Fourth Ave., NY NY 10003, from the Young Adult Services Division of the American Library Association, 50 E. Huron St., Chicago IL 60611.* Dear Kal Wagenheim: The

Best Books for Young Adults Services Division…is very pleased to inform you that your book *CLEMENTE!* has been selected for inclusion in our annual list "Best Books For Young Adults 1973". Compiled each year by a committee of librarians who work closely with teenagers in public or school libraries, the list is distributed nationally and used in recommending books to teenagers, parents and teachers…Sincerely, Eleanor K. Pourron, Chairman, Best Books for Young Adults Committee.

Dec. 2, 1974. From Kal to Dad. Dear Dad: I've been swamped with work lately, but I did want to say hello, and send along this little check. Still no new book contracts, but I have gotten a nice consulting contract for the Migration Division of the Puerto Rican government, its office in Manhattan. I will work 20 hours a week for them, about two days weekly, at a nice salary. It will keep me busy, and keep the $$$ rolling in. Also, I've been handed a rush job, to write a position paper for the Puerto Rican community in New Jersey for the state legislature, with relation to quality education for Hispanic children. It's interesting work, and good money also, and I must finish the thing by next week. I think somebody up there likes me, because both of these jobs came looking for me, as a result of phone calls from people who had heard of me, but I didn't know them. Guess that my books help in establishing my reputation. Also, I lectured before a class at the Columbia Graduate School of Journalism last week (on journalism and politics in Puerto Rico), which was also fun. The other night I attended a stamp collectors' club in Millburn NJ (I collect once in a while) and I ran into a fellow (Cohen's his name, I think) and when he heard my name he told me that he had a teacher named Wagenheim at Hawthorne Avenue school—a very *good* teacher, he added. Thought you'd like to know. Must go now. It's late and have to take the early train to Manhattan tomorrow. Much love from all of us, especially from your grandchildren David and Maria. Please write and let us know how things are going. PS. Have also seen Neal Simon occasionally, and very much enjoy his company.

1975: "*A Survey of Puerto Ricans on the U.S. Mainland in the 1970s*" published by Praeger (based on my SUNY-Buffalo graduate thesis). Described by *Choice* as "essential for all academic collections as a basic reference for study of the Puerto Rican experience on the mainland."

June 1, 1975. Excerpt from 700-word article in The NY Times. "Job Study Issued on Puerto Ricans. It Predicts Grim Struggle In The Coming

Decade." By Peter Khiss. Puerto Ricans on the mainland "face a grim struggle for economic survival in the Northeast, according to a newly published study by a Puerto Rican Government consultant. Kal Wagenheim, now a research consultant for the Puerto Rico Migration Division, said Puerto Rican incomes 'lag far behind' others. They even fell behind in relative terms during the war on poverty in the nineteen-sixties, he said....The author of two earlier books on Puerto Rico, Mr. Wagenheim began his latest study while in a graduate program at the State University of New York in Buffalo." *Note: the publication of this article pressured SUNY-Buffalo to finally grant me the Master's Degree which I had sought since completing my thesis.*

June 20, 1975. My uncle, Nat Wagenheim, told me that Isaac Bashevis Singer, a writer I'd long admired, would be appearing at a synagogue in South Orange NJ, not far from where we lived. We all attended. The auditorium was packed. Mr. Singer, a small, white-haired man in his 70s, sat on the podium and was introduced by the rabbi. He rose and read a brief excerpt from his work. The rabbi then said there were a few minutes available for questions from the audience. A young lady rose, explained that she was working on a graduate thesis on some aspect of literature, and then engaged in a complex, longwinded (endless!) question. She sat down. Mr. Singer, with a benevolent smile, and with his Yiddish accent, said "With such a question, I would give you the degree already!" The audience burst into deafening laughter. Later, I was thrilled when Mr. Singer gave me his autograph (which I framed and it now occupies a spot on the wall of my study). I will always remember that day, and the laughter that Mr. Singer inspired with his kind, funny comment.

Washington-International Communications

On July 1, 1975 I signed a contract "to advance the public relations interests of the Government of Puerto Rico in the United States." I was hired part-time, average two days weekly, for $840 per month, from July 1, 1975 through June 30, 1976 to generate news stories. The man who hired me was Scott F. Runkle, President, Puerto Rico Information Service, Suite 1103, 1825 K St NW, Washington DC 20036. I must have done some work for PRIS earlier, because I have a carbon copy of an invoice dated March 13, 1974 "for professional services...$500.00."

Paper Gold

July 29, 1975. Letter from Peter H. Wyden, Publisher, Peter H. Wyden, 750 Third Ave., New York NY 10017. Informing me that "the promotion and advertising for *'Paper Gold'* will be taken over by my present parent firm, the David McKay Co. Inc., an old friend of mine, a vice president of McKay....I have obtained an amicable divorce from McKay and will be publishing and distributing elsewhere in the future."

January 1976: My book "*Paper Gold: How To Hedge Against Inflation By Investing in Postage Stamps*" is published by Peter H. Wyden and distributed by parent company David McKay Co., 750 Third Ave, New York NY 10017. 202 pages. $8.95.

Jan 8. 1976: My dear buddy Robert Bletter (I met him in the Army in Ft. Benning in 1955) died, leaving a wife (Rosemary) and a son (Nathan). Bob, in his 40s, had been suffering from severe mental problems and I'm told was taking lithium. I believe he died of a heart attack. Some days later, I received a phone call from from Jerry Kaplan, then a Seton Hall professor of mathematics, who also lived in Maplewood NJ. Jerry told me that Bletter was editing his book at Columbia Teachers College Press, and Bletter told him he had a dear friend (me) who also lived in Maplewood. Jerry asked if I would like to join him to attend the funeral reception in New York, organized by Bletter's friend Peter Goldman. Jerry and his wife Pat have remained close friends of ours ever since.

Feb. 1976: Granted Master's Degree in American Studies from SUNY-Buffalo, following publication of my book. *Note: the head of the Puerto Rican Studies Dept. for some reason did not like me, and earlier had blocked my request to obtain a Master's Degree, based on my thesis about Puerto Ricans in the United States. However, when the NY Times published an article about the book on June 1, 1975, I contacted the head of the American Studies Dept. sent them a copy of the article, and asked once more to be granted the degree. It was issued soon after. So, I have a Master's degree, without a Bachelor's degree!*

Feb. 1, 1976. Review from *Library Journal* on my book *Paper Gold.*: "Both the philatelic neophyte and the experienced collector will benefit from his tips in stamp investment techniques as well as his analysis of specific stamps values demonstrating their dramatic rise in values over the years."

May 2, 1976. *Brief excerpt from a long NY Times book review entitled "Stamp Stories" by Christopher Lehman-Haupt, who says he "has been hoarding American postage stamps since he was a boy of 30".* "I therefore recommend that you *not* buy for the beginning stamp collector Bill Olcheski's *'Beginning Stamp Collecting,'* a solid and reasonable guide to the fundamentals of philately. And if you think the acquisitive line I've taken in this review is penny-pinching, then try reading Kal Wagenheim's *'Paper Gold: How to Hedge Against Inflation by Investing in Postage Stamps,'* wherein it is revealed that during the decade, from 1963 to 1973, the increase in value of certain United States postage stamps outpaced the rise in the Dow Jones industrial average by over 230 percent. There are some things worth being selfish about."

July 24, 1976. Op-Ed article in The NY Times. If You're 'Brown'—or Maybe Purple—You're 'White'. By Kal Wagenheim. When are Chinese Japanese? When is chocolate black? And when can you be brown, white, purple, pink and polka-bot at the same time? For these magic tricks, and more, put yourself in the hands of our United States Bureau of the Census. In a series of dress rehearsals for the 1980 decennial census, the bureau is making partial surveys in different parts of the nation. Americans are being polled by mailed questionnaires, phone calls and personal interviews. The bureau wants to record, among other things, the "race" and "origin or descent" of every American and that's where the magic tricks begin. The questionnaire offers these choices under "race": White, Black or Negro, Japanese, Chinese, Indian (American), Filipino, Hawaiian, Korean, Vietnamese and Other. If you fill in the blank space next to "Other", the Census Bureau has published a handy guide book that tells its staff how to classify these write-in entries. For example, if you list your race as "coffee" or "chocolate", the guidebook says you are "black." But if you write that are you are "brown" then you are "white." "Confused? Read on. If you write in "Oriental", you are considered Japanese. But if you write in "Yellow", you are classified as "Other." If you write in "Brazilian", the guidebook says you are "white" (this will be news to Pelé). If you're black and prefer to be white, simply write in "American," since that, according to the guidebook means "white." So does "South Africa". If you're feeling whimsical, and write in "pink" or "polka-dot" or "purple" or "spotted" or "vanilla"—or if you simply decide to list yourself as a member of the "human" race---you'll be listed as "white". There's more. The United States now has more than 11 million persons of "Spanish" origin. Manyof these persons use the catch-all word *hispano* to describe themselves. If they do, the Census Bureau calls them "white". But a *hispano* from the Dominican Republic who happens to list his national origin is "black" Hispanos from Cuba or Puerto Rico, however, are "white". After the Census Bureau expends millions of dollars in compiling this misinformation, will it be of any use? When most Americans were either European immigrants, or the descendants of African slaves, perhaps it made sense to inventory the public along "black" and "white" lines. But today, with jet travel, new patterns of immigration, and relaxed views towards racial and ethnic intermarriage, all that has changed. Many *hispanos*, for example, come from multiracial societies where the narrow terms "black" or "white" are ludicrously inadequate. "The same family may have members who have members whose skin tones range from dark brown to *café au lait*, what is called white. In Boston, we have seen tragicomic incidents where light Puerto Ricans are bused to black neighborhoods and dark Puerto Ricans are bused to white neighborhoods, creating artificial, ugly divisions among a people who have lived in relative racial harmony in their native land. Billions of dollars in Federal funds are apportioned according to population size in geographic areas. This makes it essential that there be an accurate census count in 1980. And since politics is still a very ethnic game, political leaders want their people to be counted, in order to get a fair share of attention from government policy makers. But do today's criteria make sense? Wouldn't it be a good idea to overhaul the confusing, contradictory—often absurd—system of racial categorization being used by our Government? As soon as the smoke clears after the November Presidential election, the winner ought to order a new look at the question of "race" and "origin" of our people. Perhaps a major conference of demographers, experts on race and ethnicity, and a few plain folks with common sense, would give us better answers to an old dilemma. *Kal Wagenheim is a research consultant, in New York City, with the Migration Division of the Puerto Rico Labor Department*

Sept. 1, 1976: Diploma from State University of New York at Buffalo, conferring on Kal Wagenheim The Degree of Master of Arts.

In Nov. 1976, after the election in Puerto Rico, a new political party (pro-statehood) took power. I continued to work at the Migration Division and in mid-Feb. 1977 met with Bobby Capó, the new director of the Migration Division, and learned that my consulting contract would be continued through June 30, 1977. However, I learned on March 7 that the matter of my contract could not be settled until the new Secretary of Labor came to New York on or after March 27, 1977. After losing the public relations job I decided to open a small office in New York to try to generate jobs in the same field. My good friend Marvin Schwartz lived in a studio apartment in a rent-controlled building on West 10th St. in Greenwich Village (he continues to live there). Through Marvin I obtained a studio in the building for just $120 a momth. I moved in a desk and other simple furniture and gave it a try. But business was not booming, and I learned that I could just as well work from home in Maplewood, and commute by train to Manhattan when necessary. Our good friend Judy Markov had a boyfriend attending college in New York so I let him take over the apartment. But after several months the owner's son saw that I was not using the place and told me I was not allowed to sub-let. Although the rent was modest, so was my income at the time, so I reluctantly handed back to apartment to the owner.

A Call From Aspira of America

Jan. 20, 1977. Another phone call out of the blue. Mario Anglada, who I met years ago when he worked as a chief aide to the Secretary of Education in Puerto Rico, was now the head of Aspira of America, with an office in New York. He said that his secretary Rosita would contact me for three days work starting in February.

January 1977: During this time I was working on a book about how to win at the race track. While working at the Migration Division in midtown Manhattan, during lunch hour, I dropped in at the Off-Track Betting (OTB) Parlor at Times Square. I bought *The Daily Racing Form* the day before, studied it, and had some fair luck, which inspired me to write such a book.

Feb. 6, 1977. I met with Ashley Hawken of the U.S. Information Agency (USIA), who expressed interest in producing films about Hispanics in the USA. He offered me $1,200 per show for gathering information that could be used for the films.

Feb. 10, 1977. To Dad from Kal: Dear Dad: Haven't heard from you in a long, long time and part of it is my fault, since I haven't been writing much myself. Fact is, I get so busy that the time flits by without my realizing it. We here are all fine. Olga is working on her doctoral thesis and also just received an appointment to the faculty of Newark-Rutgers, where she teaches one course in history and another in sociology. She has been working for years towards this, and so we are all quite pleased. As for me, I have been working mostly as a consultant on Puerto Rican affairs. Have had steady work on this the past two years, as my income from writing books temporarily dried up. Am now in some sort of transitional phase, trying to develop new accounts and book projects. A few things look promising. I have just agreed to work with the USIA (US Information Agency) in developing materials for a half-hour film on Puerto Rico, which will pay me well for a couple of weeks, and other odds and ends come along, too. Am also working a couple of days a week as a consultant to a small college in New York, editing their studies on bilingual education. So it is a varied, interesting life. And am also trying to work up a book idea that will merit a good enough $$$ advance that will permit me to spend more time on writing. How are you feeling. I wish you would just drop me a brief line, OK? I saw Nat & Bess, and Dora the other day at a Bat Mitzvah for Diane, the daughter of Bill & Shirley Wagenheim. I don't see much of the Wagenheims, except for Bill & Shirley, who live quite close by. Love from all of us...*Kal*

Puerto Rico Tourism Co.

March 9, 1977. Letter from Arcilio Alvarado, Director, US Division, Puerto Rico Tourism Co. in New York City to Joel Magruder, Director of Communications, Puerto Rico Tourism Co., San Juan, Puerto Rico. Dear Joel: As per our conversations, I have retained on a contract basis our mutual friend Kal Wagenheim...Kal will have the following duties: a) Research and collect all the data necessary for the total marketing study we are about to embark upon....Familiarize himself with all the travel editors, writers and other pertinent personnel within the realm of the Trade Press... His contract shall be for a period of 6 months commencing March 15, 1977, and the fee shall be $12,500—payable in equal monthly installments...I have asked Kal to report to this office today to commence a week of familiarization with the operation.

Phone Calls Out of the Blue

I received a call from Arcilio Alvarado Jr., another friend from Puerto

Rico, who had been named to direct the Puerto Rico Tourism Office at 1290 Ave. of the Americas in NY. He offered me a full-time job as public relations officer. The money was good, and the work was pleasant. My main task was to handle inquiries from American journalists who planned to travel to Puerto Rico to write about tourism. I often took them to lunch at restaurants in midtown (such as the famous 21 Club on W. 52d St), gave them advice, and helped them contact key sources on the island to insure they had a successful visit.

On March 14, 1977, I wrote to Mr. Capó that because of this unsettled situation at the Migration Division I had accepted a job offer to work with the Puerto Rico Tourism Dept. at 1290 Ave. of the Americas, with Sr. Arcilio Alvarado.

April 17, 1977. From Kal to Dad: Dear Dad: I heard just recently about your move to a new address and wanted to say hello, and let you know that all of us here are just fine. I am not the world's most regular letter writer (those of us who make our living by writing tend to shun the typewriter during off-hours) but you are often in my thoughts. Whenever you feel up to it, even a brief note will be appreciated. Everyone here is super busy. Olga (I don't know how she does it) is writing her Ph.D. thesis, teaching history at Rutgers, and still managing to keep the household going. David and Maria are very good kids and growing bigger by the day. I went through a little insecure period with my job early this year. Due to the elections and change in government in Puerto Rico in November, my consultant contract with the Puerto Rico Labor Department in New York was not renewed when it expired in January. But I kept busy with freelance writing and editing assignments, and finally, after a bit of nail-chewing landed an even *better* job. I am now director of public relations for the Puerto Rican government's tourism office in New York. Nice office. Fascinating work. Occasional business trips to Puerto Rico. Even an expense account for entertaining travel writers! And, most important of all, the salary is quite good. So 1977 has, thus far, been good to us. Am also keeping busy in my spare time writing two half-hour films for the U.S. Information Agency about Puerto Rico. They will be shown (in Spanish) all over South America on TV and in movie theatres. It's my first crack at screen writing, and am not familiar with the format, but the USIA people in Washington seem pleased with what I've given them so far. In fact, I must leave you now, because today (Sunday) I must finish up a treatment of the 2d half-hour and mail it off tomorrow. Write when you can. Love from all of us, and especially from your son... *($40 check enclosed*)

A funny memory

1977: Shortly after Doel García was named by Gov. Carlos Romero-Barcelo to be director of the Puerto Rico Tourism Co., he flew up to New York to check things out with his office there, and also the public relations firm (Haley, Kiss & Dowd) that handled the account. (I learned not long afterwards that Mr. García's sole experience with tourism was that he had once stayed at a hotel; he was said to be a failed businessman whose only "virtue" was being a fervent supporter of the Governor's political party). My good friend Jim Kiss, the account exec at Haley, Kiss & Dowd, tells me this is what happened: He arranged to have Doel García picked up at the airport and driven by limo to a luxury hotel in Manhattan. Jim was there waiting for him. When they went up to Doel's room, he said to Jim: "Okay, get me a woman." Jim was dumbfounded. "What?" he asked. Whereupon Doel said, "Isn't that what you people do?" Thinking fast, Jim looked in his phone book, picked up the phone, and dialed. A moment later, he said "Mrs. García? Hi, this is Jim Kiss. I just want you to know that Doel has arrived safe and sound here in New York, and he is dying to speak with you." He handed the phone to Doel. Not long afterwards, Doel canceled the contract with Haley Kiss & Dowd.

May 5, 1977. From Kal to Dad: Dear Dad: It was, as always, wonderful to hear from you. Such a long, long time. It appears to me that your psychiatric treatment is quite helpful and that the advice given to you about the past was quite sound. No use dredging up old, painful memories. The present, and the happiness of our dear ones, is far more important, don't you agree? Please do (as you promised) write to me again, and at greater length, if you feel up to it. Just got back from a week in Puerto Rico, where I gathered material for a Federal govt film on Puerto Rico, and did some work for my new employer, the Tourism Dept. of the Puerto Rico Govt. My new job is very challenging and I am dealing with good, decent folks, which makes me look forward to each new workday. All here at home are very busy and thriving...Am enclosing another check and, as long as my job situation stays as good as it is, I'll be able to send something around the first of each month. Always remember that there are people here, your family, who care for you, and are rooting for you to work your way out of your problems. Much love, your son…*Kal*

June 1977 (I think). Hand written letter to Kal from Dad at Hawthorne Manor, 14110 Cordary Ave., Hawthorne, Calif. 90250: Dear Kal: Thanks to you and Olga for the check. Right now I have money for the rest of the month, so don't worry about me. Note change of address. I spent about a month at the hospital, and the doctor suggested I come here. It has a couple of hundred elderly ladies and a number of men. The sitting around becomes tedious but I am trying my best by walking and taking exercises in the morning. Kal, I need more gainful activity and where will I get it. I really don't know … Give my love to Olga and the children…Love to all and a peaceful Father's Day. Love, your Dad, Harold. P.S. A story line for a TV movie of the week or theatrical release: a highly ranked baseball pitcher (Marishell?) from an obscure island in the Caribbean is urged by a delegation of his country men to come to their island as their leader, since they have disposed of the military junta (Allen Arkin type) and besides the pitcher is idolized by the entire island. He refuses to heed the call and is finally kidnapped, right before a league playoff, or world series. Everyone is in a dither. (Kal, you take it from here. Make it funny, satirical, etc. etc.)

Teaching at Columbia University

Sept. 1977: Another phone call: Teaching at Columbia University! I received a surprising phone call with a job offer from Lou Uchitelle, an old friend. We first met Lou in the 1960s, in Puerto Rico, where he was the Associated Press Bureau Chief. Lou soon after married Joan, and they relocated to Buenos Aires. After a few years, he and Joan returned to Scarsdale NY and Lou switched jobs to *The New York Times*. At that time we reconnected. In addition to *The Times*, Lou taught a course in News & Feature Writing in the Undergraduate Writing Program at Columbia University. A fellow *Times* staffer, Lawrence Van Gelder taught a second section of that course. Around then, the film *"All The President's Men"*, starring Robert Redford and Dustin Hoffman, was a big hit, inspiring many Columbia students to take courses in journalism. Maybe they, too, could help to overthrow a corrupt White House! Lou called and said so many students were applying to take the course that he and Van Gelder could not handle the volume. He asked if I would like to teach a third section, once a week. I had never taught before! I didn't even have a bachelor's degree! But I did have experience as a journalist. Lou reassured me that the course mainly involved handing out simple writing assignments and correcting the papers. And reading the work in class, inviting critiques by classmates. He gave me a copy of his syllabus. On Sept. 6, 1977, I took the train into Manhattan, the subway up to 116th Street, and went to Room 608, Lewisohn Hall, where I had a 6 p.m. meeting with Professor Dick Humphries, the head of the writing program (and a wonderful guy) and my job was confirmed, to start the following Spring.

September 1977: Olga recalls: "Rutgers again hired me, this time on a half-time line, to teach a course Puerto Rican History and to develop a Puerto Rican Studies Program that was being demanded by PRO (Puerto Rican Student Organization)...I was expected to publish, present papers atacademic conferences, edit and publish my dissertation, teach a full load and counsel students. Fortunately, life at home was becoming less demanding as the kids obtained driving licenses and managed quite well on their own."

December 1977: *My Uncle Murrey Shamburgh died, age 89, while living in a retirement home in Wilkes Barre PA. His dear wife Lily had died a few months earlier, at age 84. In my files I found my letter, dated Dec. 17, 1977 to relatives of Lily*: "Dear Jane and Jim, I don't think I can ever adequately express to you and your family how grateful I am for the loving care you extended to Uncle Murrey, at a time when he needed it most. We here feel a very special bond with your entire family; the love and care that Aunt Lily displayed, in times of crisis, towards both my grandmother and great-grandmother, and now you, towards Murrey. My wife Olga and I wish you all the happiest of holidays...if you ever pass this way, don't dare do so without letting us know, so that we can reciprocate the wonderful hospitality you've always extended to me. With fondest regards, Kal

Dec. 18,1977. Having lost my job with the Puerto Rico Tourism Co. I report to the NY State Dept. of Labor Office, in Manhattan, and begin to collect unemployment benefits for the first time in my life. The benefits are available for one year. My first check, dated Dec. 28, is $115. Until March 3, 1978, every two weeks, I received a check for $230 ($115 per week).

Olga managed to get full-time work in the History Dept. at Rutgers-Newark, which greatly reduced financial pressures. I continued freelancing, working quite a bit as U.S. correspondent for *Caribbean Business*, a weekly newspaper based in San Juan, Puerto Rico. I also worked with Haley, Kiss &

Dowd, a company seeking to promote investment in the Dominican Republic, and in Guatemala, requiring several business trips to both countries, where I gathered information and prepared press releases, helping to place articles in industrial magazines, in order to attract U.S. investment in those countries.

1977-1981: Olga recalls: "The years between 1977-1981 were extremely busy because in addition to my jobs at home and at work, I was also working on my dissertation. One of the complicating factors of those years was that I was assigned to teach American History, a course not within my specialty. Preparing for that course was one of the toughest challenges I have overcome. In order to do a decent job I was almost always sleep deprived and very tired. Finally, in 1981, after a long and arduous journey I completed the dissertation and received the Ph.D. degree in Latin American history. I was so exhausted by then that I did not even attend the graduation, a decision I later regretted. Until 1981 my job at Rutgers had been on a year-to-year contract and it included, in addition to teaching, coordinating the Puerto Rican Studies Program I had created. With the Ph.D. in hand I was offered a tenure-track position at Rutgers-Newark History Department. But this came with the understanding that I would continue to coordinate the PRS program and to teach courses in that field without additional pay. By then student interest in the program had declined and the number of courses offered constituted a minor in the discipline."

1978: Publication of *"Cuentos: An Anthology of Short Stories from Puerto Rico"*, edited by Kal Wagenheim (also translator of some stories in the collection). Schocken Publishers, NYC. "Humor, pathos, poverty and courage are just a few of the recurrent elements in the volume" (*The Nation*).

Spring 1978: As an Assistant Adjunct Professor, I taught a course in News & Feature Writing at Columbia University, and it was well received. It wasn't full-time work, the pay was modest, but it came just when I had lost my job, and marked the beginning of subsequent years of freelance work and independence. I began teaching an evening session, starting at 6 pm on Wednesday, but some time later the course was switched to the afternoon. After a few years, Lou rose higher in the *Times* staff, became so busy that he stopped teaching at Columbia, leaving the task to Van Gelder and me. I was promoted to Associate Adjunct Professor. After another few years, enrollment in the journalism course continued to shrink. The department chairman told me that since Van Gelder had seniority, he would teach the single remaining course. However, since by then I'd written and had produced a few plays, he offered me a spot teaching Structure & Style I, a popular undergraduate course in creative writing. For the next five years, I taught that course. As an adjunct, teaching just once a week, I did not see much of the other professors, many of whom were also adjuncts. Once a year the department organized a luncheon at the Faculty Club, so we did have a chance to briefly socialize with other professors. Two of them—Alan Ziegler and Emily Fragos—I believe were continued to be active as of 2013. I also have fond memories of two people who administered the program; Leslie Woodard and Dorla McIntosh, both of them efficient, kind and friendly (*My three decade stint ended in the Fall of 2006, when there were several personnel changes in the Creative Writing Program*).

June 24, 1978. From me to Mr. George Arfeld, Jack Raymond & Co. Inc., 488 Madison Ave., New York NY 10022. Excerpts from a 3-page letter. Enjoyed meeting you yesterday to discuss the new edition of the booklet *"Puerto Rico USA."* At your request, I am submitting a written estimate of the work involved, were I to undertake the job. Fortunately, I had a copy of this booklet in my personal archives on Puerto Rico and, the day before our meeting, was able to carefully review it. I fully agree with you that it is not only out of date (most material reflects the situation as of the late 1960s) but is also poorly organized, with mediocre graphics and bland, uninteresting text... My fee for this service is $8,500, which I propose be paid in three installments: (1) $3,000 upon signing of our agreement to initiate the project; (2) $3,000 upon delivery of clean first draft and photos; (3) $2,500 upon approval of final clean draft. ...if we get started by early July, I can deliver the final product by Sept. 1. (In fact, I have to. As I mentioned to you, I have just received a book contract, with the book due by Spring 1979; therefore I must devote a major portion of my time to that book starting early September...I might add that I have written seven books so far (four on Puerto Rican themes) and am proud of the fact that I have never missed a deadline.

Jews In Sports!

June 26, 1978: I received an agreement from Schocken Books Inc. of New York to write a book tentatively entitled *"Jews In Sports."* The same publisher had earlier published my biographies of Roberto Clemente and Babe Ruth. It was to be a book of 50,000 to 60,000 words. I was offered an advance of $6,000, half payable on signature of the agreement. The same day I received an advance of $3,000. Looking back many yeas later, I don't recall why I never managed to complete the book. I began some research, but became occupied with other projects and time slipped by.

Nov. 15, 1978: Review in Library Journal. "Cuentos: an anthology of short stories from Puerto Rico... Dec. 1978. 160p. bilingual ed & pref. by Kal Wagenheim. $9.50 hardcover. Paperback $3.95. Presenting a panorama of Puerto Rican life both in New York City and Puerto Rico, these stories are told by writers of acute perception and strong powers of invention. A recurring theme is the culture shock which besets Puerto Ricans upon migrating to the United States. It is given poignant expression in the story which tells how, during a power failure when the lights of the alien culture were blacked out and the moon and stars could once more be seen in the sky, Puerto Ricans flocked to the rooftops, in celebration, feeling that they had 'people again.' The Spanish texts are included, and the translations ably reflect their mood and character—*Dayle Manges, Univ. of Louisville Lib. Ky* "

March 6, 1979: Charles Wagenheim, my father's first cousin, died in Hollywood, Calif. (I learned of his death, a homicide, in a phone call from my father a few days later). A brief biography about his eventful life is below (most of it from the website www.imdb.com.). In a career comprised of hundreds upon hundreds of minor character parts on stage, film and TV, diminutive actor Charles Wagenheim was initially drawn to acting to counterbalance an acute case of shyness. Born in Newark NJ on Feb. 21, 1896., he was the son of immigrant parents. Wounded in World War I, he was compensated for an education by the government and chose to study dramatics at the American Academy of Dramatic Arts in New York, graduating in 1923. I am told that he appeared in the Yiddish Theatre on New York's Lower East Side together with Paul Muni, who later became a major star. I'm told that he and Muni went to Hollywood together. After touring with a Shakespearean company, Charlie appeared in a host of Broadway plays, several of them written, directed and/or produced by the prolific George Abbott , including "A Holy Terror" (1925), "Four Walls" (1927) and "Ringside" (1928). Following his stage role in "Schoolhouse on the Lot" (1938), Wagenheim turned indefinitely to Hollywood where his dark, graveside manner, baggy-eyed scowl, thick and unruly mustache and lowlife countenance proved ideal for a number of genres, particularly crimers and westerns. In films, he scored well when

Alfred Hitchcock chose him to play the assassin in *Foreign Correspondent* (1940). He went on to enact a number of seedy, unappetizing roles (tramps, drunks, thieves) over the years but never found the one juicy part that could have put him in the top character ranks. Usually billed tenth or lower, he was more atmospheric filler than anything else as his various cabbies, waiters, deputies, clerks, morgue attendants, junkmen, etc. will attest. Some of his better delineated roles came with *Two Girls on Broadway* (1940); *Charlie Chan at the Wax Museum* (1940); *Half Way to Shanghai* (1942); the cliffhangers *Don Winslow of the Navy* (1942) and *Raiders of Ghost City* (1944); *The House on 92nd Street* (1945); *A Lady Without Passport* (1950); *Beneath the 12-Mile Reef* (1953); and *Canyon Crossroads* (1955). One of his more promising cronies came as "The Runt" in *Meet Boston Blackie* (1941), which started Chester Morris off in the popular 40s "B" series as the thief-cum-crimefighter, but the sidekick role was subsequently taken over by George E. Stone . Of his latter filming, Wagenheim was cast in the very small but tense and pivotal role of the thief who breaks into the storefront in which the Frank family is hiding above in *The Diary of Anne Frank* (1959). TV took up much of his time in later years and he kept fairly busy throughout the 60s and 70s. Wagenheim played the recurring role of Halligan on Gunsmoke (1967-1975) and performed until the very end on such shows as "All in the Family" and "Baretta." Cousin Charlie and his wife (a psychologist) had purchased a small apartment building in the Hollywood area and lived in one of them while earning rent from the other units. In early 1979. Shortly before Charlie's death his wife had suffered a stroke and was confined to their apartment. A woman had been hired to help her. Apparently one day Charlie, age 83, came back from food shopping, entered his apartment, and surprised the woman who was in the process of going through drawers and stealing articles. Charlie began yelling at her, asking her what she was doing. Apparently the woman panicked and hit Charlie with an object that killed him.. (By sheer horrific coincidence, elderly character actor Victor Kilian, of "Mary Hartman, Mary Hartman" fame, was beaten to death by burglars in his Los Angeles-area apartment.) Even today, Cousin Charlie is seen often on TV re-runs of "Gunsmoke", where he plays Josh Halligan.

1979: Editorial and Research Consultant to the U.S. International Communicatins Agency, preparing materials for *"Ahora"* a documentary film (two half-hour shows) on the growing Hispanic population in the US.

Involved trips to New York, Washington DC, Los Angeles, Cal. and San Antonio, Texas.

May 1979: *Nuestro* magazine publishes my five-page story "Puerto Rico: Food Stamps, Apathy and Alegria', which examines the social, political and economic situation on the island. (*see my letter of June 18, 1982, about not being able to collect payment)*

Oct. 24, 1979: Flew on Pan-Am from JFK to Caracas, Venezuela for a freelance assignment. I don't recall the details, but in my calendar over the next few days I scribbled "Plaza Bolivar…". Traffic in Caracas was the worst I've seen anywhere! I flew back home on Oct. 28.

Dec. 21, 1979. My sister June and her new husband, Ed Logue, are married and we hold a big celebration at our house in Maplewood.

Jan. 9, 1980. I wrote to my father with news of June's marriage. He responded with a very touching Jewish New Year's card in which he, for the first time, included her, writing: "Kal, Olga, Maria, David, June…Happy New Year, Harold."

Feb. 1, 1980. From Kal to Dad. Dear Dad: I am still enjoying the memory of seeing you a few months ago and hope to make another trip to California sometime this year…Enclosed is a money order; will try to send these regularly. If you ever run short on cash, don't hesitate to call me at home, collect (201-762-1565). I mean that. I very much enjoyed the newspaper clips you sent me. There were lots of stimulating ideas contained in them. Olga is teaching, working on her thesis, and just received quite an honor—she was named to the Board of Trustees of the Newark Museum, in order to make the museum more sensitive to the needs of Newark's large Hispanic community. We're very proud of her. Other good news out this way is that my cousin Bill (Nat's younger son) just threw a party celebrating the fact that his eldest daughter Susan has been admitted to medical school. She is now working as a nurse, and is aspiring to more. I'm sure she'll make it. She is extremely bright, and a good person. We see quite a bit of Bill, his wife Shirley, and family. My kids, David and Maria, are doing well in high school. David now has a car, and works part time to pay for the gasoline (more than $1 a gallon!). Must go now. Keep well. You are always in our thoughts. Let's hear from you. Love from all…*Kal*

Early 1980? Undated from from Dad to Kal (handwritten). Dear Kal: I, too, felt good seeing you. I am proud of you and you are a blessing to Olga,

David and Maria and June. Thanks for the money order you gave me and sent me in the mail…the supermarket where I cash my security check would not cash a money order. I think it best to send cash although the lady here who goes to the bank and post office about 2 or 3 times managed to cash the money order at the bank. I got a "rent rebate" of two hundred dollars from the State of California which delighted me very much. You don't have to send me too much; however I haven't bought items such as shoes, slacks, a belt or two, etc. etc. I intend to spend some of the money on these items. Of course, I still dream of being in good health and productive. There are no outlets for creativity. The idea of the libraries might spark motivation to research and write. I have been reading the newspaper daily and Sunday (I take items out which might interest you and Olga). Sometimes I buy the paper, other times I wait for the Manor copy to be read and take parts of the paper to my room…I read some time ago that two pictures, one for TV and one for Theatre showing, are being made on Roberto Clemente. Will watch for future developments. One is being made on Satchel Paige…Have you ever given thought to"comic" strips, one frame character serialization of your Puerto Rican history in Spanish and English for a Puerto Rican newspaper; the Babe Ruth story for serialization in English, to coincide with the time of his birth or death, and the Clemente Story. That's about it, Kal. I pray that you and Olga, Maria and David and June and all children about you enjoy good health and be joyous for all the years to come. Love, Harold. PS. On second thought, a mail order would be safer.

May 6, 1980. From Kal to Dad. Dear Dad: Enclosed a little money order for you. We've gotten a spell of very warm, summery weather, which makes working in offices quite disagreeable (looks too pretty outside). Fortunately, my classes at Columbia are just now over with, so I will have more free time to enjoy the outdoors, although I still work 3 days a week in New York City with Aspira, where I serve as an editorial consultant. Olga is still hard at work on completing her thesis, and I think she will do so this summer. It's been a long, hard haul, but will pay off with a doctoral degree. David (who will be 18 on May 30) has a car…works part-time, and this fall will enter Newark-Rutgers U. as a freshman. We're fortunate in that he won't have to pay tuition since Olga is a faculty member. Maria (will be 17 on May 15) will be entering her final year of high school in the fall. This weekend we spent two solid days working on the lawn, raking leaves, cutting grass, watering, etc. and I have the calluses to show for it, but I enjoy the chance to get in some physical exercise…a nice form of therapy for the mind, I think. As for writing projects I don't have anything very pressing at the moment, but I may undertake polishing up the manuscript of a 19th century Puerto Rico novel which I translated some years ago. I think that some university press might find it good for their textbook list. It's a book that I very much enjoyed and it deserves a wider audience. The other day I saw Nat and Bess at a birthday party for their son Bill (he was just 50) and they both look well. They were pleased to hear that you and I had reestablished our correspondence…All our love. Your son, *Kal*

May ? 1980. Undated handwritten letter from Dad to Kal, responding to letter above. Dear Kal: I have your letter of May 6 and thanks for the money order and bringing me up to date…What is Aspira? What classes did you take at Columbia? Toward a degree? What is Olga's thesis on? A doctoral degree will definitely enhance her work situation. Maria will be 17! My, how wonderful. And David entering Rutgers! Give Olga and the children my full love! Keep well, Kal. the working of the lawn is just that—therapy. And you should be thankful for having a lawn to work. As for myself, truthfully I can't throw off boredom at times, but am making the over-all situation as well as most of us do. Again, love to all, *Harold.*

June 1980. Handwritten letter from Dad to Kal. Dear Kal: First, let me wish you a pleasant Fathers Day. May there be many many more. I saw the doctor on Thursday (once a month) and condition quite good. Blood sugar 150 (contained for my age). Hope the enclosures are entertaining, educational, etc. etc. Nothing much else. Hot weather seems to be coming in, 85 today and tomorrow. Give my love to Olga, Maria and David. Your dad, Harold

June 6, 1980. From Kal to Dad. Dear Dad: Thanks for your last letter, and the very interesting news clippings! I am enclosing a money order ($40). In answer to your question, Aspira is a non-profit agency, founded in 1961, to help Puerto Rican youngsters get through high school, into college, and eventually into rewarding careers. They have counselors, people who help with scholarships, arrange for cultural enrichment activities, etc. Aspira also gets involved in doing research on education and publishing the results. I am an editorial consultants (about 3 days a week) and help them to write proposals for funding, and edit a scholarly journal for them, which focuses on educational problems and issues among Hispanics in the U.S. I haven't been *taking* classes at Columbia, in response to your second question. For the past 2 years I have been *teaching* a class in journalism at Columbia's School of General Studies, in their Creative Writing Program. The class emphasizes practical aspects of journalism. For example, I lecture one hour a week and give the students a written assignment each week—a news article, a feature article, a review, a personality "profile," a re-write of several articles, etc. Then I read the articles, comment on them, and help the students to improve their writing. It's an enjoyable class and the students tell me it helps them, mainly because it forces them to write something every week.The fellow who started teaching the course is a good friend of mine, Lou Uchitelle, who was with the Associated Press and is now a financial editor at the New York Times. After about 1 year, the course became so popular that there were too many students (there is a maximum of 15 students per class) so Lou called me and asked if I was interested in teachinig a second section of the class. I accepted, it was late 1977 actually, and have been teaching it ever since. Last Semester, when Lou got busy, I taught 2 sections (his and mine) and it's been a nice part-time job for me and pays quite well, too. My classes ended in mid-May so I have some spare time now until they resume in September. Olga's doctoral thesis is about a revolution in Puerto Rico in the 19th century, 1868. Her major is history and, as you know, a thesis has to focus on a very particular topic, delving into it in great detail. No book has ever been written about this revolution, known as El Grito de Lares. Once her thesis is accepted (she could get here doctoral degree late this year or early next) there is a good chance that some university publisher might want to print it in book form. We have our fingers crossed... because it would really do wonders for Olga in terms of her career. Yes, Maria is 17 and is doing well in school. David graduates from high school this month, and enters Rutgers in September. Last night he took his girlfriend to the senior prom. I took a few photos and will send them when they are developed. My son Jeffrey (from my first marriage) has just graduated, too, from Boston University, with a double major in journalism and English, and with honors. Writing seems to run in the Wagenheim blood, because he has been working part-time with a weekly paper, *The Boston Phoenix*, and seems to like the Boston area, where he is living now. When I get a copy of something he's written recently I'll send it along. I correspond with him, and talk on the phone, but haven't see him in a long while, but hope to do that later this year. One of these days I'll try to get out to California. If you ever feel up to it, I would be delighted to pay your airfare to come out here and visit with us for a few days, perhaps during the summer months when the cold weather wouldn't bother you. It would be very nice. We have plenty of space here, and David and Maria and Olga would love to see you. Love from your son, *Kal*

July 14, 1980. Letter from Kal to Dad. Dear Dad: I've been so busy lately that I have a sneaky suspicion that I neglected to write to you on the lst of the month, and enclose a money order. How are you? I went to a very nice lawn party yesterday, at Cousin Bill's backyard (Nat's son). It was to celebrate Nat's 84th birthday, as well as Bess' birthday, and the birthday of Susan, Bill's daughter. The whole family was there...Nat, Bess, Greta, Harriet (Allan's first wife), Dora, and a few others...and a good time was had by all...Dora was glad to know that you and I manage to exchange letters from time to time. During the summer I've been pretty busy with Aspira, where I work as an editorial consultant...and am also helping to put together a couple of ½ hour documentary films for the Federal government...we're doing the final editing on the films which caused me to go to California when I last saw you...that's when I was doing the preliminary research for the films. Olga is busy finishing up her thesis, and hopes to have it complete by the end of the summer. My son David, who starts studying at Rutgers in September is now working hard at a gas station, saving money for a car...and our daughter Maria is relaxing this summer, taking little day trips with her friends to the seashore. Maria is quite talented. In school last semester she made two lovely items of stained glass...a mirror and a window decoration. I'm going to buy her more materials so she can also work with stained glass at home. The other day I went to my sister June's house and met a relative of the family that adopted her...a man by the name of Danny Stiles (?). He is in his 60s and now lives in Florida. He said he was a student of yours at Hawthorne Avenue School and spoke very highly of you and asked for you, although he said you probably wouldn't remember him since he was quite young then, maybe ten years old. Must go now. Work calls! Keep well. I am saving my money to see when I can get out to California and see you again. Love from all of us...

July 16, 1980. Handwritten letter from Dad to Kal. Dear Kal: I pray you and Olga and Maria and David are well. It's been hot out here, but the pleasant winds from the Pacific Ocean make it most comfortable—and very little if any of smog. It does me very good to hear of your productive routine as well as Olga making progress in her various endeavors. You are most fortunate and much Thanksgiving for you and the family. As for myself, I am pretty good. I keep occupied with walking and watching TV, reading the Los Angeles Times and cutting out items, and sending out items to you, and keeping some for myself. As for Maria and David, send my warmest affection and love. I feel you are proud of them and in this you and Olga are happy. Again, keep well. May peace and serenity be with you and the family for all time. With love, your Dad, Harold.

Aug. 11, 1980. From Kal to Dad. Dear Dad: Things have been a bit hectic lately, but I've decided to sit down and say hello, and also forward this enclosed money order ($40). All is fine here. The kids are busy. David just bought his second car (a 1972 model), he sold his other car a few weeks ago. David works hard at a gas station nearby, and enters Rutgers as a freshman in September. Maria is staying at home this summer, relaxing, also working on a lovely stained glass Star of David (she took a class in making stained glass in high school last semester and seems to enjoy it a great deal). Olga has finally finished the first draft of her Ph.D. thesis, and is forwarding it this week to her committee, which takes a great deal of pressure off of her. Later this month we will all go away for a much needed vacation, one week down the Jersey shore, at Seaside Park, and I'll be sure to send you a card from there. I saw my Cousin Bill yesterday (Nat's son) and he and his family went with us up to a beautiful state park in northern Jersey; we went swimming in the lake there and enjoyed the pretty countryside. I continue busy, going to New York a few days a week to work with Aspira, and am also busy with my small but growing business of buying and selling postage stamps for collectors. Must go now. It is my hope (just a hope mind you) that late this year we will be able to fly out to the coast (Olga and the kids have never been there), which will allow us to see you, and also to explore that part of the USA...If we do go, my guess is that it would be around the Xmas period. Love from your son, *Kalb*

Sept. 12, 1980. Letter from Kal to Dad, with $40 money order. Dear Dad: Thanks for your last letter, and for the clippings, which contained lots of interesting articles; particularly the magazine supplement about the anniversary of the city of Los Angeles. All goes well here. David has just completed his 2d week of college. They are throwing a lot of homework at him, but he is working on it diligently and I'm sure he'll do fine. Maria is in her senior year at high school and also working at home on a pretty stained glass project. Olga has finally finished her Ph.D. thesis; she handed it in to her committee, and 3 of the 4 professors on the committee have already read it and said //they liked it very much, so she is virtually assured of getting her Ph.D. and also being promoted from Instructor to Assistant Professor at Newark-Rutgers (which would mean a raise). As for me, I'm busy on a number of freelance writing projects. Night before last, to celebrate Rosh-haShanah (Jewish New Year) I didn't go to synagogue, but stayed home and baked two big tasty "Challahs", which came out great. I'm not much of a cook but for some reason I occasionally enjoy staying home and baking bread; it's relaxing, and, when completed, delicious. Must go now. This weekend I will be taking part in a stamp show in nearby Pennsylvania (I sell postage stamps to collectors, another sideline), and I have to clear away a lot of small projects before I get ready for the stamp show. Love from all of us, your son, *Kal*

Oct. 10, 1980. Letter from Kal to Dad, accompanied by $40 money order. Dear Dad: How are you? All here are fine. Olga is in the final, final throes of completing her Ph.D. thesis. She submitted a first draft of the 300-page manuscript to the 4 professors who are on the thesis committee and all 4 have told her it is a fine job. They did ask for a few minor revisions before she meets with them (perhaps in November) for an oral "defense" of the thesis, required before they certify that she has completed all requirements. We're getting close to the finale on this, and we hope to have a nice celebration later this year, because Olga has put in years of work on this. David, as mentioned previously, is in his first semester at Rutgers-Newark and is working hard. Maria is completing her senior year at high school. I haven't seen much of my sister June lately (she lives in Metuchen, 16 miles south of us) but we do speak on the phone. She is remarried quite happily (we had a big wedding celebration here in our house), is busy working as a teacher in the public schools, and her two children—Lowell and Becky—are bright, delightful children. I'll send you pictures one of these days. I have been busy with all kinds of freelance work. My main job is about 3 days a week as a consultant to Aspira, an agency that helps Hispanic youth in the field of education. I have also been teaching one day a week at Columbia University (each Thursday p.m.). And I have been active buying and selling rare postage stamps, partly for diversion, and partly as a mode of investment. I also just wound up work on a documentary film for the U.S. government about growing Hispanic political power (when I saw you last October I was just starting my research on that film) and am now doing a long article about Hispanics and bilingual education for a magazine published by the Council on Foundations. There is a very *good* chance that I'll be flying out to the West Coast on or about Christmas. Don't count on it, but don't be surprised if I turn up. I'll call you, of course, in advance, but prospects look very good, so we can get together and talk. Wish I could see more of you, but I understand how difficult it would be for you to relocate in this part of the country. Must go now. Love from all of us...*Kal*

Nov. 1980-1981: Served as consultant for Haley, Kiss & Dowd, a NYC public affairs firm involved in promoting investment and economic development in Guatemala, requiring visits to Guatemala. I recall seeing General Lucas Garcia, the military dictator. I also interviewed a colonel who was in charge of education. He said the biggest challenge was the fact that many natives in Guatemala don't speak Spanish. "So I guess you need bilingual language teachers," I said. "It's more complicated," he said. "Many people live in such isolation that there are 14 different native languages." Prepared a newsletter, press kit and other materials.

Nov. 10, 1980. Letter from Kal to Dad, with $40 money order. Dear Dad: This will be a very short letter, because I'm in the midst of work, but I wanted to say how nice it was talking to you. I have to rush today, because I must get home (I'm in New York) and go out to dinner with Olga, who today is expected to get her Ph.D. approved (she is meeting with her thesis committee for an oral defense at this very moment). I pray that all goes smoothly for her...The *L.A. Times* has promised to send me a clipping of the article I did for them on Sunday, Nov. 9, but if you find an extra copy it would always be welcome...With love from all..Your son, *Kalb*

The last visit with my father

In December 1980, I learned of bargain flights from Newark to California. On Dec. 20, we (Olga, David, Maria and I) flew to San Francisco, saw the sights, and drove down the Pacific Coast. At one point we met up with our dear friend Ernie Potvin, who had moved from Puerto Rico to California, and I recall he took us to see a hilarious gay costume parade. We later ended up in Los Angeles, where we had a memorable family gathering with my father. This was the first time he had met Olga and his grandchildren. We stayed at a hotel, and enjoyed our time together; I particularly recall a fun afternoon on Dec 28 at Santa Anita racetrack, where we bet on the horses, and had lunch.

We returned home on Dec. 29. *Note: I had been cigarette smoker (2 packs a day) for many years. I told the family I wanted to quit but found it difficult. At the airport, preparing to depart for California, I lit up a cigarette and was told this would be my last one, forever. Somehow, not being alone, interacting with family for more than a week, I was able to resist the urge to smoke. Upon our return to New Jersey I continued as a non-smoker, and found help by chewing gum and toothpicks.*

Jan. 9, 1981 (letter never mailed, found among his papers), addressed to "Kal & family" from Harold Wagenheim (Dad) to Kal. From Hawthorne Manor, 14110 Cordary Ave., Hawthorne Calif. 92050. Dear Olga, Kal, Maria and David: I pray meeting you all may be a prelude to many more gatherings in the future. I recall the letters exchanged between you, Kal, and myself. But seeing all of you as a family unit made me feel so good and with an inner peace and thanksgiving which I haven't felt in a long time. I shall remember those precious moments for all times. Olga, good health to you and creative success in your work; Kal, good health and remunerative projects in the now, and the future; good health to you Maria, and a crystallization of your dreams and aspirations; and David, good health and also mastering whatever stands before you. Love to you all, and God bless all. Harold.

Jan. 11, 1981: At 1 pm. I received a call from a woman named Debby at the Hawthorne Manor, saying my father had suffered a heart attack, that he was "stable, but critical." At 8 pm. I received another call, saying Harold E. Wagenheim died, age 77, at Hawthorne Community Hospital in Hawthorne, Calif. The Certificate of Death from the State of California gave the time at 1040 hours. Social Security No. 136-16-0162. Reports that he was a teacher for 20 years in New Jersey Public Schools, and was Widowed. His residence was listed as 14110 Cordary Ave., Los Angeles, Calif. Causes of death: Cardiogenic Shock (1 day); Acute Myocardial Infarction (1 day); Arteriosclerotic Heart Disease (10 years). Other conditions: Diabetes. That same day I sent the following Western Union Mailgram at 8:35 pm EST to Malinow & Silverman Mortuary in Los Angeles. I authorize you to remove the remains of my father Harold Wagenheim from Hawthorne Community Hospital and prepare for burial as per my instructions. I am his son and next of kin. I will assume financial responsibility. Kal Wagenheim.

On Jan. 12, 1981 my Uncle Nat and I made arrangements for my father's remains to be flown from the Malinow & Silverman Mortuary, 850 Venice

Boulevard, Los Angeles, Calif. New Jersey. We sent $1,005.80 via Western Union to cover the costs out there. It cost another $1,430 to cover costs of the funeral and burial.

Jan. 14, 1981: Obituary in *Newark Star-Ledger*. Services for Harold Wagenheim, 77, of Hawthorne, Calif. will be held at 11 a.m. tomorrow in the Menorah Chapels at Millburn, 2950 Vaux Hall Rd., Union. Mr. Wagenheim... was a teacher with the Newark Board of Education for many years, retiring 35 years ago. Mr. Wagenheim was a member of the Civic Theatre of the YMHA, Newark. Born in Newark, he lived in California for 35 years. Surviving are a son, Kalman; a daughter, Mrs. June Logue; a brother, Nathan; a sister, Mrs. Dora Seidner, and five grandchildren.

Jan. 15, 1981: Funeral, eulogy written by Nat Wagenheim, Dad's brother. He read this at the Menorah Chapels in Union NJ. Harold Wagenheim was a scholar, a teacher and an innovator of ideas and way ahead of his time. At age 24 he was a principal in a junior high school in East Rutherford, N.J. He was of fine character, a shy man, and easily hurt by the ways of the world. He had the potential of making a niche for himself as an author and director in the performing arts. But his love was for the children in his classes. Surely there must be a number of performers and writers today that owe their success to Harold for his guidance and instruction. He was so well liked and well thought of by his students that to this day he is remembered. Mention the name of Wagenheim to a clerk, bank teller, nurse or others and they would inevitably ask 'Are you related to Harold Wagenheim? He was my teacher.' Then came the words of admiration and affection they so long carried in their memories of this man. At the old YMHA that for many years graced the corner of High and West Kinney Streets in Newark, he contributed greatly by writing and staging plays, but always remained in the background, letting others take the credit and praise. We as a family urged him to assert himself and accept some approbation, but no, Harold was too reticent for that. In his youth he had close relationships with Dore Schary, Alfred Kahn, William Bendix and many others who started their careers at the old 'Y' and then eventually went on to bigger and better things.

Many years ago he and a trunk full of books he had authored took off for California. Too timid to push through the doors of the moguls, his luck ran out. Working as a salesman to keep alive, and going from job to job was too much for him. He had a complete breakdown and through the good graces of friends he was placed in a home where he spent many years. Here he lies, born before his time, and now rests in peace, no more heartaches, frustrations, or pain. He leaves a son, a daughter, brother, sister and grandchildren. May he rest in peace.

On Jan.15, 1981, my father was buried at Mt. Lebanon Cemetery, Iselin, NJ.

Haley, Kiss & Dowd

In 1981 I was hired as a consultant to do occasional writing for Haley, Kiss & Dowd, a large Mahattan-based public relations firm. I had worked earlier with one of the partners, Jim Kiss, when his firm did public relations for the Puerto Rico Tourism Co. I spent a good portion of my day working for them. I also continued teaching at Columbia, did occasional work for Aspira, and managed to squeeze in time to attend auctions for rare postage stamps.

Latin American Journalists Seminar

I had been teaching one day a week for a few years at Columbia University, and since I was bilingual I was asked to serve as the academic leader of a two-week seminar each year for visiting financial journalists from four Latin American nations, conducted by Columbia University, financed by Citibank.

Oct. 5, 1981. From Frank Wolf, Associate Dean, Columbia University, School of General Studies. Dear Kal: Ward and I are delighted that you have agreed to serve as Director of the Seminar for Latin American Journalists for 1982. Your role will be to act as the academic leader of the Seminar, to direct and stimulate discussion, to focus the questioning of people appearing before the Seminar, to introduce speakers and conclude each session, to try to impose some intellectual coherence on a varied series of meetings, etc. There will be eight participants, two journalists selected by the press associations of their respective countries—Argentina, Chile, Peru and Uruguay. In addition, Guido Minerbi, a Citibank official based in Buenos Aires, will attend...Your honorarium will be $1,500 for the period Jan. 4-15, 1982 (ten working days)... we will reimburse you for all related incidental expenses...

Waterfront Press

1982: I founded and operated Waterfront Press, a small independent publisher, operating out of my home. I called it “Waterfront” because Olga and I at the time were seriously considering moving to Hoboken NJ, where the film "On The Waterfront" was shot. We later abandoned that idea, but kept the name. Between 1982 and 1992 we published more than 20 books (several new titles and some reprints) that focus on Puerto Rico, the Caribbean and Central America. Looking back, I think my main motivation for founding the press was to publish my English translation of *"La Charca"* (The Pond), the classic 19th century Puerto Rican novel by Manuel Zeno-Gandía. Once the word spread, other books were submitted. The titles:

Benevolent masters. Enrique A. Laguerre; translated from the Spanish by Gino Parisi; introd. and notes by Estelle Irizarry. 1986.

Cuento therapy. Folktales as a culturally sensitive psychotherapy for Puerto Rican children.Giuseppe Costantino, Robert G. Malgady, Lloyd H. Rogler. 1985.

The dreaming man. Lynne Alvarez; [edited by John Wellman] .1984.

Earth and spirit: healing lore and more from Puerto Rico. Maria Dolores Hajosy Benedetti. 1989.

The gravedigger and other stories. Ramón Ferreira. 1986.

Hasta los baños te curan. remedios caseros y mucho más de Puerto Rico. María Dolores Hajosy Benedetti. 1991.

Hidden parts. by Lynne Alvarez. 1988, c1987.

The immigrant iceboy's bolero. Martin Espada; Photographs by Frank Espada

1986.

The labyrinth Enrique A. Laguerre; translated from the Spanish by William Rose; introduction and bibliography by Estelle Irizarry 1984.

Living with numbers. Lynne Alvarez, 1987.

The masses are asses. Pedro Pietri. 1984.

Papa Doc: Haiti and its dictator. Bernard Diederich and Al Burt. 1991.

Puerto Rican families in New York City: intergenerational processes Lloyd H. Rogler, Rosemary Santana Cooney. 1984.

The Puerto Rican struggle. Clara E. Rodriguez, Virginia Sánchez Korrol, José Oscar Alers, editors. 1984.

Puerto Rican youth employment. José Hernández. 1983.

Puerto Rico: the four-storeyed country and other essays. José Luis González; translated by Gerald Guinness. 1990.

Requiem on Cerro Maravilla: the police murders in Puerto Rico and the U. S. government coverup. Manuel Suarez 1987.

Somoza and the legacy of U. S. involvement in Central America. Bernard Diederich 1989.

Traffic violations. Pedro Pietri. 1983.

After a decade of zero profits, I decided to close down the publishing house. One bonus: my books were stored in the same warehouse as Markus Wiener Publishers of Princeton NJ. He learned of the closure, we met, and this led to Markus publishing several books by me and my wife Olga. I have fond memories of the time spent on Waterfront Press, the books I edited, and the authors I met. In particular was the friendship I established with Pedro Pietri, a brilliant writer, and a man with a fabulous sense of humor.

Another Phone Call: Caribbean Business

1982: Began as correspondent in US for *Caribbean Business*, a weekly newspaper in San Juan, Puerto Rico, covering news from New York & Washington DC.

This all started with a phone call from Bob Schoene, a journalist friend in San Juan, who offered me the job. I spent, on average, one day a week, covering stories that would be of interest to readers of *Caribbean Business.* About once a month I took the train to Washington DC to cover events there. This work provided me with welcome extra income, in addition to my once a week class at Columbia University, and other freelance assignments.

March 12, 1982: Attended a conference on Grenada at Medgar Evers College in Brooklyn, part of free lance work for *Caribbean Business.* Three days later, I met in New York with officials from St. Lucia for another possible story. And two days after that visited the Center For Inter-American Relations at 680 Park Ave, NYC, for more information. I also continued covering stories about Puerto Rico, Jamaica, and Panama taking place in New York and Washington DC.

1982-83: Olga recalls: "During the academic year 1982-83, I got my first partially paid sabbatical, a luxury I had never had. I took the time to move to Puerto Rico, to revise my dissertation, find a translator for the text into Spanish and find a publisher. I began the adventure by setting up my own apartment in the Condado section of San Juan, not far from the General Archives. After a very productive year I had achieved all three goals and returned to NJ just in time to board a plane for Cuba, July of 1983, where I was to form part of a group of scholars invited to celebrate the island's first war of independence

(Oct.1868-1878) against Spain. I was there because of my work on El Grito de Lares, Puerto Rico's own cry of Independence against Spain (Sept. 23, 1868) a few days before the Cuban struggle. While in Puerto Rico (1982-1983) I gave several talks on el Grito de Lares and developed lasting friendships with the well-known historians Arturo Morales Carrión and Loida Figueroa. I also met a host of younger historians and researchers, many of whom have gone on to distinguish themselves in their fields. The year back home also did a lot for my soul. By then I had been away from the island a dozen years. I secured a job offer at the University of Puerto Rico, which I had to decline because the family was unwilling to move."

March 14, 1983. I came to Cousin Rose's apartment in Irvington. A few days earlier she told me that I should come to help her gather tax materials to send to her attorney in New York, and also had some bankbooks she wanted to give me. She showed me a thick stack of savings account passbooks, bound by a rubber band. About 12 of them were from New York banks; the remainder were from New Jersey banks. "I want you to have this, this is for you," she said. I replied that Rose didn't have to give me anything, but Rose insisted, and offered to go to the bank with me if her signatures were necessary for the transfer. A short time later, she called her attorney, Abraham Goldstein, and told him she had given some books to me. I spoke with the banks in New York and they told me to provide forms signed by Rose and me. I withdrew the funds, but wasn't quite sure about her wishes. To keep the funds safe, I began to purchase tax-free municipal bonds. Sometime in April, Rosie said she had more bank books for me. She directed me to a metal file box in her closet, and said she had more bank books in a bank safety deposit box. I told Rosie that she had been overly generous, but Rosie replied "I have plenty of money." On April 5, I called her lawyer, Abe Goldstein, to report on her condition. Between March and May, Rosie gave me 22 different bank books,12 from NY City banks with deposits totaling $221,012, and 10 bank books from New Jersey banks, totaling also about $221,000.. I purchased more than $440,000 in tax-free municipal bonds. (After Rosie's death, her lawyer, Abe Goldstein reported that an additional $53,188 was found, in cash in banks and undeposited checks.).

April 13-21, 1984: Rosie's health was declining, so I took her to see a social worker, Mrs. Friedman. Then I took her to Daughters of Israel, 1155 Pleasant Valley Way, in West Orange, where Dr. Sylvia Cohen examined her.

April 29, 1983: I took Rosie to see our family doctor in Maplewood, Dr. Donald

Gilbert, because she was having difficulty walking. In particular her leg was hurting. He examined her and recommended that someone come to her house each day, to buy groceries, cook and help her. Shortly after that I called the Upjohn Company to find someone to help Rosie. On May 3, I took Rosie to see Dr. Donald Kalfus, our dentist.

May 6, 1983: Mrs. Murphy, a wonderful African-American lady, began to work for Rosie seven days a week, as a home health aide. At first, Rosie opposed the invasion of her privacy. But soon she and Mrs. Murphy were getting along so well that Rosie expressed sadness when Mrs. Murphy went home at the end of the day.

June 12, 1983, Rosie's health declined further, so we arranged to place her in the White Housing Nursing Home in Orange NJ where she was well treated for the final few months of her long, eventful life. Since Rosie had vacated her apartment, Olga and I went there to empty it out. We opened a large closet and were amazed (and amused) to find it packed from top to bottom with all sorts of small appliances! Now we understood why Rosie kept her money in so many different banks. Each time she opened an account they gave her a gift, a toaster, or some other nice household item. On June 19, I called Abe Goldstein, her lawyer in Manhattan, to update him on the situation.

July 21-22, 1983. Rose Hoffman died at age 86. The next day at noon she was honored by friends and relatives at the Menorah Chapels in Union NJ, and later was buried at Mt. Zion Cemetery, 59-63 54th Ave., Maspeth NY, in the Alper Meyer Family Circle, 14 right.

August 1983: Not long after Rosie's death, I visited the office of Abe Goldstein, her family lawyer in Manhattan, and gave him an accounting of all the funds I had deposited in tax-free bonds, to keep them safe. I told him I assumed she wanted me to have part of the the money, but wasn't sure, and didn't know what was contained in her will. He said he would be in touch with me later. I had first met Abe about ten years earlier, at the funeral of Lillian Hoffman (Rosie's sister) and between March and July I had spoken with him on the phone a few times, to express my concern about her health. I showed Abe records that I had paid from the funds $7,598 to cover the cost of Rose's care with Mrs. Murphy and the nursing home, plus utilities for her apartment.

Oct. 8, 1983: My Great-Uncle Ed Shanberg arrives from North Carolina for a one-week visit, that includes seeing my sister June, cousins Kay & Robin. One day I drove him to New York's Lower East Side, where he was born more than 80 years earlier. The old tenement building where he grew up was long gone, replaced by a high-rise apartment building. Eddie looked fondly out at the East River and said "when we were kids, in the summer, we would go swimming out there!"

Jan 19, 1984: I was required to testify concerning the funds I had been given **by** Rosie. I was advised to find a lawyer to represent me, and through a friend I hired John M. Newman, from the law firm Portzio, Bromberg & Newman of Morristown NJ to represent me. Three days earlier, Abe Goldstein, Rosie's lawyer, signed an Affidavit stating that on Nov. 15, 1974 Rosie had signed a will, prepared by Abe Goldstein, bequeathing $10,000 to the New York Association for the Blind, and the remainder of her estate in three equal parts to: the United Jewish Appeal of Greater New York; the Federation of Jewish Philanthropies of New York; and the United Hias Service, also based in New York. (She had never told me about this. I later learned that these beneficiaries were suggested by the lawyers, and Rosie agreed.) The lawyers noted that I was holding more than $400,000 in municipal bonds, plus $15,990 in dividends from the bonds I'd purchased. They claimed that Rosie was "not mentally competent" when she gave me the funds. I had made clear to Abe Goldstein that I was holding the money, until we found out what her will said. But I guess they didn't want to take any chances that I might try to steal the money, and they began the legal proceeding. *(In later testimony, Abe Goldstein said Rosie had called him and said "that she gave some books to Kal." He also said that "she appeared to be in good mental and physical health when he last saw her, and she had no trouble understanding him or being understood during their telephone conversations.")*

April 20, 1984. My great-uncle Edward Shanberg, died in Greensboro, NC. Two days later I flew down and attended the funeral and returned to Newark NJ the same day.

Beating The Races

1984: I self-published "*Beating The Races: Seven Easy Steps to Becoming a Consistent Winner*", my 173-page hardcover guide, under the Waterfront Press label, showing how to win at the track, illustrated with details of one-week of betting. I advertised the book in *The Daily Racing Form*, but sold very few copies. My interest in betting on racehorses began in the early 1970s, when I worked at the US Environmental Protection Agency in lower Manhattan. I wandered into a local OTB (Offtrack Betting Parlor) and was fascinated. Later, around 1974, when I worked with the Puerto Rico Migration Division on West 45th St., during lunch hour I often walked over the OTB parlor, then located on Times Square around West 43rd St. I would buy the Daily Racing Form earlier in the day, or the night before in New Jersey, and study the races at Aqueduct or Belmont racetracks. The OTB clients included a bunch of real characters. One of them was Willie Bongiorno, who worked as a bundler in the printing plant of the N.Y. Times on West 43rd St. After we got to know each other, Willie asked if I'd like to bet along with him on the 9th race Trifecta. The idea was to select the first three finishers in the correct order. Willie said we should take the three horses and try nine different combinations, so it wouldn't matter in which order they finished. The cost for nine was $18. So we each chipped in $9. I came back by the end of the day and discovered to my surprise that we had hit the trifecta, which paid $249! Willie gave me half. I returned home to Maplewood NJ, convinced that I would never have to work again; all I had to do was follow Willie's advice. The next day, I returned to the OTB and saw Willie poised over the sheet to select the horses for the trifecta, and he was peering out the window at the passing traffic. "Kal," he said, "the letters on that truck passing by…are they JEL or JEF?" Willie was betting on license plate letters! He did hit the trifecta now and then. He told me that lived with his wife (no children) in an apartment in west Manhattan. When he hit the trifecta, he bought a small TV for every room, the parlor, the dining room, the bedroom, even the bathroom, so he wouldn't miss any show! Another regular was a Korean gentleman, Kim, a natty dresser, with brilliantly polished leather shoes. I learned that his wife operated some kind of store a few blocks south of Times Square. Kim seemed to hit the exacta quite often, and Willie was jealous. Whenever Kim walked in, Willie would mutter "here somes Ho Chi Minh." I once asked Kim what his secret winning formula was. He replied, "Eight to one horses, they win a lot." So Kim was simply on a lucky winning streak. Later, his luck run out, and I noticed his clothes and shoes began to look rather drab. Later, when I worked at the Puerto Rico Tourism Company on Sixth Avenue near 46th Street, I still played the horses, and often had lunch at a nearby diner. One day, a man wearing glasses and a gray suit (he resembled a Certified Public

Accountant) noticed me reading the *Daily Racing Form* and nodded. We struck up a conversation. After a few lunches, he confided that he "never" played the horses, but was in fact a bookie, and all of his clients were executives in the huge Rockefeller Center Building. After playing the horses for several years, I was convinced that I could make money betting on the horses. My system was based on the idea that only two or three races of the nine each day were playable. The others were too close to call. I began betting $200 per race, and made a bit of money. I decided to try an experiment: become a full-time track gambler. I would try it for a week. I took the train out to Belmont Racetrack for seven consecutives days and bet $200 on the races I played. At the end of the week I was exhausted, and didn't lose a penny, but my profits were so sparse (about the same as working minimum wage) that I decided to abandon that career. The problem: it is possible to beat the races; my system made sense. But it requires strict discipline. On average only two or three races daily are playable. But I lacked the willpower to follow my own advice and refrain from playing marginal races. Bottom line: one needs iron will and discipline. It was no longer fun.

CARIBBEAN UPDATE: A NEW CAREER

After nearly 20 years as a freelancer, in February 1985, I launched my own monthly newsletter, *Caribbean Update*, and have been doing it ever since. The newsletter was a big risk, requiring an investment of several thousand dollars. I printed 10,000 copies of an initial issue, and rented a mailing list of companies involved in business with Latin America and the Caribbean. With the help of Olga and my children David & Maria (all of us stuffing envelopes, affixing postage) we mailed out the 10,000 free samples (labels purchased from Dunhill), offering an annual subscription for $120. I received a 1.2% response, meaning we got 120 subscriptions at $120 for $14,000, and we went on from there. Gradually I increased the subscription cost, and today (2013) it is $281 a year.

1985: I again served as coordinator for the two-week Latin American Journalists Seminar at Columbia University. A group of journalists from several countries were part of the seminar, and we had much fun. I was their guide and translator as we traveled around New York to places of interest, including the Stock Exchange and the Wall Street Journal. We usually traveled in a bus and as we did the journalists often asked me the names of specific places. I knew most of them, but as we traveled along the East Side of Manhattan I wasn't sure of the names of some of the bridges, and also wasn't sure of the names of a few other spots. So I would tell them, in Spanish, " I think it's the (name) but ***no estoy seguro*** (I'm not sure)." When the two weeks were up, the journalists gave me a gift, which I cherish. It's a small plaque that says ***"To Kal: No Estoy Seguro. L.A.J. 1985."***

June 16, 1985: My uncle Nat Wagenheim died, age 89, after a long, healthy life. He was a remarkable man. He worked for many years driving around to stores and supermarkets, making sure that his company's products were well placed. When he reached age 65 the company required him to retire, but he wasn't ready. So he went to work for another company for 14 more years. Finally, at age 79, his driving became a bit erratic and he really had to retire. But he still wasn't ready. Around 1981 Uncle Nat told his son Bill that he wanted a part-time job. Bill's store in downtown Newark was a retailer of electronics equipment, and in the basement were several technicians who repaired defective equipment. Uncle Nat became their librarian, organizing all the technical data sheets that came pouring in. Uncle Nat was such a relaxed, sensible man that family members often sought him out for advice. If someone said there was a serious problem and asked him what he thought, Uncle Nat would think for a moment, and then say "You know? A hundred years from now we're gonna laugh about this." Uncle Nat was also a very healthy man, and took all sorts of vitamins each day. Once, when we met, I asked him about vitamins and he recited a long list of supplements that I still take each morning. I buy them at The Vitamin Shoppe on Route 22 in Union NJ. They include: E-400, Folic Acid, Ecotrin Aspirin, Zinc, Saw Palmetto, Multi, Garlic, Vitamin C (prefer chewable), Glucosamine-Chondroitin, Omega Fish Oil, Calcium-Magnesium. I can't prove that these are the reason for my good health, but so far I've been fortunate.

Dec. 23, 1985: Finally, after much back and forth between lawyers, testimony of relatives and many others, an agreement was reached on Rose Hoffman's estate. Most of it went to charity. I was granted a "settlement" of about $91,000. My attorney fees of $35,000 were deducted from his amount, so I wound up with about $56,000. The money was most welcome, and it was also a great relief to see the end to the legal conflict. I was earning enough to support myself, so I invested the funds in bonds and mutual funds for my retirement. *When the settlement came I recalled the poem Rosie wrote to me around the time of my birth that "in years to come, you will collect a great sum." She was right!*

"Cousin" Gita Wagenheim

In the late 1980s, while in Washington DC with the visiting Latin American journalists, I accidentally learned of a Gita Wagenheim who had come to the USA from Riga not long before, and worked in the Latvian language department of the Voice of America. Gita explained that her father, Leon, was Jewish, her mother Christian. He wanted to move to Israel. The Mom said she might go later. Gita, working then as an actress in the Latvian state theatre, went with her Dad to Vienna, for eventual transfer to Israel. While in Vienna her Dad died of a heart attack. Gita was left alone, and since her mother was not Jewish there was no easy entry into Israel, where she had no strong desire to go anyway. She learned of a cousin, or friend, in the USA and moved there, where I met her. A few years later, Gita met and married Al Morris, a college professor, and they remain married, and travel often. I stay in touch with birthday & Xmas cards, and send her fond regards, calling her *"Masica"* (Latvian for "Female Cousin") and she calls me *"Bralens*" (Latvian for "Male Cousin").

1986: Olga was awarded tenure at the History Department of Newark-Rutgers. This followed the publication of her dissertation to positive reviews and additional published articles in academic journals. Glowing teaching evaluations and solid recommendations from scholars in my field helped to convince her colleagues in the History Dept. to recommend her for tenure. She recalls: "The tenure process is a very difficult challenge for most academics, as it keeps the candidate in limbo for oneentire year, if there are no complications. Mine went through within the year, but it was not a pleasant process."

THE WALL STREET JOURNAL

While working as the U.S. correspondent for *Caribbean Business*, in New York I came into contact with offices of various Caribbean nations, including St. Lucia One day I received a phone call from Michele Evenson, a young lady who sold advertising for *The Wall St. Journal.* She explained that the paper was planning an "advertorial" about investment opportunities in St. Lucia. She asked if I'd be interested in a week-long assignment to go to St. Lucia and develop an article for the "advertorial." She explained that the head of the St. Lucia office, based on his contacts with me, suggested that I be given the assignment. It worked out well, and Michele later assigned me to several similar projects. Michele and I met periodically for lunch in New York (often at the lovely mezzanine restaurant of the Paramount Hotel on West 46th St.), to discuss business, and also became friends. I learned that Michele was born in the southwestern US to an American father (who later passed away) and a Mexican mother. As a result, Michele speaks both English and Spanish. One day, after graduating from college, she attended a job fair, presented her credentials, and *The Wall Street Journal* hired her. She quickly rose up the ranks to take charge of advertising promotion in the Caribbean and Latin America.

In most cases I spent an average of one week in each country, gathering information via interviews with key contacts. The sections included: St. Lucia (April 9, 1986); Caribbean Travel (Oct. 30, 1986); Dominican Republic (June 22, 1987); Caribbean Travel (Oct. 29, 1987); Dominica (Dec. 2, 1987); Jamaica (June 6, 1988); Caribbean Basin Opportunities (Nov. 4, 1988); Costa Rica (1988); Mexico (Jan. 23, 1989); Venezuela (June 2, 1989); Caribbean Travel

(Dec. 1, 1989); Trinidad & Tobago (May 23, 1990); Mexico (Oct. 1, 1990); Caribbean Travel (Oct. 19, 1990); Mexico (April 12, 1991); Argentina (Nov. 18, 1991); Venezuela (Dec. 11, 1991); Argentina (Sept. 21, 1992); Mexico (Sept. 22, 1992); Mexico (Oct. 26, 1993); Argentina (Oct. 27, 1994); Mexico (Dec. 8, 1994); Argentina (April 22, 1996).I recall a funny moment. In most cases *The Wall St Journal* had a key contact in each country who helped to arrange for interviews, and also helped Michele pin down advertisers. One time, Michele and I flew down to Panama, and our "contact" there turned out to be a total failure. He didn't seem to know anybody! After a day or so of fruitless traveling around in taxis, Michele and I shrugged, laughed and flew back to New York. *C'est la vie!*

Except for the Panama "disaster," these assignments were lucrative and the trips, together with my work for *Caribbean Business*, provided me with valuable background information which would allow me to strengthen my *Caribbean Update* newsletter business, launched in early 1985. Another memorable episode. One day Michele invited me to a lunch at a rather fancy restaurant in midtown Manhattan (don't recall the name) which specialized in all sort of exotic fish dishes. For some reason I ate a rather strong pickled herring. Afterwards, prior to returning home, I called my old friend Marvin Schwartz, who lives in Greenwich Village, and suggested that we meet for coffee. We met at a diner near Sheridan Square (since closed and now a Starbuck's). I ordered coffee and a cream pie, without realizing that, in my case, pickled herring and cream pie are a "fatal" combination. After a few minutes, I began to feel faint and started moaning. Marvin, quite casually, said: "If you're having a heart attack, Saint Vincent's Hospital is just a couple of blocks away." After a few moments, the crisis passed. But ever since then I've learned not to mix pickled fish and cream pie! Some years later, Michele married, had a young daughter, Ariadne, resigned from *The Journal,* and she and her husband Scott Lindsay (an executive in the world of finance with Credit Suisse) moved to England. A few years ago, they returned to New York and we have met occasionally for lunch She is so bright, I wouldn't be surprised if, when her daughter grows older, Michele may want to return to the advertising world, where she excels.

June 2-12, 1986: Coinciding with our 25th wedding anniversary, Olga and I spent a marvelous time with Cousins Bill & Shirley Wagenheim, visiting Spain and Portugal. First we flew via Iberia from JFK-NYC to Madrid, then took the Talgo express train to San Sebastian on the north coast. There, via Avis we rented a car and drove west along the coast, stopping at different small resorts, including Santander (with its elegant casino), Ribadasella, the old quarter of Oviedo, stopping at a small jewel of a parador in Ribadeo, Portobello. Then a short visit to Portugal. Among the most memorable there was Nazaré, a coastal fishing village. Then flew back to Madrid, and finally returned to NYC on Iberia.

1987-1991: Olga recalls: "The summer following my promotion to tenure (1987) I was selected as one of twelve NEH (National Endowment for the Humanities) fellows for a summer post graduate course of study, held in St. John's College in Santa Fe, New Mexico. The course revolved around studying the Portuguese language and Brazilian history and culture. The idea for course had been proposed by Prof. Jon Tolman and a Brazilian colleague. I did well in that program and as a result was invited by the same professors to attend a course they were holding the following year in Sao Paulo, Brazil. I was unable to accept the offer. My volunteer work in the growing Latino community of New Jersey led me to meet the dynamic Gloria Bonilla Santiago, who was then (1987) seeking to establish the Hispanic Women's Task Force. I became quite active with that group and served on its board for the following five years. In that organization I had the privilege of working very closely with a very devoted group of Latina women, which included, in addition to Gloria, Maria Vizcarrondo, Wanda Garcia (Gloria's right hand throughout), Alicia Diaz, Ivette Mendez, Veronica Escala-Waldman, Carmen Jones, among others whose names I cannot remember off hand. The double mission of the Task Force was to aid professional Latina women to break through the glass ceiling and to help low-income Latina women to obtain training and useful skills that would enable them to find employment. For the former, the Task Force created a series of leadership workshops and for the latter, it pushed a law through the state legislature that would permit the creation of three multi-service centers, paid for by the state, to train the women. The centers were established in part because of the support of many legislators and the incoming governor Jim Florio. One of those centers was located at Casa de Don Pedro in Newark. The funds for the leadership workshops were diligently raised by Gloria Bonilla, often with the help of Maria Vizcarrondo and/or Ivette Mendez. The experience I gained at the HWTF and the friendships I made during those five years enriched my life in wonderful ways. I discovered that within the Hispanic communities there are incredibly talented and devoted women. Since my next promotion would depend on a different type of academic work (not on oral history or the development of the local Puerto Rican community) I continued to write and present papers on Puerto Ricans and Puerto Rico at national and international academic conferences. During the next few years I wrote and published numerous articles and book reviews. For personal satisfaction I served on the boards of the National Puerto Rican Coalition, Aspira of New Jersey and two editorial boards."

March 26, 1988. My great-uncle David Shanberg dies, at age 91, in Greensboro, NC.

Sept. 2, 1988. Letter from me to Frank Wolf, Associate Dean, General Studies, Columbia University. Dear Frank: This is to confirm that I am regretfully unable to continue in 1989 as Director of the Seminar for the Latin American/Caribbean Journalists. The growth of my Caribbean Update newsletter (which I founded in 1985) has made it impossible for me to properly attend to the demands of other major projects, such as the seminar. It has been a pleasure directing the seminar for the past seven years (the time has gone by so quickly!), and working with you, Ward Dennis, Evelyn Tavarelli, and the folks at Citibank. I have particularly fond memories of the many friends I made among my Latin American colleagues—a rare fringe benefit. Citibank and Columbia are to be congratulated for sponsoring and designing this innovative program, which has allowed so many journalists from abroad to enhance their understanding of the United States, and of American viewpoints towards their countries. All the best in future seminars. If I can be of any assistance in recruiting—or briefing—my replacement, don't hesitate to call.

Dec. 31, 1988: For New Year's Eve, Olga and & I went with our friends Shirley & Howard Stuewe to the huge cathedral in Newark at 7 pm and we heard the most beautiful choir music. What a marvelous way to welcome in the new year.

Aug. 11-12, 1989. Olga and I travel to see my nephew Lowell Stern & Juleen Savarese marry at lavish ceremony in Charlottesville, Virginia.

The 1990s Onward

March 9, 1990. My letter in The NY Times

Nicaragua Votes for End to Washington's Siege; Cuba's Turn?

To the Editor: William Safire gleefully predicts in ''Castro's Last Stand" (column, Feb. 19) the ''coming downfall'' of President Fidel Castro of Cuba. He links this event to ''the economic crisis facing his Soviet sponsors'' and other political changes sweeping the Communist world in Eastern Europe.I am neither a seer nor a booster of the Castro regime, and Mr. Safire's prediction may well come true. His views, however, appear to be based on wishful thinking and an astonishing ignorance of Cuba. President Castro, in power since 1959, has outlasted seven United States Presidents, and I am willing to make a modest even-money wager with Mr. Safire that he may still be around when President Bush completes his term in 1993. One key reason President Castro stands a chance of survival is that his Government must be viewed in its regional context. The crumbling Communist regimes of Eastern Europe were economic basket cases compared with their Western European neighbors. But Cuba, while far poorer than the neighboring United States, provides a standard of living that is comparable, and in several cases superior, to that in most other Caribbean and Central American countries. Cubans, despite limits on personal freedom and the clear (to me) shortcomings of a centralized Communist economic system, are better fed, housed and educated, and enjoy better health care than do the citizens of several nearby countries with a capitalist system. Infant mortality in Cuba, for example, is now about 11 per 1,000 births, about the same as New Zealand and Israel, far lower than that of such free enterprise neighbors as the Dominican Republic (66), Haiti (118), Honduras (70), Guatemala (60), El Salvador (60), Trinidad (20), Jamaica (18) and Costa Rica (18). And while Cuba is in the midst of a serious economic crisis, the same can be said of many of its non-Communist regional neighbors, overwhelmed by debt and inflation. Their exports command successively lower prices on the world market, and their citizens continue to migrate to the United States in search of opportunity. Third world underdevelopment is a tenacious problem that crosses ideological barriers and defies simple formulas. These facts Mr. Safire forgets or chooses to ignore. As for human rights, he is curiously selective when he rails against the ''tyranny'' in Cuba, while making no mention of murder and mayhem committed by governments in Haiti, Guatemala and El Salvador. *KAL WAGENHEIM, Maplewood, N.J., Feb. 21, 1990 The writer is editor of Caribbean Update, a monthly newsletter.*

April 16, 1990. Letter from Wendy Sherman, Henry Holt & Co., 115 W.16th St., NYC NY 10011. "Dear Kal: This is to confirm our discussion regarding your book *Babe Ruth: His Life & Legend.* Holt will proceed in our negotiations with Warner Bros. TV for the television license. The offer at present is $1,500 option plus a $10,000 purchase price…John Goodman is signed to star. NBC is the network. Per the contract, Holt retains 20% of proceeds. The agent in Los Angeles gets 10% off the top. Holt has agreed to permit you to print 2,000 trade paperback copies of the book. I'm so glad we can work together on this." *Note: The NY Times on 5/31/91 had a brief mention that "'The Babe Ruth Story'...starts shooting on Tuesday as an NBC television movie. Scheduled to be broadcast this fall, it stars Stephen Lang, who is up for a Tony award on Sunday for his role in 'The Speed of Darkness'."*

Feb. 1991: *Founded Mexico Business Monthly* newsletter, published together with *Caribbean Update* newsletter. Teamed up with my son David (then age 29). He focused on administrative and marketing, and I handled the editorial work.

1991: My 1974 biography, *Babe Ruth: His Life & Legend*, a Playboy Book Club selection, is adapted for an NBC-TV film (1991). "Graceful and anecdotal and uncommonly readable ... Wagenheim's richly detailed narrative has the power to touch off both guffaws and tears" -- Roger Angell, *The New York Times. Available as audiocassette, on-line from E-Reads.com and in paperback from Olmstead Books/LPC Group.*

Fidel Castro's Autograph!

May 21-26, 1991. Olga and I spent five fascinating days in Havana, Cuba, where we attended the annual conference of the Caribbean Studies Association. One memory: during the conference I chatted with a Cuban political scientist and asked him what he believed were the possibilities that the USA and Cuba might achieve normal diplomatic relations, thus ending the embargo. His reply was somewhat prophetic. "We are cursed," he said. "China is also a Communist country, but China has a huge population of 1 billion people and is an irresistible market for the United States. We have only 10 million people in Cuba; we are an interesting market, but not an irresistible one." Another day, José Ignacio Jimenez, a Puerto Rican gentleman married to the Venezuelan ambassador to Cuba invited us to his lovely home on the outskirts of Havana. During lunch, I commented how peaceful and beautiful it was. "Fidel loves to come here once in a while, to relax," he said. "Fidel and I have one thing in common," I said, half joking. "We both love baseball."

"Yes!" said our host, "he really does!" Back in 1973 I had written a biography of Puerto Rican baseball star Roberto Clemente, and a Mexican publisher had issued a small number of copies in Spanish translation. When I told our host that I could send a copy of the Clemente book as a gift for Fidel, he expressed interest. Around July I remembered my promise, and found a copy in our basement. I inscribed it, in Spanish, *"To Fidel Castro, from one ex-ballplayer to another, with the hope that our two countries will someday be friends,"* and mailed it to our host in Havana. I expected no reply, but in late October the mailman brought a copy of a 157-page book in Spanish, "Present and Future of Cuba: Interview With The Magazine Siempre!", a long interview with Fidel by a visiting journalist. It was accompanied by a note from Jose, saying *"Fidel had dinner with us yesterday. I had been planning to give him your book personally for quite a long time. This explains our silence. The opportunity arose after we sat down to eat. He showed great interest and appreciation as you will see by his dedicatory inscription. One of his most most attractive qualities is his capacity for individual attention when the situation arises, as was this case."* Inside the book, on the first page, Fidel inscribed it, in Spanish: *"To Kal Wagenheim, with profound gratitude for your book. We shall be friends! Fidel Castro. Oct. 28, 91"*

May 28, 1991: By accident, Olga & I met a married couple who would become dear friends over the years. Norma & Alfredo Wilk, from Buenos Aires, were vacationing a year or two earlier in Italy and they met our friends from Puerto Rico, Irma Rodriguez and her husband Orlando Samalot. They traveled together. Now, we received word from our Puerto Rico friends, saying the Wilks were coming to New York in a few days and would love to see a certain hit musical. Could I get tickets for them? I traveled often to Manhattan, so I went to the theatre box office and found good seats for May 28. On May 27, I called them at their hotel on W. 44th (they had just arrived) and told them I had the tickets. The only way to give them the tickets on time was for us to head into Manhattan and deliver them personally. We picked them up at the hotel and went down to the West Village, had a nice lunch at Sazerac restaurant. Alfredo was a doctor, head of orthopedic medicine at the municipal hospital in Buenos Aires. His wife, Norma operated a family-owned paint factory. During our lunch I asked where Alfredo's family had come from when they migrated to Argentina. "Bessarabia," he replied. That's exactly where my great-grandparents came from in 1890. We immediately bonded, and would see much more of them in future years

Oct. 12, 1991: Saw Mozart's *"The Marriage of Figaro"* at the intimate Amato Opera Theatre in the lower East Side. I am becoming a Mozart-DaPonte fan. Joining us was my sister June, who became all excited when she noticed that sitting directly behind us was F. Murray Abraham, the actor who played the role of Salieri in *"Amadeus,"* the film about Mozart.

1991: Olga was awarded a Fulbright Fellowship to Argentina, Won the Outstanding Teacher of the Year Award at Rutgers-Newark and was invited to serve as Distinguished Visiting Scholar at William Paterson University. She recalls: "The year 1991 was a particularly exciting year for me, as I went to live in Buenos Aires (August-December), where I learned a great deal about about a part of the world I knew only through books. Argentina then under the Presidency of Menem, had restructured its economy and had exchanged its currency at parity with the U.S. dollar. There was much excitement and great hopes that Argentina would become L.A.'s leader. Teaching in Argentina, where university attendance was free of charge to all who qualified, was a revelation for me. I discovered also that, students received little else from the state and that they had had a tough time finding the texts for the courses they took. Thus, in preparation for my course, called U.S. Puerto Rico Relations, I brought along many boxes of books, paid for by the Fulbright program in Washington, D.C. and which were shipped free of charge via the U.S. Embassy in Buenos Aires. I was told by the very students there that they had Xeroxed most of the readings I assigned. At the Graduate School I discovered that all university professors generally taught at more than one institution in order to make ends meet. The contact person to me at UBA by the Ford Foundation, the historian Dr. Pablo Pozzi, I saw only three times in five months because he taught at three different universities, one of them a nine hour ride by bus in the city of Rosario and another in Patagonia, an eight hour trip by plane. Because of these grueling schedules professors were hardly available and students tended to work on their own. They told me that having access to me on a regular basis was a real luxury. I found out on my first teaching night that the classroom lacked heat, chalk and erasers. I sat with my coat on for the duration of the course, and brought in my own chalk an eraser. Yet, despite the shortages and inconveniences, I found the students to be well prepared for class and very enthusiastic. Our hours together were very enlightening to me, as they constantly made made comparisons between Argentina and other places. They taught me much more than I taught them. While in B.A. I made several trips to a few outer provinces, including Cordoba, Bariloche, San Martin de los Andes. In the latter I visited a colony of Mapuche Indians, to the surprise of many Argentines, who claimed that the country had neither blacks nor Indians. My trip to Cordoba was memorable because everywhere I went I was asked to repeat myself so the listener could hear my Caribbean accent, which apparently was quite amusing. In Buenos Aires I met wonderful people that over time became long-lasting friends."

Oct. 18, 1991: I traveled to Argentina several times to be with Olga. We flew there via Newark-Miami-Buenos Aires on our first visit. I managed to obtain an assignment from the *Wall Street Journal* to prepare an "advertorial" that highlights investment opportunities in the country. We were immediately "adopted" by our friends Norma & Alfredo Wilk, who introduced us to their wide circle of friends. On the very first day, I baked a challah which I shared with our friends. Thanks to them we see much of this wonderful country, including the spectacular Iguazú Falls, and the impressive Teatro Colón opera house.. On Oct. 25, I managed to interview President Menem and Economy Minister Cavallo. I returned home Oct. 26.

1992: Olga returned to Rutgers for one semester in 1992 and then took a leave of absence during the fall in order to supervising the remodeling of our Maplewood home, carried out by Tom O'Donovan, an excellent contractor. The respite from teaching and other academic chores gave her time to reconsider what else she wished to do to advance her career. She opted to begin research for a history of Puerto Rico. That project, because of her teaching and other obligations, took nearly five years. The book (*Puerto Rico: From Pre-Columbian Times to 1900*) would be published by Markus Wiener in 1998.

July 25, 1992: Another flight to Buenos Aires, via Miami. I return on Aug. 3. The short detective novels of Simenon have become my favorite traveling companions.

Sept. 26, 1992: Flew with Olga to Madrid to attend the Inter-American Press Assocation (IAPA) conference, held there to commemorate the 500th anniversary of the discovery of America. On Sept. 29, we actually saw the King and Queen of Spain at one of the events. On Oct. 2, we flew to Seville to attend the World's Fair there. I had a terrible cold, Olga went to a local pharmacy and bought pills which made me feel well enough to walk around. I thought it was a miraculous cold cure (I later learned that in the USA it was called Alka-Seltzer Cold Plus!). Visited the Latvian pavilion, had lunch at a Korean restaurant, and dinner at the Puerto Rico pavilion. While waiting for a bus one day a thief tried to make off with Olga's purse, but other bystanders helped her hold on to it in the tug-of-war, and the thief scampered away. Returned home via Madrid on Oct. 4.

March 8, 1993. Sad news about the man who hired me to work for the New York Times in 1967. Obituary below in the New York Times.

Henry Giniger, 71, Correspondent Who Chronicled Postwar Europe

By CLIFFORD J. LEVY

Henry Giniger, a longtime correspondent for The New York Times who spent two decades chronicling the rise of postwar France before moving on to report from dozens of other countries, died yesterday at a hospital in Paris. He was 71 and lived in Boulogne, a suburb of Paris. He had lung cancer, said his daughter, Marianne Moncrief of Westfield, N.J. Mr. Giniger joined the Paris bureau of The Times in 1946 and soon became a mainstay of the paper's European coverage. Fluent in French, Spanish and Portuguese, he specialized in articles that described the political scene on the Continent as its nascent governments struggled to rebuild. He was regarded as a correspondent who thrived on breaking news events and distinguished himself in his reporting from Budapest during the Soviet invasion of Hungary in 1956 and from Algeria during the revolution there in the early 1960's. In 1965 he moved to Mexico City, from which he covered Latin America, winning an Overseas Press Club Award in 1969 for the best reporting from that region.

He then returned to Paris and in 1972 took over the Madrid bureau, covering the Portuguese revolution, the death of Franco and Spain's return to democracy. He later was head of the newspaper's bureaus in Montreal and Ottawa. In 1982 he moved to New York to work as an editor on the Week in Review section. He retired in 1987. Mr. Giniger was born on Jan. 15, 1922, in Brooklyn and attended City College before receiving a master's degree in journalism at Columbia University. During World War II he served in the Marines as a combat correspondent, writing for The Stars and Stripes newspaper. Slight of build, he once told his family that he had landed on the beach at Iwo Jima with a rifle over one shoulder and a portable typewriter over the other.

May 27, 1994: Since my wife Olga has such a large, loving family in Puerto Rico, we decided to buy an apartment in San Juan, where we could spend part of the winter months We flew to Puerto Rico, stayed at the Dutch Inn Hotel in the Condado for a week, and thanks to a very energetic realtor we found a two-bedroom apartment on the 10th floor of Condominium Torre Del Mar, at 1477 Ashford Avenue in the Condado sector of San Juan, right next to the Ashford Presybterian Hospital. The purchase price was $167,000. The apartment is a block in from the beach and has a magnificent view of the Atlantic Ocean. At the time, Olga was still working at Rutgers, so we were only able to use the apartment for a couple of weeks soon after the Christmas holidays. We soon after arranged for San Juan Vacations, a realtor, to rent out the apartment during the rest of the year. This was helpful, since they rented it on average about 6 months of the year.

August 14, 1994. My niece Rebecca "Becky" Stern and Michael McElreath marry.

May 19, 1995. Letter from James M. Stuart, Hofstra University, Hempstead NY 11550-1090. Dear Mr. Wagenheim: Thurs, April 27, Friday, April 28, and Saturday, April 29, 1995 will go down in history as the dates of one of Hofstra University's most interesting and successful conferences. Thank you for participating in *"Baseball and The Sultan of Swat."* The conference was a major league success due to the valuable support the University received from people such as you. (Note: I took part on April 27 in Forum "C-Biographers and Historians Assess The Babe," together with, among others, Robert W. Creamer, author of *Babe: The Legend Comes to Life.*

May 21-30, 1995: Olga & I went to Italy on a tour organized by ABC Tours. Wonderful stays in Venice, Florence and Rome. Diane Wagenheim, daughter of my cousins Bill & Shirley accompanied us on the trip. While in Venice, Olga's sister Maria and her husband Doug met up with us (they had earlier been in Switzerland, visiting Doug's brother Craig, who lives there with his wife). ABC Tours proved to be a comfy way to vacation. They provided air travel, first-class hotels, and bus travel between the cities. They also offer optional tours in the cities, but allow you to be on your own whenever you prefer.

Sept. 24, 1995: On occasion of my wife Olga's birthday, my sister June wrote a lovely poem, a tribute to Olga's father, Santos Jiménez, a wonderful man who played an important role in the life of Olga and the rest of his large family. June met Don Santos not long after I was reunited with my sister, in the 1970s and she came with us to Puerto Rico with her then small children, Lowell and Becky.

Poem for Olga

It was Don Santos
who wrapped her in a blanket
when she was ill
and rode with her on horseback
past the sugar cane
and rounded hills,
to the doctor's house.
And it was Don Santos
who saw to it
that she went to school
in New York, the first
of his children to leave the island,
she went the furthest. Still
returns to see him,
although he no longer
ride horses, or dances
as he used to;
Elegant, the way he held one hand
behind his back,
at his waist;
"La Danza," all around a room
filled with his in-laws,
daughters, nieces,
now on Sundays,
they bring his favorite dishes.
They surround his chair,
Lupe, Carmelo, Juanita,
they are all there.
He is their center,
once a rider of horses,
a dancer of dances,
gentle farmer,
anchor, starter;
Olga's father.

WRITING PLAYS AND FILM SCRIPTS

Somewhere in the mid-1990s, I decided to try a new genre: screenwriting. I had for some years admired the music of legendary Argentine tango idol Carlos Gardel (1890-1935), who died in a tragic plane crash at the peak of his career. I listened to his music, and researched his career, and then wrote a screenplay, "Tango King" about his life and death. After completing the first draft of the screenplay, I learned of a symposium on screenwriting at the Museum of the Moving Image in Queens NY and decided to attend. Several leading screenwriters on stage offered helpful advice, and then opened it up to questions from the audience. A few rows in front of me a young lady rose. She explained that she had recently graduated from the film school in Buenos Aires, and then asked something. At the conclusion of the symposium I approached her, and said that I, a gringo, had written a screenplay about the tango star Carlos Gardel. That's how I met Fernanda Rossi, then 28 years old, a recent arrival from Argentina. She said she was willing to look at the script, which was the beginning of our friendship, which endures to this day. I sent her the script, she replied with very helpful comments, and said that a friend of hers was enrolled in a weekly screenwriting/drama workshop with a Mick Casale, who taught at the Graduate Film School at NYU, and also provided the workshop away from NYU.

Oct. 3, 1996: Based on Fernanda Rossi's recommendation, I called Mick Casale, who lives in lower Manhattan, and joined a Thursday evening writing workshop in Manhattan, at 18 West 18th St., run by Present Tense Productions, a loosely knit group of writers and actors. We met from 7 pm. to 10 pm on Thursday nights and it cost $360 per semester (well worth it). It was quite convenient, since I taught earlier in the day at the Writing Division of Columbia University on W. 116th St. After class, I would drive down the West Side Highway, find parking on W. 18th St, at 6 pm, enjoy a light supper at a diner on 6th Ave., and then walk to the workshop, where I learned a great deal and also made friends with a number of talented writers. This was the start of my new "career" as a playwright / screenwriter, which has not earned me substantial amounts of money but has enriched my spirit.

Fernanda Rossi gradually become part of our "family." We often invited her to our home and she also visited us in Puerto Rico. Fernanda is a brilliant young lady. At first she made a living editing TV commercials. Later, after producing a documentary film about home schooling, she became a recognized expert and travels all over the US and some foreign countries, serving as a consultant to other documentary filmmakers.

Are you Julio?

A few years later, via Email I contacted Julio Orione, a journalist in Buenos Aires, who was also a tango fan. Julio then told me he was coming to New York to attend a conference. I contacted Fernanda Rossi and suggested that we meet Julio for lunch while he was in town. We met at the Paramount Hotel on West 46th St. Fernanda and I sat at a table in the mezzanine restaurant, overlooking the lobby entrance. One problem: neither of us had ever met Julio. We kept looking down, watching folks enter the lobby. I saw a man in his 40s, with a fashionable leather jacket, and decided that was him. I ran down the stairs, hurried up to the man, smiled and asked "Are you Julio." The man looked at me, smiled, and in a flirtatious tone replied "That depends!" Clearly it was not Julio. I returned to my seat. Then came another young person, also smartly dressed, and Fernanda said it was her turn. Moments later, she returned, laughing, and explained that it was a woman with a man's haircut! A few minutes later, we finally spotted Julio, who entered and looked around, and this time I went down, shook his hand, and we enjoyed a good lunch together. Some time later Olga & I went to Buenos Aires and Julio took us to lunch. We have remained in touch via E-mail ever since.

May 2, 1997: My one-act play ***"Bavarian Rage"* is** produced at Annual Off-Off Broadway Original Short Play Festival at Harold Clurman Theatre in NYC, the first time a work of mine is performed. It all began in late

1996 during Mick Casale's workshop in NYC, when I was told of the play festival. It was around the time of the OJ Simpson trial. One afternoon in Greenwich Village, while having lunch with dear friends Marvin Schwartz and Leon King at a diner by Sheridan Square in the West Village (since closed and now a Starbucks), I jokingly commented that the "dream team" of lawyers defending OJ Simpson would defend "anyone, even Adolf Hitler." They laughed. That inspired me to write the one-act play about a "dream team" of lawyers defending a man who may (or may not) be Hitler. Synopsis: Adolf Hitler alive? A wannabe "dream team" of lawyers eagerly interviews their hoped for ticket to fame, an elderly man who may—or may not—be The Fuhrer. Film rights! Book deals! Interview with Larry King! It's a bonanza! There are surprises galore in this edgy madcap comedy of shifting identities. It was accepted for the festival, and suddenly I was a playwright! I had no idea what to do next, but through members of Mick's class I somehow found a young woman, Alexandra Aristy, to direct the play, and a cast was put together. Several rehearsals were held, and I watched with awe as the actors brought life to my written lines. The play was performed at the Harold Clurman Theatre on W. 42d St., and well received but did not move on to the finals However, it was a joyous occasion, attended by friends, family and members of the writing workshop. Later, inspired by the positive feedback, I expanded the play to a full-length, and also converted it to a screenplay. Since then, the play has had modest success, with staged readings, but no actual production.

May 29, 1997: The modest success of *"Bavarian Rage"* inspired me to remain with Mick Casale's weekly workshop and continue working on other plays and screenplays. This Thursday night I brought in 30 pages of my screenplay about legendary tango singer Carlos Gardel, which the group read aloud, and provided helpful critical comments. Each Thursday I also enjoyed reading the work of other members of the group, and found that by offering critical comments to them it helped me improve my own skills. Among the skilled writers were some who became good friends: Beth Holden, Frank Verderame, Marie Trusits, Beth Novick,Victoria Janis, Sue & Tim Nolan, Kim Cummings, Alex Ladd, Fred Rosenberg, Ingalisa Schrobsdorff. *Note: Marie Trusits was working with a law firm in New York at the time, and before the workshop we often met for dinner at Portfolio, a nice restaurant just a block away on W. 19th St. Some years later, Marie* *moved to Verona NJ, became an elementary school teacher, and we remained in touch until her death in 2012.*

Beth Holden, a member of Mick Casale's writing workshop, has remained a dear friend to this day. Beth and her husband Chris Greco live in Yonkers, and she directs a writing progam at Westchester County Community College. She is also writing a graduate thesis (as of Spring 2013). Beth is a fine writer, with a great sense of humor. One of her funniest works is *"Royal Flush,"* a short play based on the life of Mr. Crapper, who helped to perfect the flush toilet. After Mick's class, I occasionally drove her to Grand Central Station so she could take the train home to Yonkers. In later years, Beth and I met for lunch at Sam's on W. 45th St. (now closed), and also at the New Leaf Café, a lovely place at The Cloisters. Beth, born in Pittsburgh PA, came to New York years ago, and had a variety of interesting jobs, including as an assistant to TV star David Letterman. She also wrote several magazine articles. At one point, she met and married Chris Greco, a sound engineer who travels near and far to cover concerts and other events. Olga and I attended their wedding in August 2000. Beth's current work-in-progress is a memoir about her and Chris's move to their home in Yonkers. First, it is for her thesis, but later I think it would make a fine novel.

June 1, 1997: Olga and I attended a wonderful 60th birthday party luncheon for my sister June at Tavern on the Green in Manhattan.

Sept. 5, 1997. I had been teaching News & Feature Writing one day a week at Columbia University since 1977, but student interest in the course declined. I was called in by the people who run The Writing Program and said that this semester there would only be one section of the course taught, instead of two. And, since Lawrence Van Gelder of *The NY Times* had been teaching the course even before I began, he would continue. However, Professors Austin Flint & Alan Ziegler, who administered The Writing Program, invited me in for a chat, and told me that, since I had recently had a play produced and had others in the works, I could remain on the faculty, teaching one section of a popular course, "Structure & Style I," an introduction to creative writing, including fiction, drama and poetry. Austin & Alan met with me, gave me a syllabus for the course, and some advice on how to run it, and I began teaching S&S I on Thursdays for nearly another decade.

1998: Not sure of the date, but I believe it was this year when our dear friend Ernie Potvin passed away in Simi Valley, California. We knew Ernie in Puerto Rico during the 1960s, and among other things he was the graphic designer for our monthly magazine *The San Juan Review*. Ernie later moved to California, and we visited him there once. Ernie was very active in the movement for gay rights. A fine writer, he self-published *"La Chancletera and other Latin Faerie tales"* a 24-page story collection that is a gem, and can be purchased on the Internet.

July 1, 1998: During the weekly workshop with Mick Casale, I wrote a one-act play *"We Beat Whitey Ford"* which has been produced a few times. Mick Casale said we should come up with a short play for a festival. Driving home that night, I thought about my friendship in high school with a fellow baseball player, Ralph Fortson, and somehow the play took shape. Later, as I lay in bed, even more ideas appeared, and by the next morning much of the play was there in my mind. Two former high school baseball teammates -- one black, one white -- meet twenty years later at Newark Airport, and seek to bridge the racial/class gulf that separates them. This is a moving, often funny, tale of friendship, of race relations in America, and of the chasm between youthful dreams and reality—between what we want and what we get. *"A nice clean... honest play... before it's through, you might feel a few emotions welling up." –Jerry Tallmer, The Village.*

July 22, 1998: I was invited to attend an HBO screening of the *"Babe Ruth"* film, based in part on my biography, at a theatre in Manhattan.

July 24-Aug. 1, 1998: We flew to Buenos Aires, spent time with dear friends. Sightseeing. One highlight was a visit to Señor Tango, a huge nightclub, which offers fine food and great tango music, including dancers. While there we also met with Julio Orione, a leading journalist from *Clarín*, a Buenos Aires daily. As mentioned previously, I had corresponded with him earlier, when we discovered we had a mutual interest: tango.

July 31, 1998. *Letter from HBO, 1100 Ave. of the Americas, NYC NY 10036-6737.* Dear Kal: On behalf of HBO Sports and Black Canyon Productions, we would like to thank you for taking the time to participate in "Babe Ruth:"...(it) will be seen on HBO the following dates and times: Aug. 16, 8 pm E/P, Aug. 19, 11:30 a.m. E/P, Aug. 20, 7:30 p.m. E/P, Aug. 22, 8 a.m. E/P. Thanks to you and the cooperation of other participants who were as gracious with their time, we were able to produce a show which we believe you can be very proud of. Enclosed please find a copy so that you may screen the program at your leisure and add it to your library…Sincerely, Ross Greenburg, Exec. Producer,, Rick Bernstein, Senior Producer, George Roy, Producer and Editor, Steve Stern, Producer and Writer.

1999: Death At Weehawken. The idea for this full-length play (later also converted to a screenplay) was born one day when I was driving along the Jersey side of the Hudson River at Weehawken NJ and I saw a small monument recalling the day when Vice President Aaron Burr shot and killed Alexander Hamilton in a duel. I researched the story at the library and wrote the script. **Synopsis:** This historical drama probes a two-centuries old mystery: what passions compelled the Vice President of the United States (Aaron Burr) and the former Secretary of Treasury (Alexander Hamilton) to engage in a fatal duel? Touching upon themes that resonate today, it is a tale of sex, jealousy, corruption, bare knuckle politics, and a scandal-hungry press, culminating in the deadly encounter, in 1804, on the west bank of the Hudson River. *(Semi-finalist in the 1999-2000 Playwrights First competition sponsored by The National Arts Club.*

1999: Republication of my English translation, from Spanish, of *"The Pond"*, a classic 19th century novel by Manuel Zeno-Gandía, by Markus Wiener Publishers, Princeton NJ. "A classic of Latin American fiction (in) a modern and colloquial translation" -- *The Nation.*

Aug. 14, 1999. My niece Rebecca Stern marries Michael McElreath.

Oct. 18, 1999. Letter to actor Eli Wallach, via his agent in NYC. Dear Mr. Wallach: I have long admired your work and I believe you would be an excellent choice for the lead role in my full-length play *'Bavarian Rage'*… Synopsis: A 'dream team' of lawyers meets in Manhattan to brainstorm a defense for their newest client; an elderly man who claims he is Abe Heller, a retired businessman (and Holocaust survivor) but may be…Adolf Hitler. The story unfolds with surprises galore, shifting from black comedy to nightmare, and back again….Enclosed are a few sample pages…

Nov. 20, 1999: The option for *"Bavarian Rage"* screenplay obtained by Jon Brown expires. He was unable to raise funds for a production.

Dec. 19, 1999: We attend a pre-Xmas party at the home of our good friends in Millburn, Jeff Ambers & his wife Lisa Hull. This is an hilarious time, as Lisa drowns us in often silly (but sometimes great) Xmas gifts that she has collected all year, by attending garage sales and discount stores.

Dec. 23, 1999. Hand-written letter from Eli Wallach: "Dear Kal

Wagenheim. Sorry for the long delay in answering your letter---but my wife & I have been involved with Anne Meara's new play *'Down The Garden Paths'*—we opened & had a great success at George St. Playhouse in NJ – and will reopen after the holidays at Long Wharf Theatre in New Haven. Your idea for the Hitler play is a good one, but I don't feel that Abe Heller's character is developed enough (from the section you sent me). For years I've had a script on Hitler called *'Mein Kampf'* by the author George T????0—it's about Hitler as a young man—but we could never get it done—Incidentally during WWII I was in France & Germany as an American officer. One of my jobs was commanding officer for 250 German POWs. Good luck on your project. Eli Wallach."

Jan. 2000: Ceased publication of *Mexico Business Monthly* newsletter after my son David. moved to Florida. I sold (for a few thousand $) the name and subscriber list to Business Monitor International, a group based in London, which publishes several newsletters. Continued publishing *Caribbean Update*.

Jan. 19, 2000. Letter to Eli Wallach: "Dear Mister Wallach: Thank you so much for your letter, concerning my play *'Bavarian Rage.'*...I am taking the liberty (forgive me!) of sending the entire script, which would enable you to take a complete look at Abe Heller, the principal character...I realize that this is a great imposition...and that you may not have the time or desire to read the entire script.. But if you are able to offer any comments at all, I would be deeply appreciative. Sincerely, Kal Wagenheim"

Feb. 21, 2000: Reading of my full-length play *"Bavarian Rage"* at the Pulse Ensemble Theatre on W. 42d St.

Feb. 25, 2000: Hand-written letter to Kal from Eli Wallach. Dear Kal Wagenheim—Sorry I took so long in reading the complete *'Bavarian Rage'*—but I was in a new play by Anne Meara---and we performed it at George St. Playhouse in New Brunswick, and at Long Wharf in New Haven. The play was a big success & we're hoping a theatre in N.Y. becomes available—so we can move it. *Bavarian Rage* is funny & somehow touching....I thought since Heller memorized Hitler's speeches he might come out of his coma & start talking to the Masses---what do you intend to do with the play? I, fortunately, have the Meara play & a new play about Sigmund Freud on my plate—so will be a busy actor for quite a while....I think you can deepen & enrich the stuff between Heller & the Lawyer-- & make realer the Hitler role so that you draw out the suspense—is he or isn't he—But you write with a sure comedic hand---I hope you can arrange readings of the play at Manhattan Theatre Club or any of the many theatre producing companies. Good luck to you – Eli Wallach.

April 9, 2000: Olga and I went with Cousin Ben Steltzer & his wife Nelly to see comedian Jackie Mason in a matinee at the Golden Theatre, W. 45th St. in New York. Excerpts from my letter to him "Dear Mr. Mason: We attended your Sunday matinee yesterday..and I must say your talent for generating laughter is as strong as ever. One of the persons laughing loudest was my wife Olga, who has a Ph.D., is a native of Puerto Rico, and who for the past 23 years has been a professor of history at Rutgers University. Would you kindly sign the enclosed cover of the Playbill and dedicate it 'to Olga'? I know she'll get a great kick out of it... *We had attended a Jackie Mason show earlier, in June 1996, and Olga also laughed, when he commented about the "happy Puerto Ricans" on television because the truth is, every time one turns on Channels 41 or 47 (which he described as the Puerto Rican channels) they always seem to be dancing.*

"I thought you might also be interested in this anecdote. In one of your earlier shows, I recall you commented that, while Jews always patronized Chinese restaurants, you never see Chinese in a Jewish deli. Well...several weeks ago, we were visiting family in Miami Beach and dropped in for a bite at Wolfie's, the landmark Jewish deli on Collins Ave (the one with the mural of dancing pickles on the wall). Two tables away, enjoying an early supper was...a Chinese couple! I immediately thought of you and commented to Olga: 'Jackie Mason has to hear about this!' Best wishes for many years of continued success." *(A few days later Mr. Mason sent me the autographed cover of Playbill saying "My love to Olga. Jackie Mason.")*

April 13-14-15, 2000: My one-act play *"We Beat Whitey Ford"* is performed for three evenings at the Pulse Ensemble Theatre on W. 42d St. in Manhattan.

May 17-28, 2000: Olga and I visit Israel via ABC Tours. We spend part of the time visiting Jorge Klainman, the Holocaust survivor, and his wife Teresa. They live most of the time in Buenos Aires, but spend some time in Israel where they have a daughter. ABC provided an excellent tour of the country. It was an interesting time, but although I am Jewish I don't feel an emotional connection with Israel. It is part of the Middle East, and my roots are European..

July 19, 2000. Caleb is born to my niece Rebecca Stern, who is married to Michael McElreath.

July 27, 2000: I appear in a brief interview in a show about Babe Ruth on ESPN Sports Century TV series documentary.

Aug. 25, 2000: We attend the wedding of our good friend Beth Ann Holden, who marries Chris Greco. They live in Yonkers NY.

Sept. 7, 2000. My dear friend and editor Leon King dies, age 75.

Sept. 20, 2000: My one-act play *"We Beat Whitey Ford"* is performed for one night at PSNBC Here on Spring St. Very well done. I invite my old pal Ralph Fortson, who inspired the lead role of Mitch, and he was moved to see the play, all about our high school days. The role of Mitch, the African-American friend, is performed very well by Harlin Kearsley, a very skilled actor.

Dec. 25, 2000-Jan. 12, 2000: Our usual winter vacation in Puerto Rico. Our good friends Pat & Jerry Kaplan come to the island and stay at a nearby hotel. We have fun showing them the sights.

2000. The Libertine Librettist/School For Lovers. The idea for this screenplay emerged in a very improbable way. I have always admired Mozart, and was reading a biography of the genius. In one brief segment, it describes his meeting with Lorenzo Da Ponte, who later became his collaborator, writing the lyrics for *"The Marriage of Figaro"*, *"Don Giovanni"* and *"Cosi Fan Tutte"*. I was shocked to learn that several years after Mozart's death, DaPonte came to America and....opened a grocery store in Elizabeth NJ! I was so intrigued that I acquired DaPonte's memoir, and a couple of books about him. **Synopsis:**The adventures of Lorenzo Da Ponte, Mozart's "libertine librettist." Jew, defrocked Catholic priest, fugitive from justice, brilliant poet, friend to Casanova, grocer, bookseller, teacher, loving husband and father, querulous complainer, tireless seeker of glory. Da Ponte's 89-year life span takes us to Venice, Vienna, London, and ends in New York, where he founds the city's first opera house.

October 2000. Fish Die By The Mouth. This screenplay was inspired by my friendship with a New Jersey building contractor, Rudy Orlandini, who had to disappear with his wife Esther and family into the Federal Witness Protection Program. Names and a number of facts have been changed, but the essence of the story is faithful to the facts. **Synopsis:**Johnny Faustino, a building contractor frustrated by his inability to obtain business in a corrupt industry, enters into a pact with a mob figure and magically prospers at first. The scheme collapses, and Johnny is caught in a squeeze between his murderous partners and the FBI, which threatens him with prison unless he testifies. A modern take on a classic legend. *(Semifinalist, Script Magazine Open Door Contest, October 2000.)*

TEACHING AT THE STATE PRISON

Oct. 20, 2000: My wife Olga, who was teaching at Rutgers-Newark, was invited to lecture on Caribbean history once a month before a group of inmates at the State Prison in Trenton NJ. I volunteered to drive her there, about a one-hour trip from our home in Millburn NJ. When we arrived, the visitor hall was packed with more than 40 inmates, eager to learn. I chatted briefly with William García, one of the inmates involved in directing the inmate education program known as Hispanic Americans for Progress (HAP). I mentioned to William that I taught a weekly creative writing workshop at Columbia University and wondered if any of the inmates would be interested in such a class. He said they would be delighted. I asked him to mail me their poems, stories and essays. He did so, and I made Xerox copies. For the next two or three years, while Olga lectured at one end of the large visitor hall, I sat with about 15 inmate/writers at a long rectangular table at the other end, and we would read aloud and critique their work. It was most enjoyable for all concerned. Eventually, Olga finished her lecture materials, but I continued to drive down on my own to direct the writing workshop. I would leave my home at 10:30 a.m., arrive about an hour later at the McDonald's across the street from the prison, sip a cup of coffee and review my notes. A few minutes before 12:30 p.m. I would park at the prison, remove everything from my pockets except my car keys, and go through the electronic detector, after which I would proceed to the classroom/visitor hall. We would wind up about two hours later. At one point I submitted some of their poems to an online literary magazine, www. jerseyworks.com. It was satisfying to them, and to me, that their work was reaching a wide audience.

2001. I wrote an historical screenplay, **Tragedy in Lafayette Square**, which I later converted to a novella in prose fiction. Synopsis: Washington DC.,1859. Was it premeditated murder or temporary insanity when an enraged Congressman, Dan Sickles, shot and killed Philip Barton Key in Lafayette Square? Key (a prominent lawyer and the son of the composer of The Star Spangled Banner) was involved in a passionate affair with Teresa Sickles, the wife of the Congressman. The nation is gripped by the ensuing "trial of the century," which raises issues of a double standard, as Sickles is revealed to be an adulterer himself. *(Finalist, 2001 New Century Writer Award).*

June 5-13, 2001: Spent vacation in Argentina with friends Shirley & Howard Stuewe. Enjoyed food & music at Señor Tango supper cljub. Visited our friends Norma & Alfredo Wilk. Had lunch with journalist pal Julio Orione. A taxi strike in Argentina complicated our departure, but we managed to walk the long, last stretch to our terminal.

Aug. 6, 2001. Reading of my play *"Bavarian Rage"* at the Chelsea Playhouse in NYC.

Aug. 15, 2001. While in Cape May NJ we learned that Olga's father, Santos Jimenez, had died. He had been in poor health for quite some time. We flew to Puerto Rico the next day and on Aug. 17 we attended the funeral and burial. We then returned to NJ. It was a very sad time. Don Santos was an exceptional man. He was born into poverty in rural Puerto Rico and was never given an opportunity to learn to read. Despite that, he worked hard on farms and his own modest property, cutting sugar cane, growing coffee and vegetables. Olga, born in 1941, was his oldest child. Then came Carlos, Juanita, Maria and Norma. Olga's mother died when she gave birth to Toña, the youngest. Don Santos remarried and with Lupe, his second wife, had four more children, Toño, Irma, Carmelo and Teresa. Despite his modest circumstances, he always worked, put food on the table and provided a safe home for his family. He also encouraged them to get a good education, and most of them have done very well. To me, Don Santos was a hero.

Sept. 8, 2001: Our friends Norma & Alfred Wilk came for a brief visit and joined us for an excellent performance of *"The Fantasticks"* at the Sullivan Street Playhouse in Greenwich Village (the play would close there after more than 40 years and re-open at a new venue in midtown).

Sept. 11, 2001: I will always remember the day when I sat home working at my desk, watching the news on TV, and seeing The Twin Towers collapse.

Later that day I saw Dr. Zablow, an oncologist at St. Barnabas Hospital. My family doctor Joseph Fretta, after my annual physical, earlier noticed that my PSA level was growing gradually each year, was now 4.0, and recommended that I see a urologist. I was examined, and it was found that I had a tiny cancerous growth on my prostate. An operation was not needed. They recommended brief radiation.

Oct. 7, 2001. My son Jeff Wagenheim and Sarah Swersey marry. A magnificent event. This was the article in *The New York Times*: "WEDDINGS; Sarah Swersey, Jeff Wagenheim. Sarah Deborah Swersey, a daughter of Alice and Burt Swersey of Stephentown, N.Y., is to be married today at her parents' house to Jeff Wagenheim, the son of Carolyn Wagenheim of Cranford, N.J., and Kal Wagenheim of Maplewood, N.J. The Rev. Susan Schultz, a Baptist minister, will perform a nondenominational ceremony.

Ms. Swersey, 36, will keep her name. She is a freelance flutist with the Cape Symphony Orchestra in Hyannis, Mass. She also teaches yoga at Brookline Adult and Community Education, a night school in Brookline, Mass., and at the Oak Square Y.M.C.A. in Brighton, Mass. She graduated from the Oberlin Conservatory and received a master's degree in flute performance from the Yale School of Music. Her father is a senior lecturer in mechanical engineering at Renssalaer Polytechnic Institute in Troy, N.Y. Her mother, who retired from teaching music in the Central Berkshire Regional School District in Dalton, Mass., gives piano lessons in Stephentown.

Mr. Wagenheim, 43, is an editor on the sports copy desk at *The Boston Globe* and is also a freelance writer. He graduated from Boston University. His father is the author of *''Babe Ruth: His Life and Legend''* (Olmstead Press, 2001) and other books, and teaches an undergraduate creative writing course at Columbia University. The bridegroom's mother, who is retired, was a bookkeeper in Clark, N.J., for Cosmair, a beauty products manufacturer.

Jan. 10, 2002: Carolyn Smith, 68, my first wife, died at her home in Cranford NJ, after a long illness. She had retired in 1999 after 12 years as a bookkeeper with Cosmair in Clark NJ. Born in Elizabeth NJ, she lived in Roselle NJ before moving to Cranford in 1985. Mass was offered at St. John the Apostle Roman Catholic Church in Linden, and burial in Mount Olivet Cemetery, Newark. At the very least, she lived to see her son Jeff marry, but unfortunately didn't live long enough to see her grandchildren.

2002. After hearing a program on National Public Radio about the development of hydrogen fuel cells, I did some research on the Internet and was inspired to write a screenplay, *"The Hydrogen Thing"*, later converted to a novella. **Synopsis:** Three scientists in different parts of the world are murdered in apparently random events. All three are pioneers in a new hydrogen fuel cell technology that will end the world's dependence on oil. Becky McLean (a young college professor) and her boyfriend Michael Stern (a journalist) stumble upon the plot (concocted by a deranged scientist and corrupt stockbroker) and are pursued by the killers in this quirky comic thriller. *Semifinalist: 10th Annual Writer's Network Screenplay & Fiction Competition.*

Feb. 5-March 13, 2002: Most mornings during a month I visited St. Barnabas, disrobed, laid on a cot, and was "zapped" with radiation. They were very efficient. I was in an out in 15 minutes. Over the next few years, my PSA level remained at 0.1, quite an improvement. I have Dr. Fretta to thank for spotting the problem before it became too serious.

May 15, 2002: I often had lunch in NY with my good pal Harvey Rosenhouse. Now he was 85 years old and didn't seem to like most of the food available at midtown restaurants, our usual haunts. I asked him what he preferred. He said on the lower East Side there were places that served good cheese blintzes. I picked him up at his place in the West 60s, we drove down to First Ave, around 9th St., parked in front of a tiny diner called Polonia. We went in, found a small table, and they had the most delicious cheese blintzes which Harvey loved. I had terrific potato pancakes with apple sauce. The whole bill was $16 for two. We returned a few times.

June 2002: We learned the sad news that our dear, generous friend Dick Friedman had died in a tragic accident when his catamaran capsized while he was at sea. We met Dick in the early 1960s when he came to run a small radio station that he later built into one of the largest on the island. Dick married Rita, a young lady from Cuba, and they had a son and a daughter. Over the years, Dick became fluent in Spanish, and helped launch the careers of several Puerto Rican artists, including Mark Anthony. He and Rita lived in a condo apartment in the Isla Verde section of San Juan, and also had a lovely weekend home out in Fajardo, where he entertained us and other friends. Dick had sold the station and retired a few years earlier, and at age 63 was enjoying life, sailing at sea, when it all came to an end. Not only his family, but also his many friends, miss him.

June 29, 2002: I appear in a brief interview about Roberto Clemente on ESPN SportsCentury TV series documentary.

July 8, 2002: Staged reading of my full-length play *"Bavarian Rage"* at the Abingdon Theatre Co. in New York.

Nov. 29-Dec. 1, 2002. Olga & I drove north about 3 hours to visit my son Jeff & his wife Sarah who now lived in a beautiful old house in Northampton, Mass. We stayed at a nearby Best Western, and had lunch on Nov. 30 with them and Sarah's parents, Bert & Alice. On the way home we stopped for lunch with cousins Bill & Shirley Wagenheim, who live in Delmar NY, near Albany.

Dec. 25, 2002-Feb. 27, 2003: Long visit to Puerto Rico. Olga is retiring from Rutgers-Newark after 26 years, so we can be away from NJ. I set up a small office in our apartment in Puerto Rico, with a laptop computer, and was able to continue working on my newsletter, *Caribbean Update*. I was also able to Email grades for my students in the class at Columbia University. Saw family and friends. Was visited by Laurie & Bud Safin, pals from Maplewood NJ.

Feb. 23, 2003: Learned that Aaron Rumi Wagenheim (my first grandson) was born to Sarah up in Northampton, Mass. 7 lbs, 15 oz.

March 2-4, 2003: Back home in NJ, we drove up to Northampton, Mass. to visit Jeff & Sarah and see little Aaron for the first time. It's only about 20 degrees there. Brrrr!

April 2003: After more than three decades at our home in Maplewood, we decide to move to a smaller place. Taxes on the Maplewood house are above $11,000, and since it is a corner house with lots of sidewalks, if we are away in winter it gets expensive to clear away the snow. My only request to Olga is that we find a place without sidewalks. Olga searches around the area and spots a small house at 116 Myrtle Ave. in Millburn, just 1 ½ miles from our current home. And it has no sidewalks! The process begins. Inspection. Putting our Maplewood home up for sale. We are helped by Irwin Semel, a lawyer specializing in home sales, and Susan Falk, an efficient realtor. There are a few open houses for realtors and homebuyers.

May 30-June 3, 2003: We learn that Olga's sister Norma, who had suffered from diabetes since childhood and was in poor health, died. On May 31 we attend the funeral in Camuy PR and return to NJ. We now begin plans to move to a new home.

June 27-29, 2003: Cousins Bill & Shirley Wagenheim invite us to join them at The Nevele, an old Catskills resort, to celebrate their 50th wedding anniversary. We attend, and have much fun. I particularly recall one aging, bent over Jewish comedian who had us all in stitches.

Olga and the HRIC

Olga retired from Rutgers in July 2003 and once free of the academic bligations devoted many long hours to designing and implementing projects in keeping with Hispanic Research & Information Center (HRIC) at the Newark Public Library. These included, among others, the establishment of the Maria De Castro Blake Community ServiceAward Dinner, teaching oral history to graduate and undergraduate students, and overseeing over the production of nearly three dozen oral histories with Hispanic leaders. Her work on these projects was done concurrently with her chairing the Organizing Committee and seeking grants for the development of the Puerto Rican Community Archives. She also focused on implementing a research phase for the Hispanic Reference Center, one of the three components of the HRIC, whose goal is to study the various Hispanic groups in the state. A grant from the NJ Legislature in 2005, obtained through the good offices of Assemblyman Wilfredo Caraballo, and with the help of his assistant Omar Perez, enabled HRIC to grant five fellowships to as many graduate students who under her training and supervision completed within two years four historical profiles of Hispanic groups in NJ. (Cuban, Colombian, Dominican, Salvadoran).

MOVING TO A NEW HOME

July 21, 2003: Moving day from our house at 52 Maple Ave., Maplewood (where we had lived in December 1971) to 116 Myrtle Ave., Millburn. The new house needs work, and there will be expenses, but with the sale of the Maplewood house we earned enough to buy the smaller Millburn home and not have a mortgage. The price was right, property taxes are lower in Millburn than in Maplewood, the house is within walking distance of the center of town and the train station to New York, and, it has no sidewalks! This is a great relief when we are away from New Jersey during the snowy winter months, and staying at our apartment in Puerto Rico. Olga contacted Tom O'Donovan, the contractor who did such a fine job on our Maplewood home, and she suggested a number of improvements in our news home. He did his usual excellent work.

November 2003. National Public Radio inspires another story. After hearing a program about Charles A. Levine, I examine microfilms of old newspapers and write *"Levine! Levine!"* as a full-length play, and later as a screenplay. **Synopsis:** This tragi-comic drama chronicles the meteoric rise and fall of brash millionaire and aviation pioneer Charles A. Levine. His brief fling with fame, as the first trans-Atlantic air passenger, two weeks after Lindbergh's historic solo flight, was celebrated with joyous Yiddish songs. *Semifinalist, 2004 Dorothy Silver Playwriting Competition.*

Oct. 7, 2003: I appear in a brief interview about the New York Yankees on ESPN SportsCentury TV series documentary.

Oct. 16, 2003. Article, including my photo, in Sonora, California weekly newspaper, with headline: "New plays in spotlight at Stage 3." "Three distinguished playwrights , whose works have been chosen as finalists in the Stage 3 Theatre Company's seventh annual Festival of New Plays, come to Sonora. Their plays were selected from more than 200 entries from across the nation and around the world... *'Bavarian Rage'*, a dark comedy, skewers our morbid fascination with the titillating and grotesque and the people who get rich from it...What if Adolf Hitler surfaced in New York having posed all these years as a Holocaust survivor? Greed and morality go head to head as a 'Dream Team' of high-profile lawyers scramble all over each other to mount a defense for one of the most hated men in history...'Bavarian Rage' will play on Sunday at 2 p.m." *Note: my play was very well received in one of the three staged readings, but did not win. However, the Stage 3 folks flew me out to California, all expenses paid, and it was a great experience. I flew from Newark to San Francisco on a 7 am flight on Oct. 18, and was picked up and driven to Sonora. I returned from San Francisco on a late10 pm flight to Newark on Oct. 19.*

May 6-9, 2004: Our dear friend Tere Ortiz dies suddenly at home. She had apparently been in excellent health, but suffered an aneuryism. Tere leaves three daughters: Ana, Laura and Mayna. We flew to Puerto Rico and attended a very touching ceremony when her ashes were planted in a beautiful forest.

May 12, 2004. *To Peter Brook, Honorary President, Directors Guild of Great Britain, Acorn House, 314-320 Gray's Inn Road, London WC1X 8DP England.*

Dear Mr. Brook: You probably don't remember me, but I have a very fond memory of our first (and only) meeting. In 1961, I (age 26) had recently arrived in Puerto Rico and rented a small room upstairs from La Botella Bar/ Restaurant in Old San Juan. Shortly afterwards, you arrived with your family, and Mr. Chuck New, the owner of La Botella, asked if I could find another place to live, since "a Mr. Brook and his family" required living quarters while he was working on a new film, *"Lord Of The Flies"*. I was living out of a suitcase and easily found another place to live. A few days later, we met in front of La Botella (through Chuck New) and, in a lovely gesture, you invited me next door to Sam's Patio for lunch. Over the years many people have commented on your great talent in the fields of theatre and film. I tell them that, to me, even more important was the fact that you were so kind to invite a young man to lunch. I am now 69 years old. At age 60, after a long career in journalism, I became interested in dramatic writing and have authored several plays and screenplays. Two of the plays have been produced Off-Off Broadway and one of the screenplays is under option. Enclosed is a bio sketch with summaries of my work. I know how busy you must be, but if any of my work is of the slightest interest, kindly let me know via a note or Email and I would be delighted to submit it. And, if course, if you are ever in New York (I live 30 minutes outside the city) perhaps someday I can reciprocate and invite you to lunch! With kindest regards and best wishes...*Kal Wagenheim*

May 26, 2004. *Handwritten note on card of Theatre Des Bouffes Du Nord, 37 bis, boulevard de la Chapelle, 75010 Paris.* Dear Kal Wagenheim: Reading your very moving letter how vividly La Botella sprang to life again! You certainly have been fully active ever since. Thank you for writing—my activities here are very full, so I must decline any temptation to look at new projects. With best wishes, Peter Brook.

Sept. 20, 2004: A small Hollywood production company buys a 6-month option on my script about legendary tango star Carlos Gardel (1890-1935). He loved the script, but was unable to raise the funds for what would be an expensive period piece.

Oct. 16, 2004: *"Bavarian Rage,"* my full-length play, is given a staged reading by the HRC Theatre Company in Hudson NY.

Oct. 17, 2005: My dear pal Marvin Schwartz stars as a serial killer in a low-budget horror film *"I Hate You"* in preview at the Pioneer Theatre, East 3rd St., and Avenue A. This is a very low budget film, and they couldn't afford to pay actors. My son David and my friend Beth Holden are among those murdered in the film. Another friend, Marie Trusits, and I appear briefly in a scene shot at Columbia University. And pal Chuck Corbett also appears in a funny moment. *(The film is on* www.imdb.com*)*. I have a tiny part in one scene, where I am a college professor leading a writing class, and Marvin talks about killing people, as though this is a piece of fiction he's working on. One funny anecdote which didn't make it into the movie. Marvin wanted me to be one of his victims. We were to shoot the scene at his apartment building on West 10th St. I was to carry a cellphone, walk down the steps into the small lobby. Marvin was there waiting for me. He would hit me with a club, I would fall, and he would stab me to death. They even found a second-hand shirt for me to wear with bloodstains. So I am sitting there on the lobby floor, with the blood-stained shirt; Marvin is standing over me with a knife, to finish me off, while Nick Oddo, the director, is filming. Just then, into the lobby walks a delivery guy (Fedex or UPS) carrying a package. He is shocked. Nick quickly explains: "We're just making a movie." The delivery guy relaxes, says "OK, that's cool." He drops off the package, heads to the door and says "You can kill him now!" I still laugh about that funny moment, which never made it into the film.

December 1, 2004: My dear friend Harvey Rosenhouse dies, age 84.

Jan. 1, 2005: I appear in a brief interview on ESPN 25: Who's #1, TV series documentary about the Best MLB teams.

March 17, 2005. My letter published in The NY Times. As a biographer of baseball's most famous homerun slugger, *Babe Ruth: His Life & Legend,* first published in 1974, I am amused by the brouhaha over the use of steroids by the current crop of baseball stars. back in the Babe's day, he 'bulked up' his physique—not with steroids—but with plenty of hotdogs and beer. Although the current crop of sluggers have eclipsed the Babe's single season and career homerun records, I think one statistic will prove how much he still towers above the crowd. In 1920, Babe Ruth hit more homeruns than fourteen of the sixteen teams in the major leagues. He beat at least one entire team in twelve different seasons. No one has ever approached that degree of dominance of the sport, and I don't think anyone will.

2005. One of the best writers I met when teaching the workshop at the NJ State Prison in Trenton was Eugene Thomas. We have remained in touch over the years and I encouraged him to keep writing. He wrote a novel, *"Lucky For Me,"* which I have been sending out to publishers on his behalf (he later self-published it). Also, with his written permission I've converted it to a screenplay and am circulating it to producers. Synopsis: Lucky For Me. Screenplay. Violence and drugs surround Charles "Lucky" Dumas, an African-American teenager, growing up on the gritty streets of the inner city. His hardworking mother (a waitress in a diner), and his father (in prison for murder) struggle to keep him on the straight and narrow. Lucky survives a number of crises, including a failed romance, gang rumbles, and the death of his two closest friends. In a rousing finale, he delivers an emotional, inspiring valedictorian speech at his school. Despite the odds, he seems on his way to success. Screenplay adapted, with his written permission, from the novel by Eugene Thomas. *Quarterfinalist, 12th Annual Writers Network Screenplay & Fiction Competition, 2005; Quarterfinalist, 2005 Fade In Magazine Awards. WGAE#I20668*

April 6, 2005. My first grand-daughter, Rebecca Ananda Wagenheim, is born to Jeff and Sarah.

June 22-26, 2005: ***"Coffee With God"*** **my one-act play**, is produced at First Annual Chester Horn Short Play Festival, American Theatre of Actors, NYC. A man is seated in a diner, enjoying a bagel with cream cheese and a cup of coffee, when God, carrying a laptop computer, sits next to him and orders the same. Their conversation ranges from playful (finding parking in Manhattan) to heartbreaking (why loved ones die all too soon). This play was inspired by the tragic loss of my mother at age 22, when I was just two years old. Much of the material is derived from letters she wrote to relatives in North Carolina shortly before her death. The play apparently appeals to anyone who has suffered loss in his/her life and has been produced numerous times.

July 14-24, 2005: Olga & I visit northern Spain and have a marvelous time with Javier & his wife Pilar. We stay with them (they treat us royally) and they drive us all around. This is a fabulous part of Spain, with old towns (Pamplona, Viana), cathedrals, beautiful countryside. They also have lovely friends. A great place, and a great time.

Aug. 16, 2005. Dear Mr. Wagenheim, The National Baseball Hall of Fame ad Museum would like to thank you for donating the oral history interviews that you conducted for your book *Babe Ruth: His Life and Legend*. They are fine additions to our film, video and recorded sound collection. Helen R. Stiles, Library-Technical Services.

Nov. 18, 2005. My one-act play *"Coffee With God"* is produced at Gettysburg College in Gettysburg PA as part of an undergraduate play festival. The young lady directing the play asks if it is OK if God can be portrayed by a female, since they didn't have many male actors. I approve, and decide to drive out there, spend the night at a nearby motel, and watch the play. I try to reserve several hotels/motels in Gettysburg and see that all are booked. Are so many folks coming to see my play? No. It's the same time as the anniversary of Lincoln's Gettysburg Address, and thousands of tourists are coming to tour the battleground. I call the Chamber of Commerce and they find me an OK motel on the outskirts of town. I attend the play, which was quite good, and God was portrayed by a lovely young blonde gal. Also, I was paid $500 as a prize!

July 28-20, August 3-5: My one-act play *"Coffee With God"* is performed at the Jersey Voice Short Play Festival in Chatham, NJ, and the role of God ia performed by an African-American male.

2006: The writing workshop for inmates at the New Jersey State Prison in Trenton lasted until 2006, when the prison authorities canceled the program. It seems that cellphones were being smuggled into the prison. The authorities panicked and canceled all volunteer programs, including mine. The actual guilty parties were guards who smuggled in the cellphones, charging $500 apiece. Perhaps one or two inmates were involved in marketing them on the inside, but it was unfair and unwise to cancel an educational program because of a couple of guilty persons. I later found out that when an inmate wishes to call a relative on the outside, it is a collect call, and the rate is about 10 times the normal phone rate. This racket between the phone company and the prison is why many inmates' families are willing to shell out $500 for delivery of a cellphone to their incarcerated family member. When I tried to renew the workshop, I was told there was "no need" for such a program in the prison. Frustrated, I compiled a 70,000-word manuscript of writings by the inmates (poems, stories, essays), under the title *"Inside Out: Voices From New Jersey State Prison"*. I had a small publisher print the paperback

Sept. 19, 2006. My dear friend Charles "Chuck" Corbett, dies in New York, age 75. I did get to visit him one last time on Sept. 9 at St. Vincent's Hospital. Despite his poor health, Chuck displayed his usual tough, good humor.

Oct. 18-30, 2006: Jorge & Teresa Klainman arrive from Buenos Aires. I met them years earlier in Argentina. A few years later, Jorge sent me a small self-published Spanish-language memoir about his surviving the Holocaust during this youth in Poland. I was impressed, and made an English-language translation. I obtained an agent, who submitted it to several major publishers. They praised the book, but said the market for such books was not good at the time. I found a self-publishing firm, Xlibris, and they produced a paperback, "The Seventh Miracle." It is available online at www.amazon.com, and from the publisher, www.xlibris.com. The Klainmans stayed at our house during their visit. We had a lively reception for him at our home, where he & Teresa met our friends. He spoke about the book at the Millburn Middle School, at Ramapo College, and at a community college in Passaic NJ (the latter thanks to our friend Ernesto Díaz, a teacher and friend). He would speak and I would offer an English translation. Thanks to these appearances, a few hundred books were sold. The students and teachers loved Mr. Klainman. He and Teresa wanted to visit New York City. On Saturday Oct. 28 we attended a marvelous matinee performance of the Broadway musical "Chicago." We had obtained great half price seats at TKTS. Prior to the performance we enjoyed lunch at the Broadway Lounge on the 8th floor of the Marriott Marquis Hotel, overlooking Times Square. A funny moment: Mrs. Klainman looked down and was shocked. There below, surrounded by tourists snapping photos and throwing dollar bills into his guitar was...The Naked Cowboy! A tall fellow, wearing scanty underwear, boots, and a cowboy hat. When we went downstairs, Mrs. Klainman was sure to take his picture. The next day, we returned to New York, this time to Battery Park City in lower Manhattan, and visited the very impressive Museum of Jewish Heritage-A Living Memorial to the Holocaust. They returned to Buenos Aires the next day. We have remained in touch since then, and Jorge Klainman continues to speak about his book at various venues in Argentina, and Israel.

GOODBYE TO COLUMBIA

Dec. 7, 2006: My relation with the Columbia University Writing Program ceased after nearly 30 years, due to budget changes in the program, resulting in layoffs of numerous adjuncts, including me. I taught once a week during the Spring and Fall semesters, and in the final two years taught only the Fall semester, spending the early part of the year in Puerto Rico. *Note: I had been planning to retire from Columbia in a year or so anyway, so I was not upset by this. However I was saddened by the fact that some of the talented younger adjuncts who were earning $10,000 a year for one weekly class were let go. The money helped them survive, as they patched together various jobs.*

2007: My one-act play, *"Coffee With God"* was acquired for publication by Dramatic Publishing Co. It has since been produced more than 40 times at colleges, high schools and community theatres in the USA, Canada and Ireland. *I later converted it to short story, which was a finalist in the 2009 Prose Series Contest of Sol Books.*

Feb. 3, 2007: To Louis S. Auchincloss, 111 Park Ave., Apt. 14-D, New York NY 10128-1234. Dear Mr. Auchincloss: This is a fan letter, and a confession! First, the confession. For several years I have taught a course in creative writing at Columbia University. During the final class of each semester I discuss with students the prospects for pursuing a career in writing. And, knowing of your achievements, I often cite you as an example of someone who has managed to be a prolific writer while also pursuing a career in law. However, I am ashamed to admit that I had never read your work..Finally, I said to myself, enough! I went to the public library in Millburn and was delighted to find dozens of your works. I borrowed one: *Manhattan Monologues*. And I am loving it! Marvelous! Slowly, I will work my way through the various shelves of your books. Three years ago, I wrote *"Coffee With God,"* a somewhat autobiographical play which has been performed several times at drama festivals in venues ranging from Manhattan to Minnesota to Northern Ireland. Recently, I converted it into a short story format (I think it works better as a play). By way of thanks to you for your wonderful work, I am hereby "inflicting" a copy of my story upon you. No need to return it, or to reply. I hope it provides you with a few moments of enjoyment. With kindest regards, *Kal Wagenheim*

Feb. 6, 2007. Dear Mr Wagenheim: I was very much complemented by your letter and very pleased that you were finding some pleasure in my work. Of course it is true that I practiced law for many years, but I retired at age 69 and have since devoted the bulk of my time to writing, so that, at 89, I almost feel that I have spent my life as a full time writer. Indeed, I have two books coming out in 2007, the second of which, a novel, *"The Headmaster's Dilemma,"* due out in September, is in my opinion one of my better efforts. I have never had anything to do with courses in creative writing, which hardly existed when I started, but my friends Vance Bourjaily and Jack Legett, who taught them in Iowa, did much to persuade me that it was a worthy field, provided the student has a real gift, to begin with. And I agree with you that drama, whether on the stage or screen, should be included. Writing is writing, after all, and plays are peculiarly subject to being improved by analysis and planning. I don't know about poetry. Perhaps that had be left to the poets. Yet look what Pound did to The Waste Land. I liked your story, though I think it is better as a play than a story. It is a bit sentimental, and that is more effective behind the footlights than on the harshly printed page. Your gift for dialogue is fine; a good actor could do a lot with God. I have also written plays but unsuccessfully. A one act play, The Club Bedroom, done on Channel 13 and off Broadway is my sole production! My new book of stories, *The Friend of Women,* due out in April, has one a one act comedy on which I would love to have your opinion. *Sincerely yours, Louis Auchincloss.*

Published Feb. 7, 2007 in the Columbia University Spectator

As a young man, I often sought advice from my Great-Uncle Murrey Shamburgh, who worked as a bartender in downtown Newark, N.J. He was a slender, confident man, with dazzling, neatly combed gray hair and an ever-present cigar clenched between his teeth. He walked with a pronounced limp, a souvenir of his adventures on the battlefields of France during World

War I. Once, I asked his opinion about a particularly contentious issue. Murrey, born and raised on Manhattan's Lower East Side, chuckled and responded with a typical blend of English and Yiddish: "Opinions are like tuckuses-everybody's got one." That bit of sage advice has served me well over the years, particularly when it comes to judging the relative worth, or lack thereof, of any creative work. Recently, I was told that Columbia is creating an undergraduate major in creative writing. And I ask: "why?" The announcement for the major states that courses will study the works of many illustrious authors, including Borges, Cortázar, Nabokov, Baldwin, Ellison, Garcia Márquez, Babel, Bellow, Lawrence, Kafka, McPhee, Spark, Flaubert, etc., which leads me to ask: did any of these literary greats major in creative writing as undergraduate students? I search in my memory for the name of any accomplished authors who majored in creative writing as undergraduates. Marianne Moore? Walt Whitman? William Kennedy? Isaac Bashevis Singer? Joseph Heller? Flannery O'Connor? James Joyce? Thomas Wolfe? Oscar Wilde? Norman Mailer? Toni Morrison? Help me! I can't think of one! I am, by no means, in the same league as the famous folks mentioned above. But I was a reporter for the *New York Times*, have had several books published (including a translation from a classic 19th-century novel), and have had a few plays produced off-off-Broadway. Confession: I only completed two years of college! I didn't hang around long enough to major in anything! Despite that, Columbia saw fit to hire me 30 years ago as an adjunct, first to teach journalism and, later, creative writing. It has been an enjoyable ride these past three decades, and along the way, I've come across a number of remarkable writers. I have a hunch that those who immerse themselves in creative writing at the undergraduate level will emerge as erudite literary critics, or perhaps professors of literature, but there is no evidence-none!-to demonstrate that such an early plunge into that pool will help improve the actual craft of writing. The announcement for the major states, "Only through a deep analysis of outstanding and diverse works of literature can the creative writer build the resources necessary to produce his or her own accomplished creative work." To suggest that there is "only" one path to success in creative writing is not only 100 percent wrong but smacks of pretentious baloney. Well, perhaps I'm being a bit harsh. Janet Maslin, in the *New York Times* (Feb. 2, 2007), writes a touching tribute to the prolific pulp-fiction giant Sidney Sheldon, who died recently. She comments: "He achieved his effects by using a secret weapon: his nostalgic appreciation of Thomas Wolfe, Sinclair Lewis, Ernest Hemingway, F. Scott Fitzgerald and their storytelling skills. Thus equipped, and endlessly interested in the rich, powerful and tragic, he brought class to trash." Oops! Did I commit an unpardonable gaffe, mentioning Sidney Sheldon in a University newspaper? Was he too "popular" (300 million books sold) to merit mention in the hallowed halls of academe? Some friendly advice to undergraduates who may want to pursue writing as a career or a vocation: Do not major in creative writing! Instead, gain some real life experience in the workplace. Take courses in "reality" subjects: law, history, anthropology, medicine, biology, psychology, etc. Later, if you wish, pursue writing, perhaps in graduate school, perhaps not. But write! Look deep inside yourself and seek out your own very personal, unique literary voice. It's there, believe me! I offer a few possible role models that might inspire you: Louis Auchincloss, the author of 57 novels and non-fiction works and former president of the American Academy of Arts and Letters, who also pursued a career in law; Wallace Stevens, the brilliant poet, who was also an insurance company executive; and William Carlos Williams, another great poet, who was also a medical doctor and delivered more than 2,000 babies during his career. I also wonder why a new creative writing major in the year 2007 would choose to exclude drama and film from genres worthy of study. What would old Bill Shakespeare, or Arthur Miller, or Lillian Hellman have to say about that? There is something undeniably "quaint" about the decision to ignore screenwriting. Before Johannes Gutenberg came along and invented the printing press, most tellers of tales did so verbally around the campfire, with a small enrapt audience. I am sure that, at the time, some grumbled about the "newfangled" idea of printing words onto paper. Then, in the 20th century, someone invented movies, and we still see a few stubborn folks clinging to the past, denying film screenwriting entry into the sacred land of "great literature." Perhaps, in a century or two, they will see the light. What also concerns me is that, while the current undergraduate writing program accepts 900 students a year and is constantly overbooked, the new program will only be able to handle 700 because of budget limitations. I ask myself: what about those 200 undergraduates who are denied access to exercise their creative writing skills? Among those 200, I wonder, is there another budding Jack Kerouac or Allen Ginsberg? (Both of these guys, by the way, studied at Columbia but were not creative writing majors.) Shouldn't Columbia-with all its resources-offer more, not fewer, choices? Of course, you might disagree. As Uncle Murrey always said, "Opinions are like tuckuses-everybody's got one."

March 2007. National Banana Week. My one-act play. A clueless Number 43 and VP Cheney discuss major issues, including how to pronounce "nuclear" in this very short White House comedy. *Staged reading, The Theater Project, Cranford NJ, March 2007. Cast: 6 (2 males).*

April 21, 2007. Mother's Day In Hell. One-act play. Two Jersey mobsters (Jewish & Italian), a brothel madame (African-American) and Britain's Lord Cornbury, the corrupt, cross-dressing first governor of New Jersey (1706) -- all long dead -- have bribed the Devil and his underlings and live in comfort in the VIP Lounge of the New Jersey Wing of Hell. They are joined by a Latino mobster (just killed in a mob war) and plan to develop a Vegas-style casino. Life is good, but Mother's Day is coming, and they are anxious and weepy for another glimpse of their beloved moms. *Cast: 6 (4 males, 2 females). Staged reading: April 21, 2007 by The Theater Project at Union Couny College, Cranford NJ.* Note: The idea for this play was inspired by a column in *The Star-Ledger* newspaper, pointing out the long history of corruption in New Jersey, started with the cross-dressing first governor under the British Crown.

Adios, Joe

Oct. 29, 2007: My beloved friend Joe Guzmán, dies of a heart attack in Vega Alta, Puerto Rico, age 85. He was born Dec. 7, 1922. I spoke with his dear wife Lidia after learning the sad news; she told me he would be cremated later in the week. Joe lived a long, eventful life , and in some ways he was my role model; he proved to me that one could rise from very modest circumstances and by using his vivid imagination and taking risks he could be successful. We met one afternoon, around the time I had the *San Juan Review* magazine (1964-1966), I was standing outside Talleres Graficos Interamericanos, the printing plant in Puerta de Tierra that published our magazine. Our magazine wasn't doing well, and my co-editor Augusto Font had left and was editing *Caribbean Traveler*, a magazine for passengers on Caribair flights to the region. He needed an ad salesman, and a mutual friend had recommended a fellow named Joe Guzmán. That afternoon, I met Joe, a man in his 40s, well-dressed in a gray suit & tie, polished shoes, resembled a guy who might fit well as a cast member of *The Sopranos*. Joe shook my hand and asked me, "Kal, can you tell me, what is a column inch?" My God, I thought, here is a guy who is going to be an ad salesman, and he doesn't even know what a column inch is! I soon learned that I had underestimated Joe. That meeting was the beginning of a long, wonderful friendship. Joe rose to success by means of sheer guts and ingenuity. On top of all that, he was funny as hell. Joe once told me that he was born in Vieques, an offshore island municipality of Puerto Rico, and was so poor that he joined the U.S. Army in order to get a pair of shoes. After his military service, Joe traveled widely, lived in New York, worked in the Merchant Marine, and in the 1960s came to Puerto Rico, with a plan to settle down. Despite his lack of experience, Joe was a successful ad salesman, but the magazine eventually folded when the airline was sold. At one point we took Joe out to Camuy to meet Olga's family, and he loved it. I recall a funny moment in particular. One afternoon we visited Olga's father, don Santos, who lived on his modest farm. He served us each a glass of rum and then invited us outside to a shady area beneath the plantain plants. Don Santos proudly showed us some of his coffee plants. We sat there quietly, in the shade, sipping rum. Then Joe, in a voice reminiscent of Frank Sinatra, began to sing softly *"Strangers in the night…."* Don Santos did not understand English, but he graciously smiled, nodded, and we relaxed in the shade, sipping our rum. Not long afterward Joe met Lidia, a family friend from Camuy, and they married and started a family. Without a job, Joe decided to… become a farmer! Through Lidia he managed to lease some land out around Camuy and hired a bunch of young men to plant *calabazas* (squash) and other vegetables. Within a year, Joe's farm was an important source of squash on the island. Once I went to visit Joe and he said he had to drive in to San Juan to claim damages at the Agriculture Department for rain that affected his crop. He knew all the angles and didn't miss an opportunity to earn money! Before setting out, Joe had some fellows fill up the trunk of his big car with plantains. On the way to San Juan, we pulled over to a roadside gas station/grocery store. In a few minutes Joe exchanged the plantains for a tank full of gasoline! Then Joe developed very serious back pains, was hospitalized, and had to give up farming. After a while he developed another idea. In the Miramar section of San Juan was a huge government motor vehicle agency, where drivers had to renew their licenses. On Fernandez Juncos Ave., near the entrance, a friend had a small photo shop. Joe patched together $500 for a

Polaroid camera and other equipment, and found an elderly doctor qualified to give eye exams to drivers. Joe then hired young men to stand out on the street and wave cars in for the exam. The business boomed, and although years later it moved to the new motor vehicle agency in Carolina, I believe his children continue to run it. As the years passed Joe retired, and he and Lidia lived in a beautiful country home in Vega Alta, about 40 minutes west of San Juan, which was complete with a spacious swimming pool. Olga and I visited them a few times, and we would take a short drive to a beautiful beachfront resort in Dorado for lunch. Around the time of Joe's 80th birthday, he suffered a severe stroke, and could barely speak. But with time, as he exercised daily in the swimming pool he recovered his ability to speak. To me, Joe was like an inspiring older brother. I could confide in him on any question, and depend upon his good judgement and support. I miss Joe, but I cherish the many wonderful memories...the times of laughter in particular! *Note: Another dear friend, Barry Levine, professor at Florida International University, was also close to Joe and wound up interviewing him at length, and achieving publication of a fine book all about Joe's eventful life (changing his name, of course). The book is called "Benjy Lopez: A Picaresque Tale of Puerto Rican Emigration and Return" and it recounts the early adventures of Joe Guzmán. He had many more adventures in later years. (The book was recently republished by Markus Wiener of Princeton NJ and can be obtained on www.amazon.com.)*

Nov. 8-9-10, 2007. My one-act play National Banana Week is produced as part of the Kaleidoscope Kabaret, an evening of short plays at the Theater Project, Union County College, Cranford NJ. In this short White House comedy, a clueless number 43 and VP Cheney discuss major issues, including how to pronounce "nuclear." Number 43 keeps saying "NOO-kyoo-ler"!

2008: *"Cuentos: Stories From Puerto Rico"* reissued by Markus Wiener Publisher of Princeton NJ. Twelve stories by six outstanding Puerto Rico writers, with original Spanish and English translation on facing pages.

Sept. 26, 2008: My Email to: PEN American Center, 588 Broadway, Suite 303, New York NY 10012 Dear PEN: I was pleased to learn that Amiri Baraka has received a PEN Beyond Margins Award for his book "Tales of the Out & Gone." As a fellow Newarker of the same generation (he is just one year older than me), I prefer to call him by his birth name LeRoi Jones. It's good to see that LeRoi continues to write, and is no longer in the mental hospital. At least that's where I thought he was, when he wrote "Somebody Blew Up America," his poem about the 9/11 terror attack. In one line he wrote: "Who told 4,000 Israeli workers/ at the Twin Towers/ to stay home that day/why did Sharon stay away?" (I'll bet the Carnegie Deli in Manhattan was mobbed by those survivors during lunch that day.) In one wacky rant against imperialism LeRoi railed at the killers of "Neruda and Allende," claiming they were one and "the same." Salvador Allende, the democratically elected President of Chile, died of a gunshot wound during a right-wing overthrow of his government. Pablo Neruda, the brilliant Chilean poet, died quietly in bed, not from a bullet, but from prostate cancer. Moving down the page, LeRoi asks "who overthrew Bishop?" This is a reference to Maurice Bishop, the popular Prime Minister of Grenada. In 1983 Mr. Bishop was overthrown and, along with several colleagues, murdered, not by right-wingers, but by a hardline Stalinist group led by Deputy Prime Minister Bernard Coard. (In October 1999, Mr. Coard read a statement on Grenada radio, accepting responsibility for the murders and apologizing to relatives of the victims). LeRoi is so far off on his facts that one wonders if his self-professed Marxism stems from Karl or Groucho. I suspect that at least part of LeRoi's anger stems from the fact that, while the work of Langston Hughes and James Baldwin will be revered forever, he may be relegated to a footnote as a pedestrian kvetch.

Nov. 8, 2008: My one act play, "Wishful Thinking" has a staged reading by the Theater Project, Union County College, Cranford NJ. The ghost of President Nixon visits the White House Oval Office and chats with President Dubya on March 8, 2008, one day before the U.S. invasion of Iraq and tries to dissuade him.

Feb. 2009: *"Inside Out: Voices From New Jersey State Prison,"* is published by Wingspan Press, of Livermore CA. Website: www.wingspanpress.com. This powerful book contains poems, stories, memoirs and commentaries by forty-three inmates at New Jersey's maximum security prison. Compiled and edited by Kal Wagenheim, who as a volunteer directed a creative writing workshop in the prison for five years, until it was shut down—without any reason provided--by the authorities. Readers of this book will discover the talent residing behind the prison walls, and also how so little is being devoted to prepare these men for life on the outside, which is harmful not only to the inmates and their families, but also to society as a whole.

Praise from readers

"The idea of being locked away for 10 years, 20 years, LIFE is a nightmare to most of us, an almost inconceivable bad dream. Well, here are the daily inhabitants of that bad dream, poetic in their description of its badness. Fascinating stuff...(the) jail cell writers in 'Inside Out' take us into dark and lonely rooms that we can only imagine. Now we can imagine much, much better." – *Leigh Montville, author of numerous books, including best-selling biographies of Babe Ruth and Ted Williams.*

"Moving stories and poems that come from the heart. It is hard to believe that people in such dire circumstances can create such lovely work. I must also believe that this was an excellent form of anger management for the authors; having the chance to pour their hearts out in a positive way. This program might well be transplanted to other institutions." – *Theo Bensen, Research Program Specialist II, California Dept. of Corrections and Rehabilitation, Sacramento CA.*

Profits from the sale of *"Inside Out"* will be donated to non-profit organizations that promote inmate training and rehabilitation and prisoner-reentry efforts. 188 page paperback. *To order : Contact* www.amazon.com. *$14.95 plus shipping. ISBN 978-1-59594-294-4. Copyright 2009.*

Dec.28, 2009: I was invited to speak about my book "*Clemente!*" in the Bronx by Danny Torres, a school teacher and sports writer. He told me that for the past nine years, each December, people gather to honor the memory of Roberto Clemente, who died in a plane crash on Dec. 31, 1972, while trying to fly relief supplies to earthquake victims in Managua, Nicaragua. After my talk Danny said it would be wonderful if my Clemente book, long out of print, could be reissued. A few days later, I contacted Markus Wiener, who publishes my Puerto Rico history books from his press in Princeton NJ, and he agreed to reissue the Clemente book, providing I could write a new Prologue, add a new cover, and new photos.

April 19, 2010: Olga organized a huge surprise party for me at Echoqua Restaurant off Highway 22 in Springfield, to celebrate my 75th birthday, two days in advance. I had no idea. Earlier I had been told by our friend & neighbor Lisa Hull that she would have a small birthday party for me two days later.

So on April 19, my son David and his dear girlfriend Cynthia came in from Manhattan and we headed for Echoqua for what thought would be a quiet dinner just for the four of us. But when we arrived I was shocked to see more than 40 relatives and friends! Even my journalist buddy Larry Luxner drove more than 4 or 5 hours up from Maryland to attend. When I thanked him Larry cracked "I'll go anywhere for free food." Another funny moment. One friend, Ernesto Díaz, asked me how old I was, I said "75" and Ernesto said I didn't look it. Sitting nearby was another friend, Sam Delgado, who wisecracked "you don't look a day over 74." Perhaps most touching of all is that my son Jeff, his wife Sarah, and their two kids (my grandkids) came all the way down for the party. Sarah played the flute, Aaron played the violin, Rebecca read a story with me, and Jeff read aloud a really funny "roast" about me.

June 10, 2010: My screenplay *"Interview at Weehawken*" about the Hamilton-Burr duel is chosen as a finalist for the Hoboken International Film Festival. I'm invited to attend the awards ceremony, a gala affair at a theatre in Teaneck NJ attended by hundreds. I didn't win, but while there met Stuart & Shelly Goodman. He's a TV producer of a show called *Manhunters"* on A&E, and a nice guy.

My letter in the June 30, 2010 issue of The Independent, a NJ weekly.

Tea Party today, what's next?

The success of the Tea Party in the USA should inspire other concerned citizens to organize and voice their views. A few ideas: The Bee Party, for those who adore natural honey; the Brie Party, for lovers of fine cheese; the Cee Party, for students with just average grades; the Dee Party, for students on the brink of failure; The Fee Party, for lawyers unhappy over their incomes; The Flea Party for itchy folks; The Flee Party, for agorophobes who always feel trapped; The Free Party, for cheapskates who hate to pay for anything. The Gee Party, for folks who are easily impressed; the Glee Party, for folks who are always overjoyed; the Hee-Hee Party, for folks who love to laugh; the Key Party, for folks always getting locked out of their homes; the Knee Party, for folks who suffer from arthritis; the Me! Party, for folks with low self-esteem who feel ignored; the Pee Party for folks plagued by frequent urination; the See Party, for folks with poor eyesight; the Tee Party, for frustrated golfers; the Tree Party, for lovers of shade; and The Wee Party, for folks who are dismayed by the tiny size of certain intimate parts of their body, including the brain. New ideas welcome! *Kal Wagenheim, Millburn*

MY FIRST NOVEL

July 28, 2010: My novel, *"The Secret Life Of Walter Mott,"* is published by All Things That Matter Press (based in Maine). It's 1959. Walter Mott, a shy bachelor, lives secretly in his office at the Security Insurance Co., in a bid to save money and retire early. Then he falls in love with a co-worker, and his plans change. Dramatizes the conflict between the yearnings for freedom and security. Oh, after an interlude with a striptease dancer, he also infects hundreds of his coworkers with the crabs. I wrote the first draft of this novel more than 30 years ago under the title *"The Home Office."* It was inspired by my pleasant, boring job at the Prudential Insurance Co. in Newark in 1956-58. I stuffed the manuscript in a filing cabinet and forgot about it. Around 2009 I saw that a TV series called *"Mad Men"* set in 1960 was a big hit, and it inspired me to pull the pages out of the filing cabinet; I retyped and revised it, and sent it to a few publishers. Finally one of them accepted...my first novel! *On July 28, 2010, the screenplay version was declared a semifinalist in the AAA Screenplay Contest, sponsored by Creative Screenwriting Magazine.*

August 2010: *"Clemente!"* my 1973 biography of the first Latino Hall of Fame baseball star was reissued with new material, cover & photos and a new title, *"Clemente! The Enduring Legacy"*, by Markus Wiener Publishers of Princeton NJ. The original edition was an American Library Association Selection as One of the Best Books of the Year for Young Readers. "The classic stuff of sports tragedy, the athlete dying young...the man beyond the ball field," Roger Kahn, *The Chicago Tribune*. Much of the new, expanded prologue was based on valuable information provided to me by Danny Torres and Luis Rodriguez-Mayoral (I acknowledge them in the book).

Oct. 29, 2010. Olga and I sold our 10th floor condo apartment at Torre Del

Mar in the Condado sector of San Juan, which we purchased in 1994. We had mixed feelings. It is a beautiful place, with fabulous ocean views, in the middle of a great neighborhood. But at most we were spending two to three months there, and the rest of the year the apartment remained empty, and we incurred substantial costs of maintenance, hurricane insurance, utilities, etc. So we reluctantly sold it to a nice couple who were renting in the same building. We will, of course, be returning to Puerto Rico, where Olga has a large, loving family. By investing the funds from the sale of the apartment, we can in future rent an apartment there. and perhaps in the very same neighborhood, where numerous rentals are available.

The passing of Wilfrid Sheed

January 22, 2011 at 2:46pm: I learned the sad news about the death of Wilfrid Sheed. Back in 1969, when I lived in Puerto Rico, working as a journalist, he came to the island, a mutual friend connected us, and Olga and I showed him around. When I wrote a biography of Roberto Clemente in 1973 he was kind enough to write the Foreword for the book (in addition to being a well recognized writer, he was also a huge baseball fan). The book has just been reissued with a new prologue ("Clemente! The Enduring Legacy") and his Foreword is still there, a reminder of his generous words.

May 1, 2011. Email from Christopher Lehmann-Haupt: Dear Mr. Wagenheim: Back on January 22—far too long ago for my response—on the occasion of Bill Sheed's death and my obit of him, you were good enough to send me his Foreword to your bio of Roberto Clemente. I had never read it and am better off now for having corrected that oversight (thanks to you). It told me more about Clemente than I had ever known, and more besides that—typical of Bill. I never had an encounter with him over the years (and we had many) when he didn't listen to anything I said without holding it up to to the bright light of his intelligence, twisting and turning it to see if it had more facets than he at first had dismissed it for lacking, and commenting ironically on what was left. John Leonard freely borrowed throwaway lines from him, including the title of his (John's) first collection, "This Pen for Hire." Thanks so much for taking the trouble to acknowledge my piece and send me this. Best, Christopher L-H."

50 YEARS MARRIED

Olga, retired from the Newark-Rutgers History Dept. (after 27 years), for the past decade has been super-busy as a volunteer and co-founder of the Hispanic Research & Information Center at the Newark Public Library. She and her co-volunteers raise money and direct a program to gather historical materials (oral histories, documents, letters, photos) of the large, growing Hispanic population in New Jersey (more than 1 million of the state's 8 million residents are Hispanic and they are growing in diversity, starting mainly with Puerto Ricans, Cubans and Dominicans, but now including Peruvians, Mexicans, Ecuardorians, etc. etc.) I keep busy publishing my monthly newsletter *Caribbean Update* (launched in February 1985) and also continue writing plays, screenplays and prose works. I also enjoy attending plays in NJ and NY. We are both blessed to be near the Millburn Free Public Library, which has a fabulous collection of books and films on DVD.

June 10, 2011: Today is the 50th wedding anniversary for Olga and me. In the morning I gave Olga a card and a gift she loves...dark chocolates! We plan to attend a dinner party with friends and some family on June 14 in Metuchen NJ near my sister June's house. But tonight we have a quiet celebration. We are treated to dinner by Olga's wonderful, generous brother Carlos Jimenez at the nearby Charlie Brown's Steakhouse in Millburn NJ.

June 14, 2011: I call my sister June "The Elsa Maxwell of Metuchen" because she really knows how to organize a party, this time to celebrate Olga and my 50th wedding anniversary. We arrive around 5:30 pm. at June & Ed's house together with our dear friends Nancy Diaz, Jeff Ambers, and his wife Lisa Hull. Soon afterwards, my son David and his lovely partner Cynthia Besteman arrive from Manhattan in a rented auto. Ed serves me my usual bourbon & water. There are delicious hors d'ouvres. Once everyone is gathered, June pours champagne and we all drink a toast. Shortly before 7 pm we drive a few blocks away to The Metuchen Inn, a lovely restaurant with a long history, where we enjoy a delicious dinner. I am surprised (and delighted) when June & my son David pick up the tab! Looking back to 1961, it's been a long eventful ride with Olga.

I was raised by two wonderful women—my grandmother and great-grandmother—and not long after they went up to Heaven I met Olga. I am a lucky guy!

Feb. 20, 2012: My one-act play *"Mother's Day In Hell"* had a staged reading at the Villagers Theatre in Somerset NJ. It was truly a fun evening, as the talented cast wore costumes, which is rare for staged readings.

The Roberto Clemente statue in Newark

My wife Olga gave a copy of my new Clemente biography to Luis Quintana, a Newark City Councilman, and a great admirer of Clemente. He then bought 100 copies of the book, organized a dinner with business leaders, and launched a fund raising campaign to erect a bronze statue of Clemente in Branch Brook Park, where there is already a Roberto Clemente Little League. He raised thousands of dollars and I put him in touch with Susan Wagner, the sculptor who created the bronze statue of Clemente in Pittsbugh. In June the statue was unveiled in the park during a huge celebration and parade.

June 12, 2012: *Email from Susan Wagner, sculptor of the Roberto Clemente bronze statues in Pittsburgh Pirates Stadium, and on June 3 in Branch Brook Park, Newark NJ.*

Hi Kal: I didn't get to speak to you very much during the unveiling, so much hub-hub. I wanted to thank you for giving me the opportunity to sculpt Roberto in Newark. It's been a dream of mine for many years to be able to sculpt him again, he was just my second sculpture and I am self taught. Us artists are our worst critics so I always wished I could do this better, or that differently. So because of you my wish came true. I think it's much better than the first. And I was so happy that Newark has him. I knew last year how much this meant to all of Newark when I heard Councilman Quintana's voice over the phone. It was so sincere. I couldn't help but say yes. I had a speech written but everyone said the same thing. I didn't want to sound redundant. But the message is on the plaque and will be there for a long time. I hope my statue will continue to inspire. This is why I wanted to sculpt Roberto many years ago. I don't know baseball at all. I did fall in love with his heart and spirit. I wanted them to quote Roberto and they did, but little did I know they quote this all the time! So thank you for opening this door for not only me but for all of Newark. Sincerely, Susan Wagner.

6-12-12. *My reply.* Hi Susan! It's great hearing from you. The unveiling of your great Clemente statue in Newark was a wonderful, inspiring event. The photo of your statue in Pittsburgh is on the cover of my book *"Clemente: The Enduring Legacy."* Here's wishing you all the best in the future! Fond regards, Kal Wagenheim.

6-12-12. *Email from Luis Rodriguez Mayoral a very helpful source for my Clemente book, now retired, living in Arlington, Texas. I forwarded to him the email from Susan Wagner (above).* Dear Kal. I'm happy Ms. Wagner has communicated with you. Your book is also a "statue" honoring Roberto. God works in unique ways...you being from the US...your wife being Boricua...and your book has given the readers a beautiful way of keeping the true Roberto alive for only He knows how many generations. A statue is a great honor...but a statue cannot tell the story of Roberto and statues do not speak. Feel proud...Kal...the enduring legacy of Roberto created by you is alive. Un abrazo, Luis..You have done more for the island than 99% of the cloned plastic-ignorant politicians we've had in our history...Frente en alto...siente orgulloso y mis respetos a tu distinguida esposa...ambos son unos Gigantes Boricuas en el mundo de la letras..Luis...Dios los bendice.

July 31, 2012. My dear friend Marie Trusits, while crossing Bloomfield Ave. in Verona NJ (near her apartment), was struck by a car at 8:45 p.m, and was taken to the University Hospital in Newark, where she died. I learned of the tragedy the next morning when her friend Linda Cerino called me. Marie was a sweet, kind, talented person, who had worked as an actor, and also wrote plays. My wife Olga loved her, and so did my daughter Maria. When I emailed mutual friends the next day I received touching replies. Nancy Diaz said Marie was "a beautiful, talented and lovely friend." Susannah Nolan wrote: "Marie was one of the first actors who worked with PTP (Present Tense Productions) and personally played the main characters in my first 2 produced plays. She was also part of the writers' group for bit. She was wildly beautiful and wildly talented and I hope she rests peacefully." Lisa Hull wrote: "Marie was an extraordinary woman—gifted, beautiful, warm, gracious, determined." My son Jeff wrote "Sorry to hear this. I remember

Marie. A very sweet woman. So sad." Gary Glor wrote: "Such a sweet and charming lady. Mark and I are shocked and saddened." My son David called me, and also expressed his sadness. My friend Beth Ann Holden commented "What I remember most about her was her laugh. I loved it.... Life is so fragile." Marie would have celebrated her 55th birthday on Sept. 14, 2012. Linda gave me the phone number of Marie's brother Kenneth, and I contacted him, asking to learn about plans for the funeral.

Aug. 7, 2012. Olga and I attended the funeral for Marie Trusits at the Higgins Funeral Home in New City NY, and then the Mass at St. Anthony's Church in Nanuet NY, after which she was buried in the nearby cemetery, close to her deceased parents. A number of friends attended.

Aug. 26, 2012: Enjoyed the musical comedy *"Menopause"* with Olga and our good friend Nancy Diaz in a packed house at the Count Basie Theatre in Red Bank NJ. Afterwards, we enjoyed dinner at an Irish bar-restaurant in downtown Red Bank.

One sad note: I had also bought a ticket for Marie Trusits, to celebrate her 54th birthday on Sept. 14, but she died on July 31, and the seat next to me was empty.

Sept. 13, 2012: I resume attending the Thursday night dramatic writing workshop run by Mick Casale at 18 W. 18th St. in Manhattan. It's a group of about 15 people who write plays and screenplays. We read the scripts, and make comments. Mick also teaches at the NYU graduate film school. I first joined Mick's group back in 1997 and it inspired me to write a number of plays and screenplays. I usually take the 4:27 pm train from Millburn to NYC Penn Station, arriving at 5 pm, then take the #1 subway down to W. 18th St., and eat a light supper (usually pea soup, bagel with cream cheese and coffee) at the Hollywood Diner (16th St., 6th Ave) then attend the workshop from 7 to 10 pm. Recently I tired of the diner and found a small, charming place called Telegraphe Café on W. 18th, near 6th Ave., where I enjoy a soup and tasty sandwich, and walk a block east for coffee at The City Bakery on W. 18th, across the street from my class. After class, I catch the 10:51 pm train from Penn Station back to Millburn.

Sept. 21, 2012. Shortly after Marie Trusits died, as a form of thereapy, I typed her one-act play *"Flirt"* and emailed it to the Brief Acts Company, explaining that she had passed away and it would be wonderful if they could produce her play, as a kind of tribute. They had done a great job producing my one-act "Wegotdates.com"in Sept 2009, and I thought they might be interested. I was delighted to learn that they would include it in their "Whispers of Fall" series of one-acts, to be performed Sept. 21, 22, 23 at the Sonnet Theatre, The Producers Club, 358 W. 44th St, NYC. After the first night, I sent the email below to Eric Leeb, who directed *"Flirt"*. "Dear Eric: I just got home to Jersey after seeing *"Flirt"* with my son David and sister June. I have a hunch that Marie Trusits was smiling down from Heaven when she saw you and your talented cast take her words and give such enjoyment to the audience. Please share this message with the cast! I plan to see the final performance on Sunday with my wife Olga, who was also a dear friend of Marie's. Gratefully, Kal Wagenheim"

Oct. 21, 2012: Olga and I are honored, along with eight other folks, by the Institute of Puerto Rico, a cultural organization based in New York, founded in 1946. The ceremony was during a luncheon at Scaletta Restaurant, 50 W. 77th St., close to the Museum of Modern History. The invitation came from Mr. Ben Pacheco, President and editor of *Alborada Boricua*, a cultural magazine. We met some good people during the event. Our dear friends Virginia Sanchez and her husband Chuck Korrol also attended. Previous honorees include Jose Ferrer, Raul Julia, Geraldo Rivera, Enrique Laguerre, and Willie Colon.

Nov. 17, 2012: Was invited to attend a VIP screening of *"Universal Babe,"* a new documentary film about Babe Ruth by Byron Hunter, at the Executive Screening Room of *The New York Times*, 40th St. and 8th Ave. Event time: 6:30-8:30 pm. The film focuses upon "the humanitarian acts" of the Babe. A couple of years ago I was interviewed by the producers, and appear for a few minutes in the one-hour film which was very well researched, and includes footage of the Babe being friendly with young children, with Asians during his visit to Japan, with African American baseball players (at a time of racial segregation) and with Hank Greenberg the Jewish homerun slugger. There was a large crowd, including Danny Torres, a Bronx schoolteacher and sportswriter who was instrumental in getting my Roberto Clemente biography reissued. I met several interesting folks there, and was told by Byron that in near future I would receive a copy of the film. *The event was originally scheduled for Nov. 2, but postponed due to Sandy, the storm that caused power outages and flooding in much of New York and New Jersey.*

Feb. 5, 2013: I learned later via email that my one-act play *"Coffee With God"* was produced at Lake of the Wood High School in Baudette, Minnesota. I received an email from the drama director, Joyce Washburn, about the production. She mentioned that the student who plays Kal (Shawn Stull) "had lost his mother two years before, and it was emotional at the time, for our small community." And for the third time in the history of the play thus far the part of God was played by a female (Allyssa Poolman). The waitress is played by Elizabeth Fraser. *(See photo above)*

April 18, 2013: I received a contract from All Things That Matter Press (they published my novel *"The Secret Life of Walter Mott*"), offering to publish a new book which I submitted a few weeks earlier. *"School for Lovers & Other Tales"* is a collection of four novellas, which include *"School For Lovers," "Tragedy in Lafayette Square," "Death at Weehawken"* and *"The Hydrogen Thing."* They said the book could be published in late 2013 or early 2014. *In early June 2014, I corrected PDF proofs of the book and am waiting for the book to be issued later in the year.*

May 9, 2013: Attended a fabulous event with Olga at Mayfair Farms banquet hall in West Orange NJ, organized by the Hispanic Research & Information Center (HRIC) of the Newark Public Library (Olga is a founding member). More than 200 people attended, money was raised for the HRIC, people enjoyed the food, the dance music,, and were able to connect with many dear friends. The event is held every two years.

August 30, 2013. *My letter in the Star-Ledger*

By The Donald, for The Donald

I see that Donald Trump's financially struggling Taj Mahal Casino Resort in Atlantic City is betting on strippers to attract gamblers. Perhaps The Donald should enroll in Trump University to learn how to boost profits. He claims his school is "guaranteed" to help. *Kal Wagenheim, Millburn*

Sept. 15, 2013. I learn that my one-act play " *Coffee With God"* will be produced at two more venues in near future: Nov 1-17, 2013. Serendipity Players, 714 E. 17th St., Vancouver , WA , 98663 US, Venue: El Presidente Restaurant, Vancouver, WA, and Oct. 24, 2014, Bowdon High School, 504 West College St. Bowdon , GA , 30108 US. Venue: Bowdon High School, Bowdon, GA. With these two that makes 45 productions at high schools, colleges and community theatres in the USA, Canada and Ireland.

Nov. 7, 2013. *My letter to The Item, the weekly newspaper in Millburn NJ, responding to their article.* To the editor: To "honor" the memory of W.R. Whittingham, who in 1931 opposed creation of a library in Millburn, saying libraries are "hotbeds of Anarchism and Communism," now that the library on Nov. 16 celebrates its 75th anniversary, I suggest we name the men's toilet at the library after him.

Nov. 27-29: Olga and I spent three wonderful days attending a 50th birthday celebration for my nephew Lowell Stern. The event was organized by Lowell and his lovely wife Juleen Savarese, and nearly 30 relatives attended. On Nov. 27, our friend Jeff Ambers drove us to Newark Penn Station and in 3 hours we reached Washington DC, where Lowell picked us up and took us to our hotel. It started at 6 pm. with a pizza dinner and drinks at the Executive Hospitality Room at the Marriott Residence Inn in Arlington VA, the great hotel where Olga and I and several others stayed. On Thursday Nov. 28, we celebrated a delightful buffet Thanksgiving Dinner at J. Gilbert's Restaurant in McLean VA. On Friday, Nov. 29, we attended the Birthday Dinner at the Stardust Room of the Wildfire Restaurant in McLean VA. Marvelous food, and folks sang and laughed and hugged. Saturday, Nov. 30, we were taken to Juleen & Lowell's home in Arlington VA-, where we enjoyed a brunch and then Lowell drove us to the train station. We arrived at Penn Station, Newark NJ, where Jeff Ambers picked us up and took us home. Looking back, it was such fun.

And 2013 was not only the 50th anniversary of Lowell's birth; in Sept. 2013 (40 years earlier) is when I found my sister June and her two children, Lowell (then 10) and Becky (then 6). Upon our return, I sent this email to our hosts:

"Dear Juleeen & Lowell: Olga and I returned safe & sound to NJ a little while ago and we want to thank you so much for organizing such an absolutely marvelous birthday party, an occasion where our large family enjoyed hugs, stories, laughter, music, great food and drink. It was wonderful seeing all the good folks again, and we thank you, thank you, thank you! Much love... Uncle Kal (& Olga)"

Dec. 12, 2013. *My letter in the Star-Ledger*

Obama's handshake: Cuba vs. China

The best analysis I've heard of U.S.-Cuba relations was in 1991. My wife and I were in Havana, attending a conference of the Caribbean Studies Association. I asked a Cuban political scientist about the possibility that the United States and Cuba might normalize relations.

"We are cursed," he said. "China, like us, is a Communist nation. But China has a billion people and is an irresistible market for the U.S. economy. We have only 10 million people. We are an interesting market, but not irresistible to Washington."

Kal Wagenheim, Millburn

Dec. 29, 2013-Feb. 27, 2014: Olga and I spent two pleasant months in Old San Juan, enjoying the warm weather (quite a contrast with the snow in New Jersey), combining work with enjoyable visits with family and friends. Through Richard Holm, a local realtor, we found a cozy apartment in La Puntilla, a quiet part of the old city, facing San Juan Bay and the cruise ship piers. Most days Olga took a bus to El Archivo or El Capitolio, gathering research materials for an ambitious book project on Puerto Rican Nationalist women, many of whom spent years in jail after their revolutionary activity in the 1950s. I had wi-fi access, a good laptop computer, and was able to continue working on my monthly newsletter, *Caribbean Update*, which I distribute via email (I ended the printed edition a month earlier). We also spent fun time with Olga's sisters Toña, Lolin, Juanita, brother Carlos, stepmom Lupe, and a bunch of other relatives. We also saw a few good friends, including Carmen Lugo, Laura Magruder, Augusto & Diana Font, Irma Rodriguez and her husband Orlando Samalot. Old San Juan, consisting of seven square blocks, is like Greenwich Village in the summer time, with the SuperMax supermarket near City Hall, an enormous CVS Pharmacy by the cruise ship pier, and good restaurants. Among the best were El Jibarito on Calle Sol (a casual friendly place that specializes in Puerto Rican food) and Triana on Recinto Sur (which offers great Spanish food). Also enjoyed lunch in the elegant interior patio of the Hotel El Convento. One nice feature of Old San Juan nowadays is "El Trolley" an open air covered bus, which passes by every 15 minutes and offers free service.

Esssential Tremors: Some time in late 2013 or early 2014 (not sure when) I experienced a strange health episode. For a brief moment I lost my ability to speak, and I noticed that when I tried to grip something with my left hand, it trembled. I found a urologist, a Dr. Joseph Sobelman , with an office in Livingston NJ. He examined me and said I did not suffer from Parkinson's, but had a much milder problem called "Essential Tremors." He recommended the following treatment: (1) walk at least 30 minutes every day; (2) drink a shot of brandy after dinner. I've been following his recommendation, The tremor in the left hand continues, but I am fine otherwise. To walk, I decided to drive each morning to the nearby The Mall at Short Hills, the home to many elegant stores. Short Hills is one of the wealthiest communities in the country, and the stores in the mall illustrate that. Each morning I see a number of folks, mostly elderly but some young, strolling to exercise in the mall. There is gentle background music playing. As I walk along I see stores such as: Abercrombie & Fitch, Alain Mikli, ALDO, Allen Edmonds, Ann Taylor, Anne Fontaine, Anthropologie, Apple, Aritzia, Au Bon Pain, Aveda, Bnana Republic, Max Azriam, bebe, Bloomingdale's, Brighton Collectibles, Brooks Brothers, Brookstone, Burberry, BVLGARI , Cartier, Chanel, Coach. Crabtree & Evelyn Crate & Barrel, Dior, Dolce & Gabbana, Emporio Armani, Furla, General Nutrition Center, Geox, Giorgio Armani, Godiva Chocolatier, Gucci, GUESS, Gymboree. Henri Bendel. Hermès. Hollister Co., JJ. Crew, Janie and Jack, Johnston & Murphy , La Maison du Chocolat, Legal Sea Foods, Links of London, Louis Vuitton , Macarons and Cookies, Macy's, Miu Miu, Molton Brown, Montblanc . Mulberry, Neiman Marcus, Nordstrom, Orologio, Pandora, Papyrus, Paradise Pen, Ralph Lauren, Saks Fifth Avenue, Tiffany & Co., Van Cleef & Arpels, Victoria's Secret. Victorinox, Vineyard Vines, White House | Black Market Williams-Sonoma. YellowKorner. And I look forward to my brandy each night after dinner!

May 14, 2014. I attend a marvelous matinee performance of the musical comedy *"A Gentleman's Guide to Love & Murder"* at the Walter Kerr Theatre in Manhattan. It stars Jefferson Mays. After the show I mailed him a copy of the Playbill asking him to autograph it, and he did sign and return it. I saw him a few years ago when he starred in *"I Am My Own Wife."*

June 8, 2014: To celebrate the 70th birthday of our good friend Jeff Ambers, Olga, Nancy Diaz and I attended a marvelous party at The Spanish Tavern, on McWhorter St, in Newark's Ironbound section. Good food and drink, and great music and comments by Jeff's many friends and family members.

Remembering Eli Wallach

Eli Wallach (1915-2014) was not only a fine actor, but also a kind, generous human being. Years ago I wrote a one-act play, *"Bavarian Rage"*, which had a short production off-off Broadway. It was about an elderly man who was arrested and accused of being Adolf Hitler. He is defended by a wannabe "dream team" of lawyers, who think that this is their ticket to fame. In this dark comedy it is later revealed that the elderly man, who calls himself Abe Heller, was not Hitler, but a retired Jewish actor who also hoped that with the trial he could become famous. I decided to expand the play into full-length and sent the script to Eli Wallach, thinking he would be perfect as the elderly "Hitler".

I never expected to hear from him, and was surprised and delighted to receive his hand-written letter, which said: "Sorry I took so long in reading the complete *'Bavarian Rage'*, but I was in a new play by Anne Meara & we performed it at George St. Playhouse in New Brunswick, and at Long Wharf in New Haven. The play was a big success and we're hoping a theatre in NY becomes available so we can move it. *'Bavarian Rage'* is funny and somehow touching...I fortunately have the Meara play, and a new play about Sigmund Freud, so will be a busy actor for quite a while...I think you can deepen and enrich the stuff between Heller and the lawyers and make realer the Hitler role so that you draw out the suspense—is he or isn't he. But you write with a sure comedic hand. I hope you can arrange readings of the play at Manhattan Theatre Club, or any of the many theatre producing companies. Good luck to you. *Eli Wallach.*"

Since then I've had several staged readings of the play and also converted it into a screenplay. Not long after I received Mr. Wallach's letter I attended a gathering of theatre folks in Manhattan and met his daughter Roberta. I told her about his wonderful letter and said *"Your dad is a real mensch"*. He certainly was.

June 2014: My new book, a collection of 4 novellas, is published.

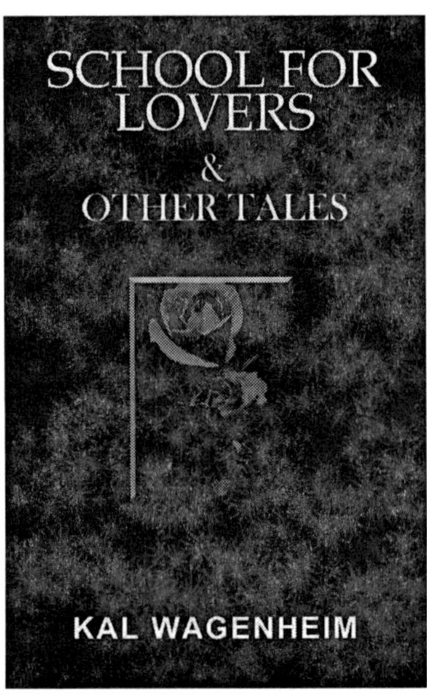

SCHOOL FOR LOVERS. The adventures of Lorenzo Da Ponte, Mozart's "libertine librettist." Jew, defrocked Catholic priest, fugitive from justice, brilliant poet, friend to Casanova, grocer, bookseller, teacher, loving husband and father, querulous complainer, tireless seeker of glory. Da Ponte's 89-year life span takes us to Venice, Vienna, London, and ends in New York, where he founds the city's first opera house. TRAGEDY IN LAFAYETTE SQUARE. Washington DC.,1859. Was it premeditated murder or temporary insanity when an enraged Congressman, Dan Sickles, shot and killed Philip Barton Key in Lafayette Square? Key (a prominent lawyer and the son of the composer of The Star Spangled Banner) was involved in a passionate affair with Teresa Sickles, the wife of the Congressman. The nation is gripped by the ensuing "trial of the century," which raises issues of a double standard, as Sickles is revealed to be an adulterer himself. DEATH AT WEEHAWKEN. This story probes a two-centuries old mystery: what passions compelled the Vice President of the United States (Aaron Burr) and the former Secretary of Treasury (Alexander Hamilton) to engage in a fatal duel? Touching upon themes that resonate today, it is a tale of sex, jealousy, corruption, bare knuckle politics, and a scandal-hungry press, culminating in the deadly encounter, in 1804, on the west bank of the Hudson River. THE HYDROGEN THING. Three scientists in different parts of the world are murdered in apparently random events. All three are pioneers in a new hydrogen fuel cell technology that will end the world's dependence on oil. Becky McLean (a college professor) and her boyfriend Michael Stern (a journalist) stumble upon the plot (concocted by a deranged scientist and a corrupt stockbroker) and are pursued by the hitmen.

"Kal Wagenheim is just as at home in Old New York and Jeffersonian Washington as he was in 'Mad Men' territory in his previous book. Kal's books are time machines."--*Bill Mesce, author of "Precis – A Collection of Short Stories", among others.*

"In the four narratives that make up *'School For Lovers & Other Stories'* Kal Wagenheim has adroitly and entertainingly managed to give us lessons in American history and the latest in energy technology, as well as an appreciation of opera lyrics and a thriller plot. He has brought to literary life none other than Wolfgang Amadeus Mozart, George Washington, Alexander Hamilton, Aaron Burr and a host of other captivating and empathetic real-life and fictional characters." *–Robert Friedman, author of "The Surrounding Sea" and three other novels.*

"Kal Wagenheim presents his readers with little slices of life, populated with dear and quirky people who soon earn a spot in our hearts. He is an unusually gifted author, who writes with ease and gentle humor. He deserves a place alongside other great storytellers like Richard Russo and Richard Ford."--*Professor Elizabeth A. Hull, Chair, Political Science, Rutgers University, author of "The Disenfranchisement of Ex-Felons."*

"Mr. Wagenheim's brilliant writing is built on firm research, dramatically presented characters (with their complex motivations, relationships, and interactions) and consistently interesting stories. Here are rewarding examples of novellas that enlighten as well as entertain." -- *Professor of Psychology, Robert Roth, Kean University (retired), author of 22 books, including "Ego, Self, Person, Contest."*

"Your prose and story-line are like a cascade that crashes down…and then up, as if it were just a rush of spray. Love it!" --*Professor Elpidio Laguna-Diaz, Rutgers University, Language Dept.*

"Never at a loss for ideas, Kal writes with a love for humanity. In every work his characters celebrate what it means to be alive, even when caught in circumstances about and beyond the ordinary. His message is always inspiring, told with an elegance of the master of writing (and life) that he is." *--Mick Casale, Professor, Tisch School of the Arts, New York University.*

Not many non-fiction writers successfully transition into the world of the imagination and fiction. Kal Wagenheim—editor of magazines about the Caribbean, stringer for the *New York Times*, biographer of Babe Ruth and Roberto Clemente, chronicler of Puerto Rican history—has done so with a bang. First were his plays, including the powerful *Coffee with God*, then his comic novel *The Secret Life of Walter.* And now we are greeted with *School for Lovers & Other Stories*, a collection of four novellas that start from a fact or two in history and end up as vivid tales that enmesh the reader. Good reads!" *--Barry B. Levine, Founding Professor Emeritus, Sociology & Anthropology, Florida International University. His latest book is "Reflections on a Puerto Rican Life."*

ALL THINGS THAT MATTER PRESS
www.allthingsthatmatterpress.com

June 28, 2014. Olga and I drove north towards Albany to meet my dear cousins Bill & Shirley Wagenheim, who now live in a lovely senior community called Beverwyck, in Slingerlands NY. We enjoyed lunch there with them, and also present was Betty, their 92-year old friend who lives in the same place, and Robyn Pforr Ryan and her husband Dennis. Robyn is a pal of Betty's and is working with her on developing a novel based on her life. Robyn was a student in my journalism class at Columbia Univ. Now a lawyer, married with 3 kids, she posted this photo (taken by her husband Dennis) on Facebook with the message below. A souvenir of a great day! Robyn wrote: "The gifts of a great teacher can last a lifetime. Den and I had a great lunch this weekend with one of my college profs, from like 1988?, and his wonderful wife Olga. Kal Wagenheim, a super creative and talented writer and a super mensch. (He volunteered to teach creative writing to prisoners in Trenton for yrs and yrs),was my only journalism prof ever & I still remember his contagious passion for writing & journalism and my assignments in his class (one was to do an obit on someone still alive; I did Diane Sawyer). But the biggest gift of his class was Kal's kind encouragement over the years as we kept in touch; at one point I left writing for law, of course, convinced & determined I was done with writing. Just keep it in yr mind as something that you always have in you, said Kal, always in this encouraging way that actually helped me grow something in me that i didn't see but now is so important to me. Thank you Kal! His wife Olga is a whole other inspirational story. What a mensch she is. She co-founded an oral history projecy in NJ that is now a great archive of Hispanic oral historiea housed at Newark Public Library."

* * *

Oct. 4, 2014. My good friend Jack Krupnick, who lived in Trenton NJ, died. He would have been 77 years old on Nov. 15, 2014. I learned of his death a few days after it happened from Arlene Schenerman, a dear friend of his. In an email she sent me she said he died on Yom Kippuer, adding that "It is sad that great men die on a Jewish holiday. I was told this when my husband Irving died on the eve of Rosh Hashonah, 1999. I believe it is true."

* * *

I no longer commute to Manhattan with the frequency that I did years earlier, when I taught at Columbia once a week, or even more often when I had full-time jobs in the city. However, I do take occasional trips into Manhattan, most of the time on the train from Millburn to Penn Station. I sometimes attend Mick Casale's Thursday night writing workshop on W.18th St. As a member of The Dramatists Guild, I receive invitations to free staged readings and sometimes for free seats at Off-Broadway shows. Recently I've also attended free staged readings by playwrights at New Dramatists, on W. 44th St. I very much enjoy these trips, reading a book on the train to and from the city. Also, while in New York, if time permits, I have a bite at the Broadway Lounge, on the 8th floor of the Marriott Marquis Hotel on W. 45th St, which offers a spectacular view of Times Square. Thin crust pepperoni pizza, a glass of Malbec red wine, and an espresso coffee are my usual meals there. I enjoy live theatre, and each year attend a number of plays, both in New Jersey and Manhattan. Also, for the past 15 or so years Olga and I have been subscribed to the New Jersey Opera Company in Princeton NJ. In July we've attended two or three Sunday matinees, which are about equal in quality to the New York City Opera Company (sadly, the opera company shut down a couple of years ago).

Every few weeks I take the train to Penn Station in New York, #1 subway down to Sheridan Square, and meet my old pal Marvin Schwartz in front of the Starbucks. From there we walk a few blocks east to Sammy's Noodle Shop, a Chinese restaurant on 6th Ave., near W.10th,which offers a bargain lunch for $7.95, including soup, a huge entrée (my favorite is chicken with broccoli, garlic sauce, white rice), tea, and of course a fortune cookie. I always enjoy spending an hour or so with Marvin, who continues to live in the same rent-controlled studio apartment on W. 10th St. There are 20 studios in the building. 17 of the tenants now pay market rate ($2,800 per month for the tiny place), but Marvin and 2 others are still protected by rent control and pay about $460 a month. "They're waiting for us to die!" says Marvin.

Some evenings Olga and I join our dear friends Lisa Hull and her hubby Jeff Ambers, and Nancy Diaz at the Parkwood Diner in Maplewood. Food is good, prices are reasonable, and we laugh a lot. Lisa usually orders the same entrée, a large dish of warm goat cheese salad. So when the waitress hands her the menu, I simply bleat "baaaaaah!"

When our dear friend Nancy Diaz retired from Newark-Rutgers she sold her apartment in West Orange and moved south to Concordia, a 55-and-up community in Monroe Township, off Exit 8-A on the Jersey Turnpike. She has a beautiful home, next to a golf course, which she plays on often. Nancy has a fabulous collection of films on DVD, including Agatha Christie's *"Miss Marple"* series. Olga and I drive down there occasionaly (the trip takes 45 minutes), have lunch at a nearby diner, and then enjoy a "Marple-ous" time in Nancy's home.

A few years ago Olga and I attended a party together with Ernesto Diaz, a good friend. He took pictures of us and later said he had posted them on Facebook. I knew nothing about Facebook, but soon became a member and am now actively involved. Via Facebook I am in contact with family and friends in the USA and worldwide, including son Jeff & and his wife Sarah up in Northampton, Mass., and son David and his partner Cynthia in Manhattan. Recently, David (who works as a realtor) has become quite active with a camera and posts lovely photos of New York on Facebook.

In another positive development, through good friend Nitza Tufino, I met Claudia Miranda, a talented young graphic designer. Copies of my San Juan Review monthly magazine, published between 1964 and 1966, were sitting ignored in my garage. Claudia digitized all 33 issues, and they are now available, page by page, on a new website: www.sanjuanreview.com. It is also on Facebook. Many people have expressed pleasure over this rescue of the articles, photos and drawings that appear in the magazine.

Olga and I are not super-wealthy but we are financially comfortable, and we have a few folks to thank for their good advice. When Olga began working at Rutgers they automatically deducted a tiny percentage of her salary for her pension. But a good friend at Rutgers, Maria Blake, told her she could deduct a much larger portion of her salary. She did so, the dollars continued to multiply, and now that she is retired the investment is handled very responsibly by TIAA-CREF. In my case, when I began my newsletter in the 1980s, Irv Roberts (college classmate with a background in accounting) advised me to start a SEP-IRA, where I could deduct up to 20% of my salary and invest it. Then my cousin Bill Wagenheim suggested that I invest in mutual funds, and he said to only invest in funds which have a 4-star or 5-star rating by Morningstar. I did so and over the years the dollars have grown. Olga and I each month take funds out to help cover expenses, but the money continues to grow.

For many years on Friday afternoons, although I don't attend a synagogue, I tuned in to Radio WQXR, which at 5:30 broadcast the services from Temple Emanu-El in Manhattan, to hear the mourners' kaddish honoring departed loved ones. A few years ago the station went public and ceased these broadcasts, but I was delighted to learn that I could access the prayers on the internet website of the synagogue: www.emanuelnyc.org So on Friday afternoons, in my office at home, I sit at my desk, listen to the service, and gaze at photos nearby of my great-grandmother Ida, my grandmother Lillian, my mother Rozlon and father Harold, my Aunt Lucille, grandma's Cousin Rose, and a few dear friends, including Ralph Fortson and Marie Trusits. It is a time of great peace for me.

Grandkids Aaron & Rebecca when they were much younger. In 2014 they are 12 and 10.

Each Mother's Day, I try to visit the grave of my Mom, Rozlon Wagenheim, who died on May 31, 1937, at age 22. The grave is located at Bnai Israel old Jewish cemetery off South Orange Ave., in Newark NJ. Directions: Drive eastward down South Orange Ave, through South Orange, to Newark. Drive beneath the bridge of the Garden State Parkway. The cemetery is on the left hand side at 616 South Orange Ave. It has an entrance there. Continue past that entrance, take the first left turn, Whitney St. (a dead end). Go to end of street, ignore the pile of debris, there is an opening at end of fence. Enter the cemetery. My mother's gravestone is in the front row, facing the fence. Looking at it from the street, it is the 9th grave, and usually has a couple of stones atop it, which I placed during previous visits. The cemetery is owned by Sanford B. Epstein Inc, which also has other cemeteries in NJ. They are located at 731 Boulevard, Kenilworth NJ 07033. 973 373 0144. I (Kal) have purchased a place to be buried at the cemetery near my mother's grave.

2014: Looking back, it's been a fabulous ride thus far. I'm blessed to have been raised by a loving family. I feel grateful to know Olga's great family; stepmom Lupe, her sisters Dolores (Lolin), Maria, Juanita, Teresa, brothers Carlos and Carmelo, and their families. And I've been blessed to have a marvelous wife, Olga, three wonderful children (Jeff, David and Maria) and two terrific grandchildren (Aaron, Rebecca), sister June, her children Becky and Lowell, and other dear relatives and friends. Mine, thus far, has been an accidental, lucky life.

Recent photo of wife Olga and me,
married for 53 years.

Kal Wagenheim (born in Newark, N.J in 1935) is a journalist (formerly with The New York Times and currently editor of Caribbean UPDATE monthly newsletter), author and translator of eight books, and ten plays and screenplays. His biography of Babe Ruth was a Playboy Book Club selection and was adapted for an NBC-TV film. His novel, "The Secret Life of Walter Mott"was published in 2010 by All Things That Matter Press, which in 2014 also published his collection of four novellas, "School For Lovers & Other Tales". His biography of Roberto Clemente, first published in 1973, was re-issued with new material in 2010 by Markus Wiener Publishers. His one-act plays, "The Dream Team," "We Beat Whitey Ford", "Wegotdates.com", "Purple Heart" and "Coffee With God" have been produced at various venues in New York and elsewhere. "Coffee With God" has been published by the Dramatic Publishing Co. and is being produced at festivals and schools in the USA, Canada and Ireland. His poetry and fiction have been published in the online literary magazine www.jerseyworks.com. His nonfiction articles have been published in The Nation, and The New Republic. He has also taught journalism and creative writing at Columbia University and The State Prison in Trenton NJ. Member: PEN American Center and The Dramatists Guild of America. Film producers may access his screenplays on the website www.inktip.com Details on his website: www.kalwagenheim.com

CPSIA information can be obtained at www.ICGtesting.com
Printed in the USA
LVOW07s0222071214

417557LV00001B/2/P

9 781595 945495